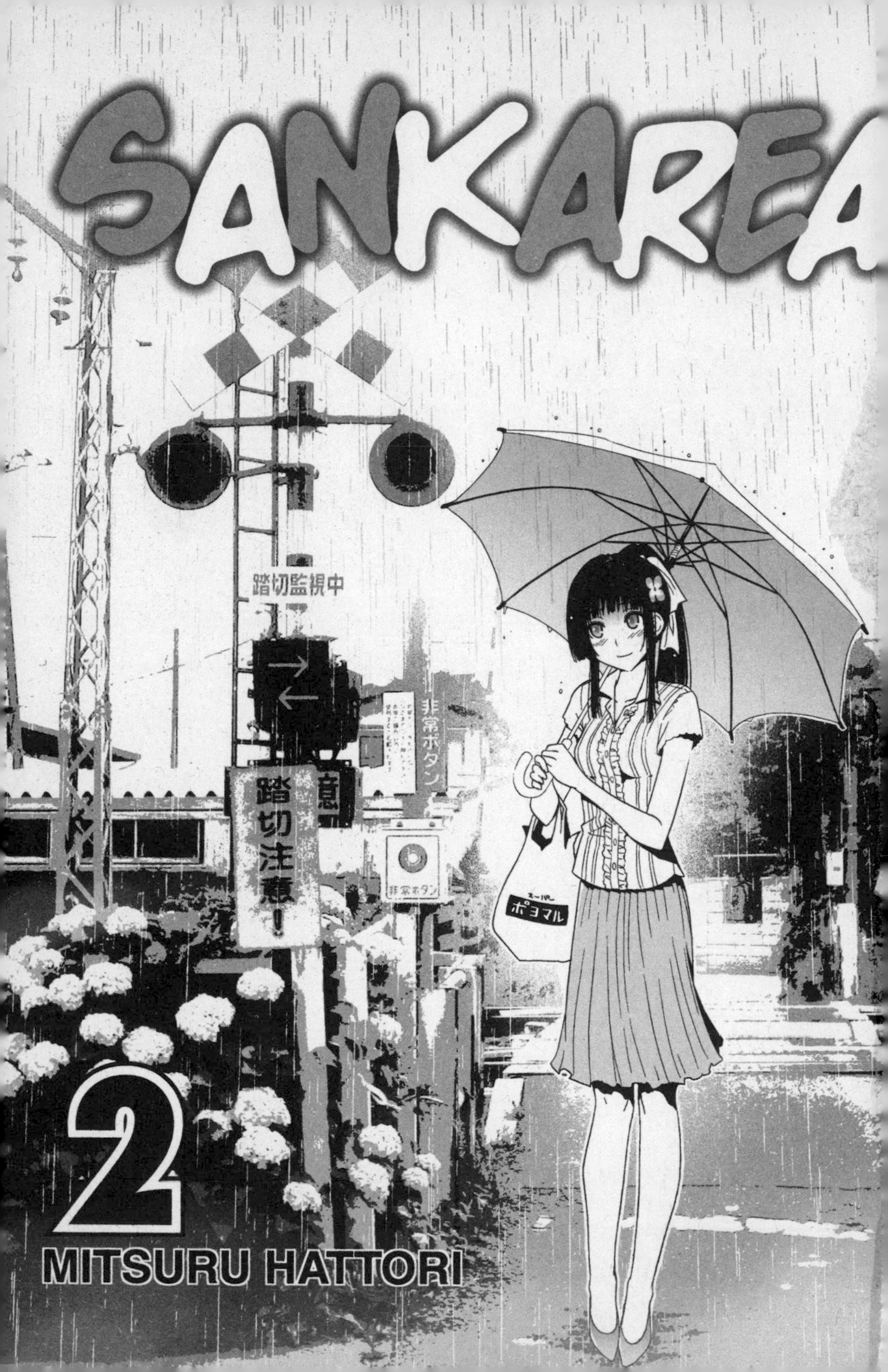
SANKAREA
踏切監視中
踏切注意!
非常ボタン
非常ボタン
ポヨマル
2
MITSURU HATTORI

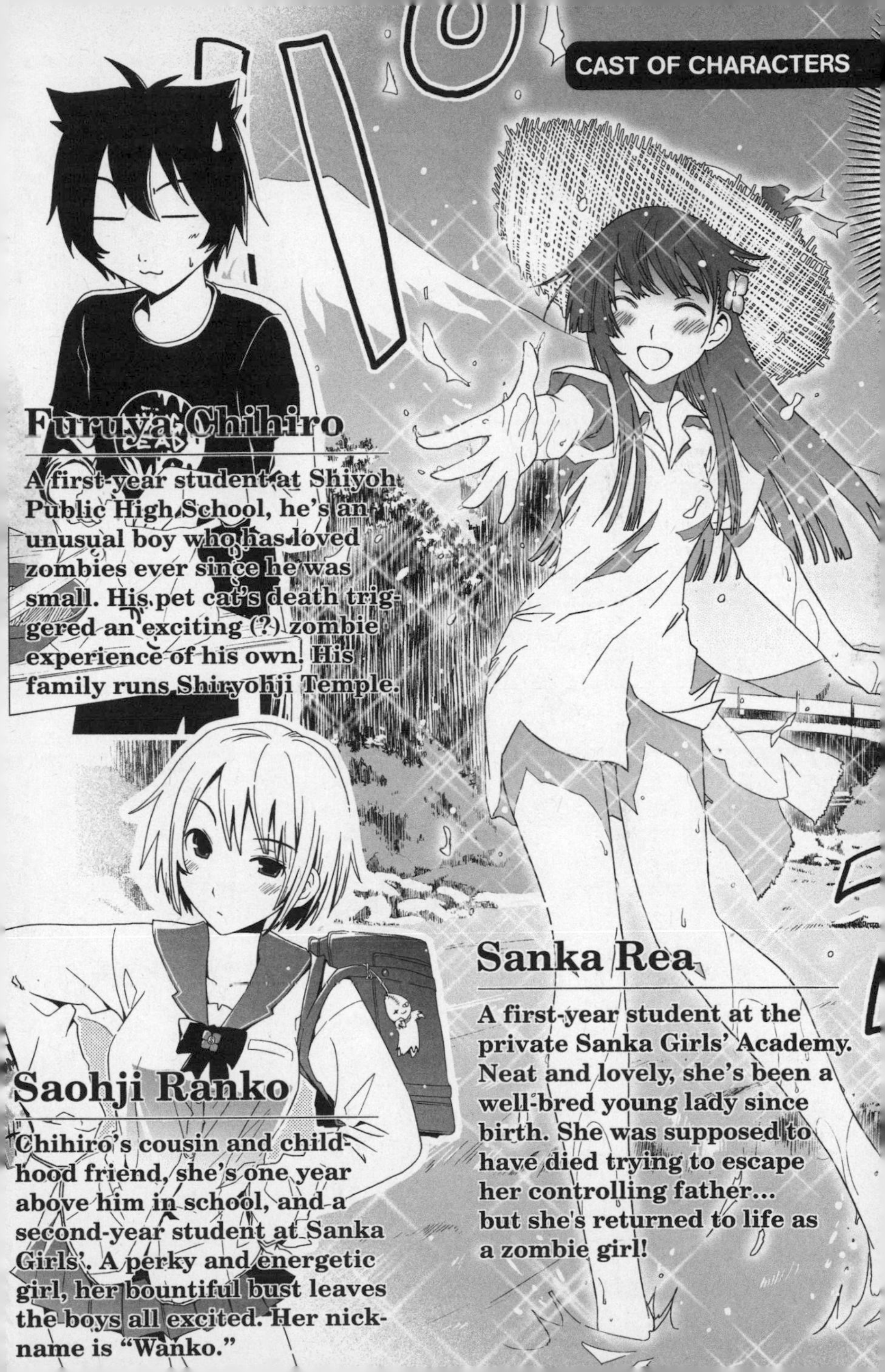

Furuya Chihiro

A first-year student at Shiyoh Public High School, he's an unusual boy who has loved zombies ever since he was small. His pet cat's death triggered an exciting (?) zombie experience of his own. His family runs Shiryohji Temple.

Sanka Rea

A first-year student at the private Sanka Girls' Academy. Neat and lovely, she's been a well-bred young lady since birth. She was supposed to have died trying to escape her controlling father... but she's returned to life as a zombie girl!

Saohji Ranko

Chihiro's cousin and childhood friend, she's one year above him in school, and a second-year student at Sanka Girls'. A perky and energetic girl, her bountiful bust leaves the boys all excited. Her nickname is "Wanko."

THE SANKA FAMILY

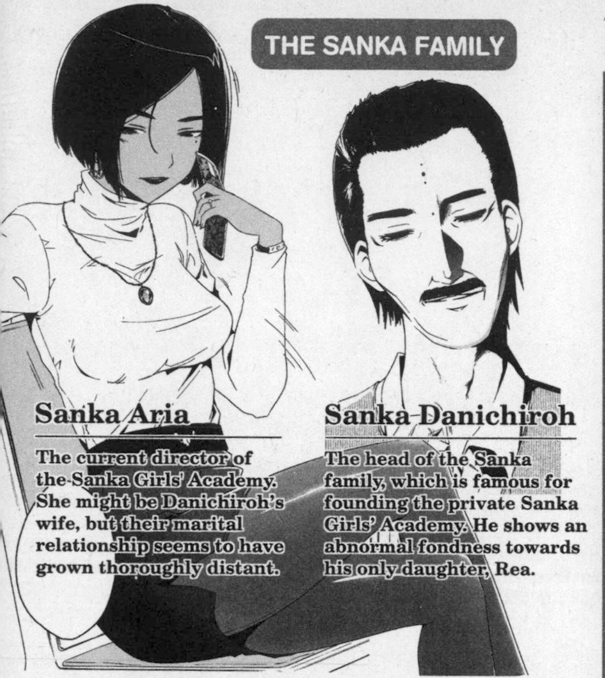

Sanka Aria

The current director of the Sanka Girls' Academy. She might be Danichiroh's wife, but their marital relationship seems to have grown thoroughly distant.

Sanka Danichiroh

The head of the Sanka family, which is famous for founding the private Sanka Girls' Academy. He shows an abnormal fondness towards his only daughter, Rea.

CHIHIRO'S FRIENDS

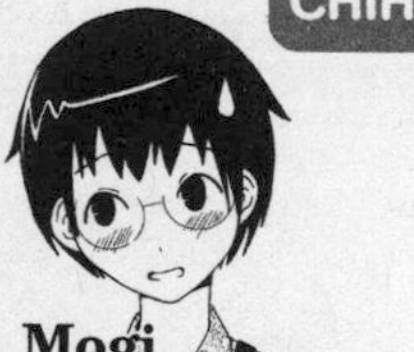

Mogi

He's got a timid personality that completely matches his appearance.

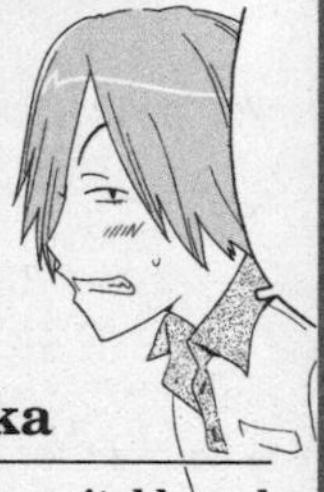

Yasutaka

He is easily excitable and constantly wants to get closer to the young ladies of Sanka Girls'.

STORY

The summer breeze carries the fragrance of hydrangeas. When his cat dies, Furuya Chihiro, a boy with a bizarre affection for zombies, becomes obsessed with bringing him back to life. He meets Sanka Rea, a girl deeply troubled by her father's rules, and the two attempt to complete a mysterious elixir together. However, Rea, who has incurred her father's wrath, drinks the poisonous elixir out of despair... and the next day, she falls from a cliff and dies! But, as it turns out, the elixir works. Rea becomes a zombie, and is miraculously revived!! And so Chihiro's dream of life with a zombie girl becomes reality.

THE FURUYA FAMILY

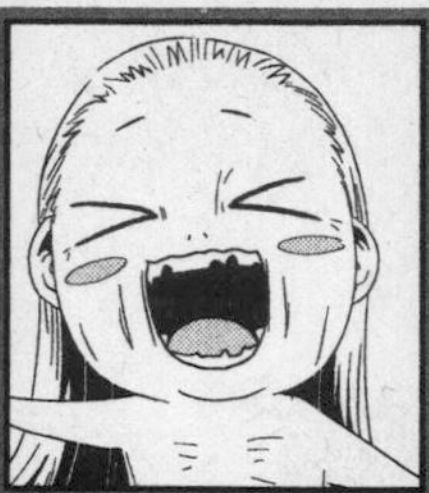

Grandpa

The most mysterious organism (?) in "Sankarea." He somehow seems to know about the "reanimation" phenomenon, but... could he really be the person holding the key to what comes next?

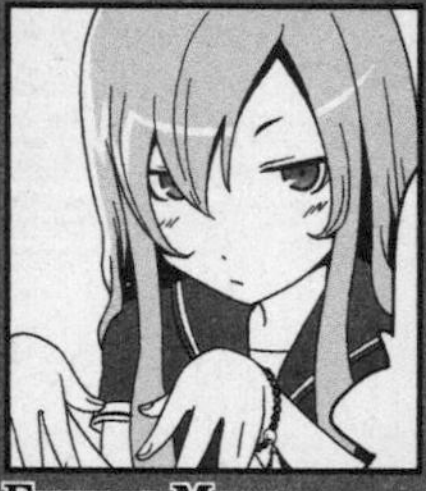

Furuya Mero

A calm and collected first-year middle school student, she presides over the chores in the mostly male Furuya household. A real Japanese-style girl, she reads the Heart Sutra for fun and is able to wear both traditional cook's clothing and the white robes of the dead in a stylish manner.

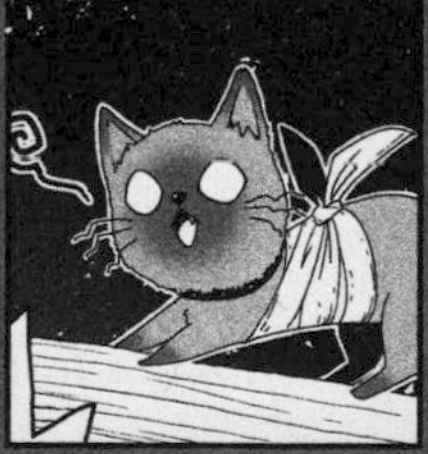

Bub

A cat that Chihiro brought home a long time ago. He was hit by a car and killed, but the elixir Chihiro and Rea made brought him back to life!

MITSURU HATTORI presents

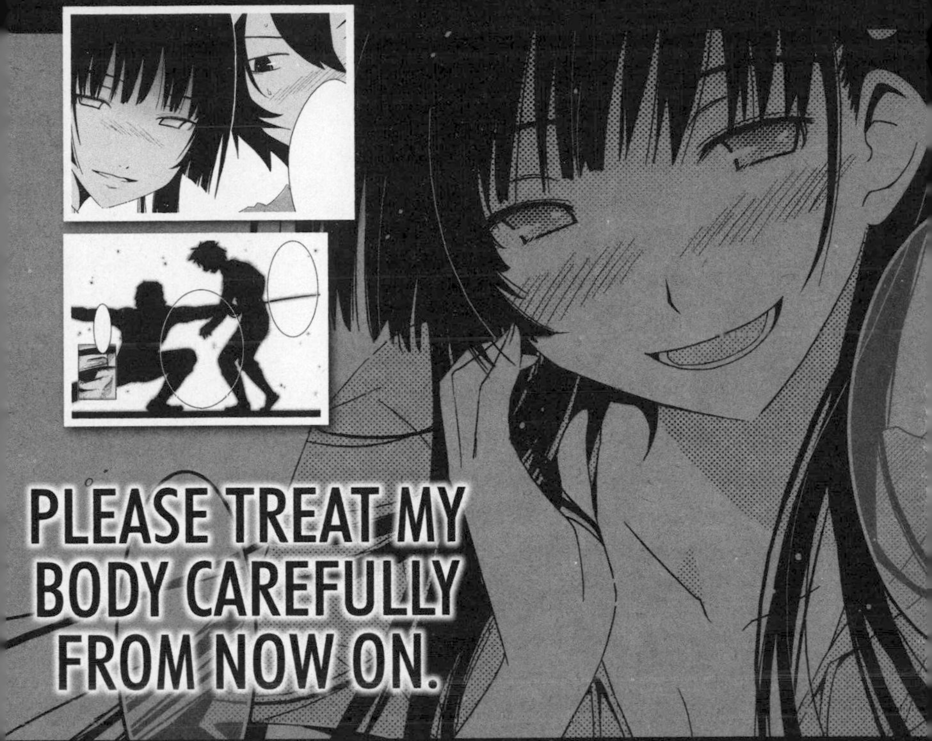
PLEASE TREAT MY BODY CAREFULLY FROM NOW ON.

CONTENTS

SERIALIZED IN BESSATSU SHONEN MAGAZINE, MAY TO SEPT. 2010.

SANKAREA 2

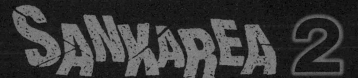

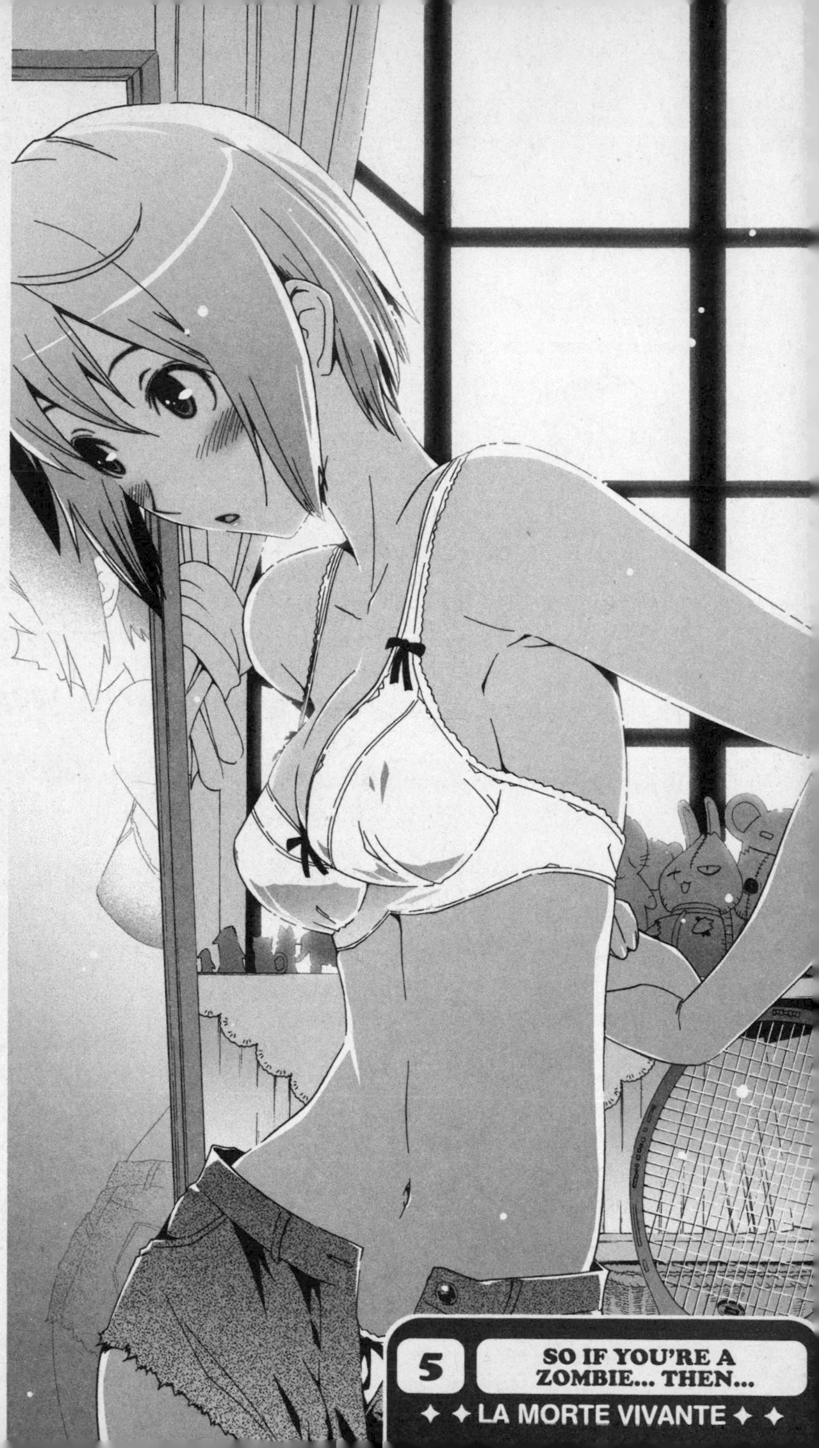
5
SO IF YOU'RE A ZOMBIE... THEN...
✦ ✦ LA MORTE VIVANTE ✦ ✦

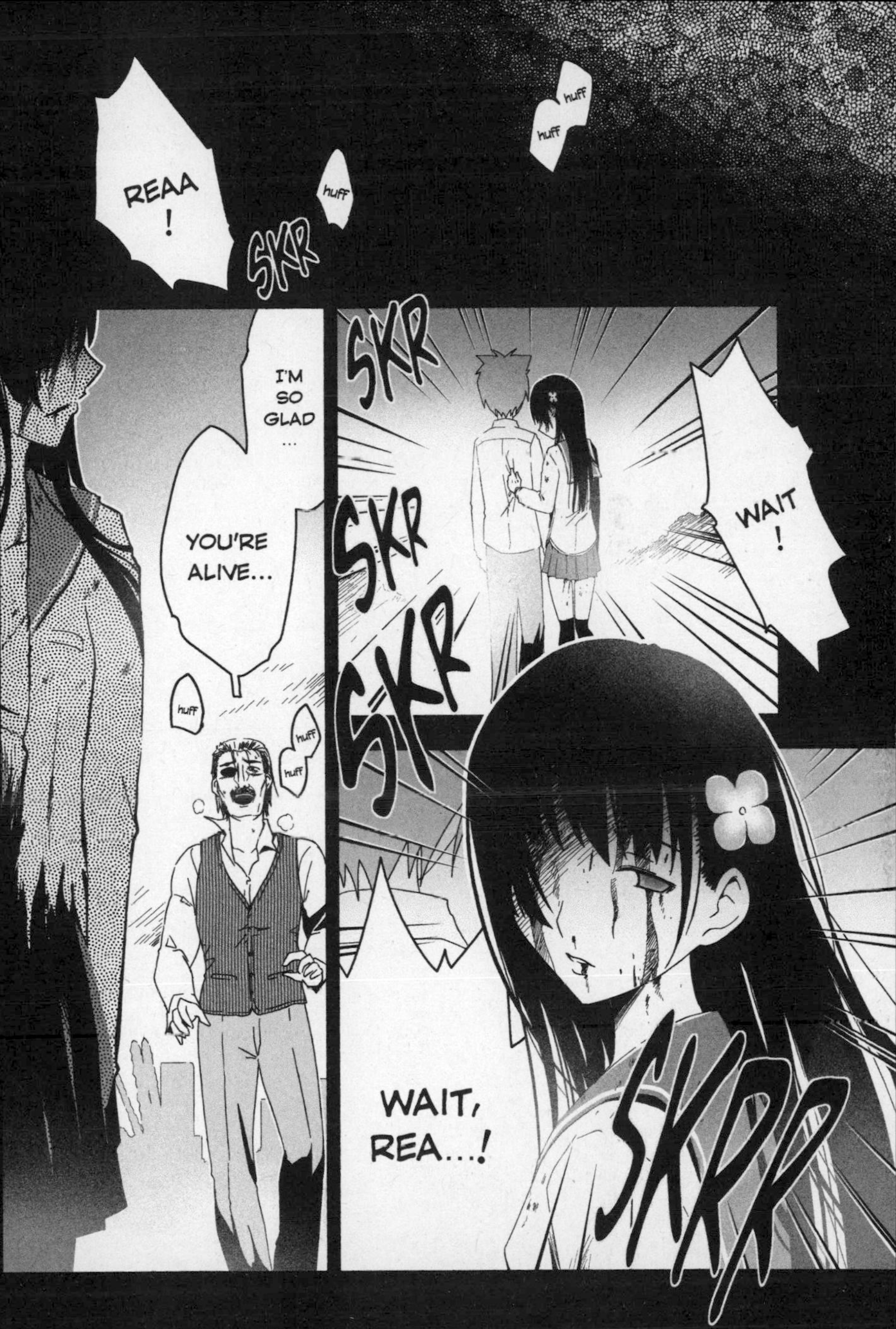
huff
huff
huff
REAA
!
SKR
WAIT
!
SKR
SKR
SKR
SKRR
WAIT, REA...!
I'M SO GLAD...
YOU'RE ALIVE...
huff
huff
huff

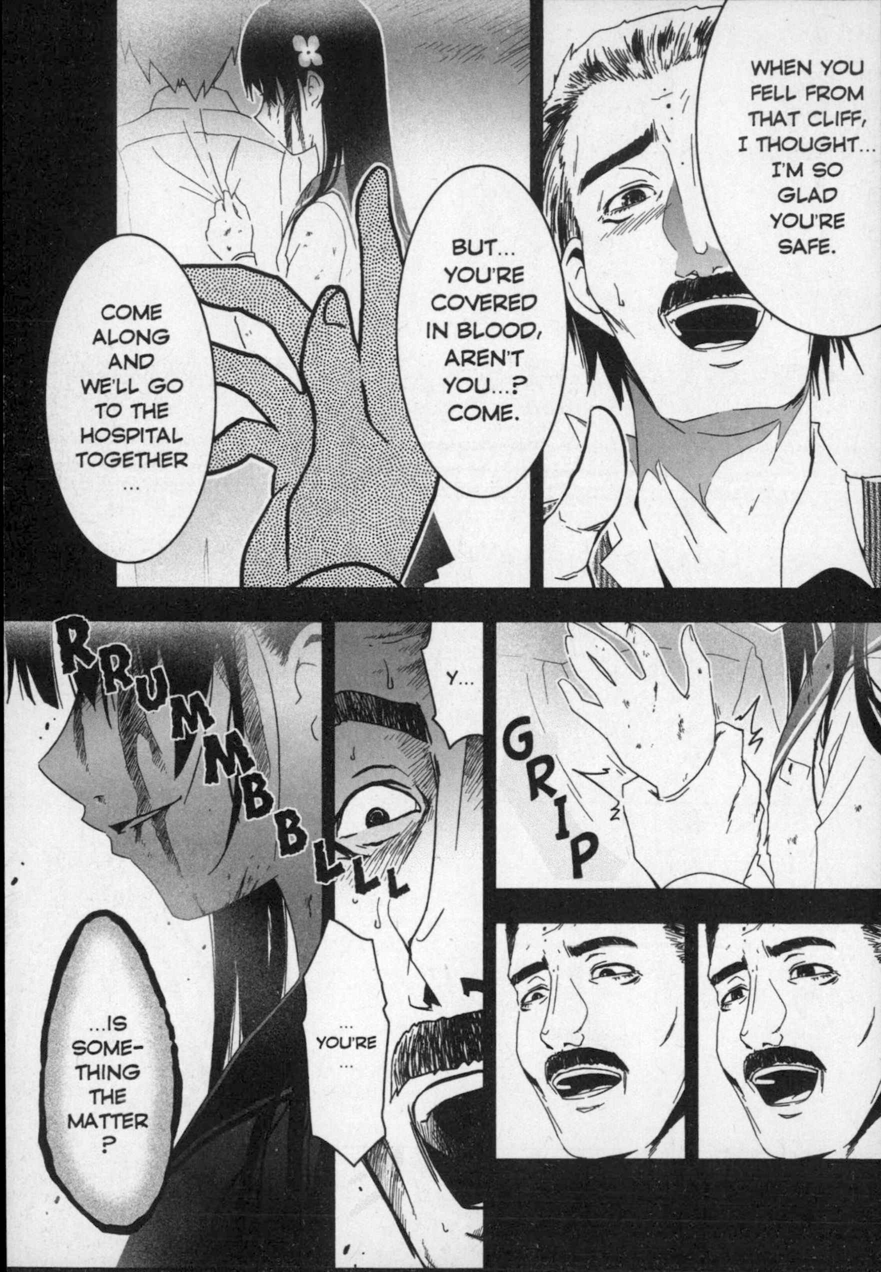
WHEN YOU FELL FROM THAT CLIFF, I THOUGHT... I'M SO GLAD YOU'RE SAFE.
BUT... YOU'RE COVERED IN BLOOD, AREN'T YOU...? COME.
COME ALONG AND WE'LL GO TO THE HOSPITAL TOGETHER ...
GRIP
Y...
... YOU'RE ...
RRUMMBBLLLL
...IS SOMETHING THE MATTER ?

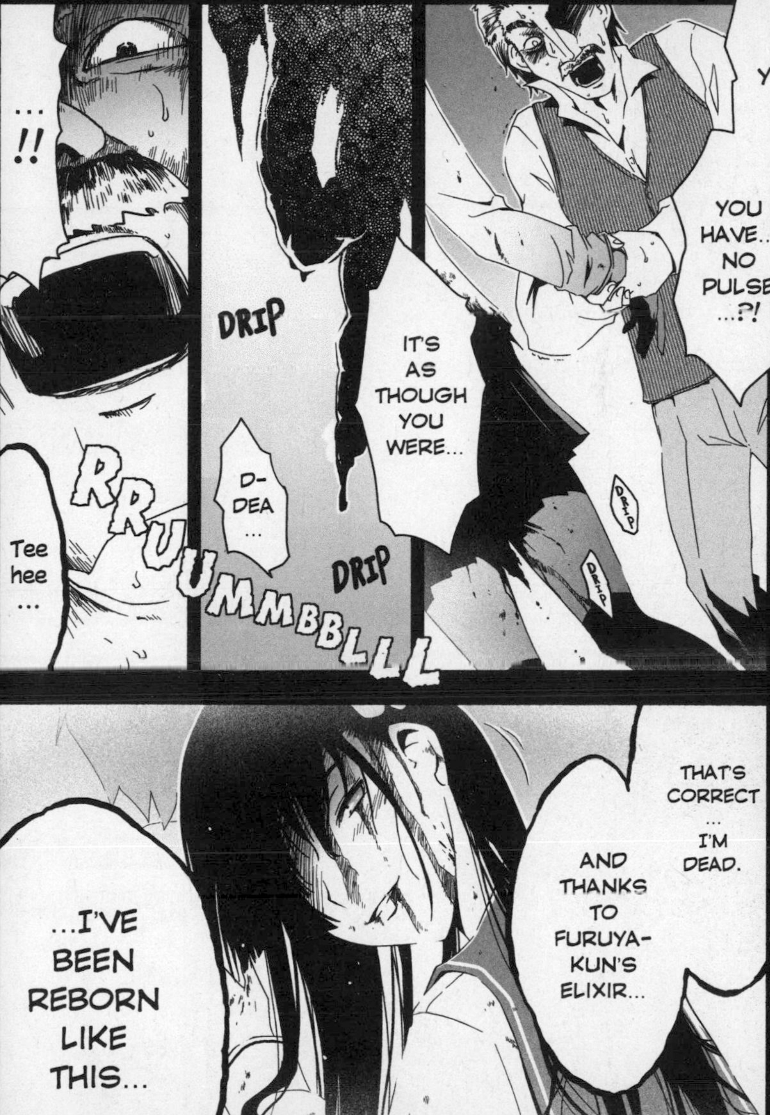
Y...
YOU HAVE... NO PULSE ...?!
IT'S AS THOUGH YOU WERE...
DRIP
DRIP
DRIP
D-DEA ...
DRIP
... !!
Tee hee ...
RRUUMMBBLLL
THAT'S CORRECT ... I'M DEAD.
AND THANKS TO FURUYA-KUN'S ELIXIR...
...I'VE BEEN REBORN LIKE THIS...

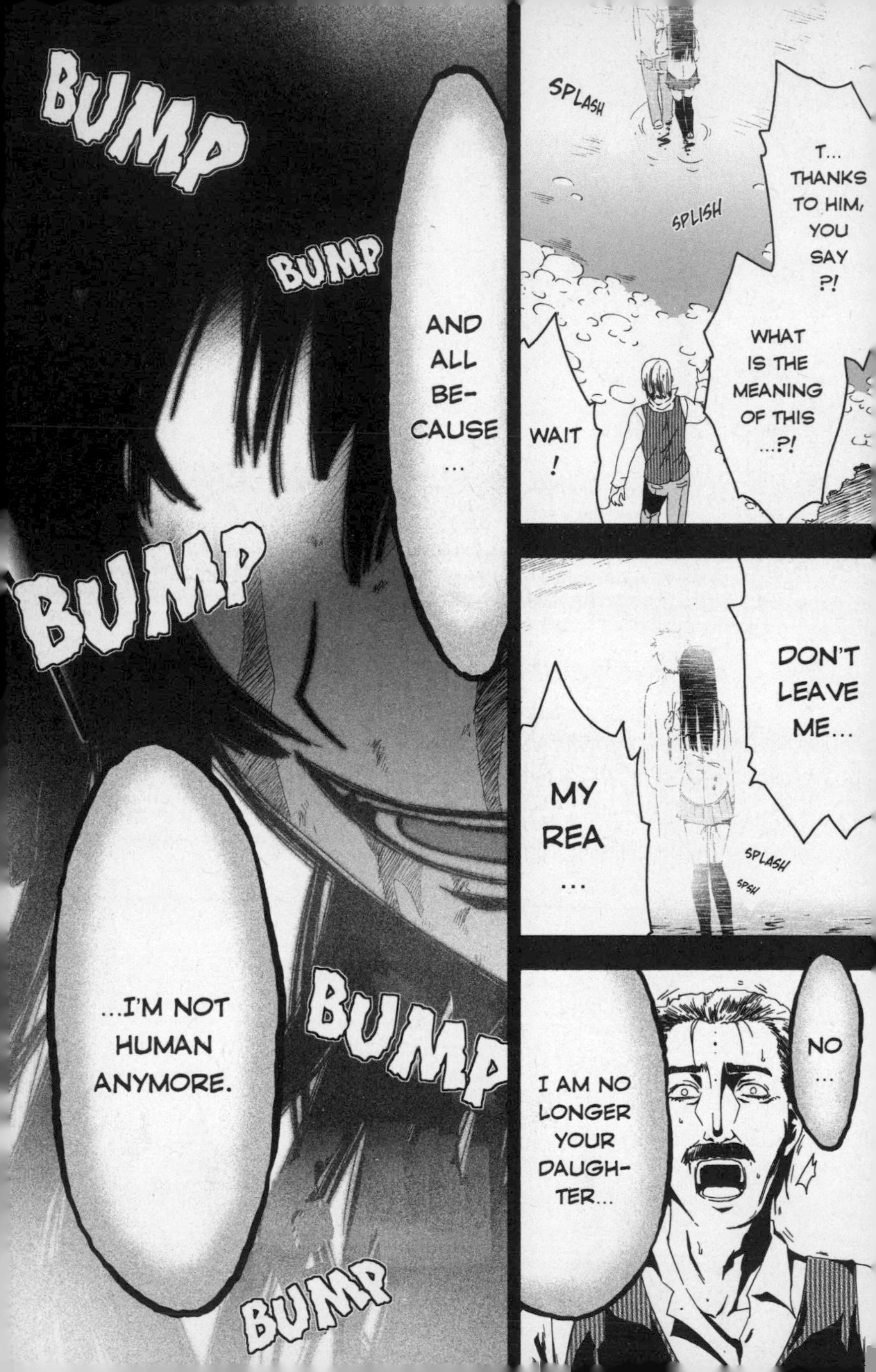
T... THANKS TO HIM, YOU SAY ?!
WHAT IS THE MEANING OF THIS ...?!
SPLASH
SPLISH
WAIT !
DON'T LEAVE ME...
SPLASH
SPSH
MY REA ...
NO ...
I AM NO LONGER YOUR DAUGHTER...
AND ALL BECAUSE ...
BUMP
BUMP
BUMP
...I'M NOT HUMAN ANYMORE.
BUMP
BUMP

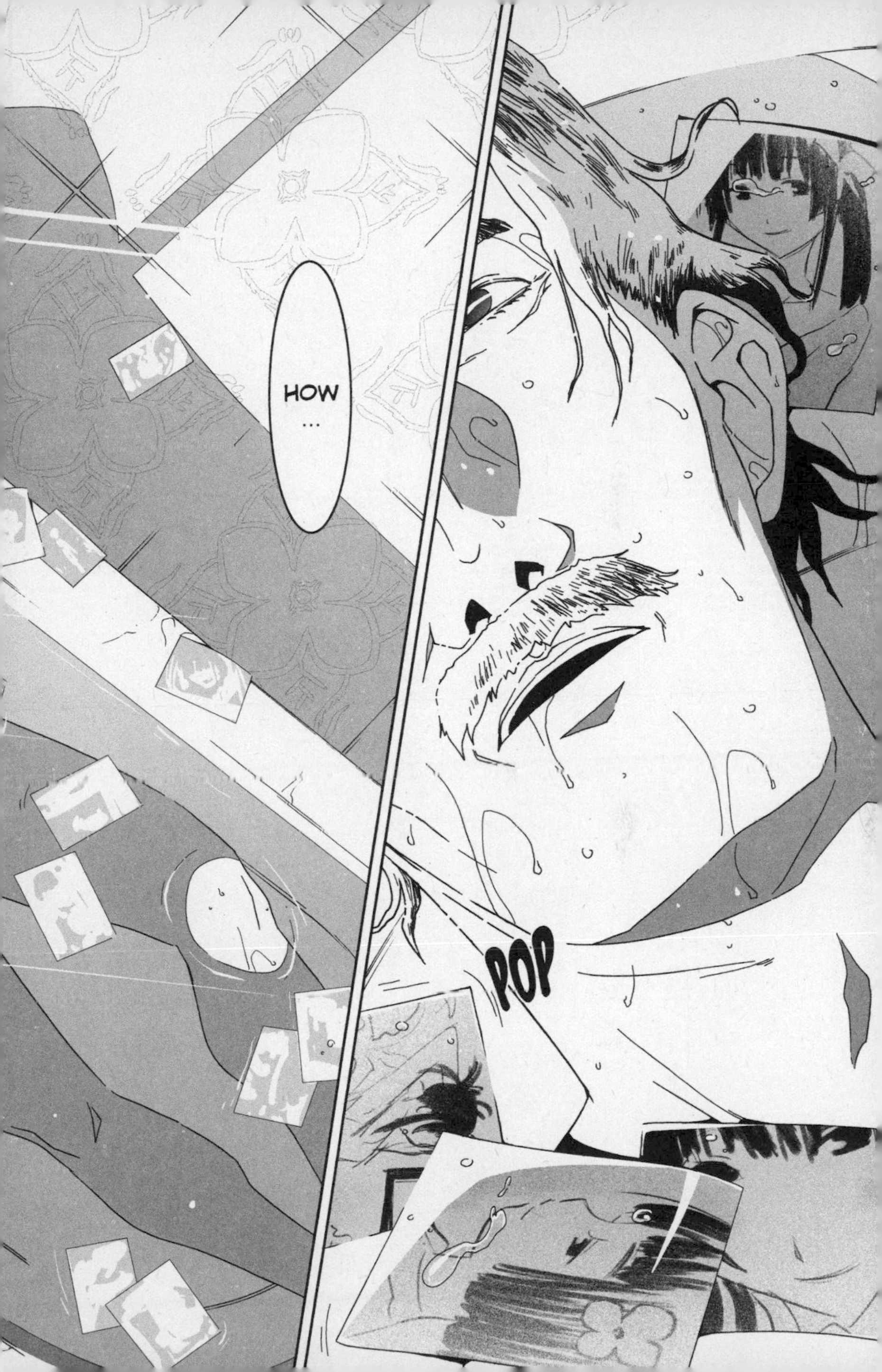
POP
HOW
...

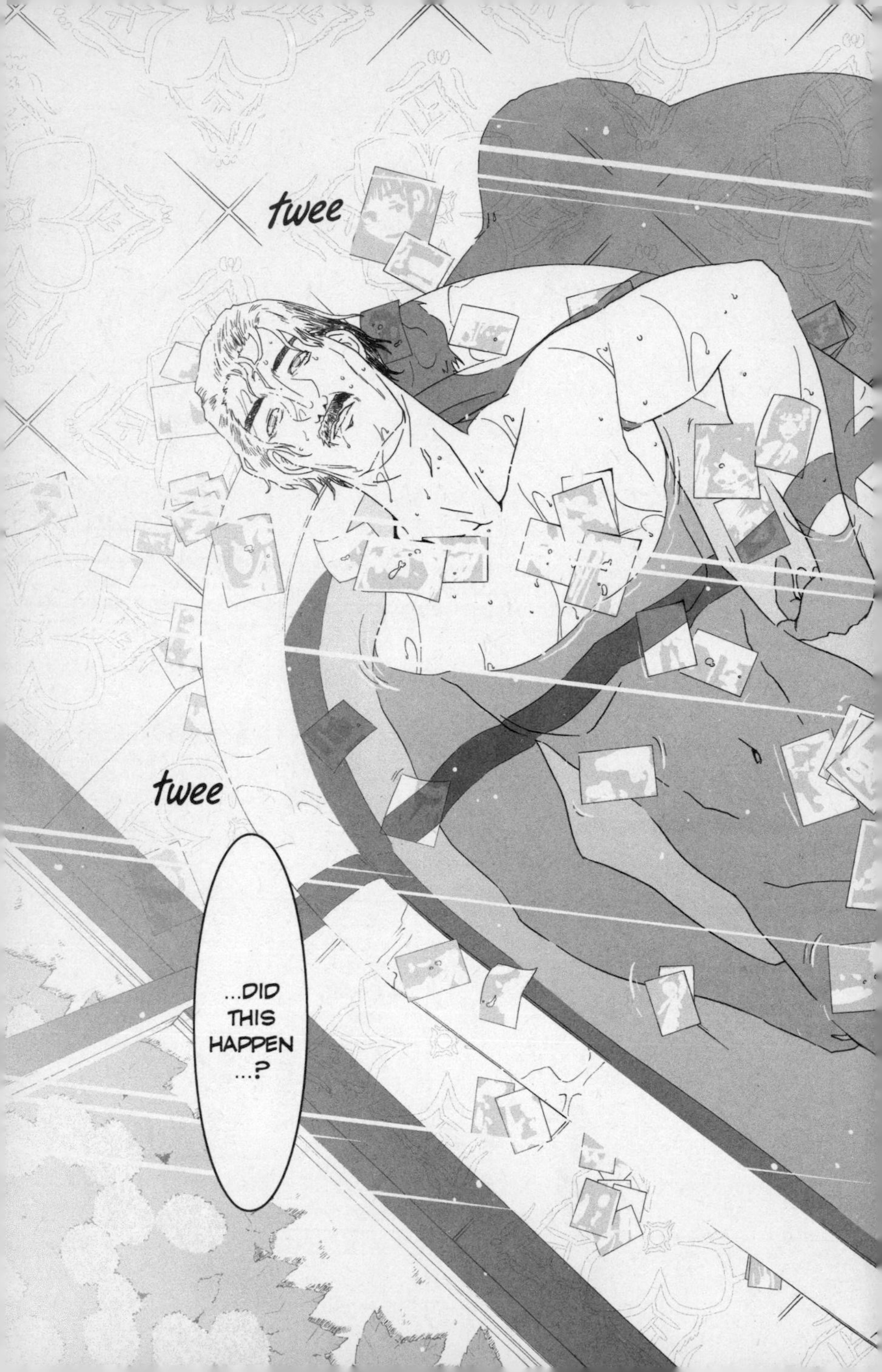
twee
twee
...DID THIS HAPPEN ...?

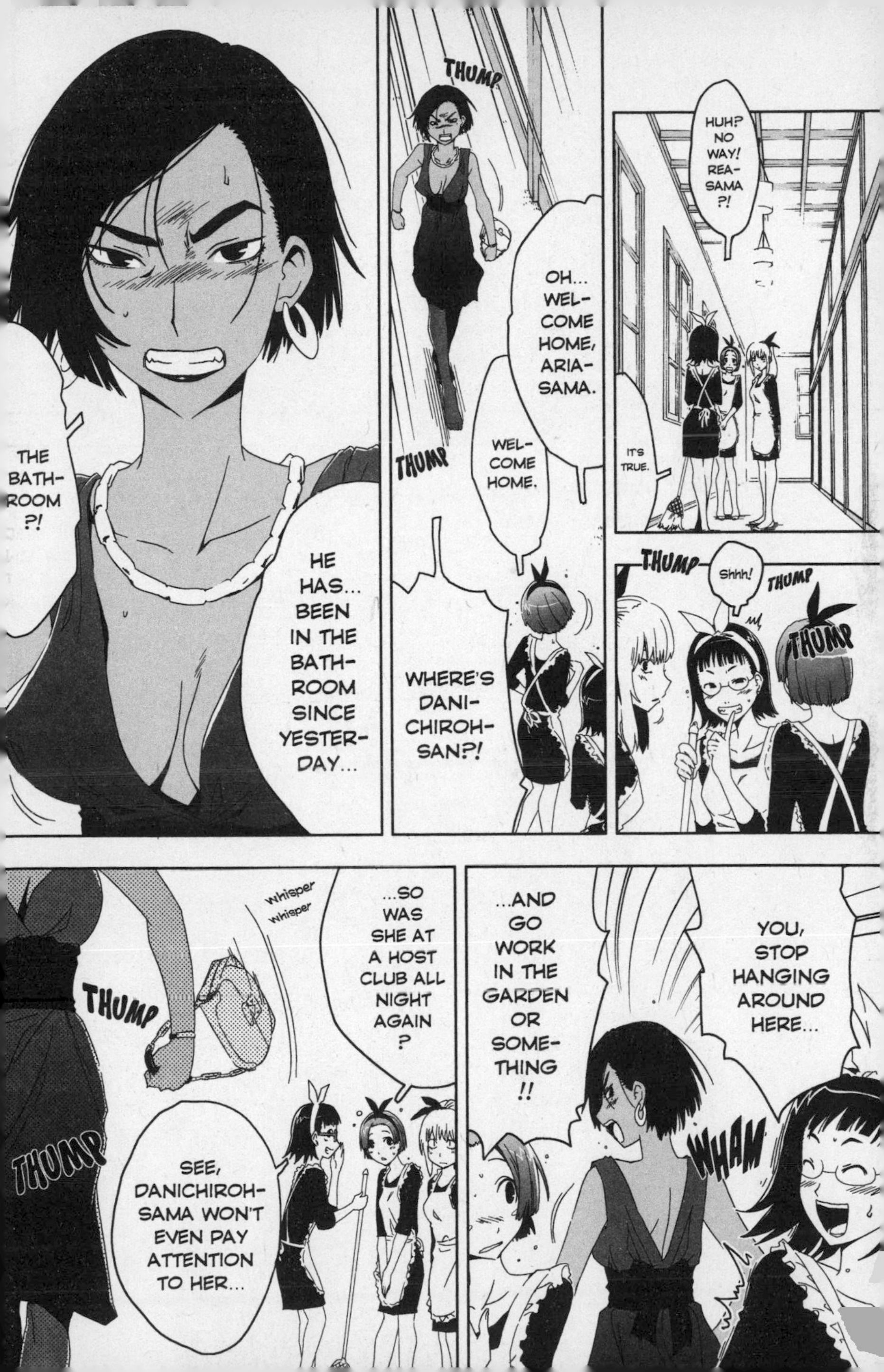
HUH? NO WAY! REA-SAMA?!
IT'S TRUE.
THUMP
Shhh!
THUMP
THUMP
THUMP
OH... WELCOME HOME, ARIA-SAMA.
WELCOME HOME.
THUMP
WHERE'S DANICHIROH-SAN?!
HE HAS... BEEN IN THE BATHROOM SINCE YESTERDAY...
THE BATHROOM?!
YOU, STOP HANGING AROUND HERE...
...AND GO WORK IN THE GARDEN OR SOMETHING!!
WHAM
whisper whisper
...SO WAS SHE AT A HOST CLUB ALL NIGHT AGAIN?
THUMP
SEE, DANICHIROH-SAMA WON'T EVEN PAY ATTENTION TO HER...
THUMP

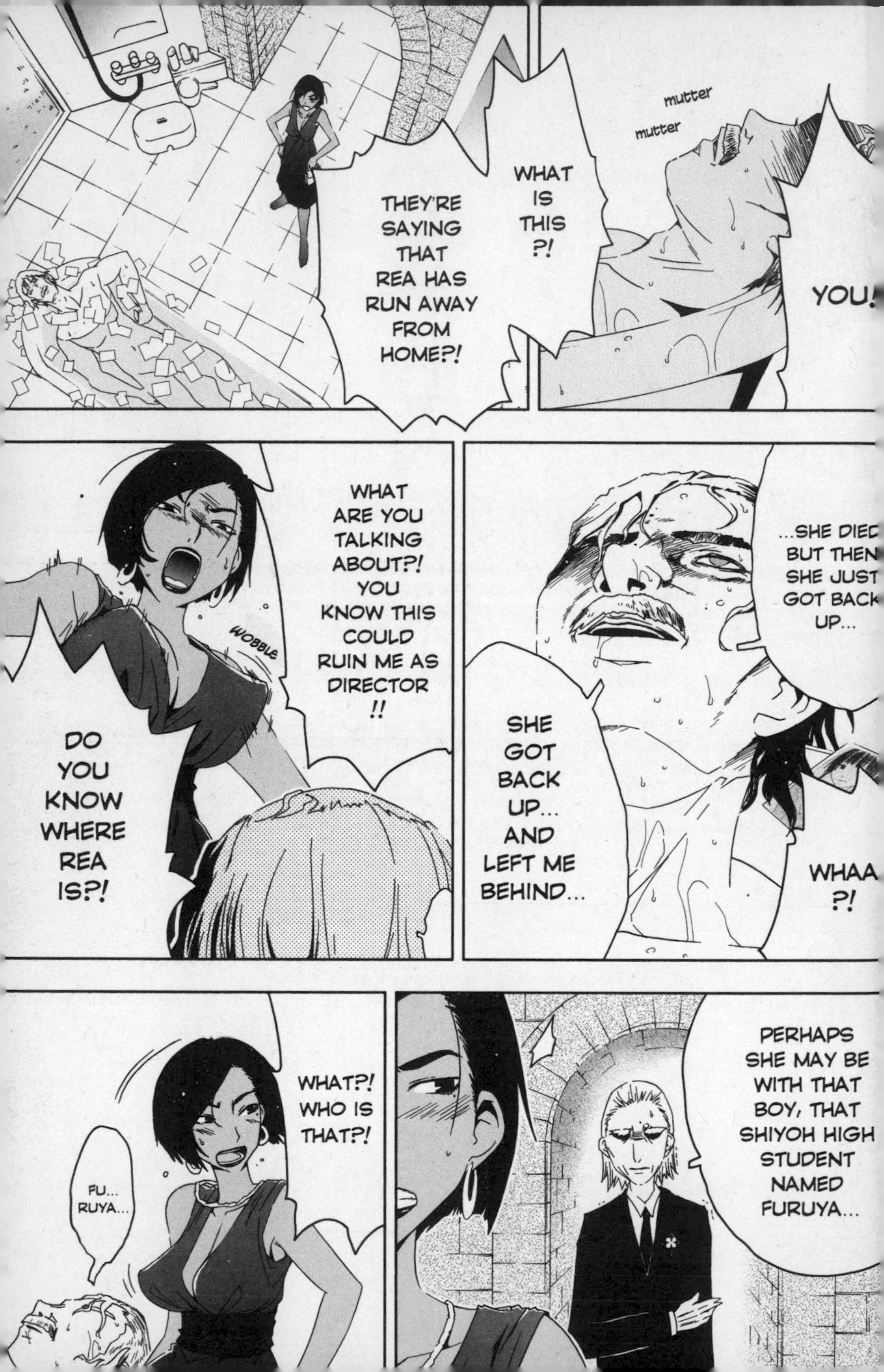
mutter
mutter
YOU!
WHAT IS THIS ?!
THEY'RE SAYING THAT REA HAS RUN AWAY FROM HOME?!
...SHE DIED BUT THEN SHE JUST GOT BACK UP...
WHAA ?!
SHE GOT BACK UP... AND LEFT ME BEHIND...
WHAT ARE YOU TALKING ABOUT?! YOU KNOW THIS COULD RUIN ME AS DIRECTOR !!
WOBBLE
DO YOU KNOW WHERE REA IS?!
PERHAPS SHE MAY BE WITH THAT BOY, THAT SHIYOH HIGH STUDENT NAMED FURUYA...
WHAT?! WHO IS THAT?!
FU... RUYA...

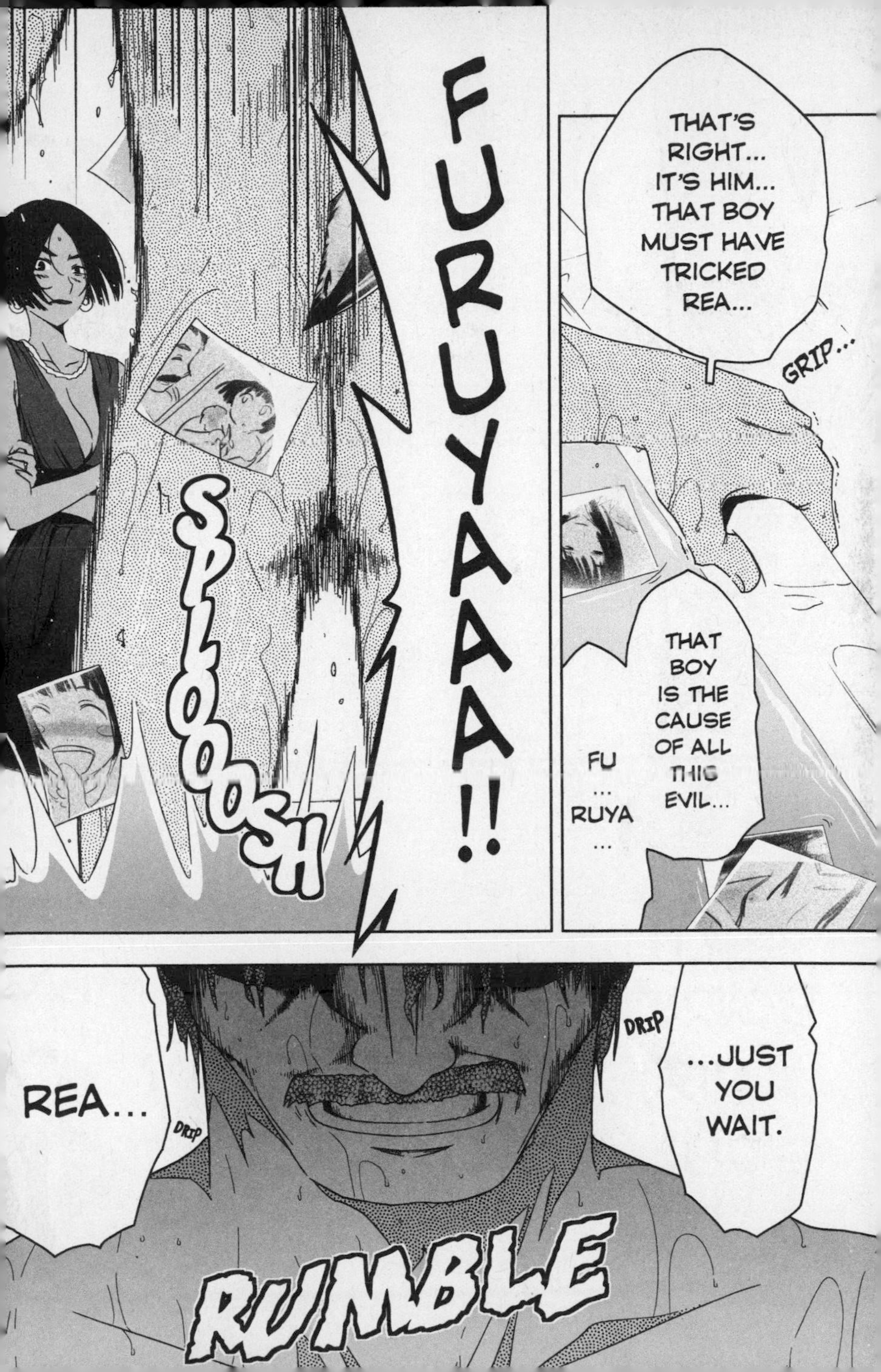
THAT'S RIGHT... IT'S HIM... THAT BOY MUST HAVE TRICKED REA...
GRIP...
THAT BOY IS THE CAUSE OF ALL THIS EVIL...
FU ... RUYA ...
FURUYAAA!!
SPLOOOSH
DRIP
...JUST YOU WAIT.
REA...
DRIP
RUMBLE

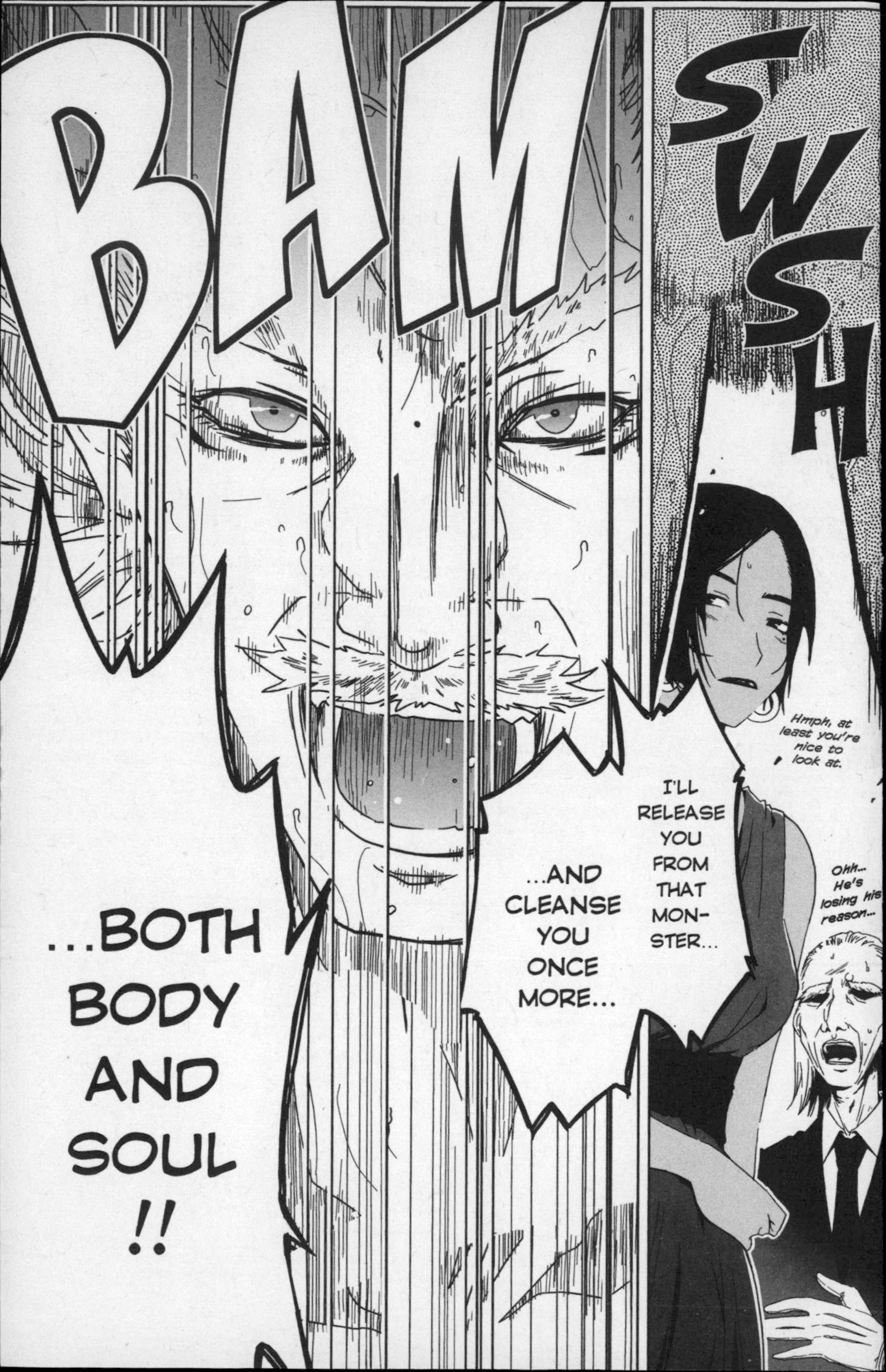
SWSH
BAM
Hmph, at least you're nice to look at.
I'LL RELEASE YOU FROM THAT MON-STER...
...AND CLEANSE YOU ONCE MORE...
...BOTH BODY AND SOUL!!
Ohh... He's losing his reason...

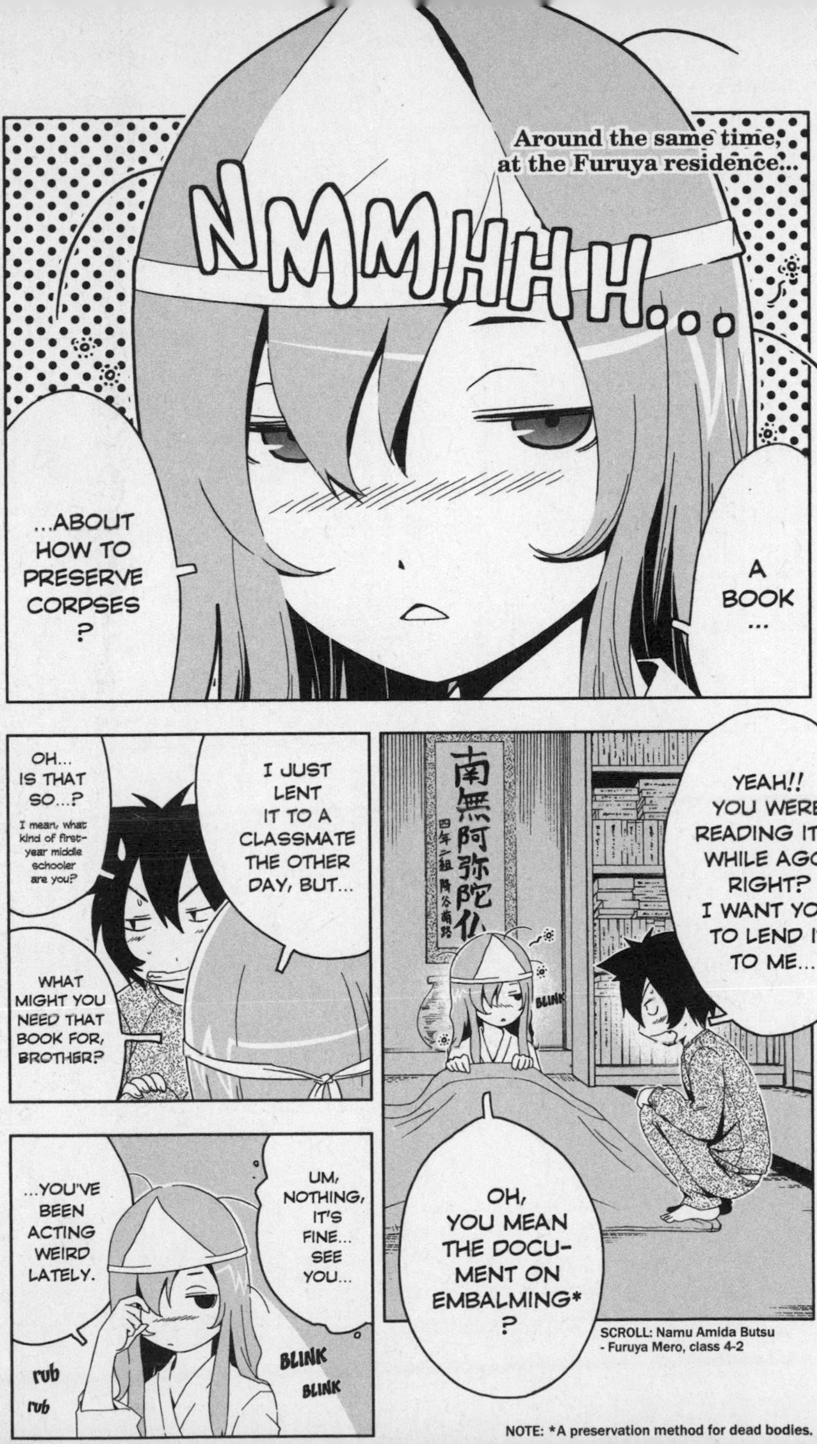
Around the same time, at the Furuya residence...
NMMHHH...
A BOOK ...
...ABOUT HOW TO PRESERVE CORPSES ?
YEAH!! YOU WERE READING IT A WHILE AGO, RIGHT? I WANT YOU TO LEND IT TO ME...
南無阿弥陀仏
四年二組 降谷萌路
BLINK
OH, YOU MEAN THE DOCU- MENT ON EMBALMING* ?
I JUST LENT IT TO A CLASSMATE THE OTHER DAY, BUT...
OH... IS THAT SO...?
I mean, what kind of first- year middle schooler are you?
WHAT MIGHT YOU NEED THAT BOOK FOR, BROTHER?
UM, NOTHING, IT'S FINE... SEE YOU...
...YOU'VE BEEN ACTING WEIRD LATELY.
BLINK
BLINK
rub
rub
SCROLL: Namu Amida Butsu
- Furuya Mero, class 4-2

NOTE: *A preservation method for dead bodies.

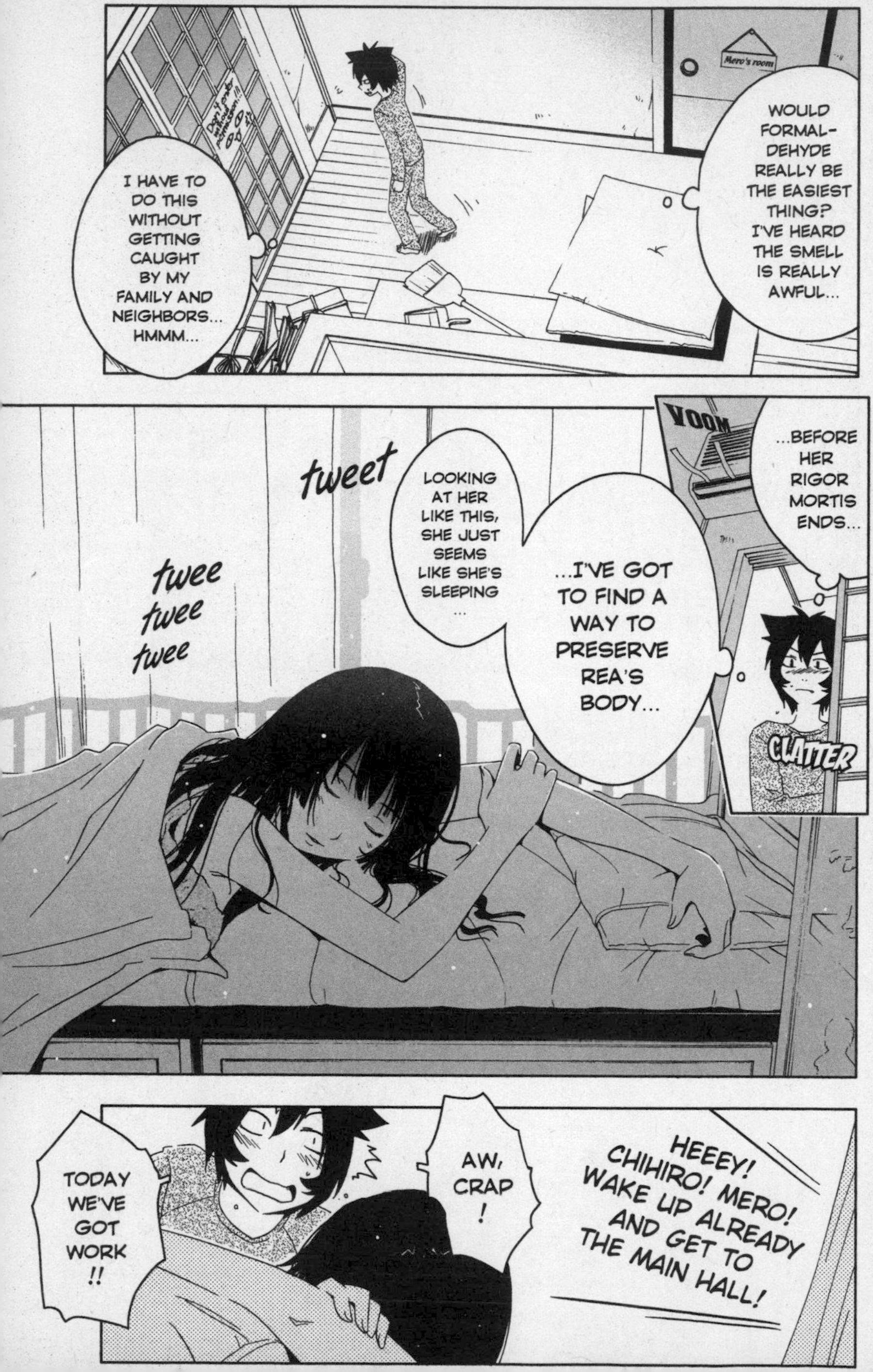
Mero's room
WOULD FORMAL-DEHYDE REALLY BE THE EASIEST THING? I'VE HEARD THE SMELL IS REALLY AWFUL...
I HAVE TO DO THIS WITHOUT GETTING CAUGHT BY MY FAMILY AND NEIGHBORS... HMMM...
VOOM
...BEFORE HER RIGOR MORTIS ENDS...
CLATTER
...I'VE GOT TO FIND A WAY TO PRESERVE REA'S BODY...
LOOKING AT HER LIKE THIS, SHE JUST SEEMS LIKE SHE'S SLEEPING ...
tweet
twee twee twee
HEEEY! CHIHIRO! MERO! WAKE UP ALREADY AND GET TO THE MAIN HALL!
AW, CRAP !
TODAY WE'VE GOT WORK !!

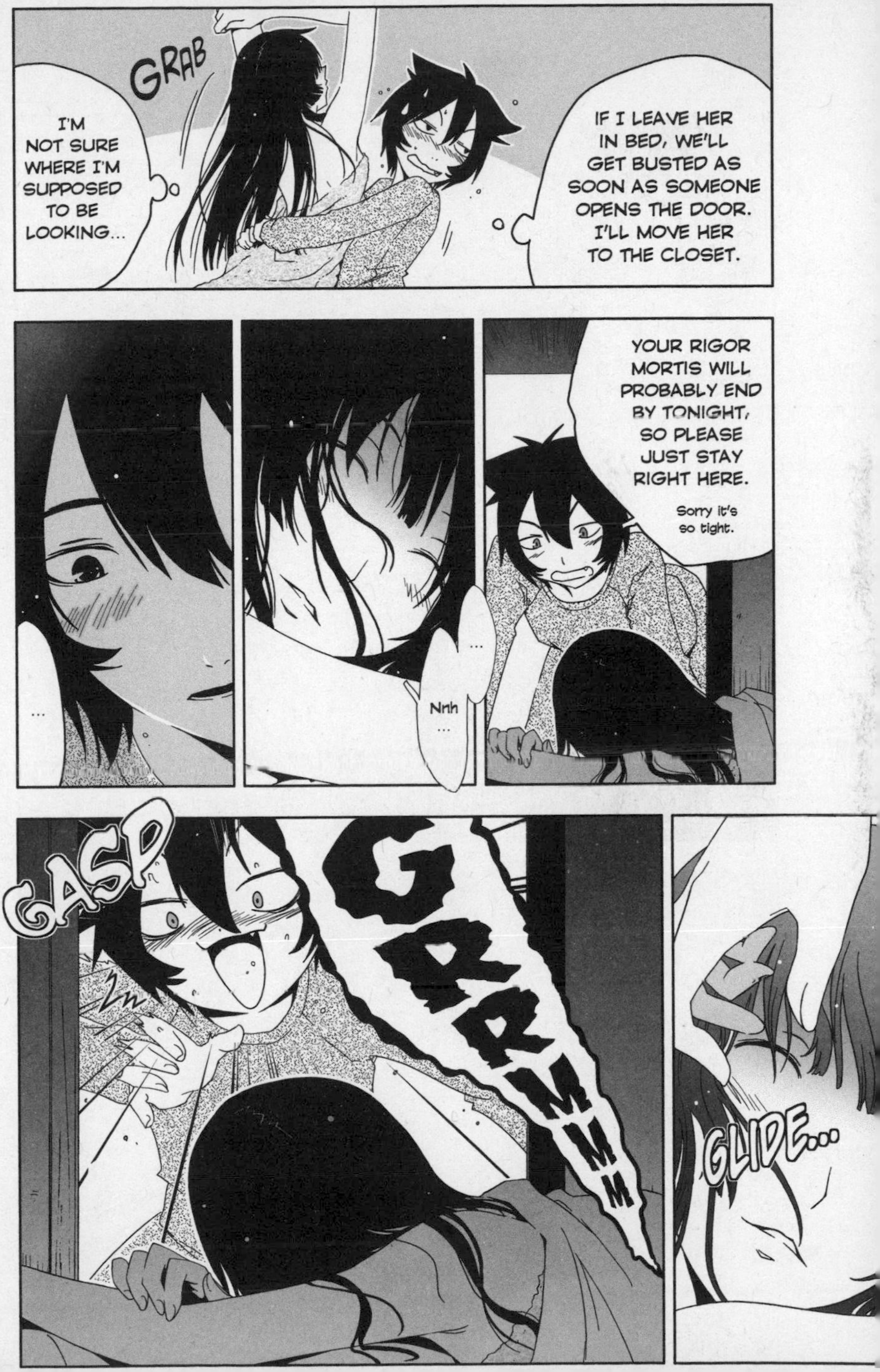
IF I LEAVE HER IN BED, WE'LL GET BUSTED AS SOON AS SOMEONE OPENS THE DOOR. I'LL MOVE HER TO THE CLOSET.
GRAB
I'M NOT SURE WHERE I'M SUPPOSED TO BE LOOKING...
YOUR RIGOR MORTIS WILL PROBABLY END BY TONIGHT, SO PLEASE JUST STAY RIGHT HERE.
Sorry it's so tight.
...
Nnh ...
...
GLIDE...
GASP
GRRMMM

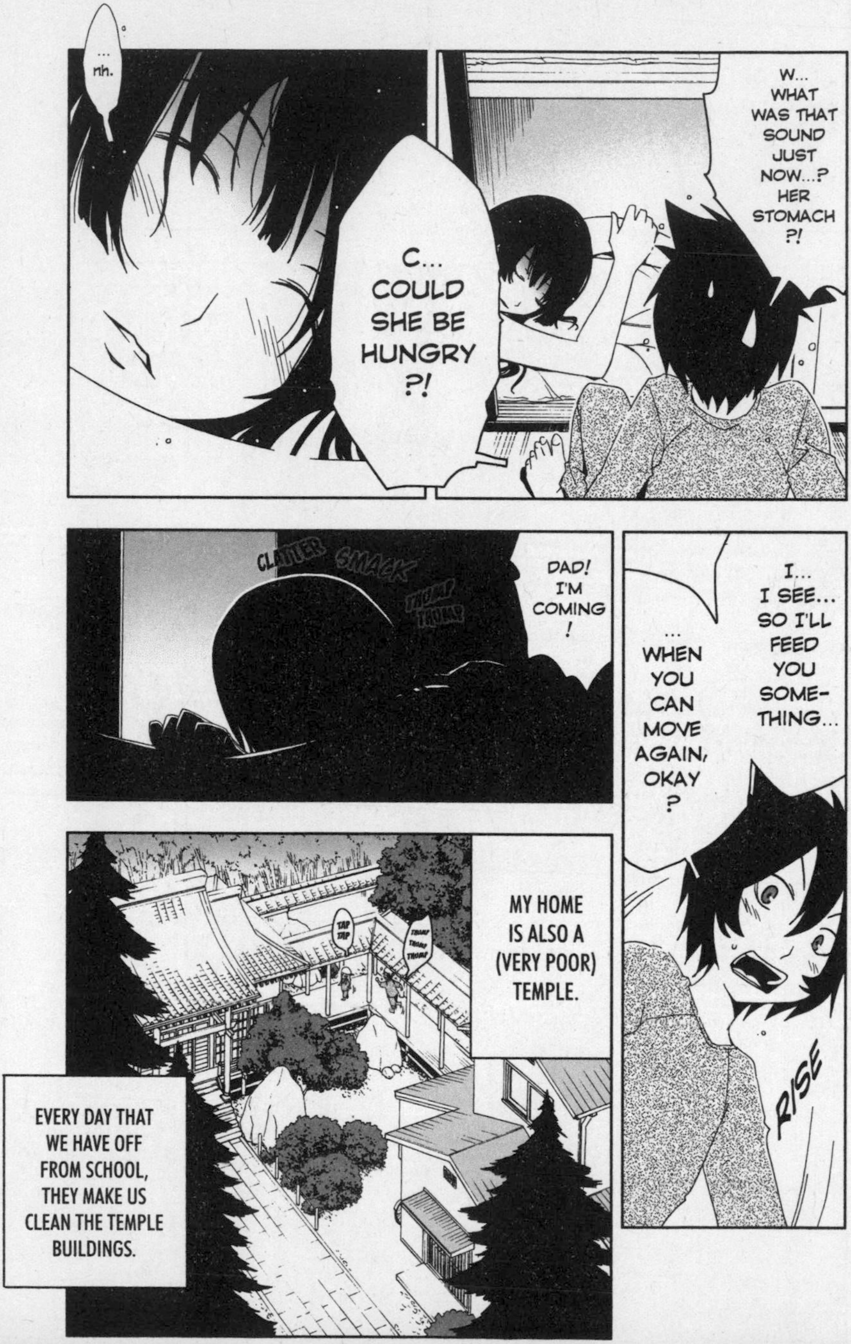
W... WHAT WAS THAT SOUND JUST NOW...? HER STOMACH ?!
C... COULD SHE BE HUNGRY ?!
... nh.
I... I SEE... SO I'LL FEED YOU SOME-THING...
... WHEN YOU CAN MOVE AGAIN, OKAY ?
RISE
DAD! I'M COMING !
CLATTER
SMACK
THOMP THOMP
MY HOME IS ALSO A (VERY POOR) TEMPLE.
THOMP THOMP THOMP
TAP TAP
EVERY DAY THAT WE HAVE OFF FROM SCHOOL, THEY MAKE US CLEAN THE TEMPLE BUILDINGS.

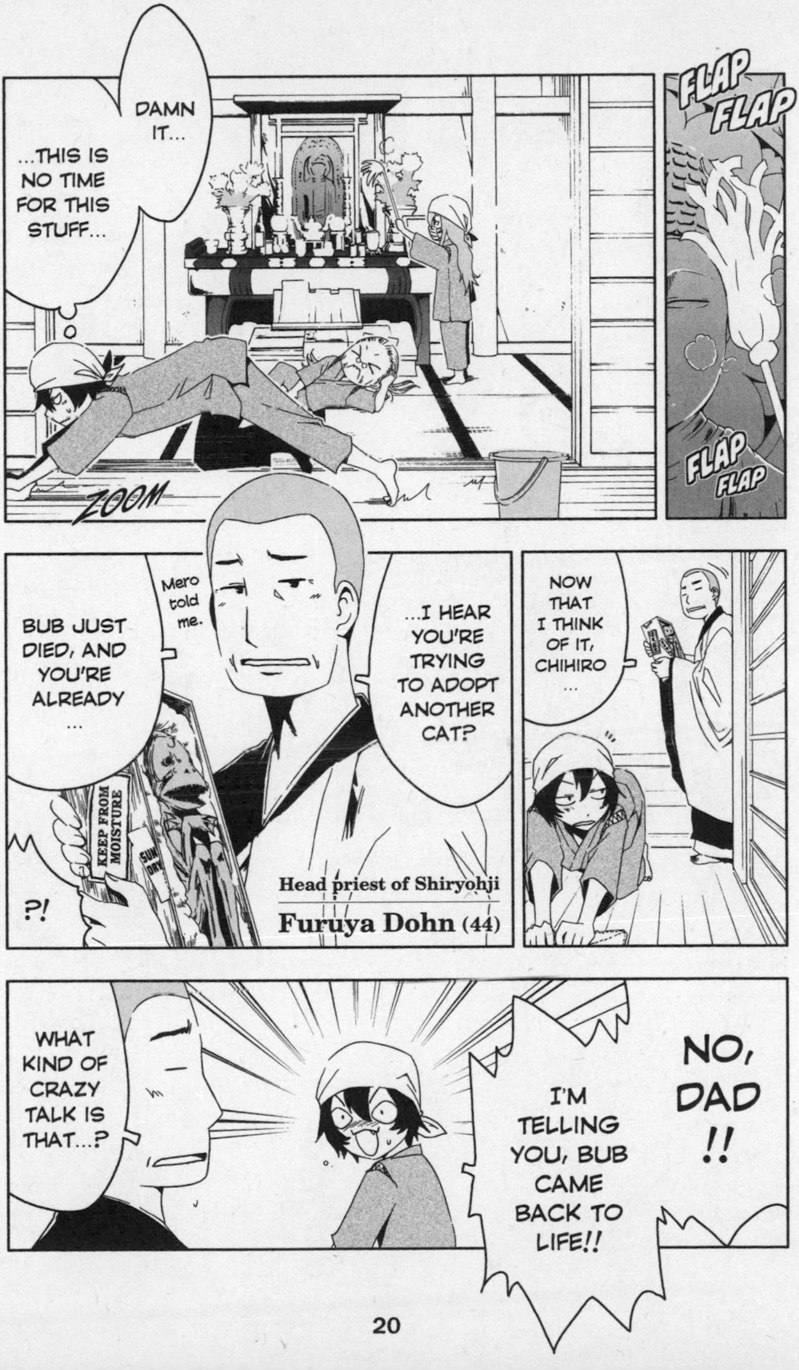
FLAP FLAP
FLAP FLAP
DAMN IT...
...THIS IS NO TIME FOR THIS STUFF...
ZOOM
NOW THAT I THINK OF IT, CHIHIRO ...
...I HEAR YOU'RE TRYING TO ADOPT ANOTHER CAT?
Mero told me.
BUB JUST DIED, AND YOU'RE ALREADY ...
KEEP FROM MOISTURE
SUN DRY
?!
Head priest of Shiryohji
Furuya Dohn (44)
NO, DAD!!
I'M TELLING YOU, BUB CAME BACK TO LIFE!!
WHAT KIND OF CRAZY TALK IS THAT...?

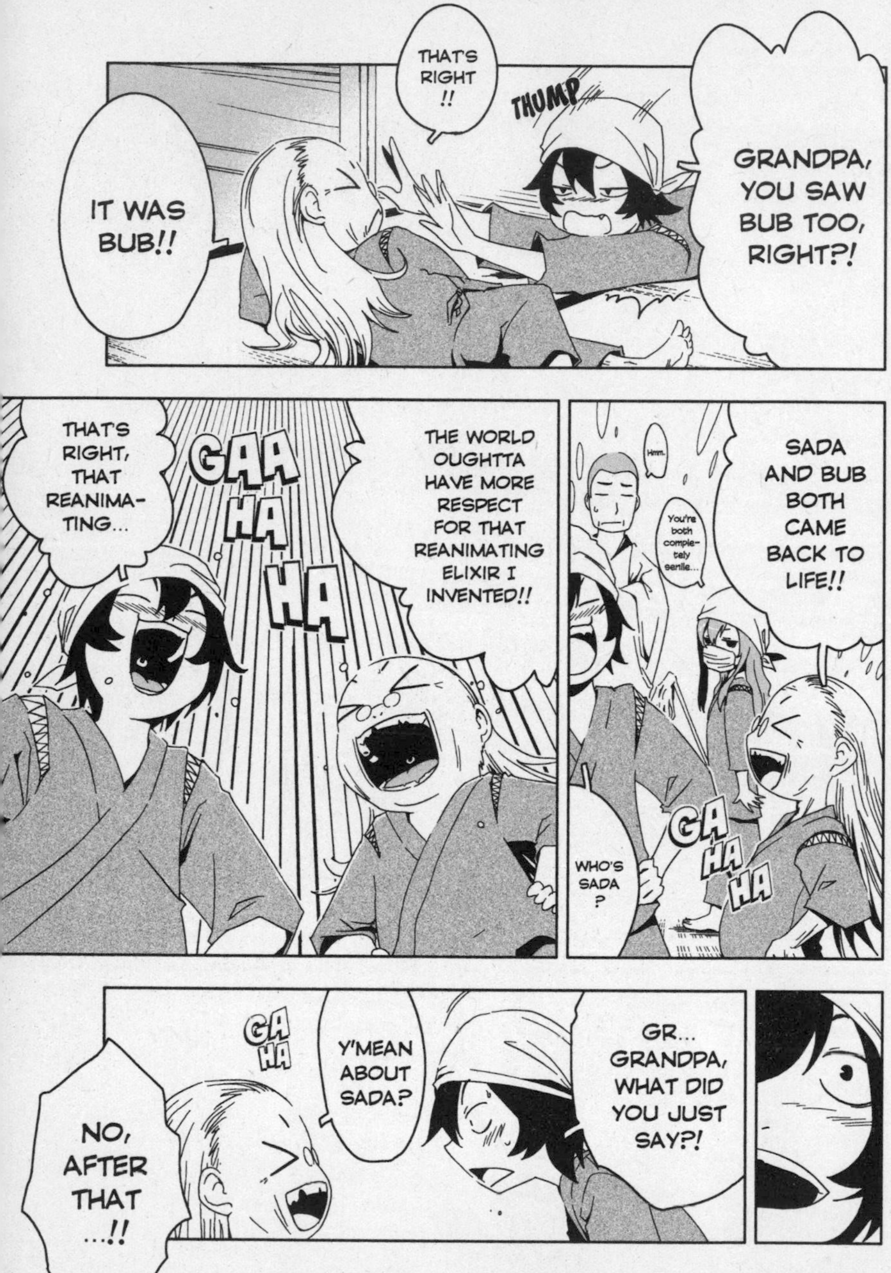
GRANDPA, YOU SAW BUB TOO, RIGHT?!
THUMP
THAT'S RIGHT !!
IT WAS BUB!!
SADA AND BUB BOTH CAME BACK TO LIFE!!
Hmm.
You're both completely senile...
GA HA HA
WHO'S SADA ?
THE WORLD OUGHTTA HAVE MORE RESPECT FOR THAT REANIMATING ELIXIR I INVENTED!!
GAA HA HA
THAT'S RIGHT, THAT REANIMA-TING...
GR... GRANDPA, WHAT DID YOU JUST SAY?!
Y'MEAN ABOUT SADA?
GA HA
NO, AFTER THAT ...!!

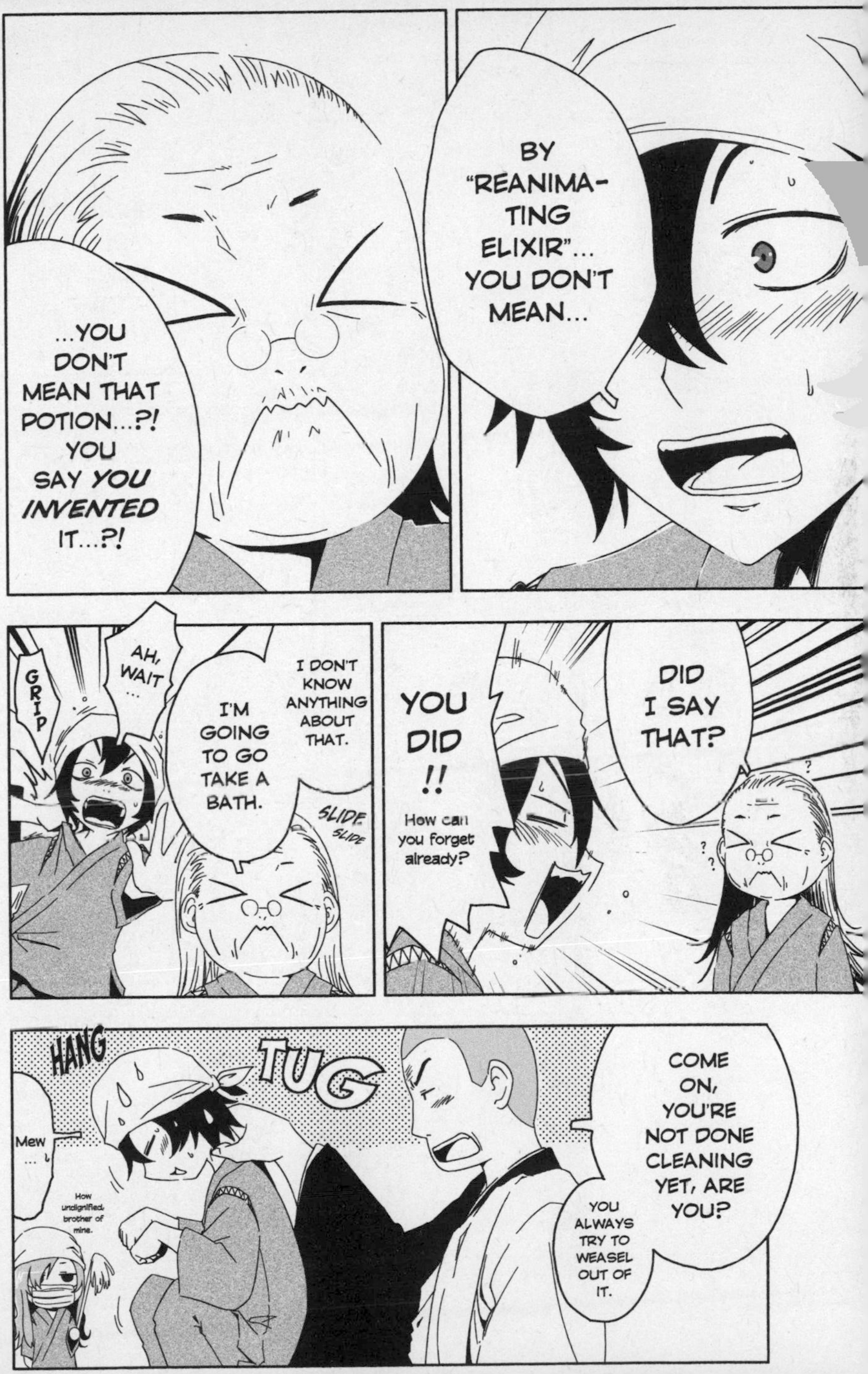
BY "REANIMATING ELIXIR"... YOU DON'T MEAN...
...YOU DON'T MEAN THAT POTION...?! YOU SAY *YOU INVENTED* IT...?!
DID I SAY THAT?
YOU DID!!
How can you forget already?
I DON'T KNOW ANYTHING ABOUT THAT.
I'M GOING TO GO TAKE A BATH.
SLIDE SLIDE
AH, WAIT...
GRIP
COME ON, YOU'RE NOT DONE CLEANING YET, ARE YOU?
YOU ALWAYS TRY TO WEASEL OUT OF IT.
TUG
HANG
Mew...
How undignified, brother of mine.

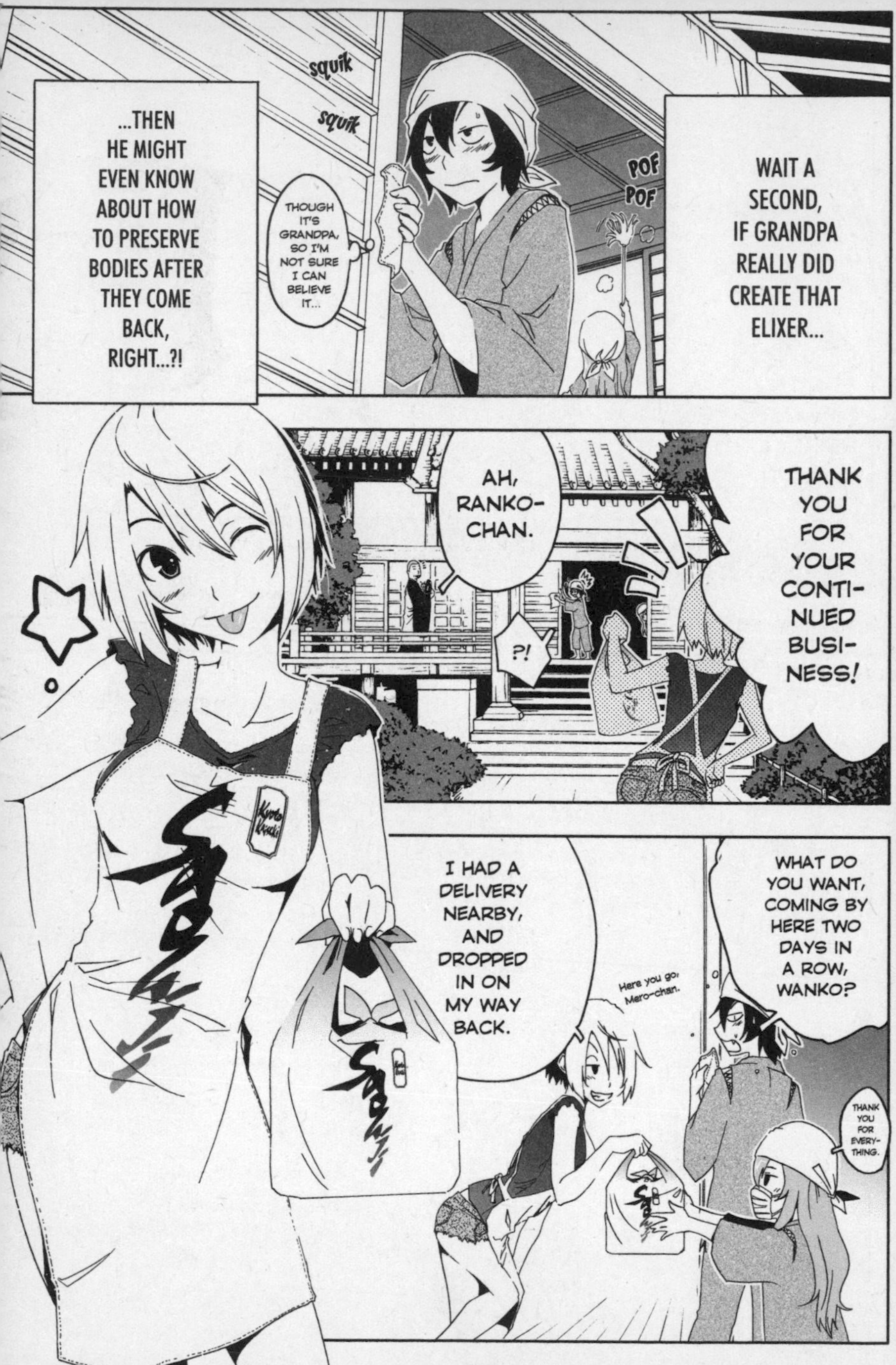
WAIT A SECOND, IF GRANDPA REALLY DID CREATE THAT ELIXER...
POF POF
squik squik
THOUGH IT'S GRANDPA, SO I'M NOT SURE I CAN BELIEVE IT...
...THEN HE MIGHT EVEN KNOW ABOUT HOW TO PRESERVE BODIES AFTER THEY COME BACK, RIGHT...?!
THANK YOU FOR YOUR CONTI-NUED BUSI-NESS!
AH, RANKO-CHAN.
?!
WHAT DO YOU WANT, COMING BY HERE TWO DAYS IN A ROW, WANKO?
I HAD A DELIVERY NEARBY, AND DROPPED IN ON MY WAY BACK.
Here you go, Mero-chan.
THANK YOU FOR EVERY-THING.

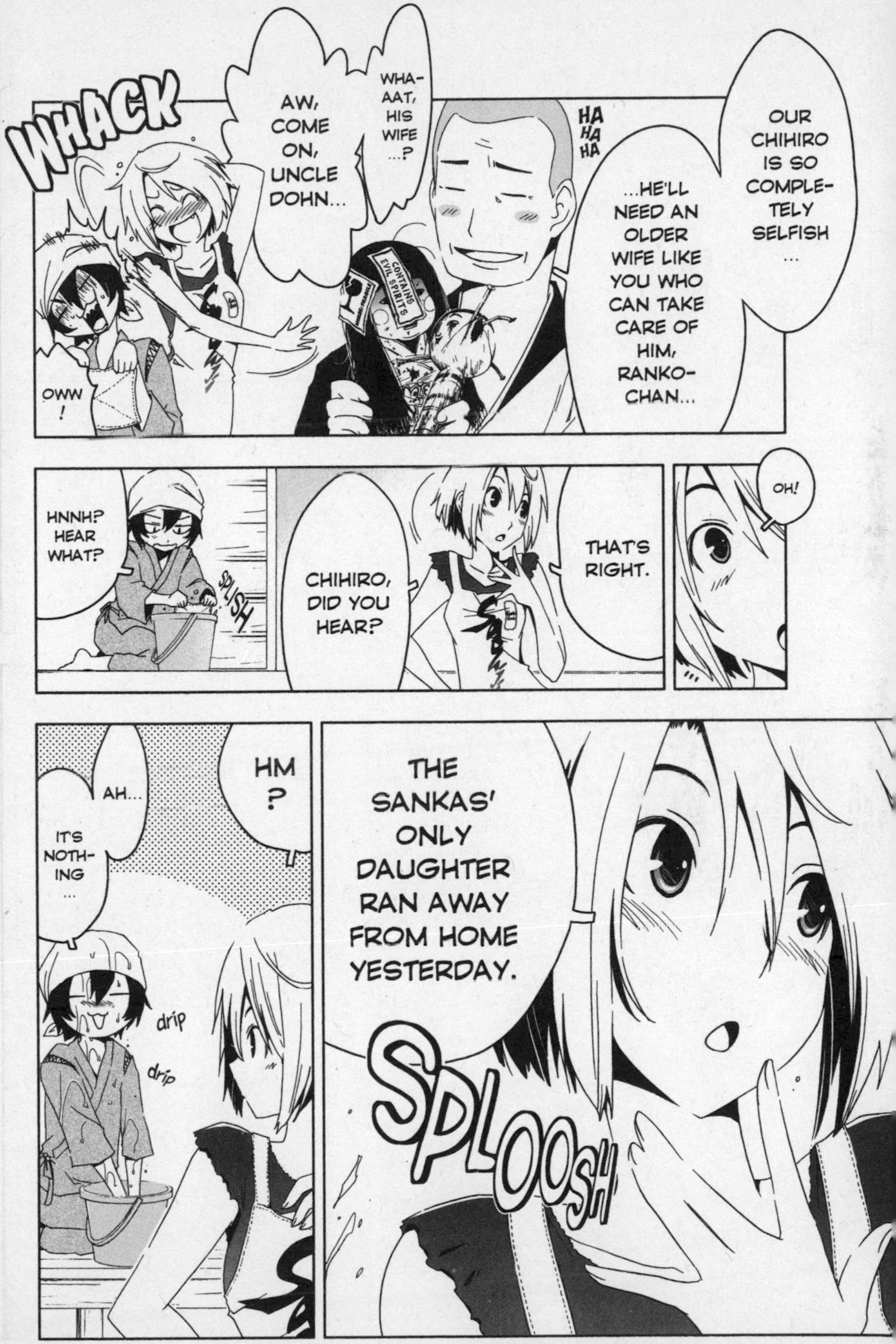
OUR CHIHIRO IS SO COMPLETELY SELFISH...
...HE'LL NEED AN OLDER WIFE LIKE YOU WHO CAN TAKE CARE OF HIM, RANKO-CHAN...
HA HA HA
WHAAAT, HIS WIFE...?
AW, COME ON, UNCLE DOHN...
WHACK
CONTAINS EVIL SPIRITS
OWW!
OH!
THAT'S RIGHT.
CHIHIRO, DID YOU HEAR?
HNNH? HEAR WHAT?
SPLISH
THE SANKAS' ONLY DAUGHTER RAN AWAY FROM HOME YESTERDAY.
SPLOOSH
HM?
AH...
IT'S NOTHING...
drip
drip

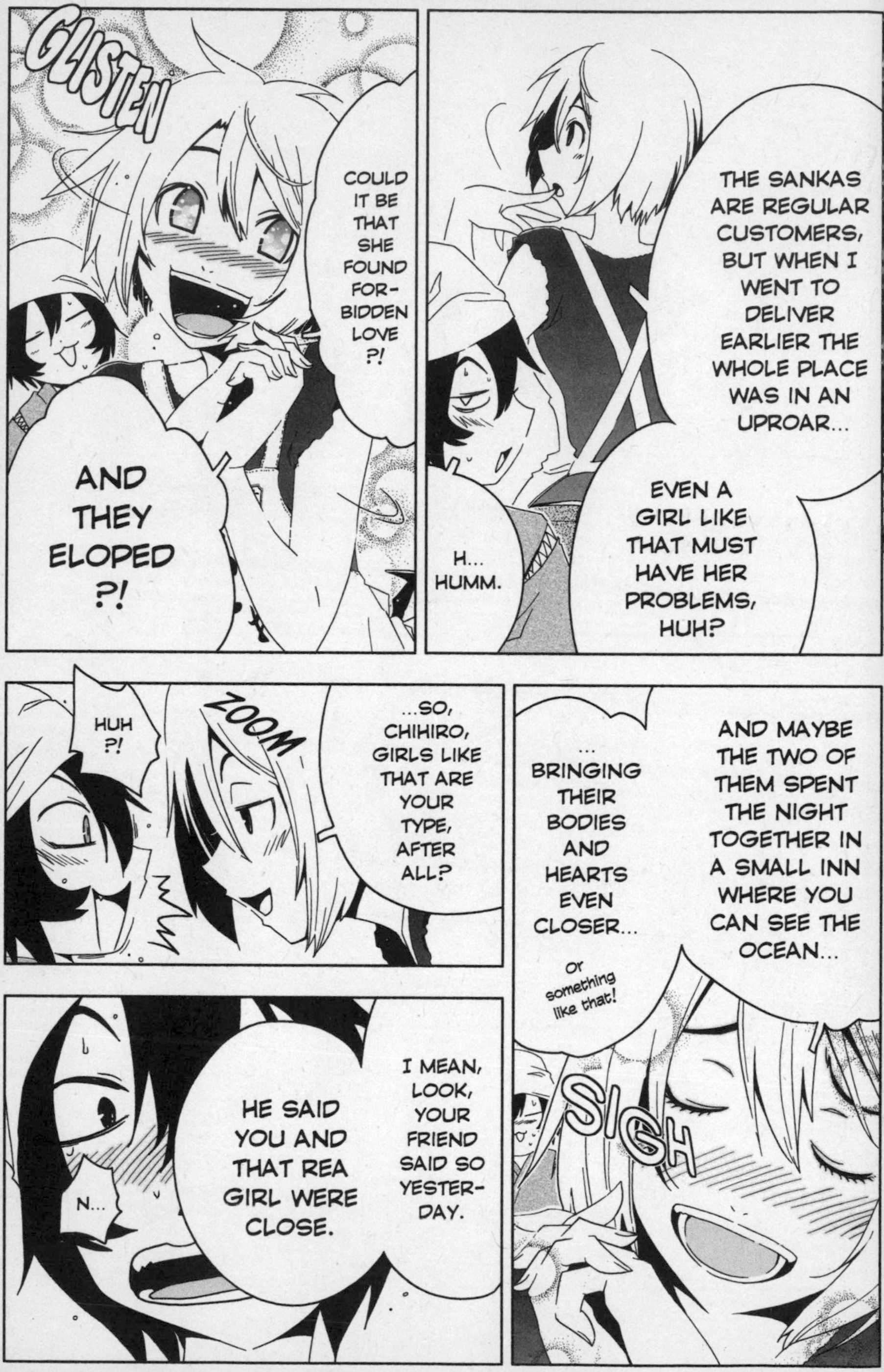
THE SANKAS ARE REGULAR CUSTOMERS, BUT WHEN I WENT TO DELIVER EARLIER THE WHOLE PLACE WAS IN AN UPROAR...
EVEN A GIRL LIKE THAT MUST HAVE HER PROBLEMS, HUH?
H... HUMM.
GLISTEN
COULD IT BE THAT SHE FOUND FOR-BIDDEN LOVE ?!
AND THEY ELOPED ?!
AND MAYBE THE TWO OF THEM SPENT THE NIGHT TOGETHER IN A SMALL INN WHERE YOU CAN SEE THE OCEAN...
...BRINGING THEIR BODIES AND HEARTS EVEN CLOSER...
Or something like that!
SIGH
ZOOM
...SO, CHIHIRO, GIRLS LIKE THAT ARE YOUR TYPE, AFTER ALL?
HUH ?!
I MEAN, LOOK, YOUR FRIEND SAID SO YESTER-DAY.
HE SAID YOU AND THAT REA GIRL WERE CLOSE.
N...

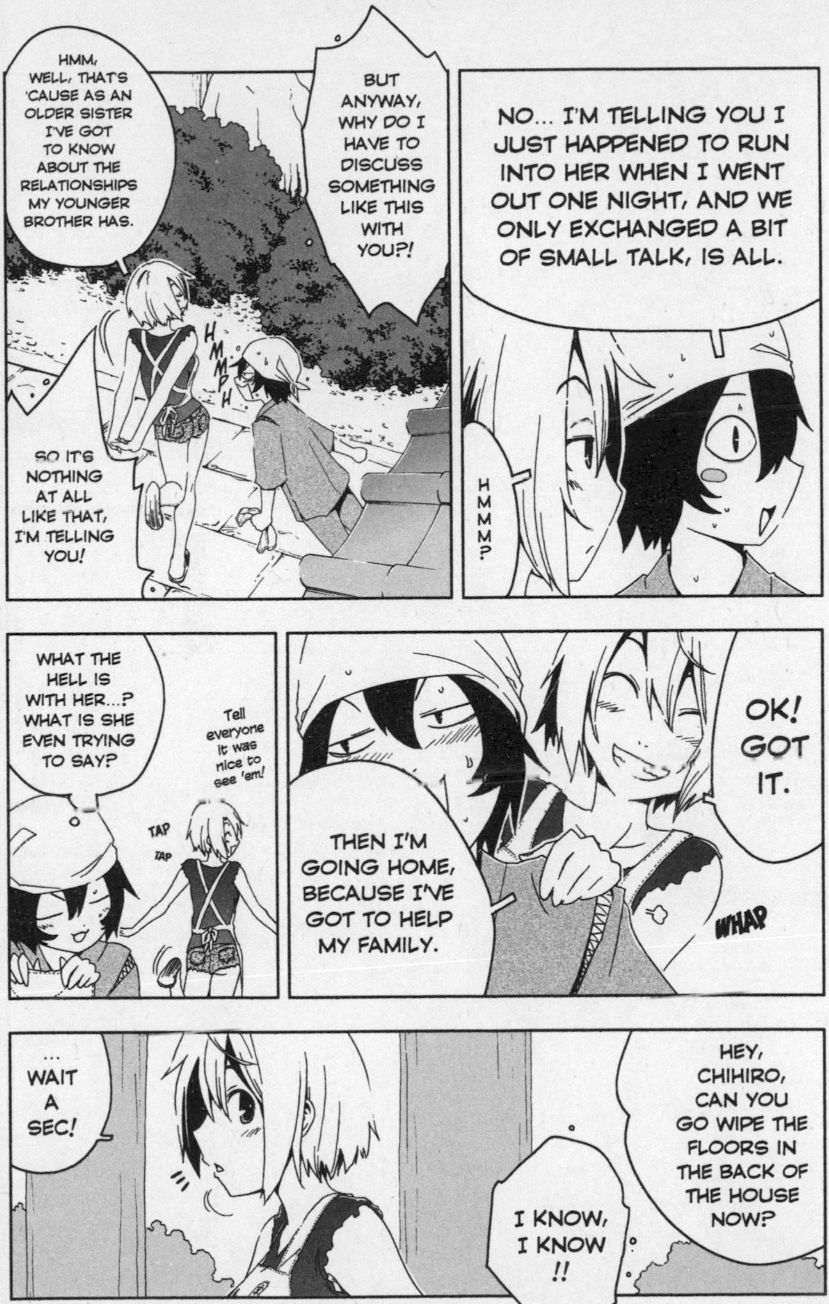
NO... I'M TELLING YOU I JUST HAPPENED TO RUN INTO HER WHEN I WENT OUT ONE NIGHT, AND WE ONLY EXCHANGED A BIT OF SMALL TALK, IS ALL.
HMMM?
BUT ANYWAY, WHY DO I HAVE TO DISCUSS SOMETHING LIKE THIS WITH YOU?!
HMM, WELL, THAT'S 'CAUSE AS AN OLDER SISTER I'VE GOT TO KNOW ABOUT THE RELATIONSHIPS MY YOUNGER BROTHER HAS.
HMMPH
SO IT'S NOTHING AT ALL LIKE THAT, I'M TELLING YOU!
OK! GOT IT.
WHAP
THEN I'M GOING HOME, BECAUSE I'VE GOT TO HELP MY FAMILY.
Tell everyone it was nice to see 'em!
TAP
TAP
WHAT THE HELL IS WITH HER...? WHAT IS SHE EVEN TRYING TO SAY?
HEY, CHIHIRO, CAN YOU GO WIPE THE FLOORS IN THE BACK OF THE HOUSE NOW?
I KNOW, I KNOW !!
... WAIT A SEC!

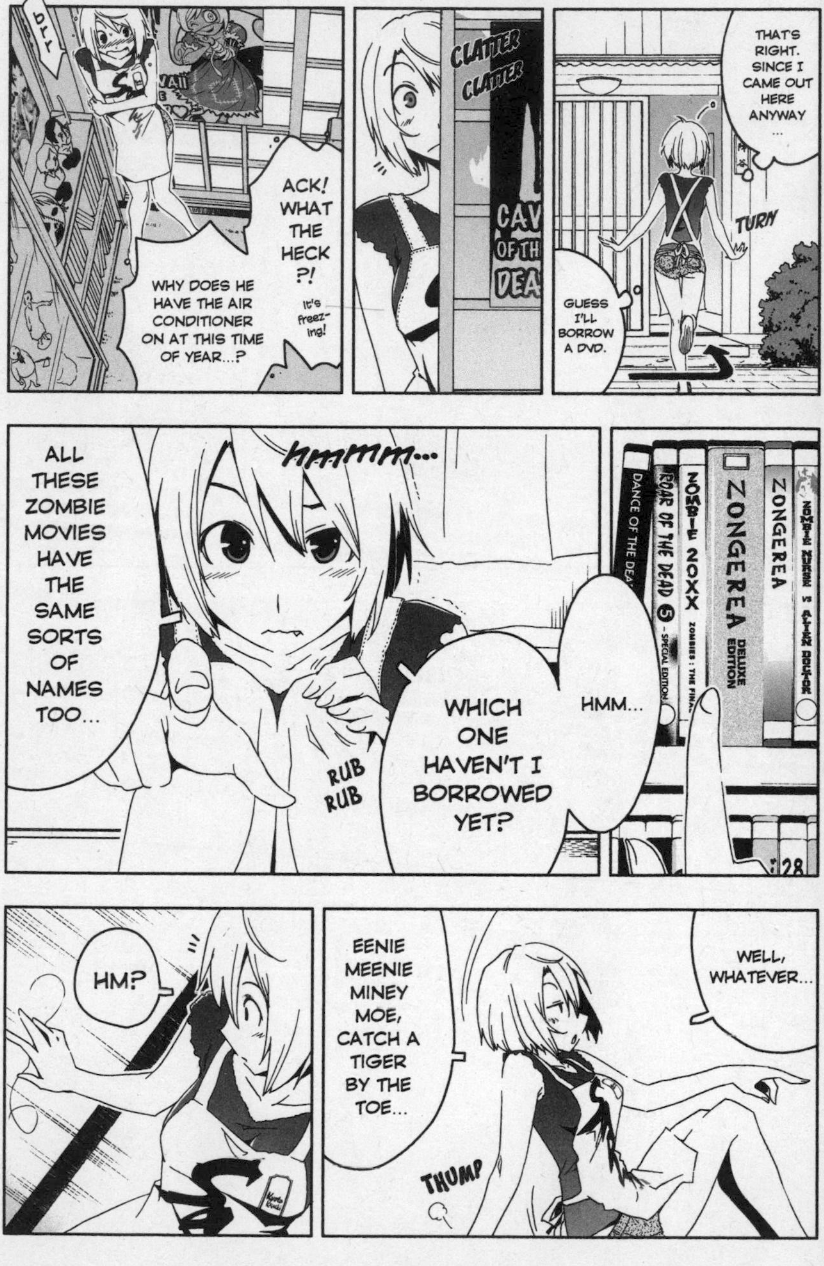
THAT'S RIGHT. SINCE I CAME OUT HERE ANYWAY ...
TURN
GUESS I'LL BORROW A DVD.
CLATTER CLATTER
CAVE OF THE DEA
ACK! WHAT THE HECK ?!
It's freezing!
WHY DOES HE HAVE THE AIR CONDITIONER ON AT THIS TIME OF YEAR...?
ZOMBIE NURSE VS ALIEN DOCTOR
ZONGEREA
ZONGEREA DELUXE EDITION
ZOMBIE 20XX ZOMBIES : THE FINAL
ROAR OF THE DEAD 5 - SPECIAL EDITION
DANCE OF THE DEA
hmmmm...
ALL THESE ZOMBIE MOVIES HAVE THE SAME SORTS OF NAMES TOO...
HMM...
WHICH ONE HAVEN'T I BORROWED YET?
RUB RUB
WELL, WHATEVER...
EENIE MEENIE MINEY MOE, CATCH A TIGER BY THE TOE...
THUMP
HM?

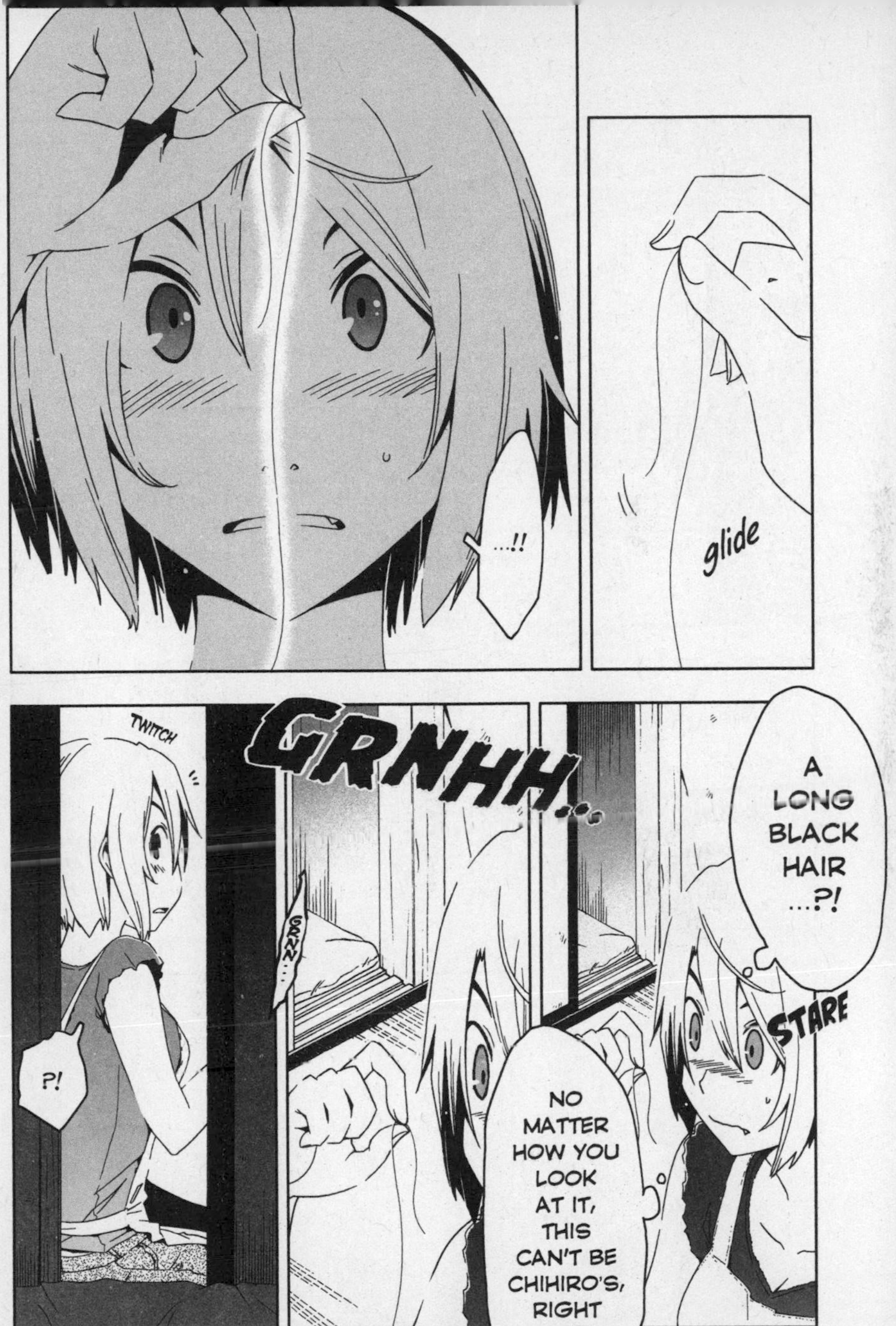
glide
...!!
A LONG BLACK HAIR ...?!
STARE
NO MATTER HOW YOU LOOK AT IT, THIS CAN'T BE CHIHIRO'S, RIGHT ...?
GRNHH...
GRNN...
TWITCH
?!

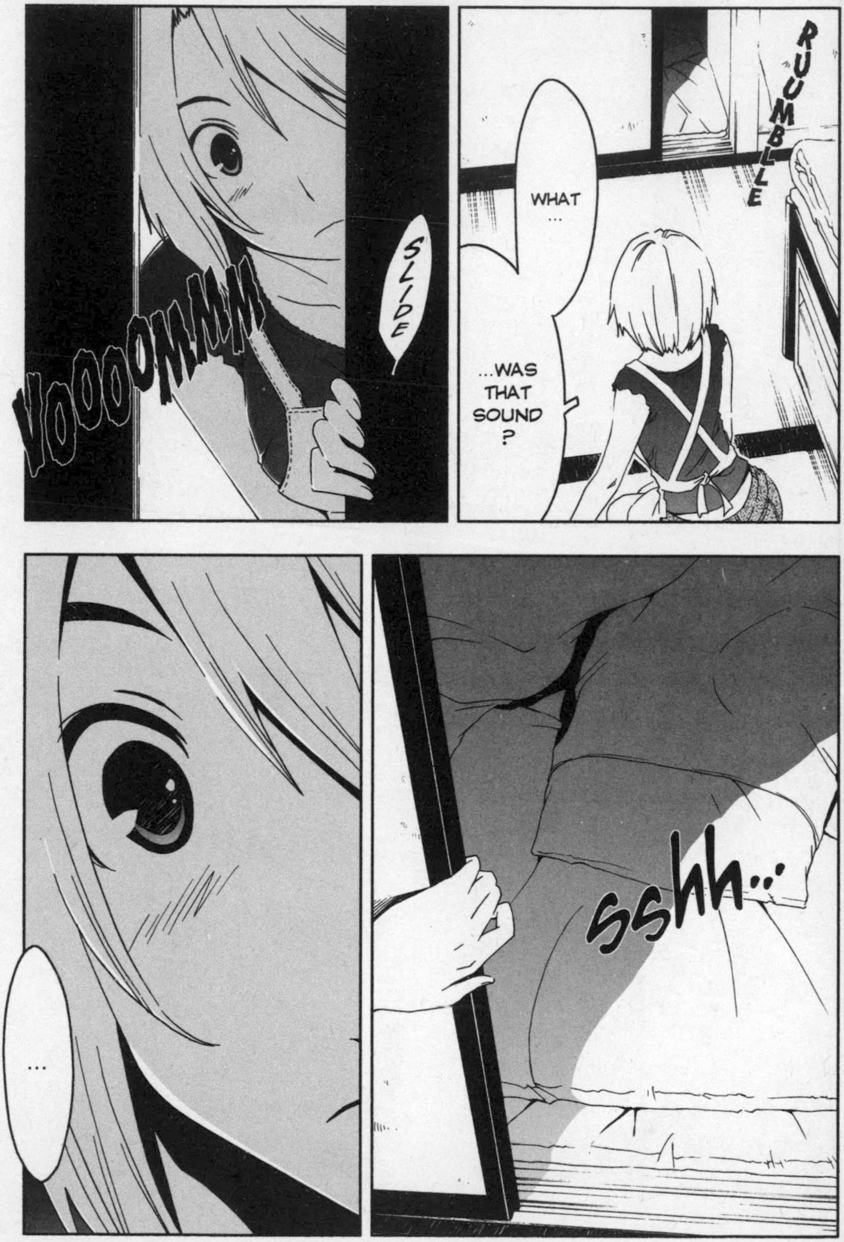
RUUMBLLE
WHAT ...
...WAS THAT SOUND ?
SLIDE
VOOOOMMM
sshh...
...

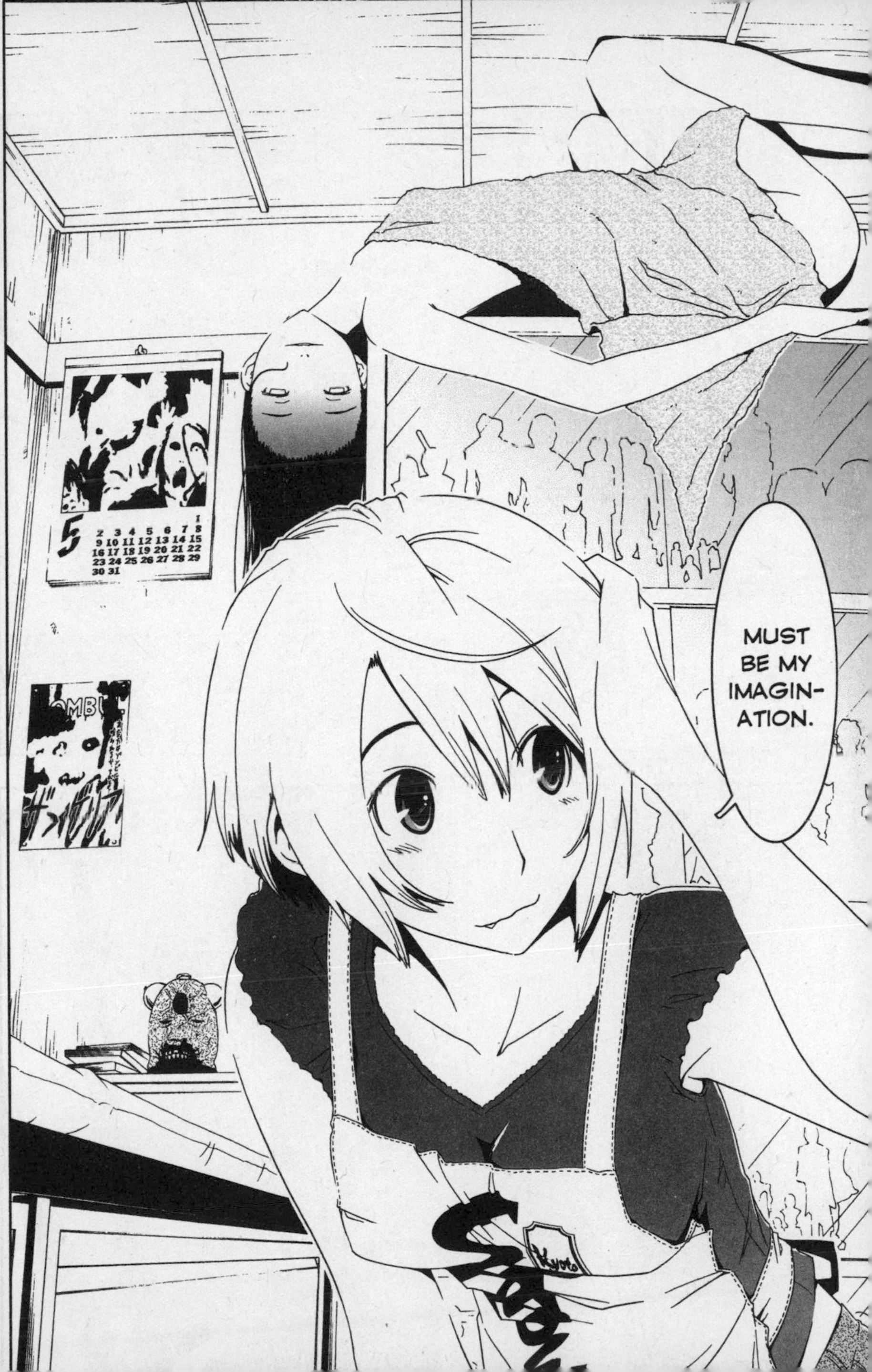
MUST BE MY IMAGIN-ATION.

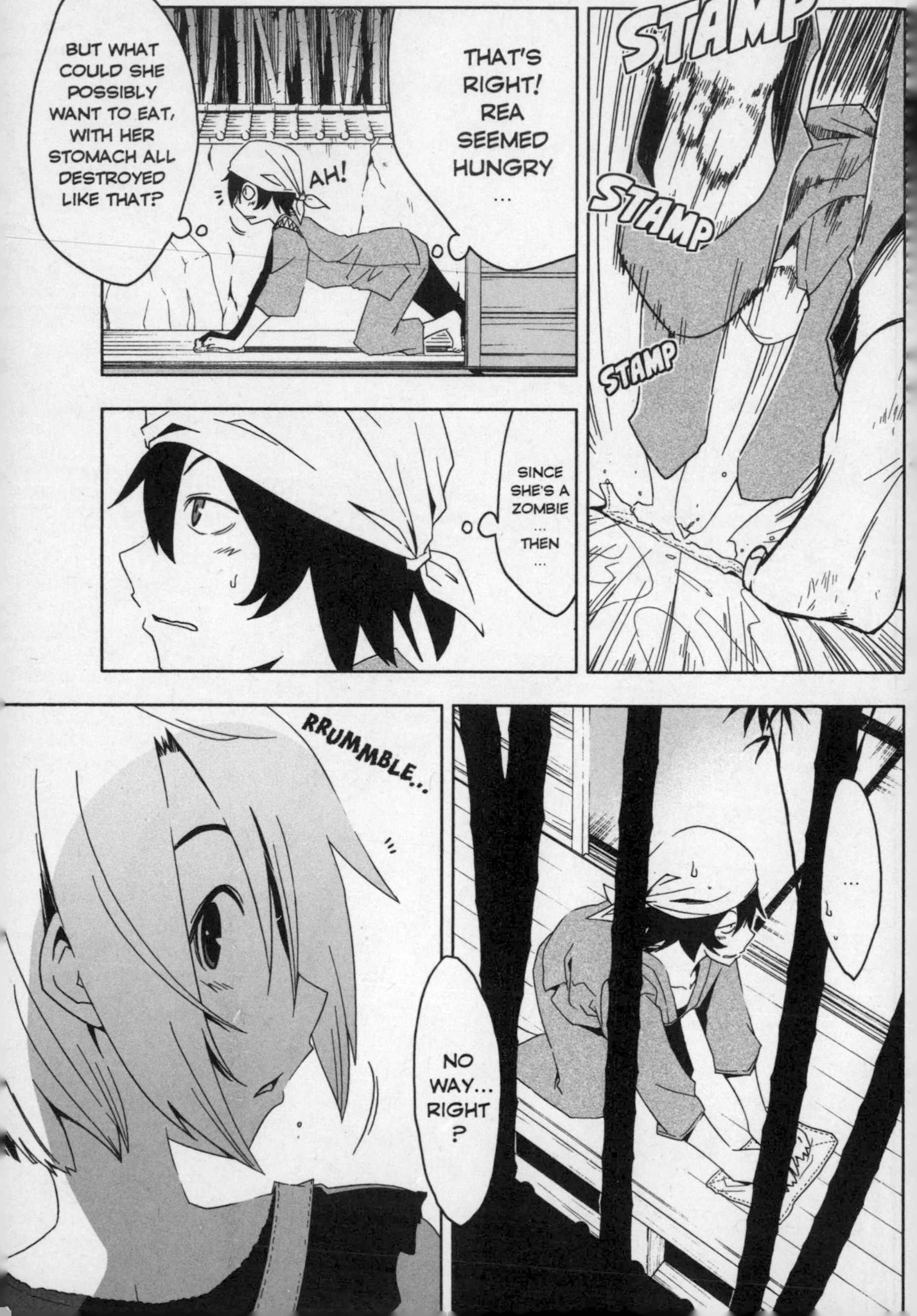
STAMP
STAMP
STAMP
AH!
THAT'S RIGHT! REA SEEMED HUNGRY …
BUT WHAT COULD SHE POSSIBLY WANT TO EAT, WITH HER STOMACH ALL DESTROYED LIKE THAT?
SINCE SHE'S A ZOMBIE … THEN …
…
NO WAY… RIGHT?
RRUMMBLE…

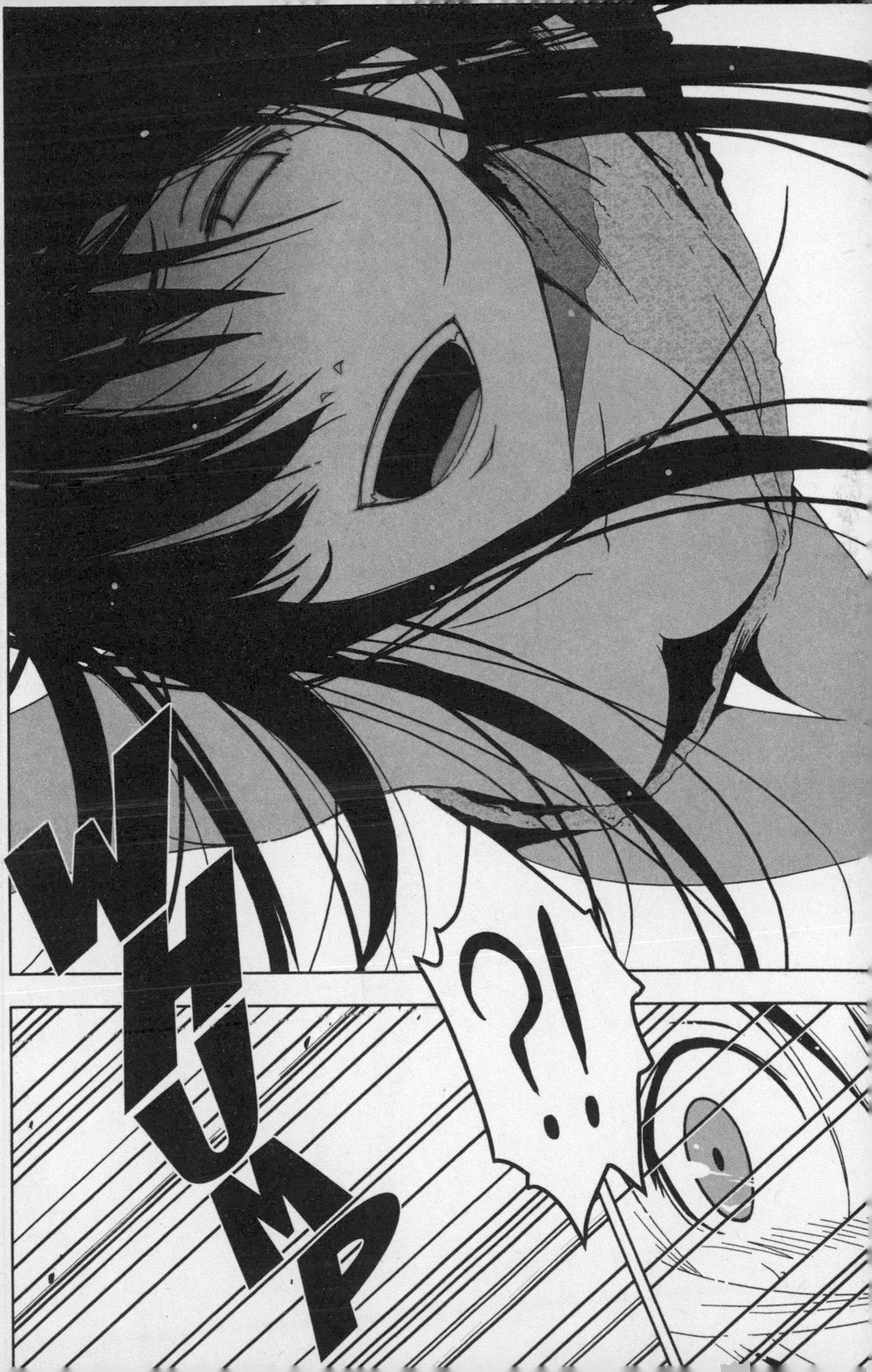
WHUMP
?!

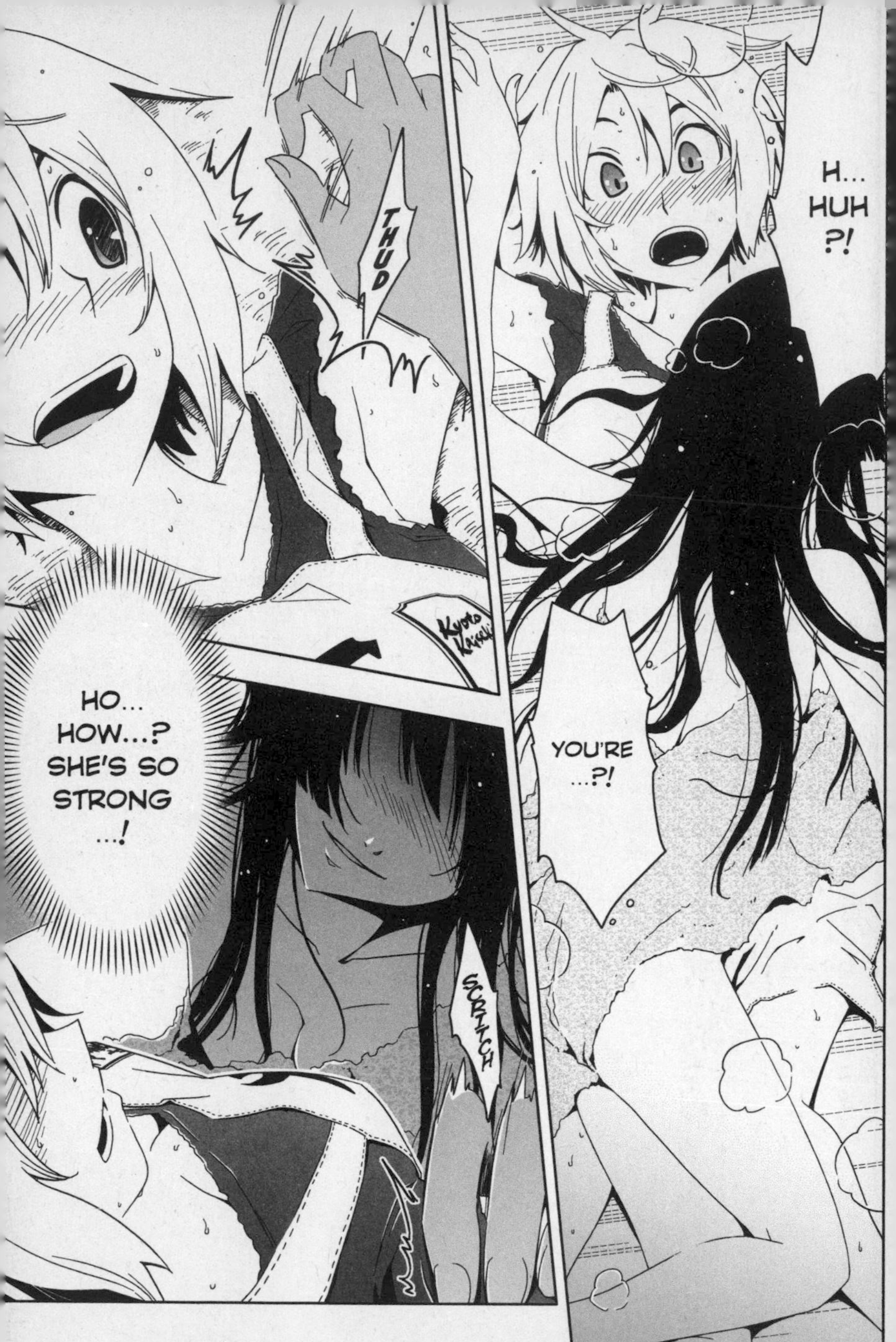
H... HUH ?!
YOU'RE ...?!
THUD
Kyoto Kaisei
HO... HOW...? SHE'S SO STRONG ...!
SCRITCH

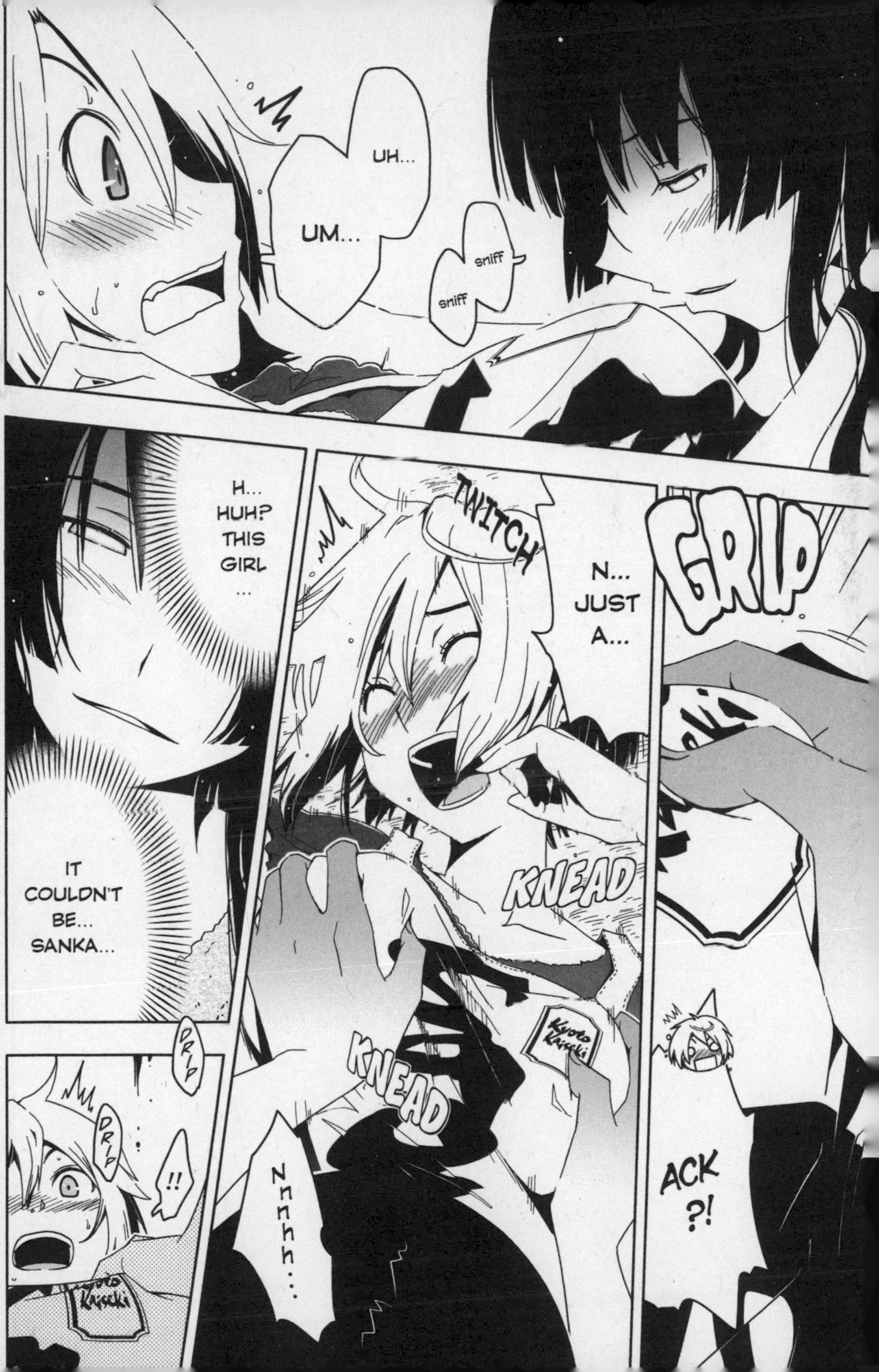
sniff
sniff
UH...
UM...
GRIP
ACK ?!
TWITCH
N... JUST A...
KNEAD
Kyoto Kaiseki
KNEAD
Nnnhh...
H... HUH? THIS GIRL ...
IT COULDN'T BE... SANKA...
DRIP
DRIP
!!
Kyoto Kaiseki

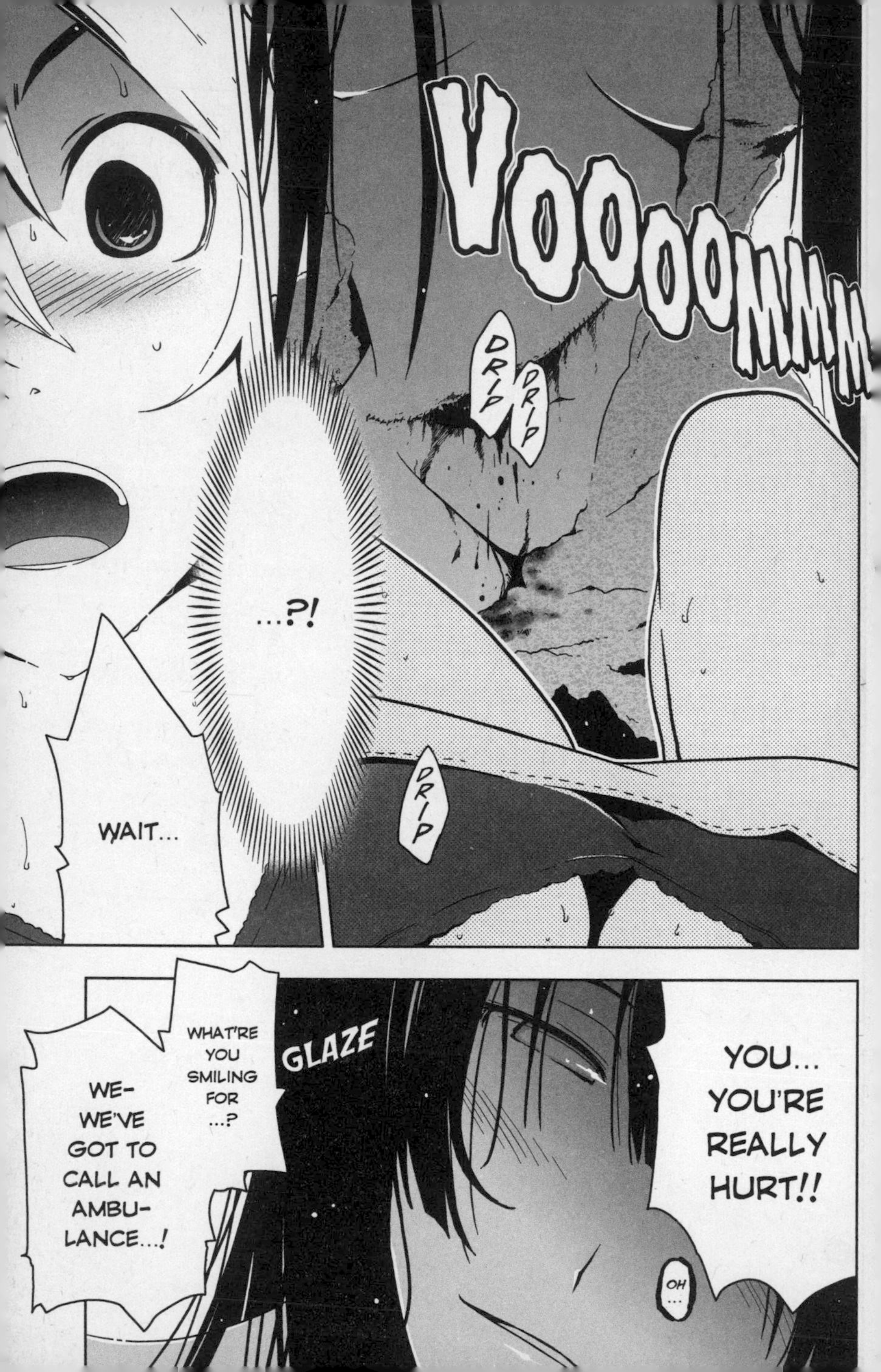
VOOOOMMM
DRIP
DRIP
...?!
DRIP
WAIT...
YOU... YOU'RE REALLY HURT!!
OH...
GLAZE
WHAT'RE YOU SMILING FOR...?
WE- WE'VE GOT TO CALL AN AMBULANCE...!

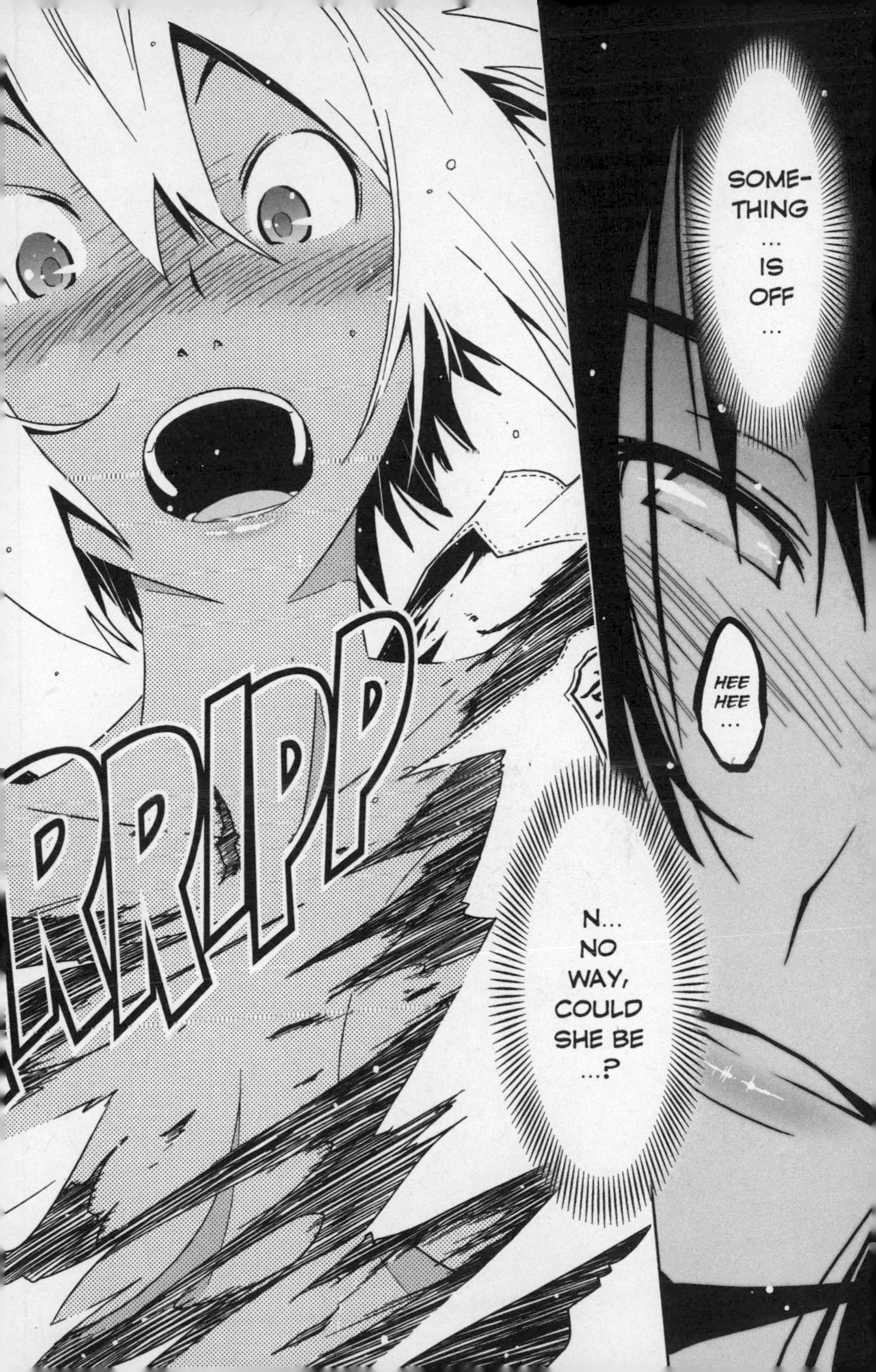
SOME-THING ... IS OFF ...
HEE HEE ...
N... NO WAY, COULD SHE BE ...?
RRIPP

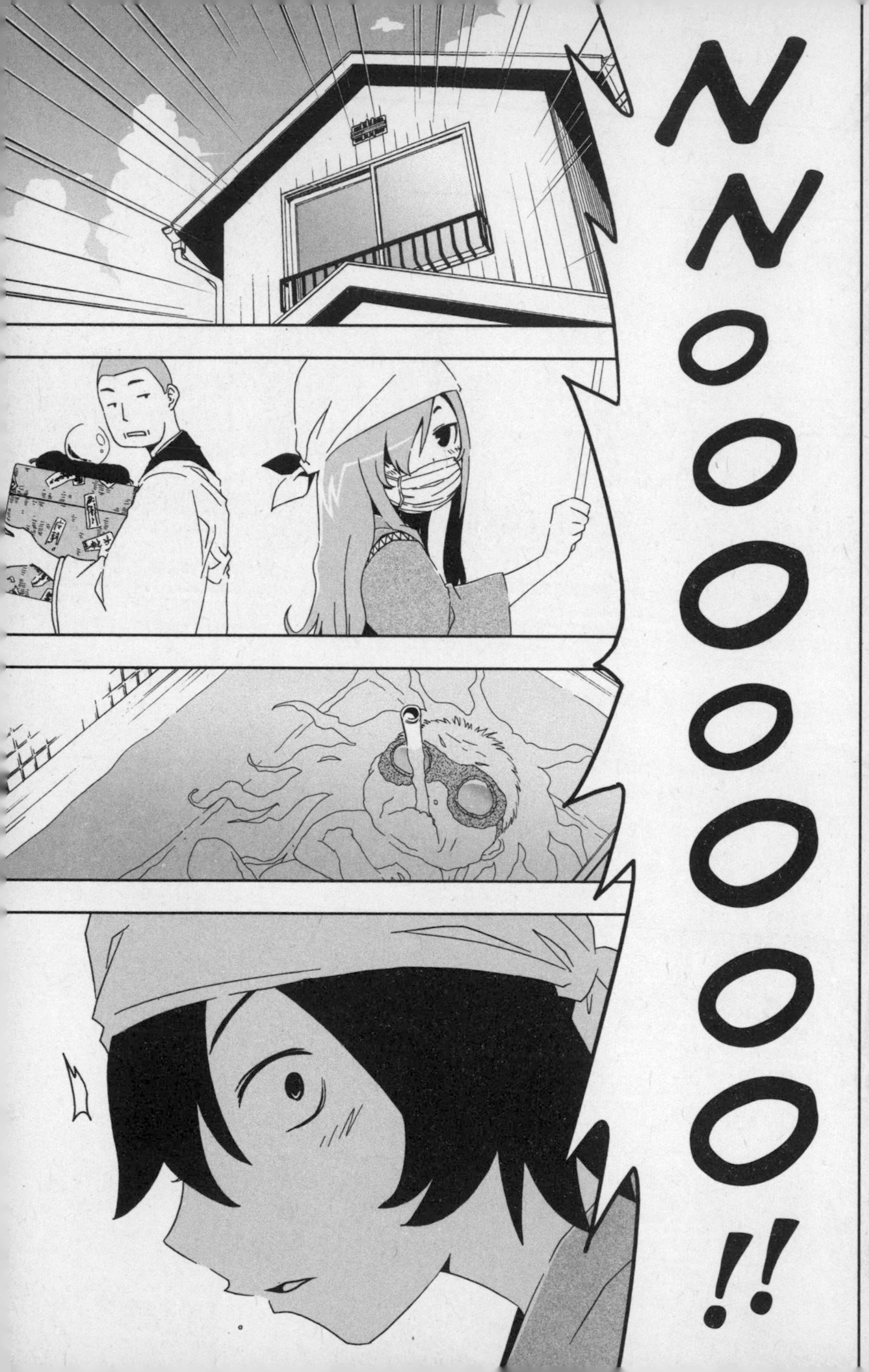
NNOOOOOOO!!

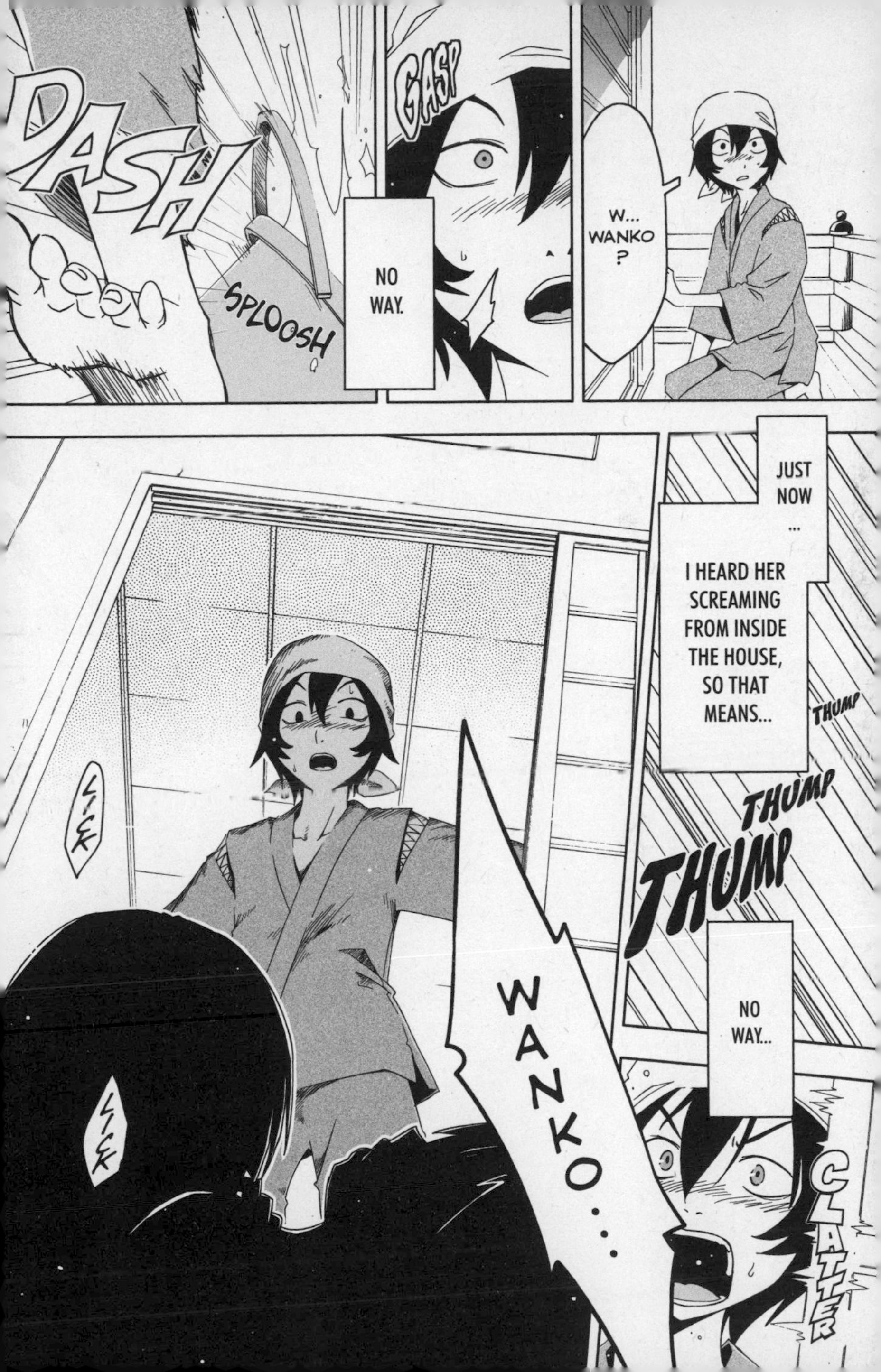
W... WANKO ?
GASP
NO WAY.
DASH
SPLOOSH
JUST NOW ...
I HEARD HER SCREAMING FROM INSIDE THE HOUSE, SO THAT MEANS...
THUMP
THUMP
THUMP
NO WAY...
CLATTER
WANKO...
LICK
LICK

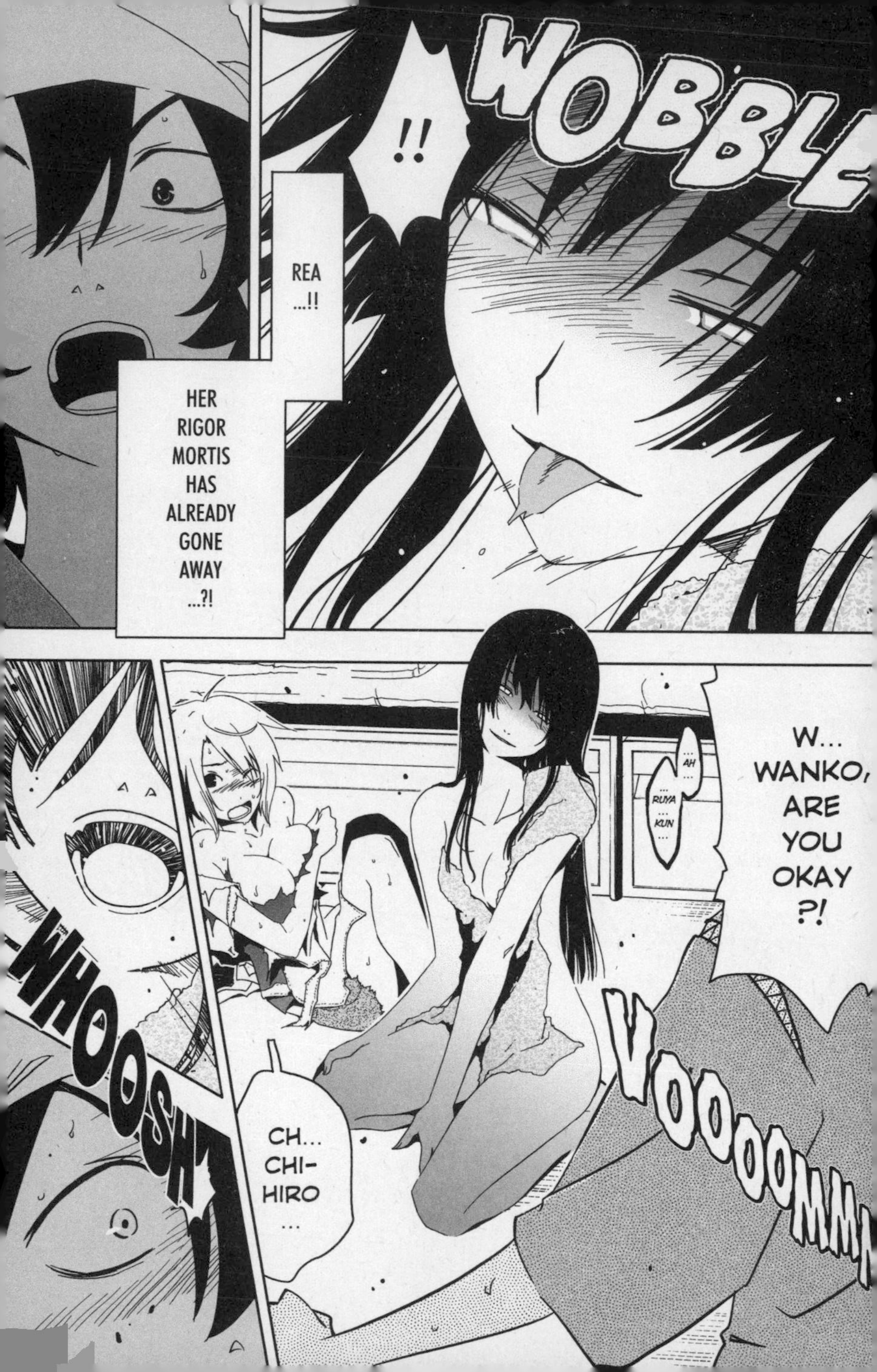
WOBBLE
!!
REA ...!!
HER RIGOR MORTIS HAS ALREADY GONE AWAY ...?!
W... WANKO, ARE YOU OKAY ?!
...AH...
RUYA ...KUN...
CH... CHI-HIRO ...
VOOOOMM
WHOOSH

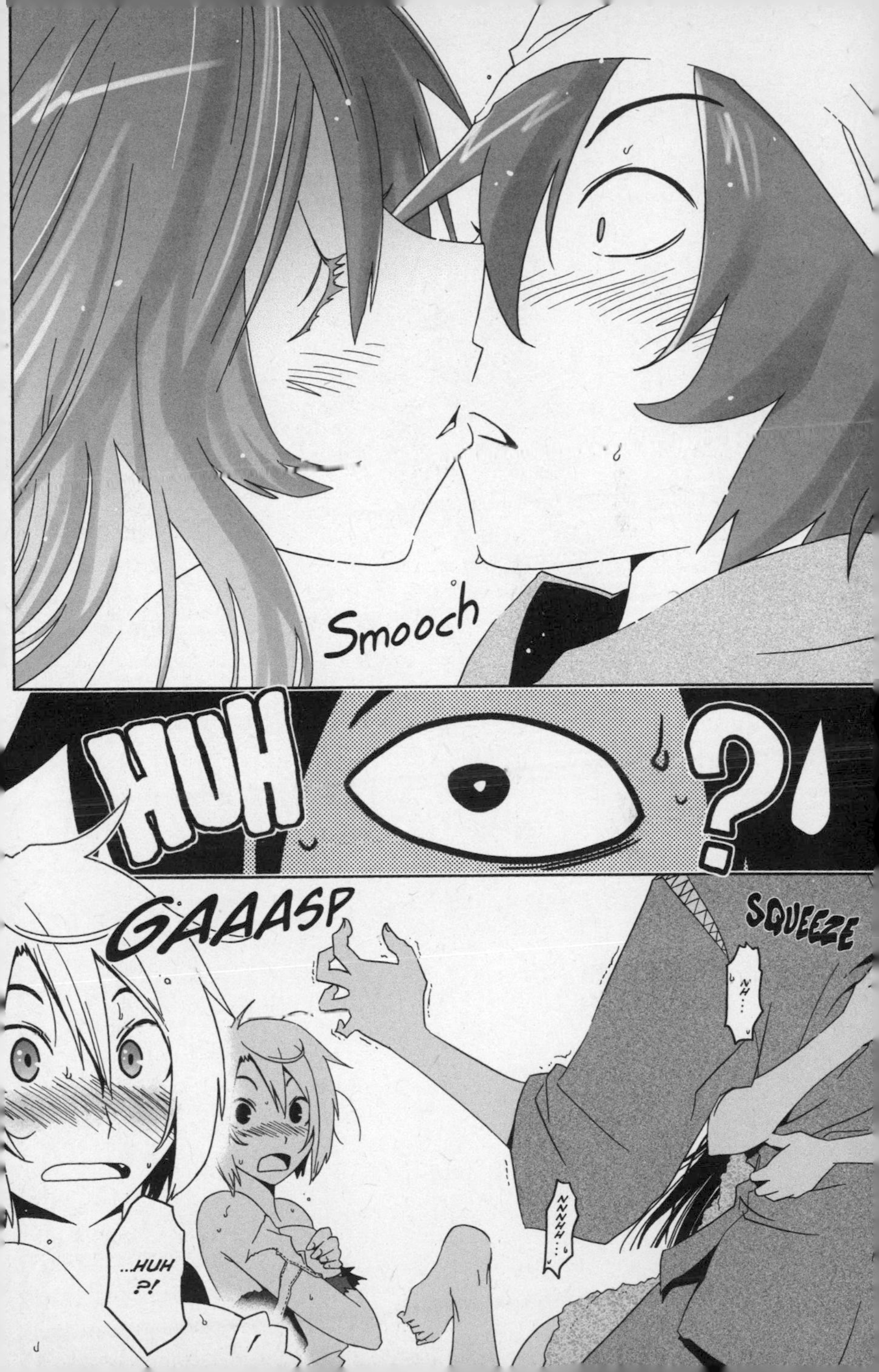

Smooch
HUH?
SQUEEZE
NH...
NNNH...
GAAASP
...HUH ?!

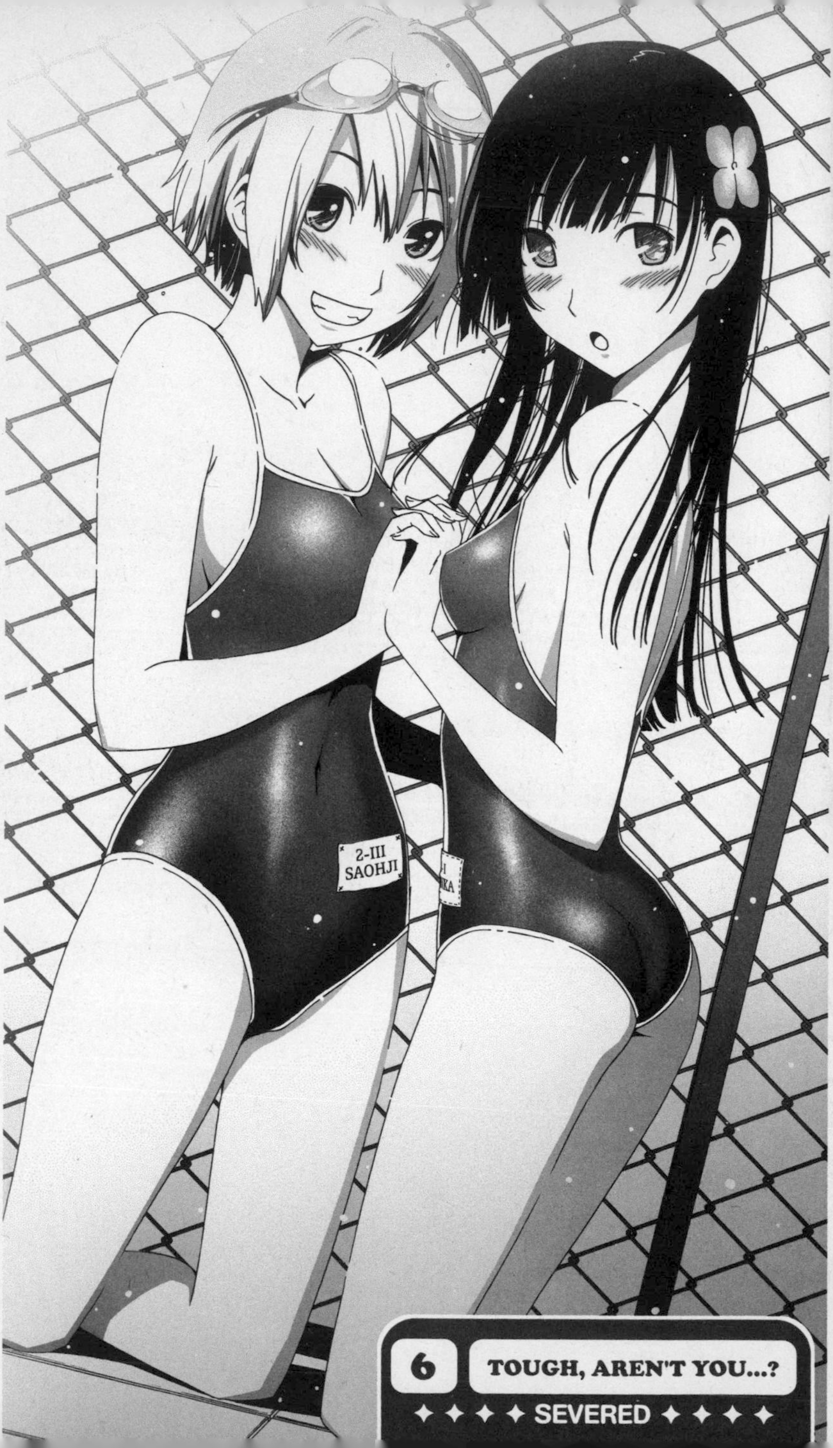
2-III
SAOHJI
6
TOUGH, AREN'T YOU...?
SEVERED

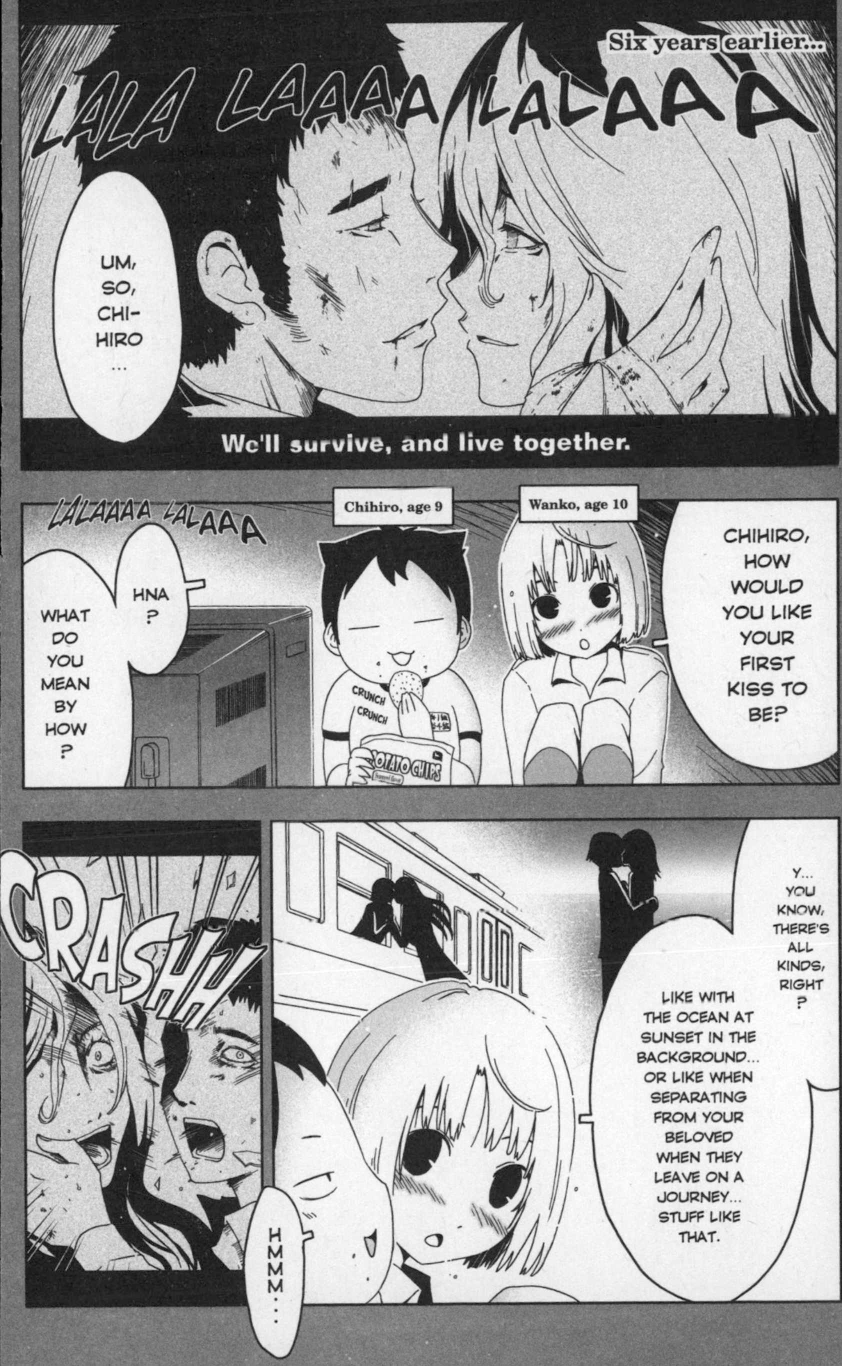
Six years earlier...
LALA LAAAA LALAAA
UM, SO, CHI-HIRO ...
We'll survive, and live together.
CHIHIRO, HOW WOULD YOU LIKE YOUR FIRST KISS TO BE?
Wanko, age 10
Chihiro, age 9
CRUNCH CRUNCH
HNA ?
WHAT DO YOU MEAN BY HOW ?
LALAAAA LALAAA
Y... YOU KNOW, THERE'S ALL KINDS, RIGHT ?
LIKE WITH THE OCEAN AT SUNSET IN THE BACKGROUND... OR LIKE WHEN SEPARATING FROM YOUR BELOVED WHEN THEY LEAVE ON A JOURNEY... STUFF LIKE THAT.
HMMM...
CRASHH

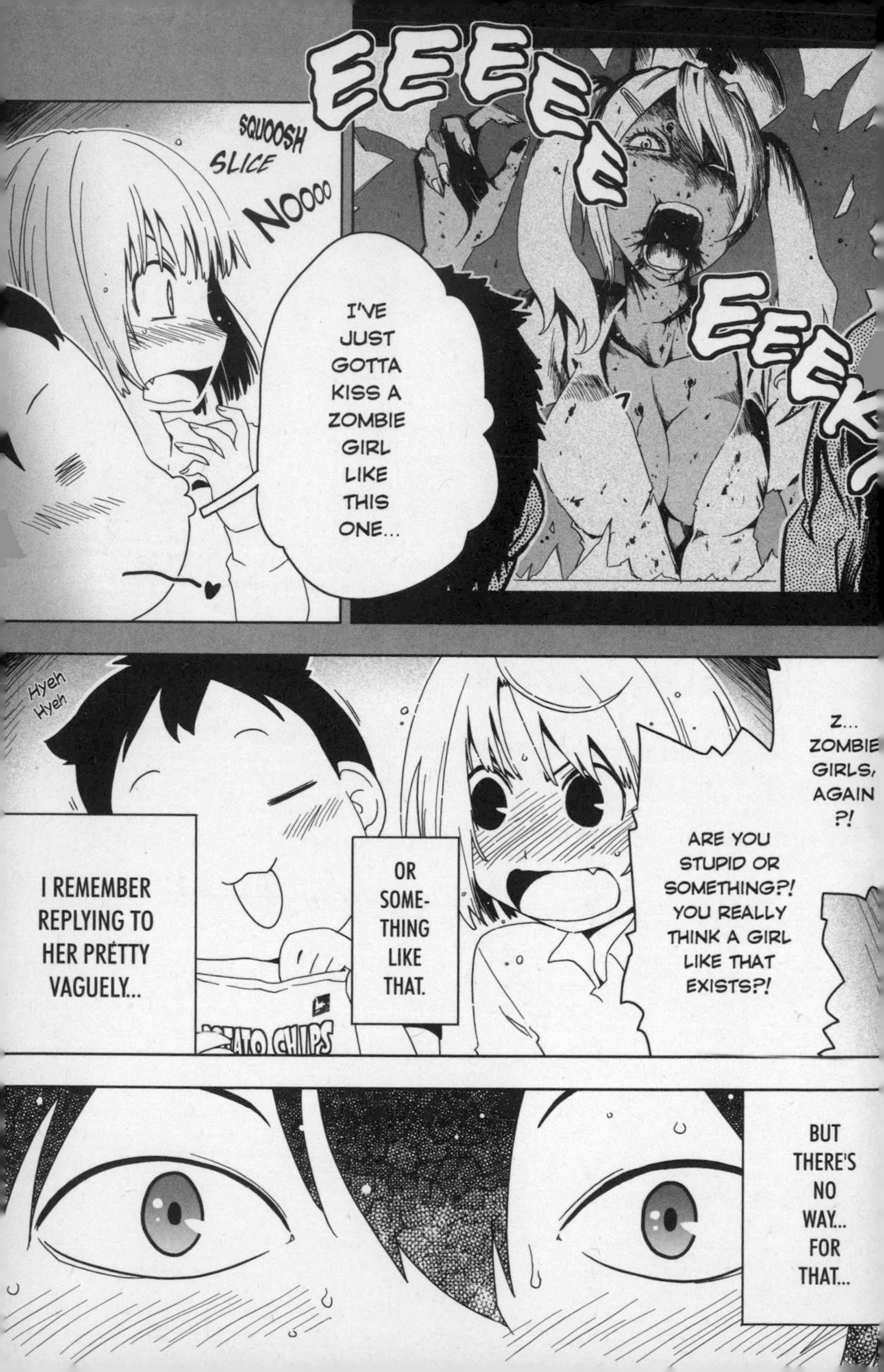
EEEEEE
EEEK
SQUOOSH
SLICE
NOOOO
I'VE JUST GOTTA KISS A ZOMBIE GIRL LIKE THIS ONE...
Z... ZOMBIE GIRLS, AGAIN?!
ARE YOU STUPID OR SOMETHING?! YOU REALLY THINK A GIRL LIKE THAT EXISTS?!
OR SOME-THING LIKE THAT.
I REMEMBER REPLYING TO HER PRETTY VAGUELY...
Hyeh Hyeh
BUT THERE'S NO WAY... FOR THAT...

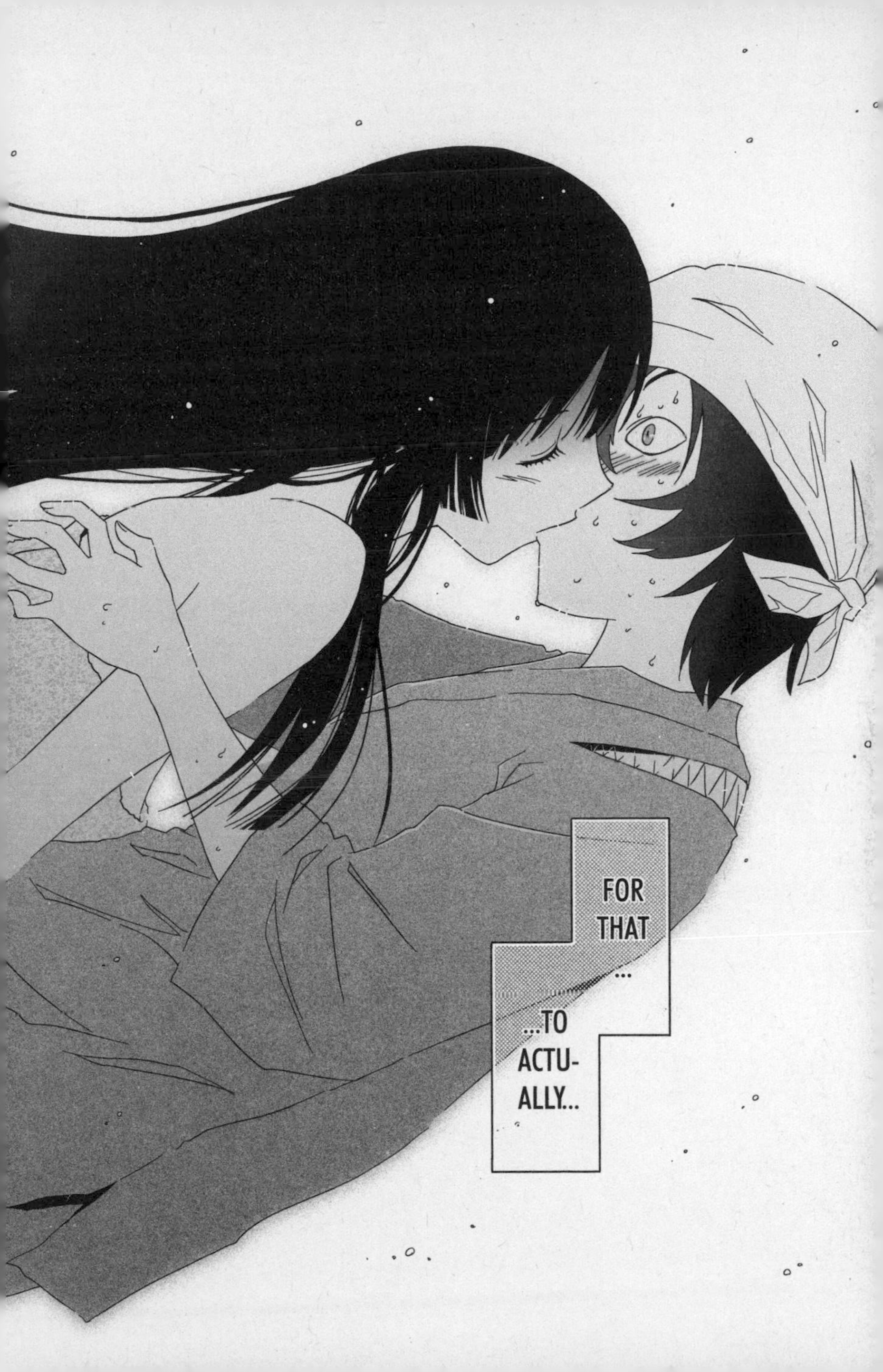
FOR THAT...
...TO ACTU-ALLY...

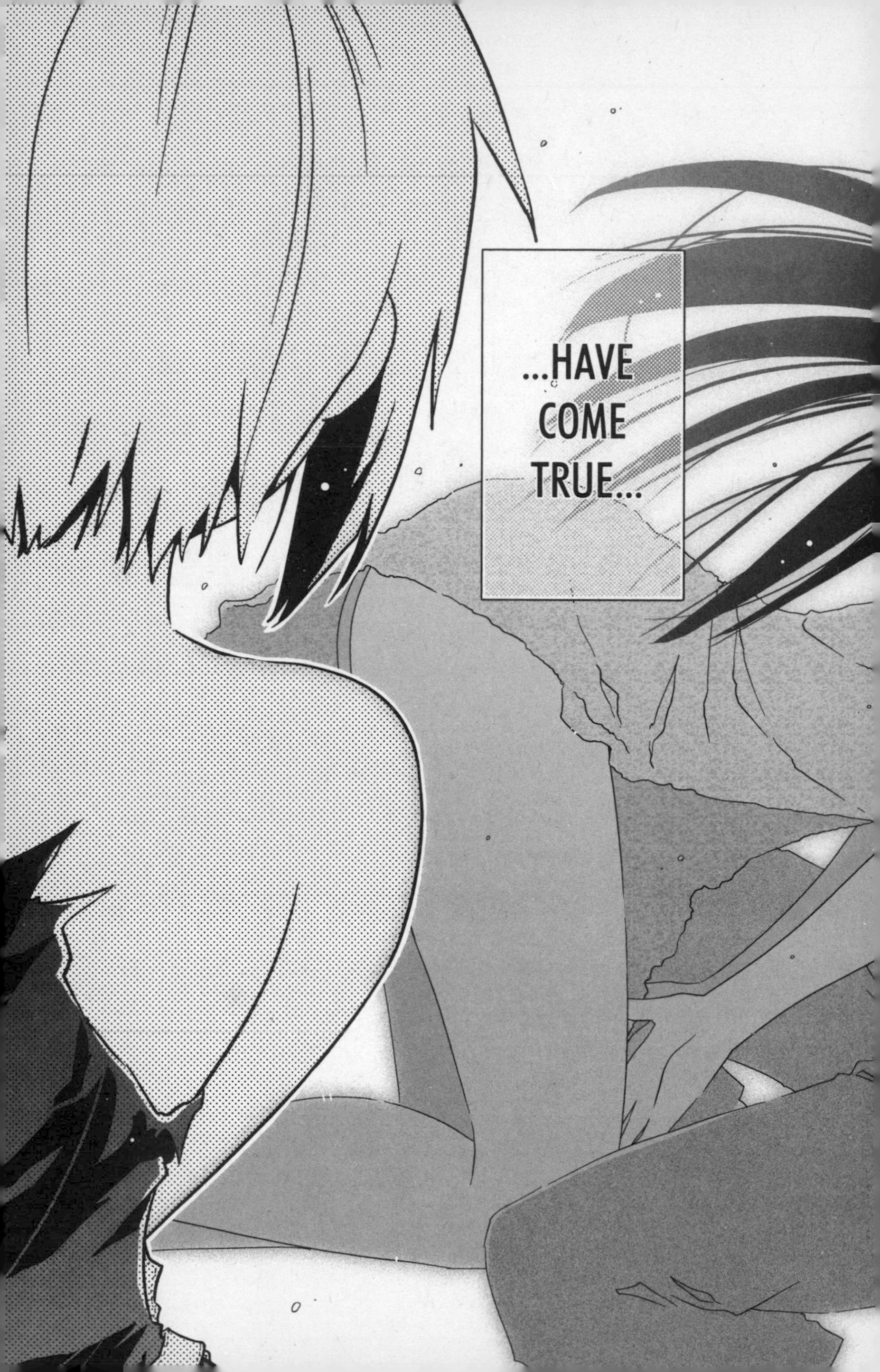
...HAVE COME TRUE...

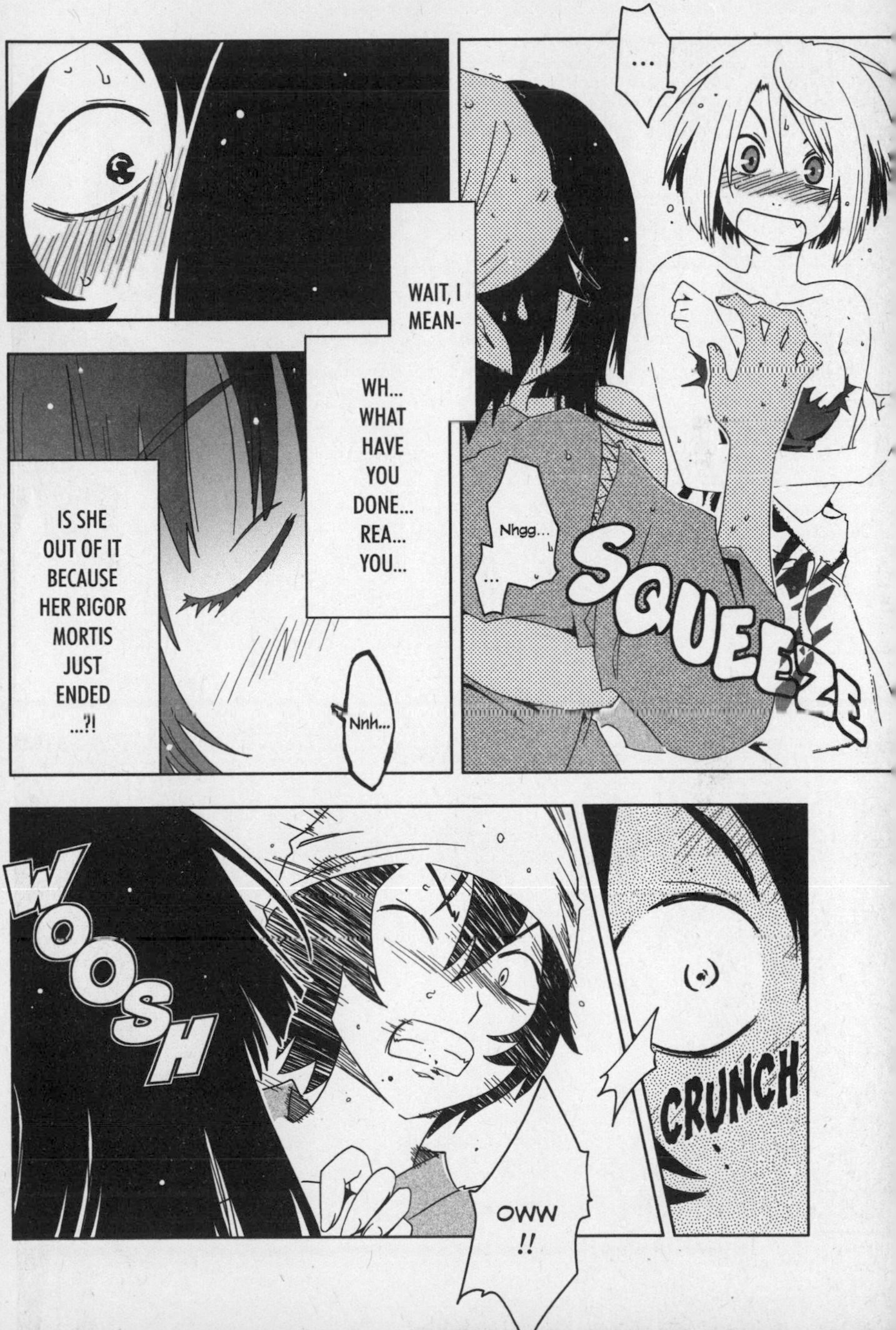
...
WAIT, I MEAN-
Nhgg...
...
SQUEEZE
WH... WHAT HAVE YOU DONE... REA... YOU...
Nnh...
IS SHE OUT OF IT BECAUSE HER RIGOR MORTIS JUST ENDED ...?!
CRUNCH
OWW !!
WOOSH

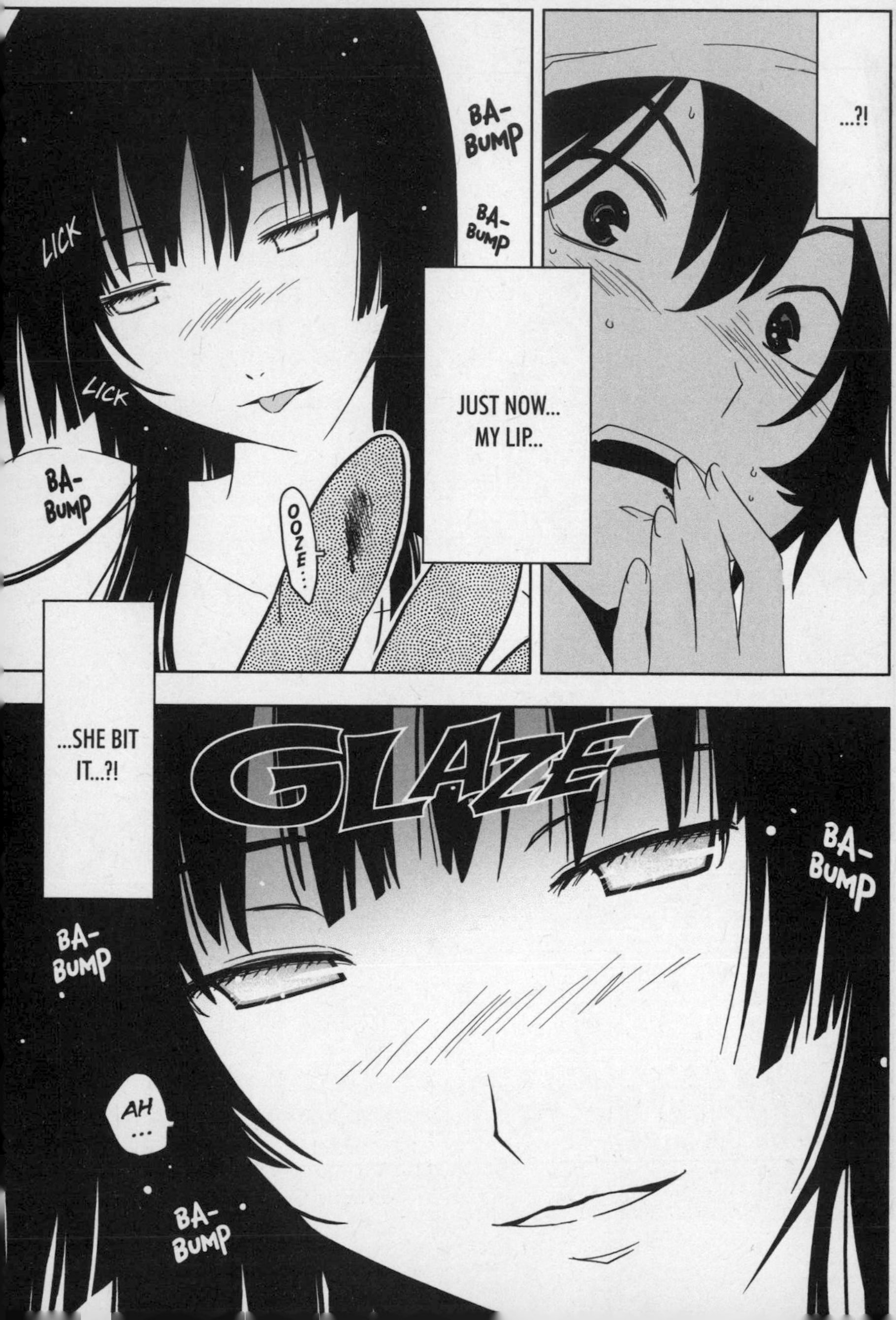
...?!
JUST NOW... MY LIP...
BA-BUMP
BA-BUMP
LICK
LICK
BA-BUMP
OOZE...
GLAZE
...SHE BIT IT...?!
BA-BUMP
BA-BUMP
AH...
BA-BUMP

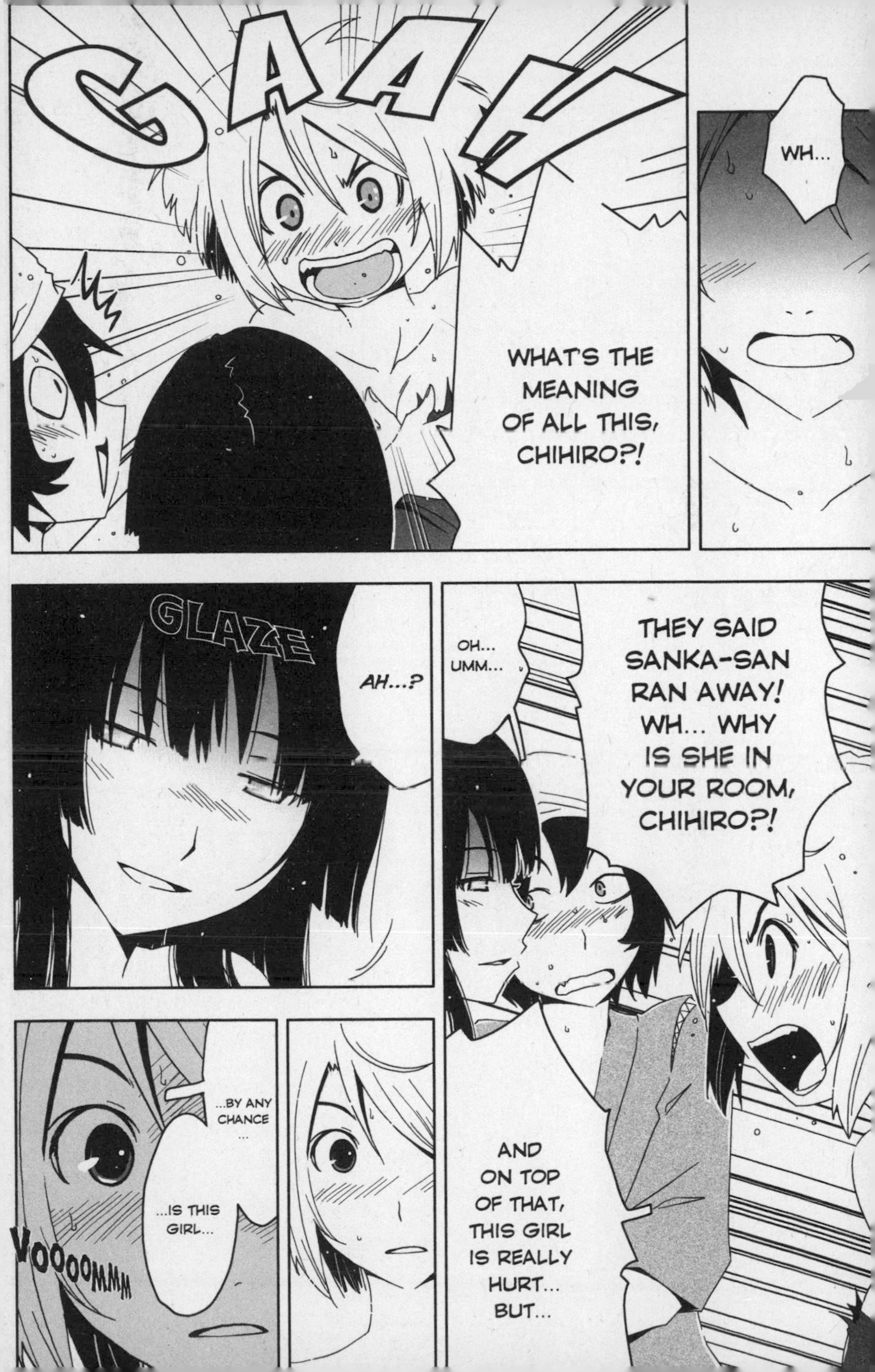
WH...
GAAH!
WHAT'S THE MEANING OF ALL THIS, CHIHIRO?!
THEY SAID SANKA-SAN RAN AWAY! WH... WHY IS SHE IN YOUR ROOM, CHIHIRO?!
OH... UMM...
AND ON TOP OF THAT, THIS GIRL IS REALLY HURT... BUT...
GLAZE
AH...?
...BY ANY CHANCE ...
...IS THIS GIRL...
VOOOMMM

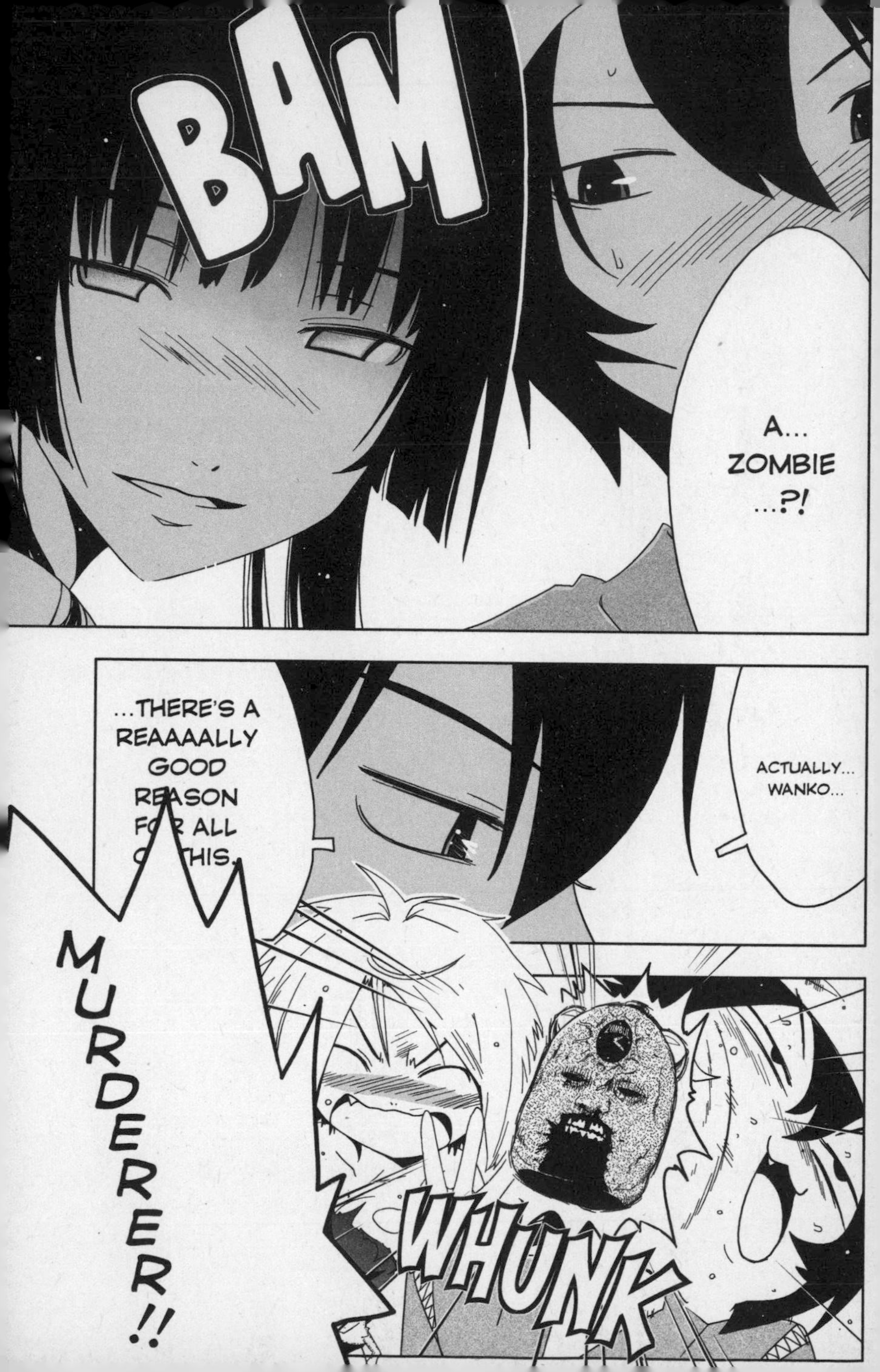
BAM
A... ZOMBIE ...?!
ACTUALLY... WANKO...
...THERE'S A REAAAALLY GOOD REASON FOR ALL OF THIS.
WHUNK
MURDERER!!

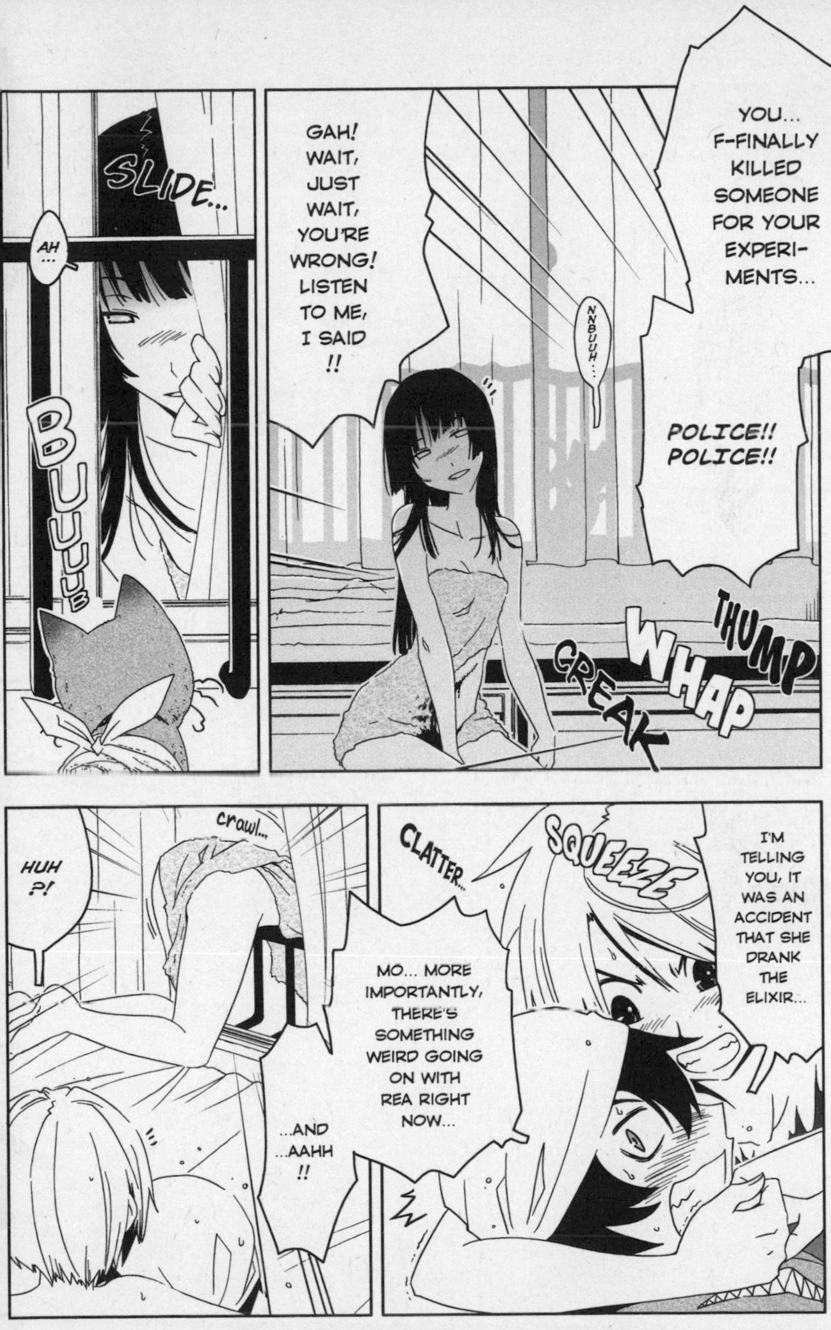
YOU... F-FINALLY KILLED SOMEONE FOR YOUR EXPERIMENTS...
GAH! WAIT, JUST WAIT, YOU'RE WRONG! LISTEN TO ME, I SAID!!
NNBUUH...
POLICE!! POLICE!!
THUMP
WHAP
CREAK
SLIDE...
AH...
BUUUUB
I'M TELLING YOU, IT WAS AN ACCIDENT THAT SHE DRANK THE ELIXIR...
SQUEEZE
CLATTER...
MO... MORE IMPORTANTLY, THERE'S SOMETHING WEIRD GOING ON WITH REA RIGHT NOW...
...AND ...AAHH!!
crawl...
HUH?!

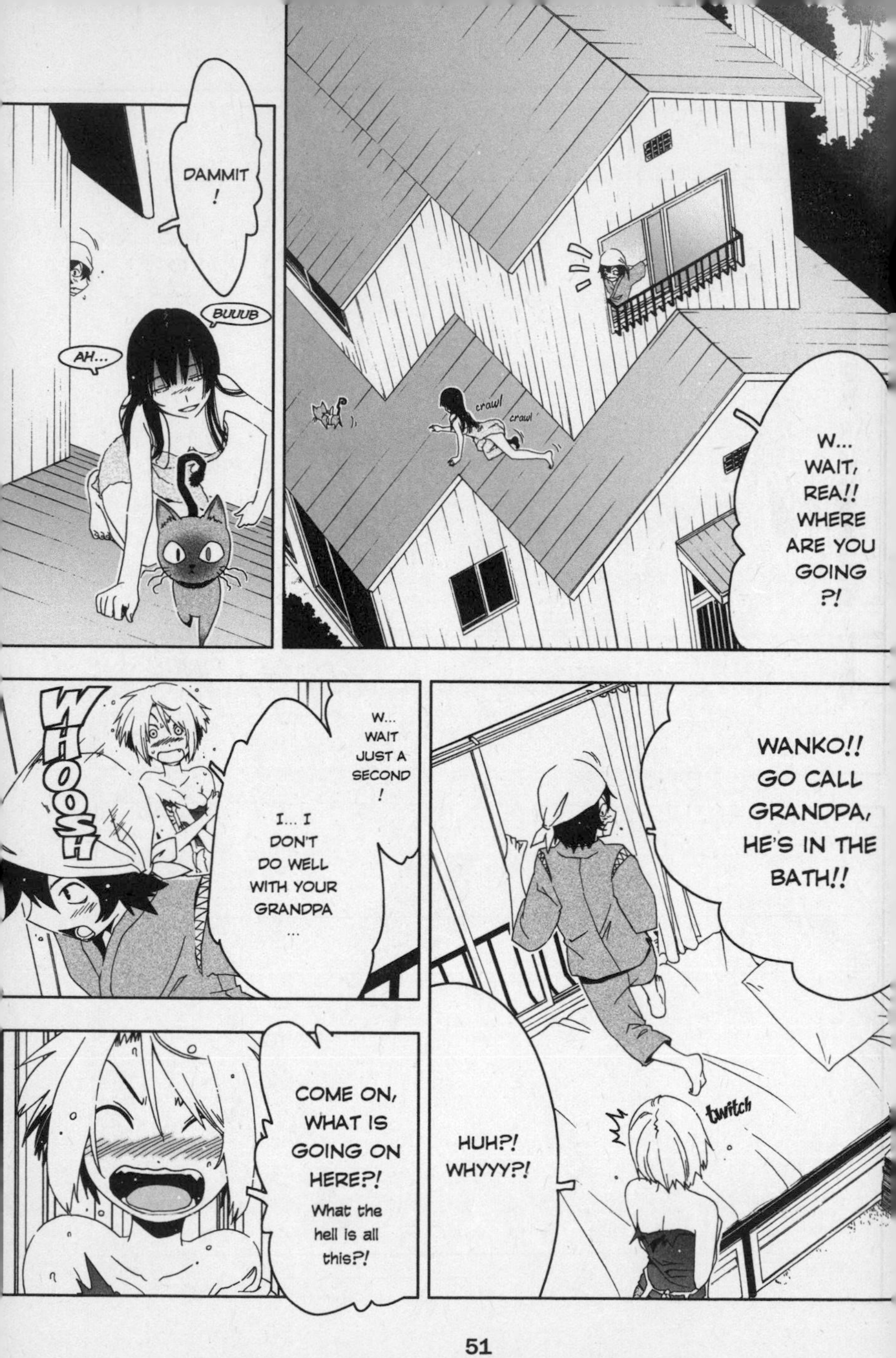
W... WAIT, REA!! WHERE ARE YOU GOING?!
crawl
crawl
DAMMIT!
BUUUB
AH...
WANKO!! GO CALL GRANDPA, HE'S IN THE BATH!!
HUH?! WHYYY?!
twitch
W... WAIT JUST A SECOND!
I... I DON'T DO WELL WITH YOUR GRANDPA...
WHOOSH
COME ON, WHAT IS GOING ON HERE?!
What the hell is all this?!

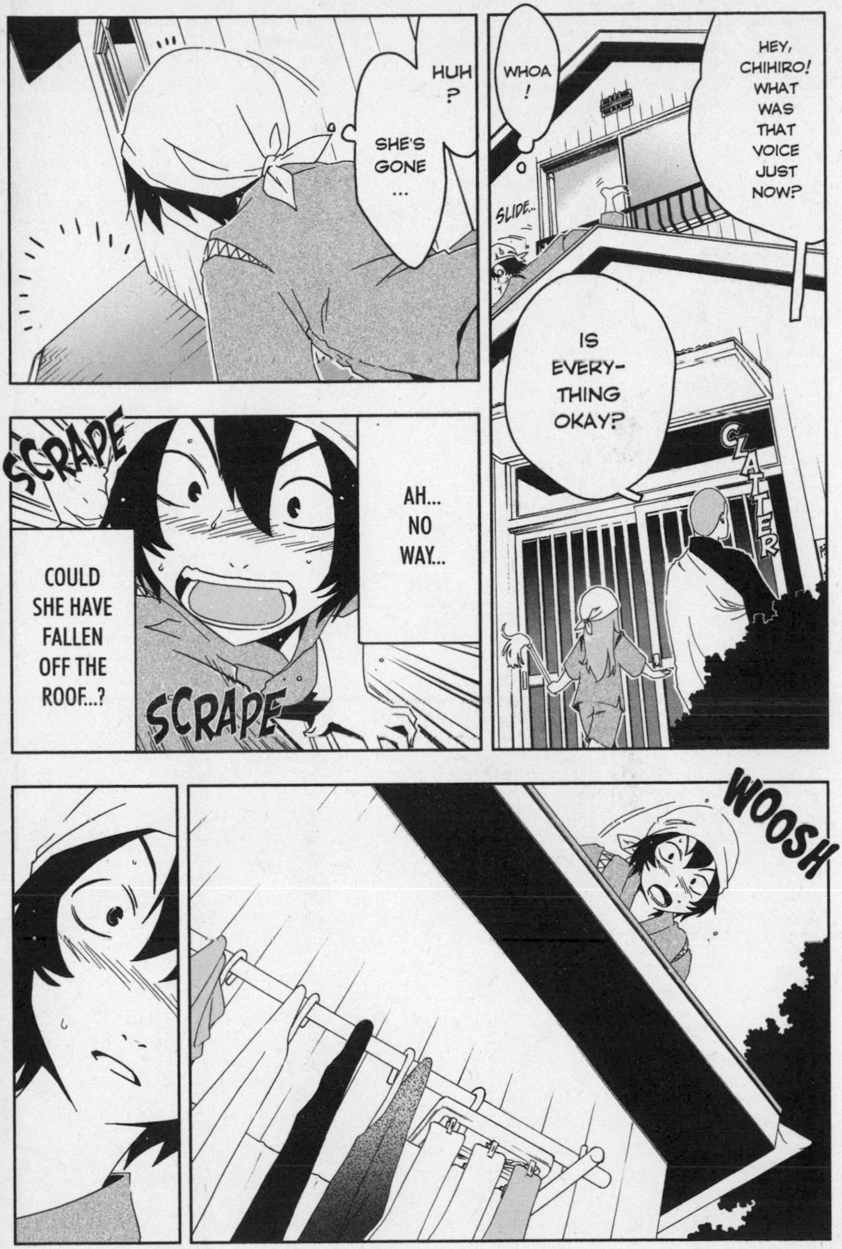
HEY, CHIHIRO! WHAT WAS THAT VOICE JUST NOW?
WHOA!
SLIDE...
IS EVERY-THING OKAY?
CLATTER
...
HUH?
SHE'S GONE...
AH... NO WAY...
SCRAPE
COULD SHE HAVE FALLEN OFF THE ROOF...?
SCRAPE
WOOSH

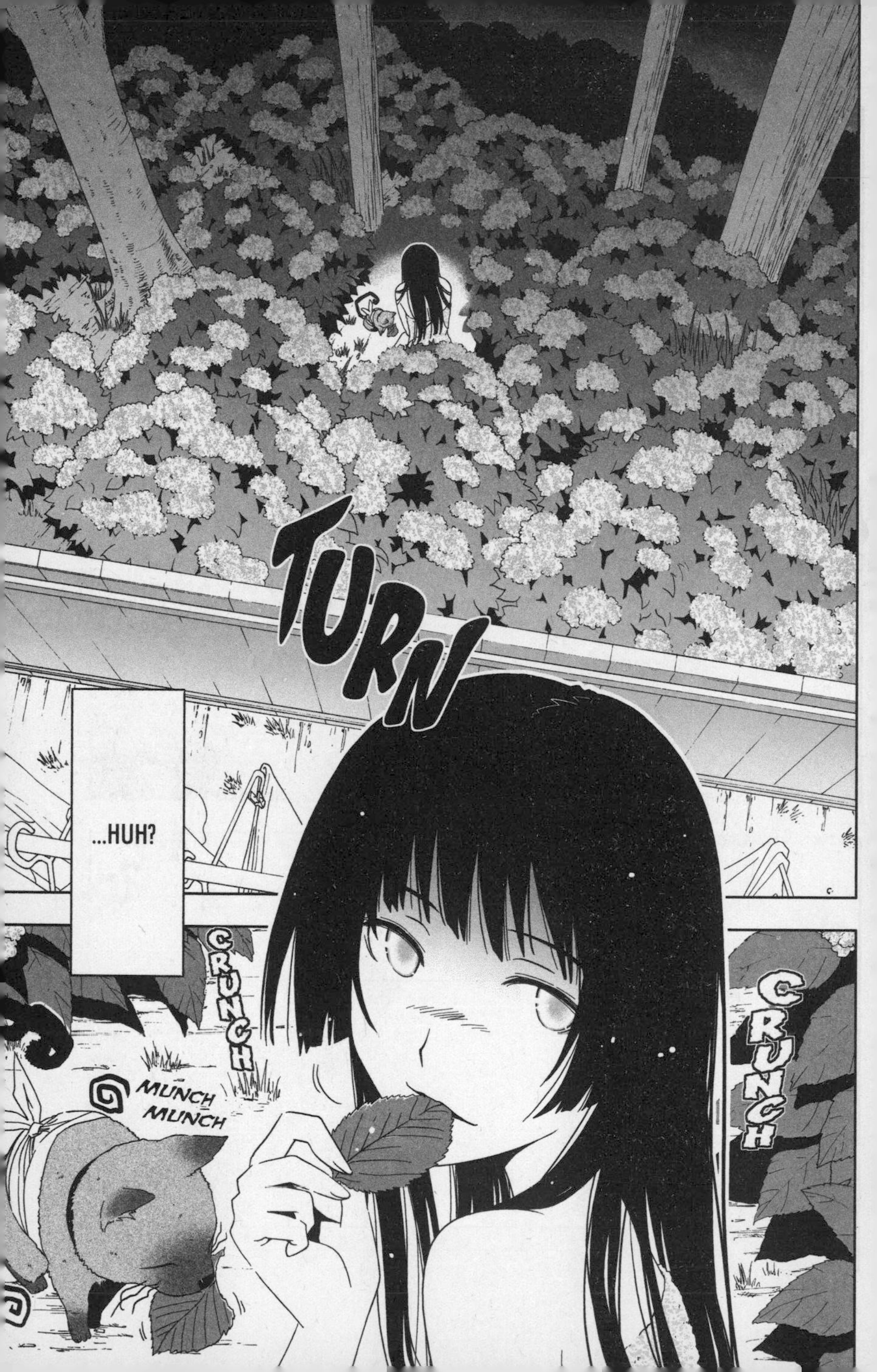
TURN
...HUH?
CRUNCH
CRUNCH
MUNCH MUNCH

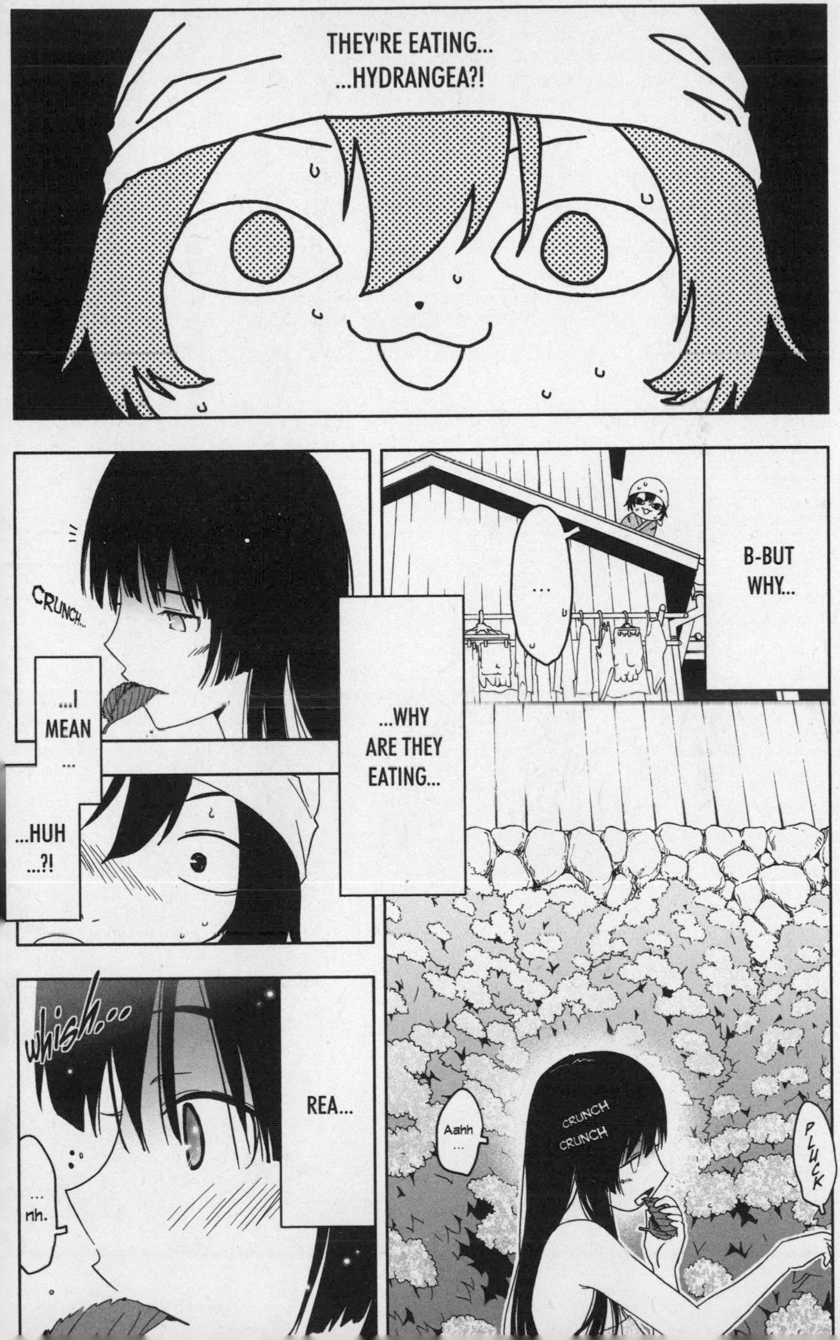
THEY'RE EATING... ...HYDRANGEA?!
B-BUT WHY...
...
...WHY ARE THEY EATING...
Aahh ...
CRUNCH CRUNCH
PLUCK
CRUNCH...
...I MEAN ...
...HUH ...?!
whish...
REA...
... nh.

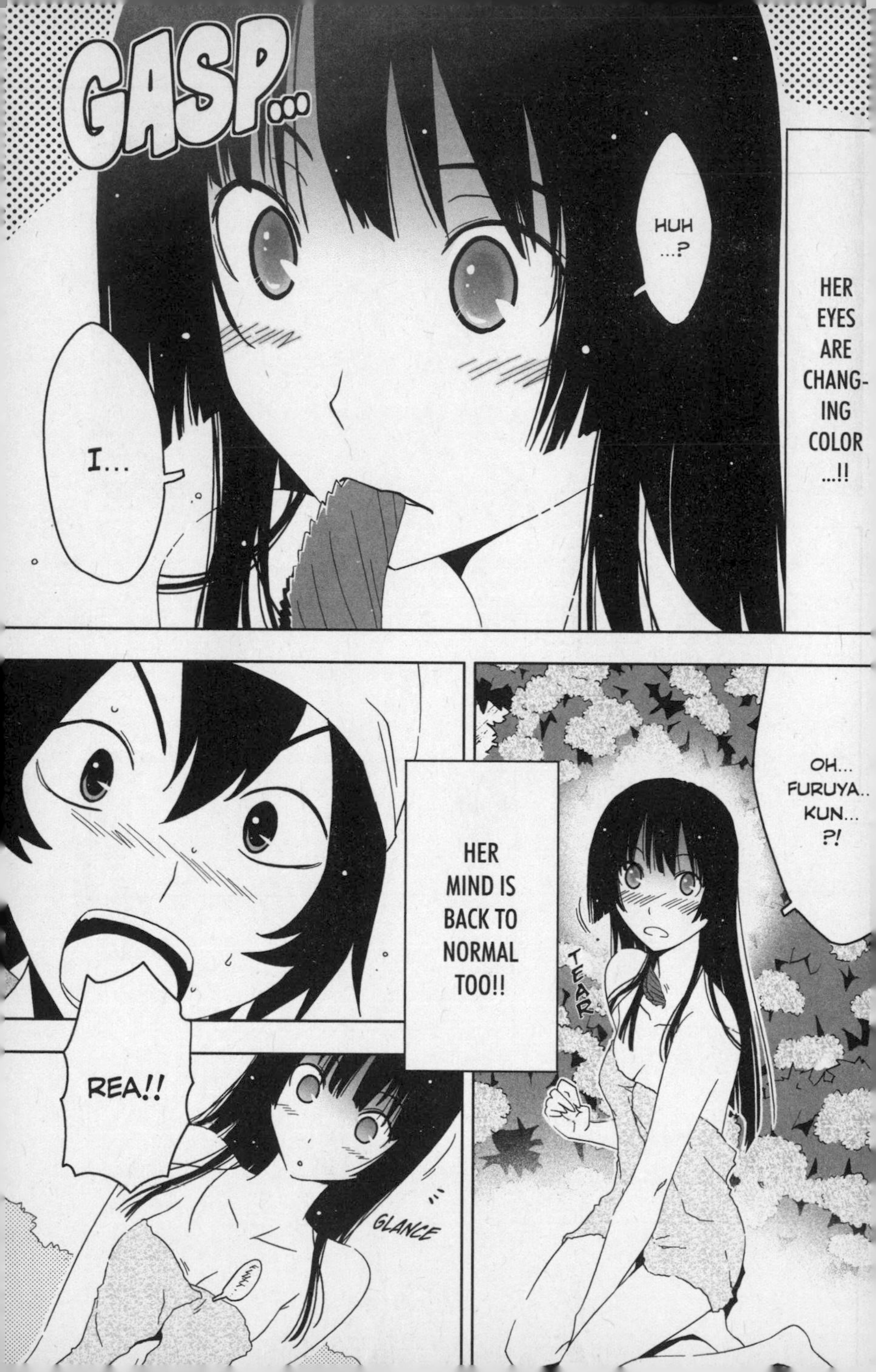
HER EYES ARE CHANGING COLOR ...!!
HUH ...?
GASP...
I...
OH... FURUYA.. KUN... ?!
TEAR
HER MIND IS BACK TO NORMAL TOO!!
REA!!
GLANCE

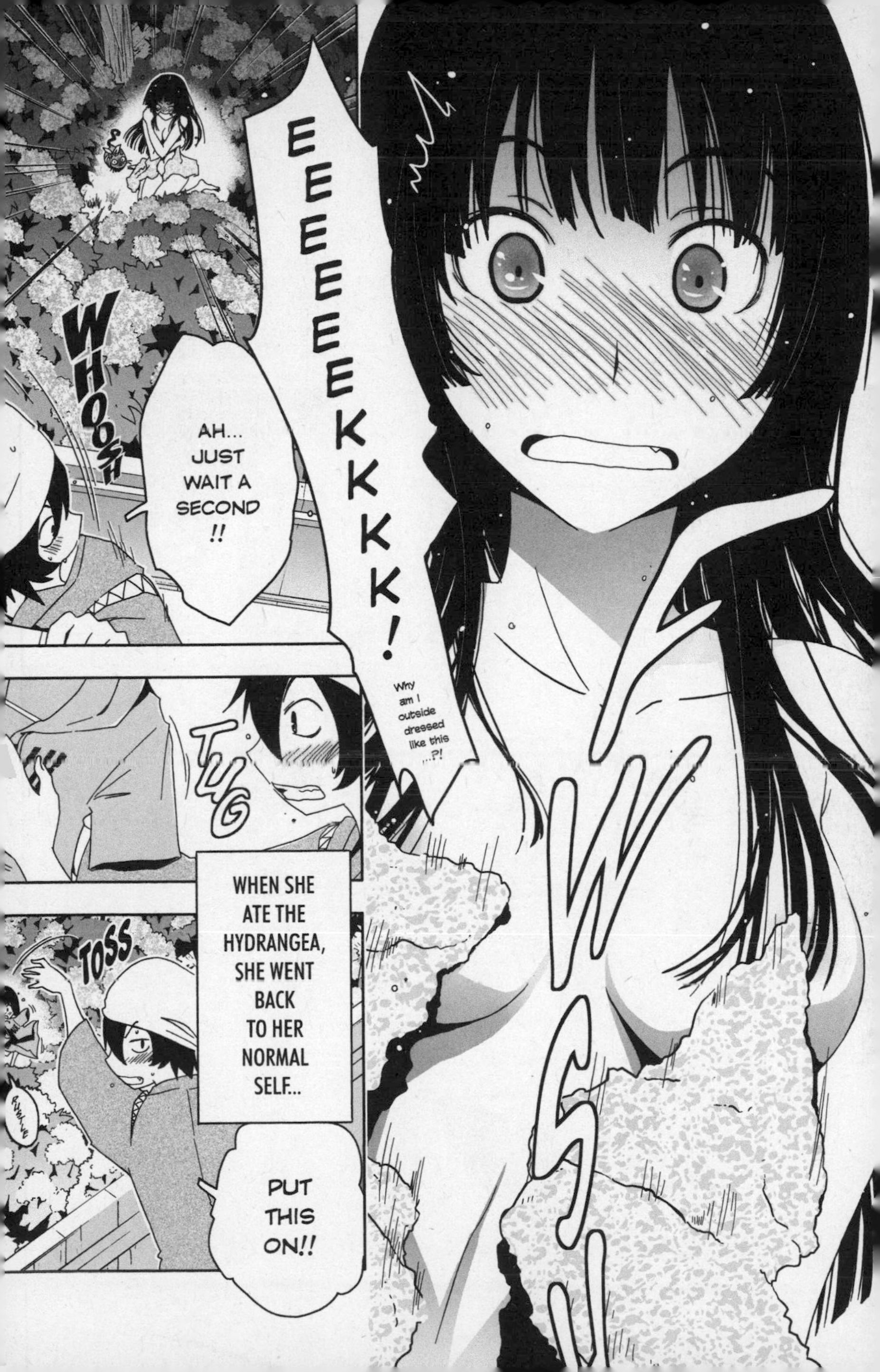
EEEEEEKKKK!
Why am I outside dressed like this ...?!
WHOOSH
AH... JUST WAIT A SECOND!!
TUG
WHEN SHE ATE THE HYDRANGEA, SHE WENT BACK TO HER NORMAL SELF...
TOSS
RUSTLE
PUT THIS ON!!

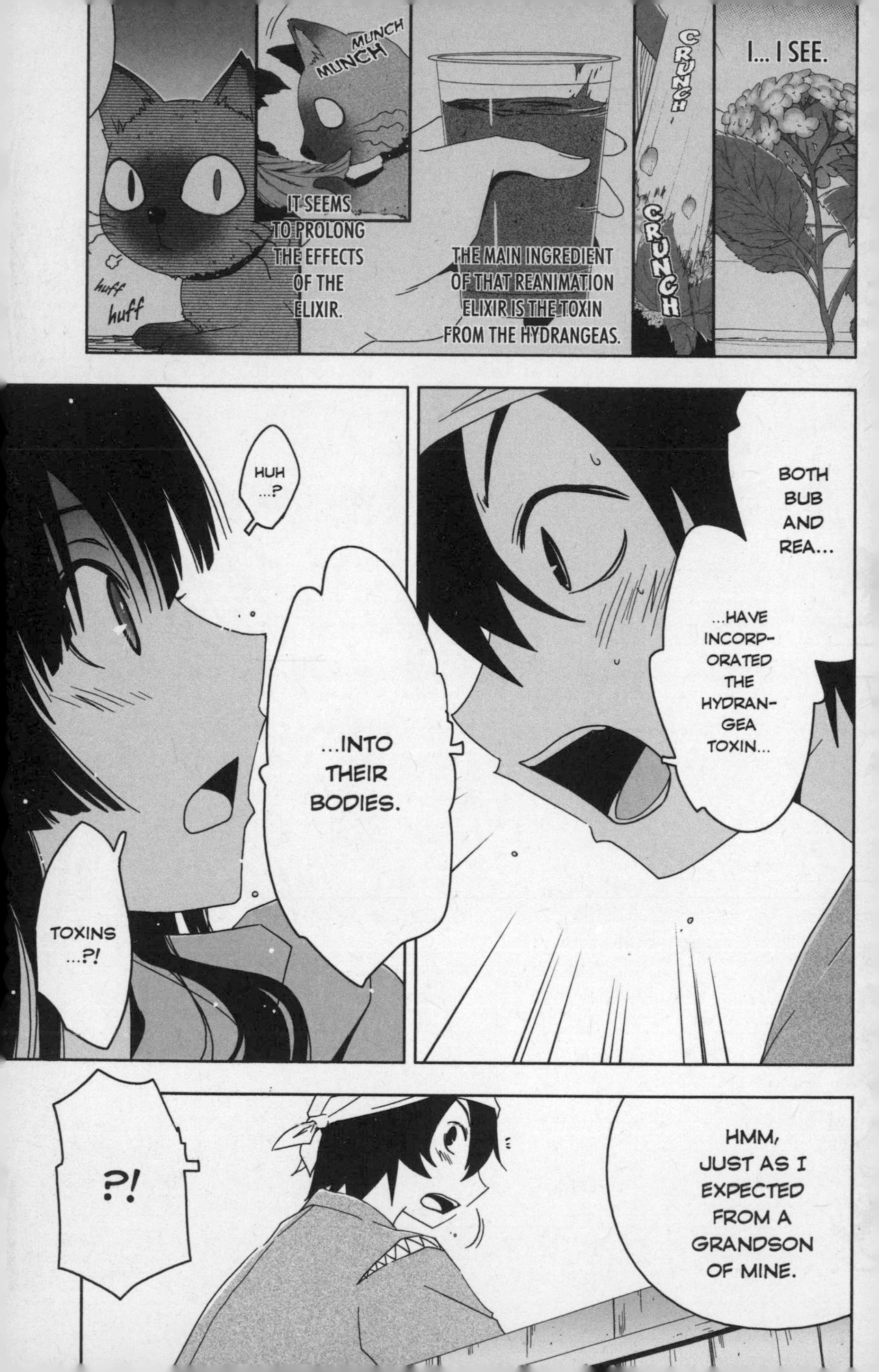
I... I SEE.
CRUNCH
CRUNCH
THE MAIN INGREDIENT OF THAT REANIMATION ELIXIR IS THE TOXIN FROM THE HYDRANGEAS.
MUNCH MUNCH
IT SEEMS TO PROLONG THE EFFECTS OF THE ELIXIR.
huff huff
BOTH BUB AND REA...
...HAVE INCORPORATED THE HYDRANGEA TOXIN...
...INTO THEIR BODIES.
HUH ...?
TOXINS ...?!
HMM, JUST AS I EXPECTED FROM A GRANDSON OF MINE.
?!

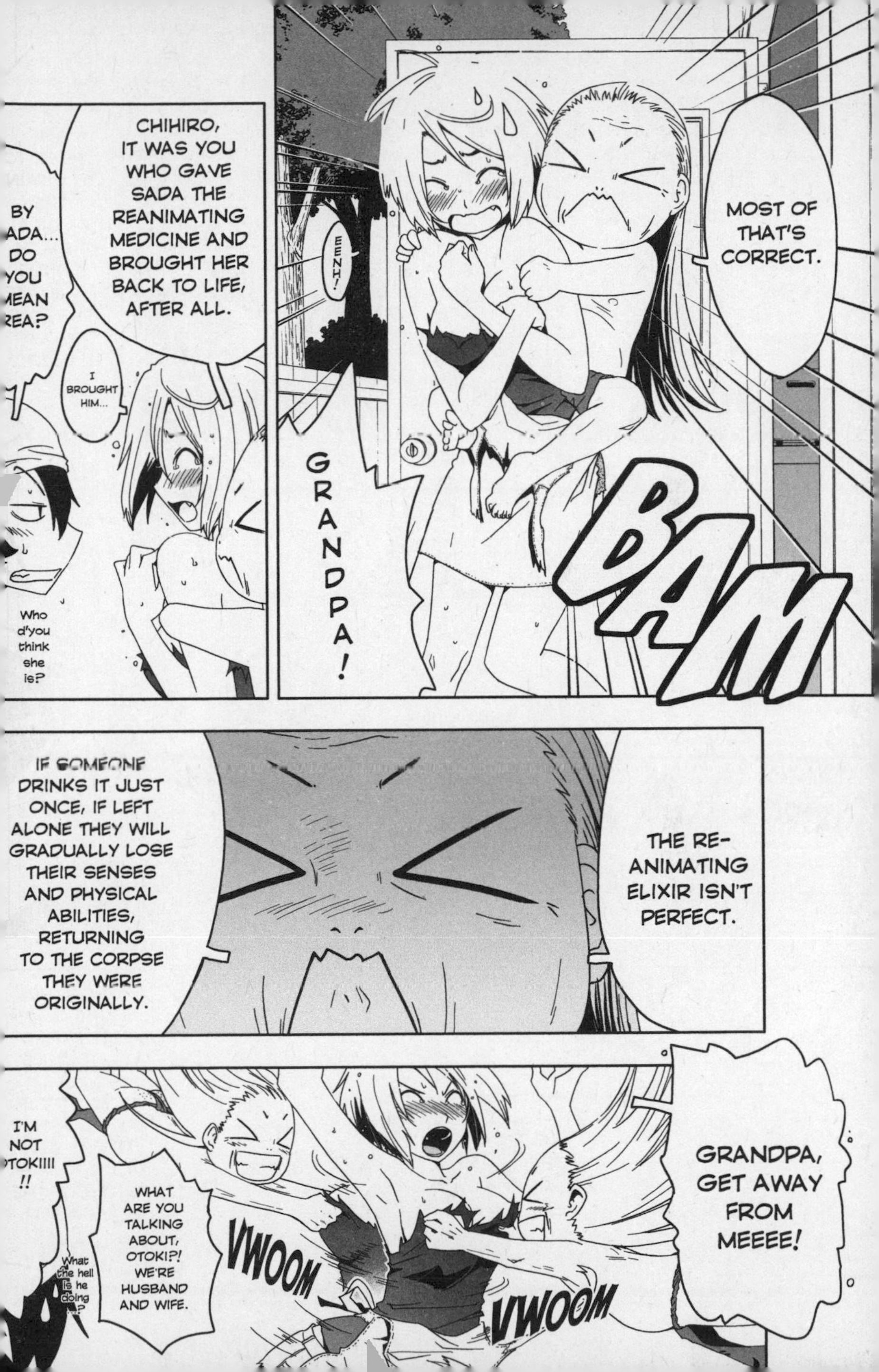
MOST OF THAT'S CORRECT.
EENH!
GRANDPA!
BAM
CHIHIRO, IT WAS YOU WHO GAVE SADA THE REANIMATING MEDICINE AND BROUGHT HER BACK TO LIFE, AFTER ALL.
BY ADA... DO YOU MEAN REA?
I BROUGHT HIM...
Who d'you think she is?
THE RE-ANIMATING ELIXIR ISN'T PERFECT.
IF SOMEONE DRINKS IT JUST ONCE, IF LEFT ALONE THEY WILL GRADUALLY LOSE THEIR SENSES AND PHYSICAL ABILITIES, RETURNING TO THE CORPSE THEY WERE ORIGINALLY.
GRANDPA, GET AWAY FROM MEEEE!
VWOOM
VWOOM
WHAT ARE YOU TALKING ABOUT, OTOKI?! WE'RE HUSBAND AND WIFE.
I'M NOT TOKIIII!!
What the hell is he doing?

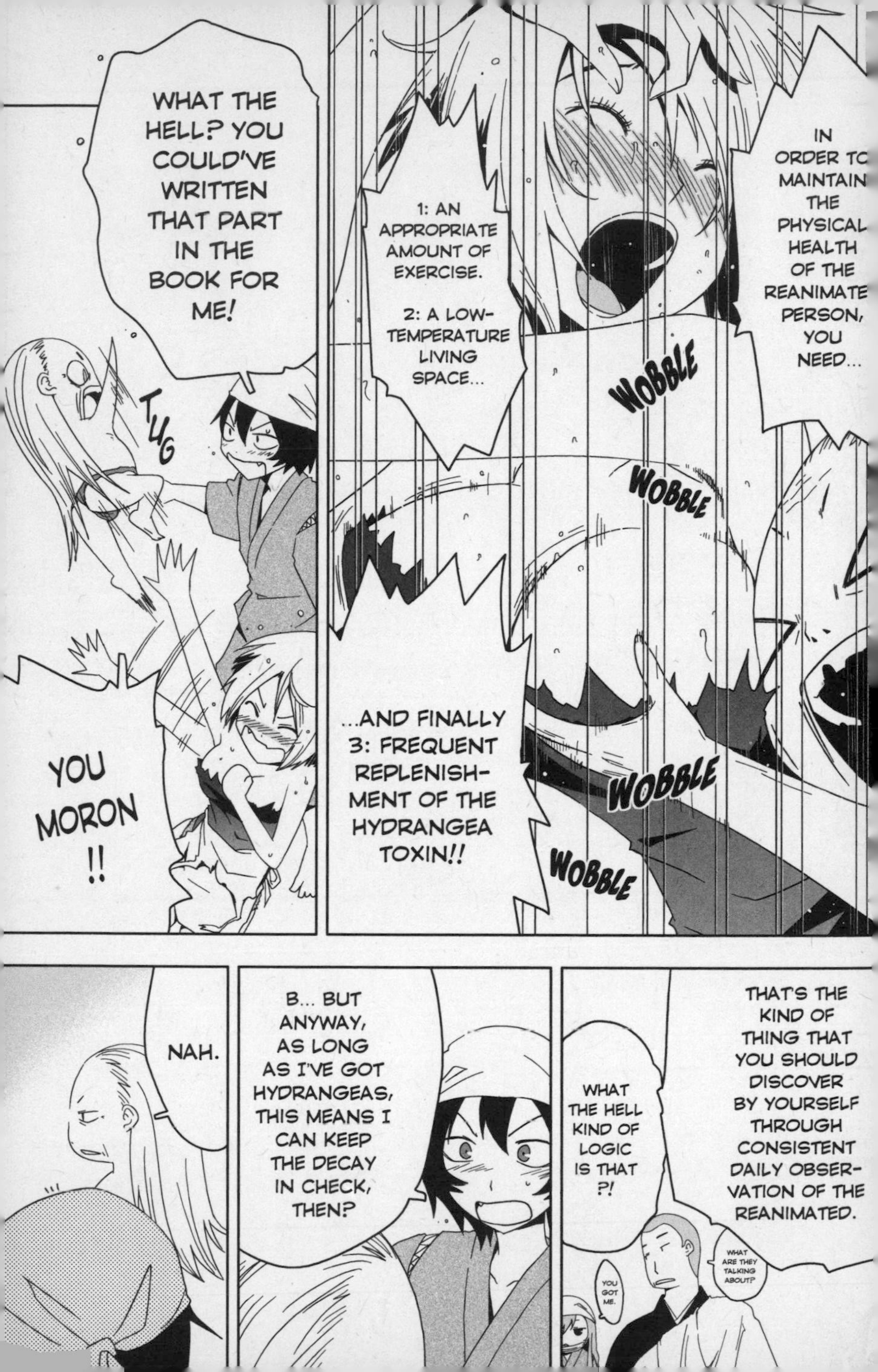
IN ORDER TO MAINTAIN THE PHYSICAL HEALTH OF THE REANIMATE PERSON, YOU NEED...
1: AN APPROPRIATE AMOUNT OF EXERCISE.
2: A LOW-TEMPERATURE LIVING SPACE...
WOBBLE
WOBBLE
WOBBLE
WOBBLE
...AND FINALLY 3: FREQUENT REPLENISHMENT OF THE HYDRANGEA TOXIN!!
WHAT THE HELL? YOU COULD'VE WRITTEN THAT PART IN THE BOOK FOR ME!
TUG
YOU MORON !!
THAT'S THE KIND OF THING THAT YOU SHOULD DISCOVER BY YOURSELF THROUGH CONSISTENT DAILY OBSERVATION OF THE REANIMATED.
WHAT THE HELL KIND OF LOGIC IS THAT ?!
WHAT ARE THEY TALKING ABOUT?
YOU GOT ME.
B... BUT ANYWAY, AS LONG AS I'VE GOT HYDRANGEAS, THIS MEANS I CAN KEEP THE DECAY IN CHECK, THEN?
NAH.

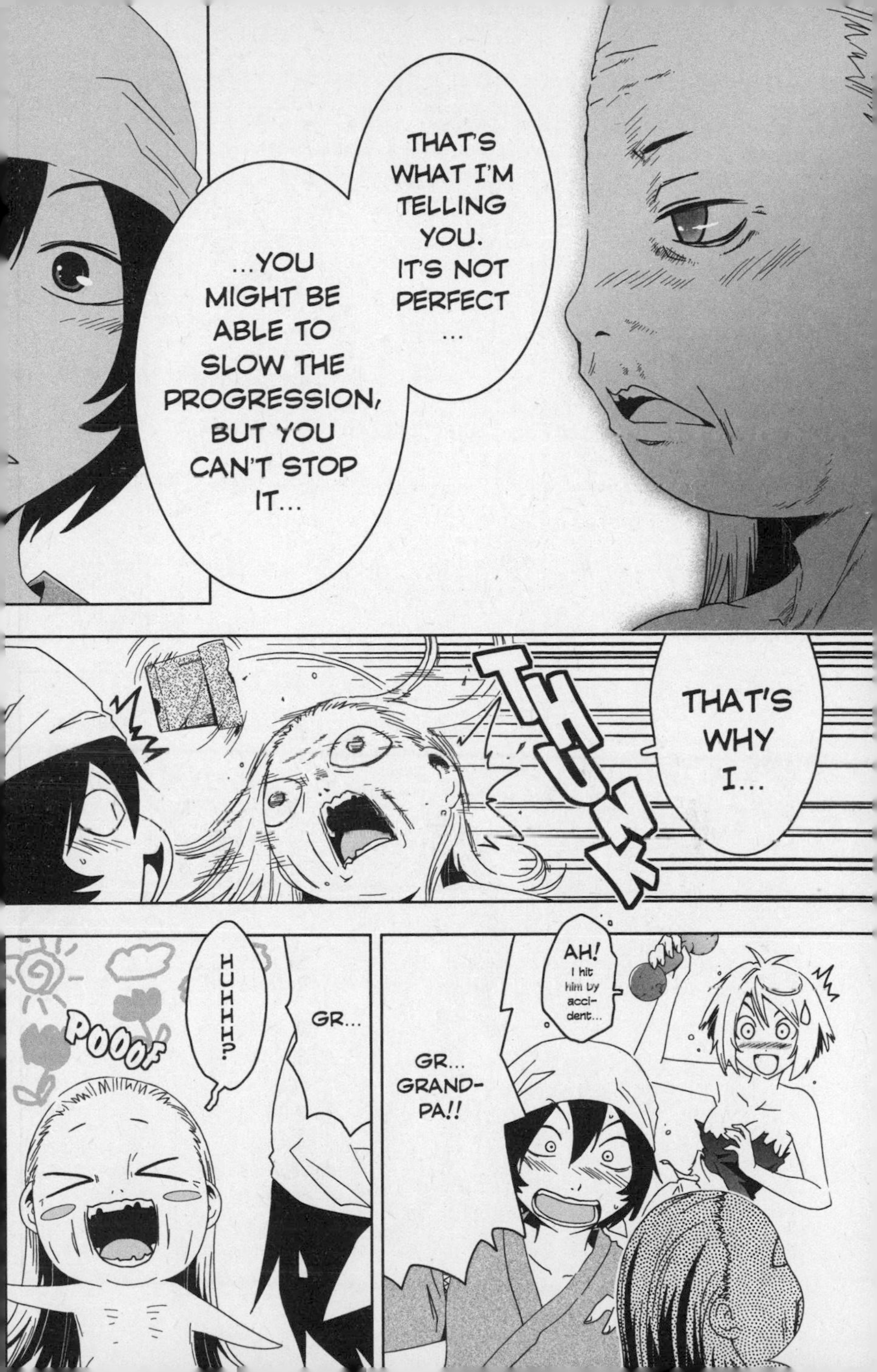
THAT'S WHAT I'M TELLING YOU. IT'S NOT PERFECT ...
...YOU MIGHT BE ABLE TO SLOW THE PROGRESSION, BUT YOU CAN'T STOP IT...
THAT'S WHY I...
THUNK
AH! I hit him by acci-dent...
GR... GRAND-PA!!
GR...
HUHHH?
POOOF

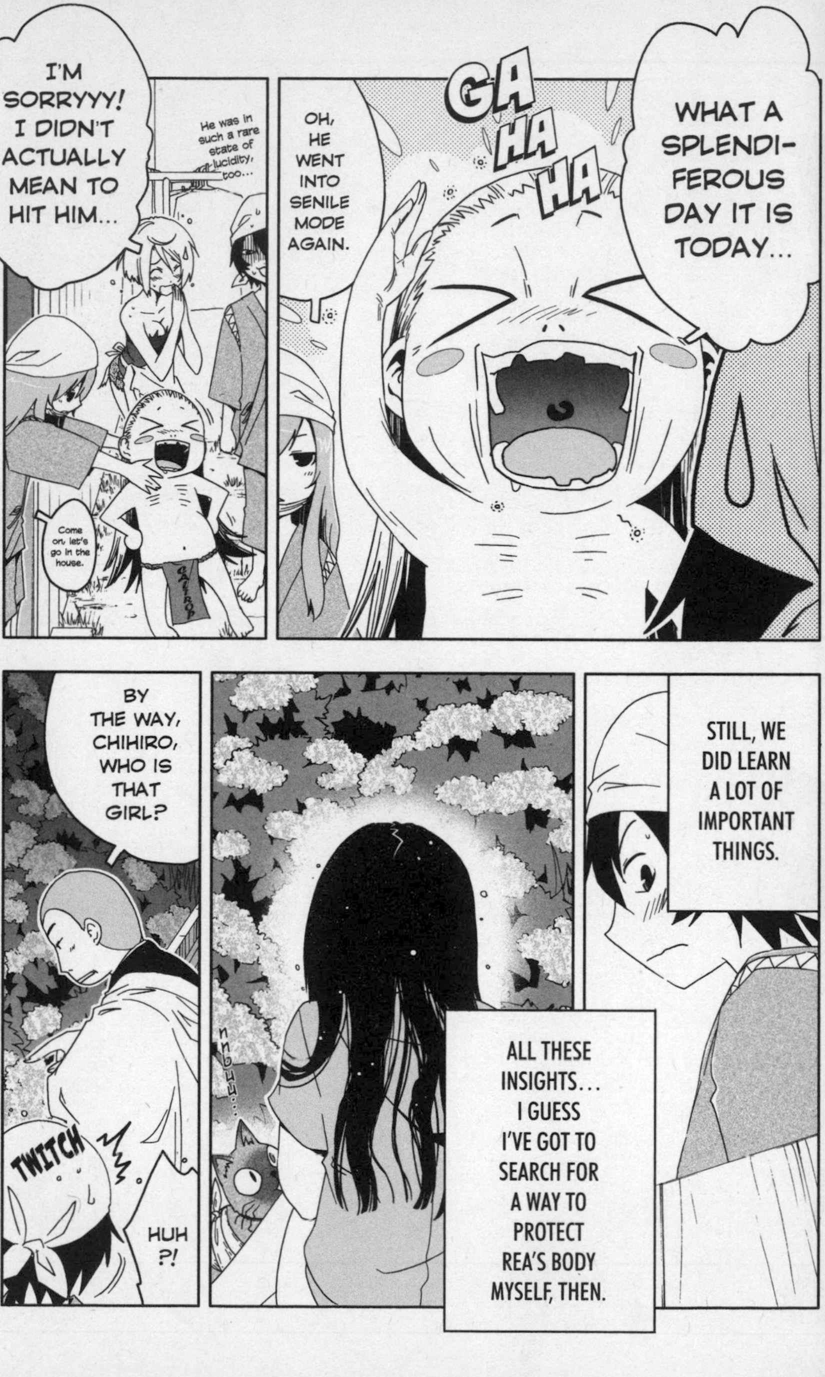
WHAT A SPLENDIFEROUS DAY IT IS TODAY...
GA HA HA
OH, HE WENT INTO SENILE MODE AGAIN.
I'M SORRYYY! I DIDN'T ACTUALLY MEAN TO HIT HIM...
He was in such a rare state of lucidity, too...
Come on, let's go in the house.
STILL, WE DID LEARN A LOT OF IMPORTANT THINGS.
ALL THESE INSIGHTS... I GUESS I'VE GOT TO SEARCH FOR A WAY TO PROTECT REA'S BODY MYSELF, THEN.
nnbuu...
BY THE WAY, CHIHIRO, WHO IS THAT GIRL?
TWITCH
HUH?!

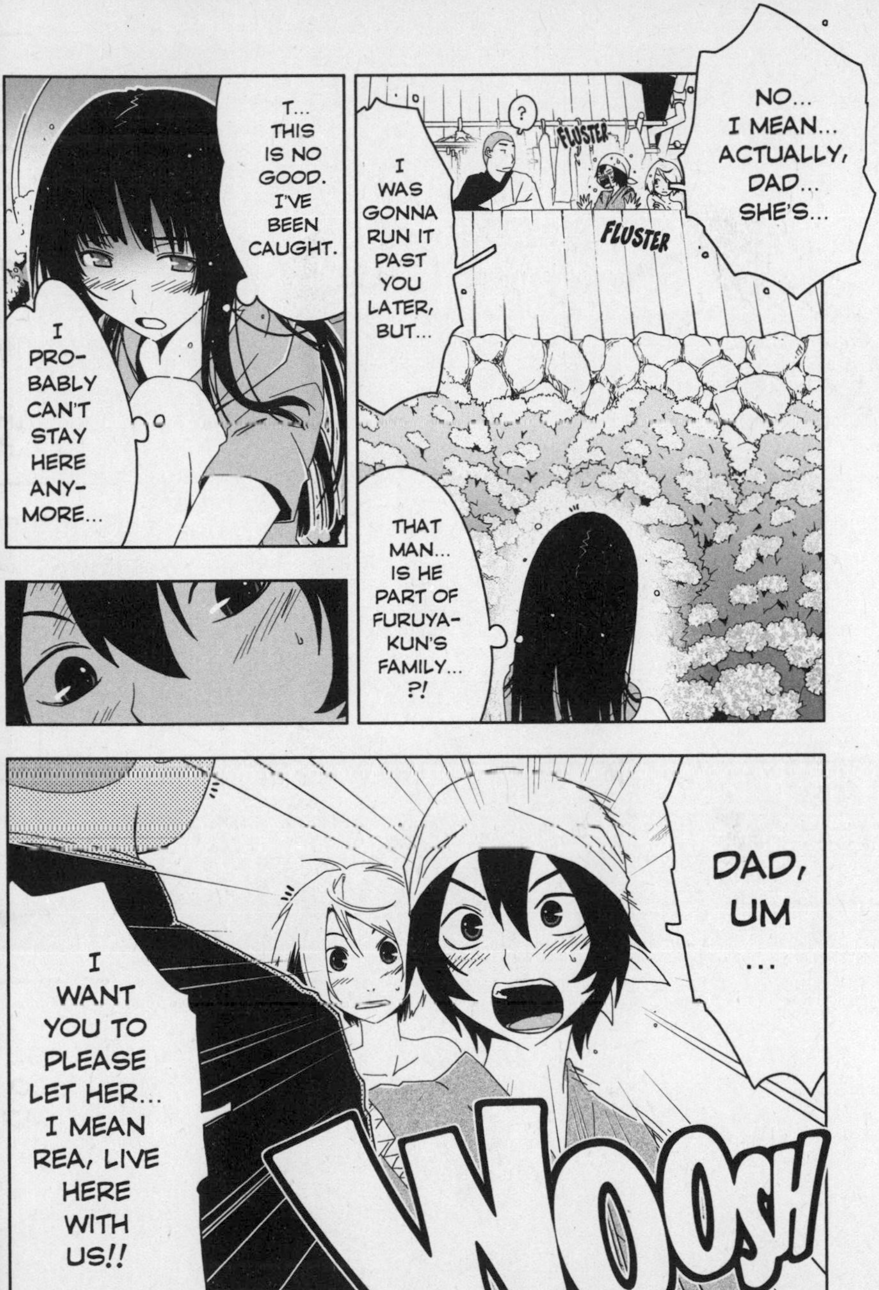
NO... I MEAN... ACTUALLY, DAD... SHE'S...
?
FLUSTER
I WAS GONNA RUN IT PAST YOU LATER, BUT...
FLUSTER
THAT MAN... IS HE PART OF FURUYA-KUN'S FAMILY...?!
T... THIS IS NO GOOD. I'VE BEEN CAUGHT.
I PROBABLY CAN'T STAY HERE ANYMORE...
DAD, UM ...
WOOSH
I WANT YOU TO PLEASE LET HER... I MEAN REA, LIVE HERE WITH US!!

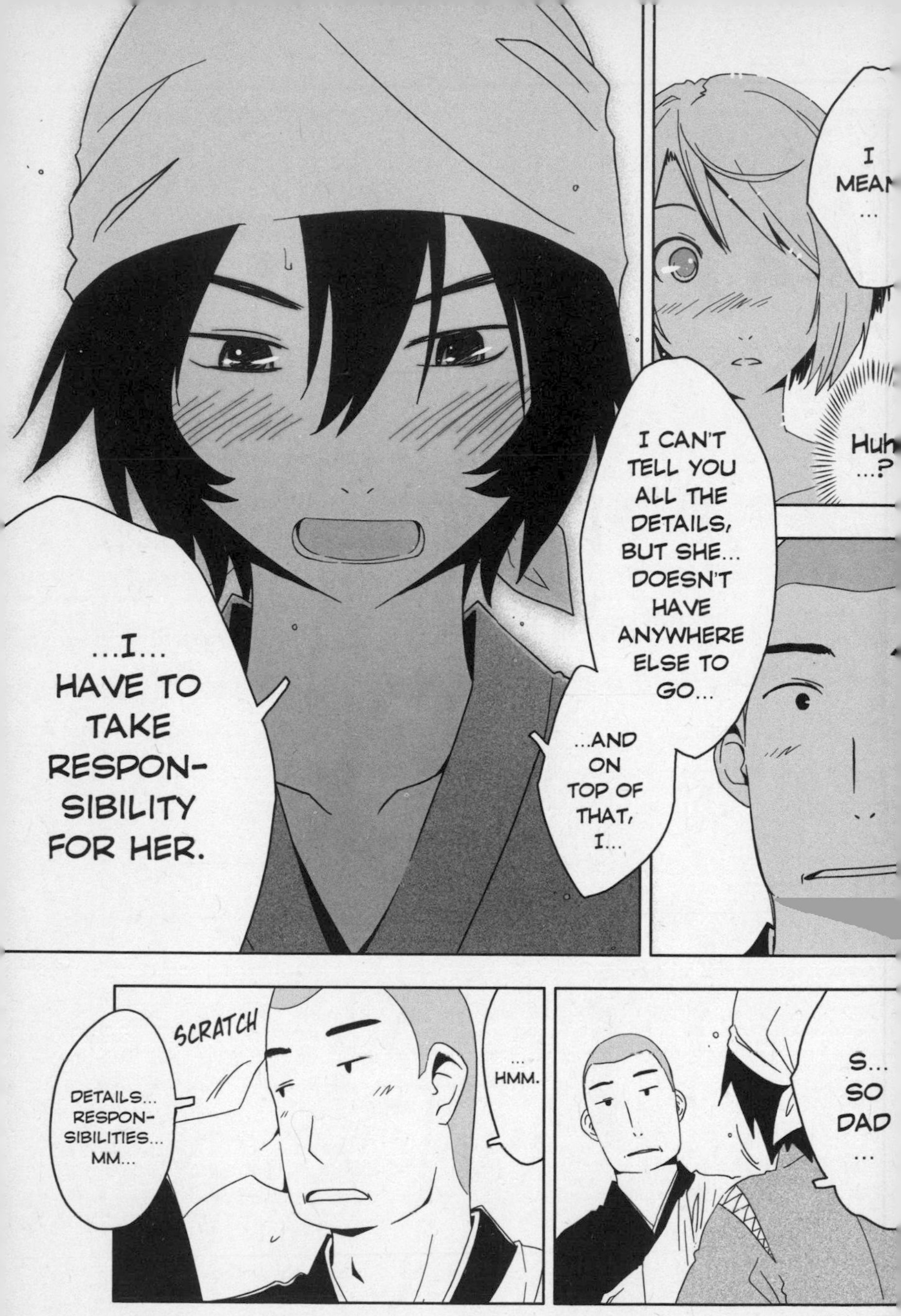
I MEAN ...
Huh ...?
I CAN'T TELL YOU ALL THE DETAILS, BUT SHE... DOESN'T HAVE ANYWHERE ELSE TO GO...
...AND ON TOP OF THAT, I...
...I... HAVE TO TAKE RESPON-SIBILITY FOR HER.
S... SO DAD ...
... HMM.
SCRATCH
DETAILS... RESPON-SIBILITIES... MM...

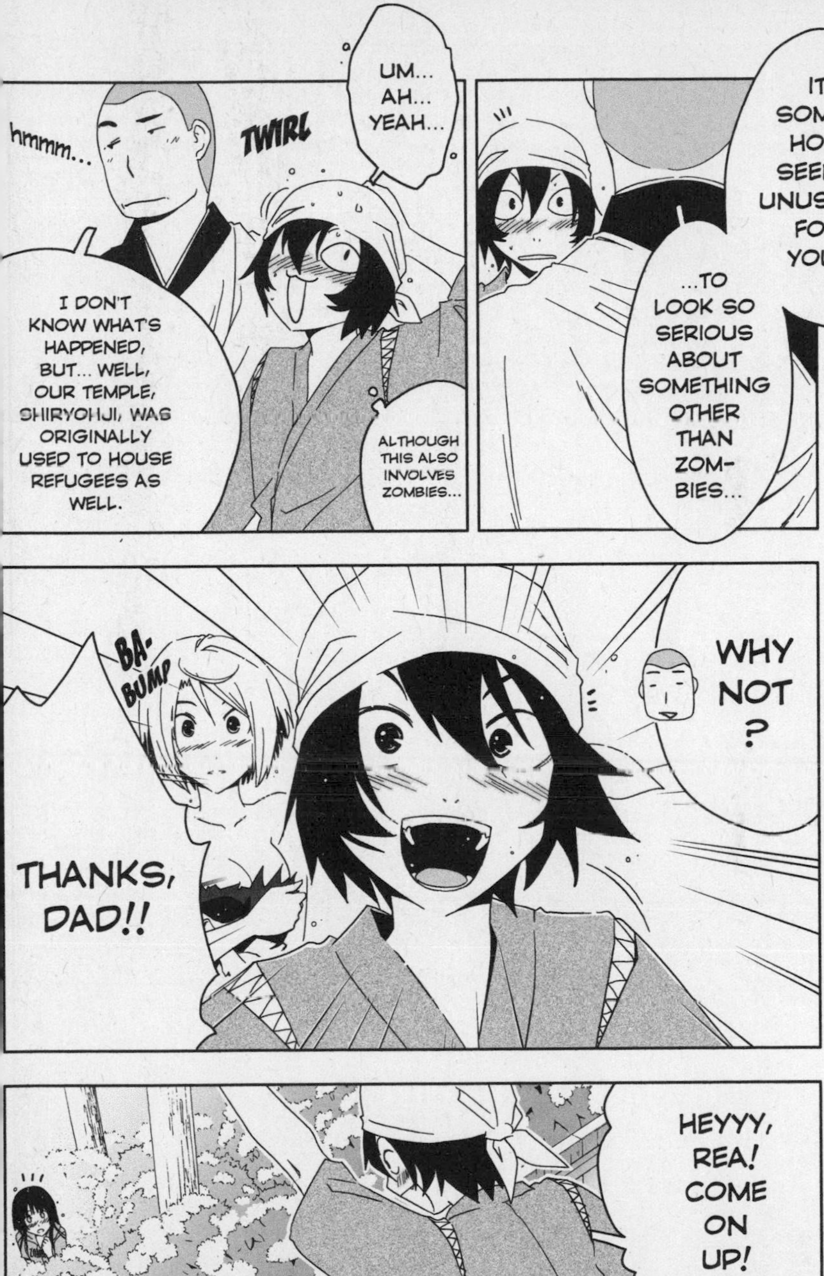
IT SOMEHOW SEEMS UNUSUAL FOR YOU...
...TO LOOK SO SERIOUS ABOUT SOMETHING OTHER THAN ZOMBIES...
UM... AH... YEAH...
TWIRL
hmmm...
I DON'T KNOW WHAT'S HAPPENED, BUT... WELL, OUR TEMPLE, SHIRYOHJI, WAS ORIGINALLY USED TO HOUSE REFUGEES AS WELL.
ALTHOUGH THIS ALSO INVOLVES ZOMBIES...
WHY NOT?
BA-BUMP
THANKS, DAD!!
HEYYY, REA! COME ON UP!

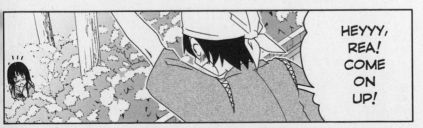

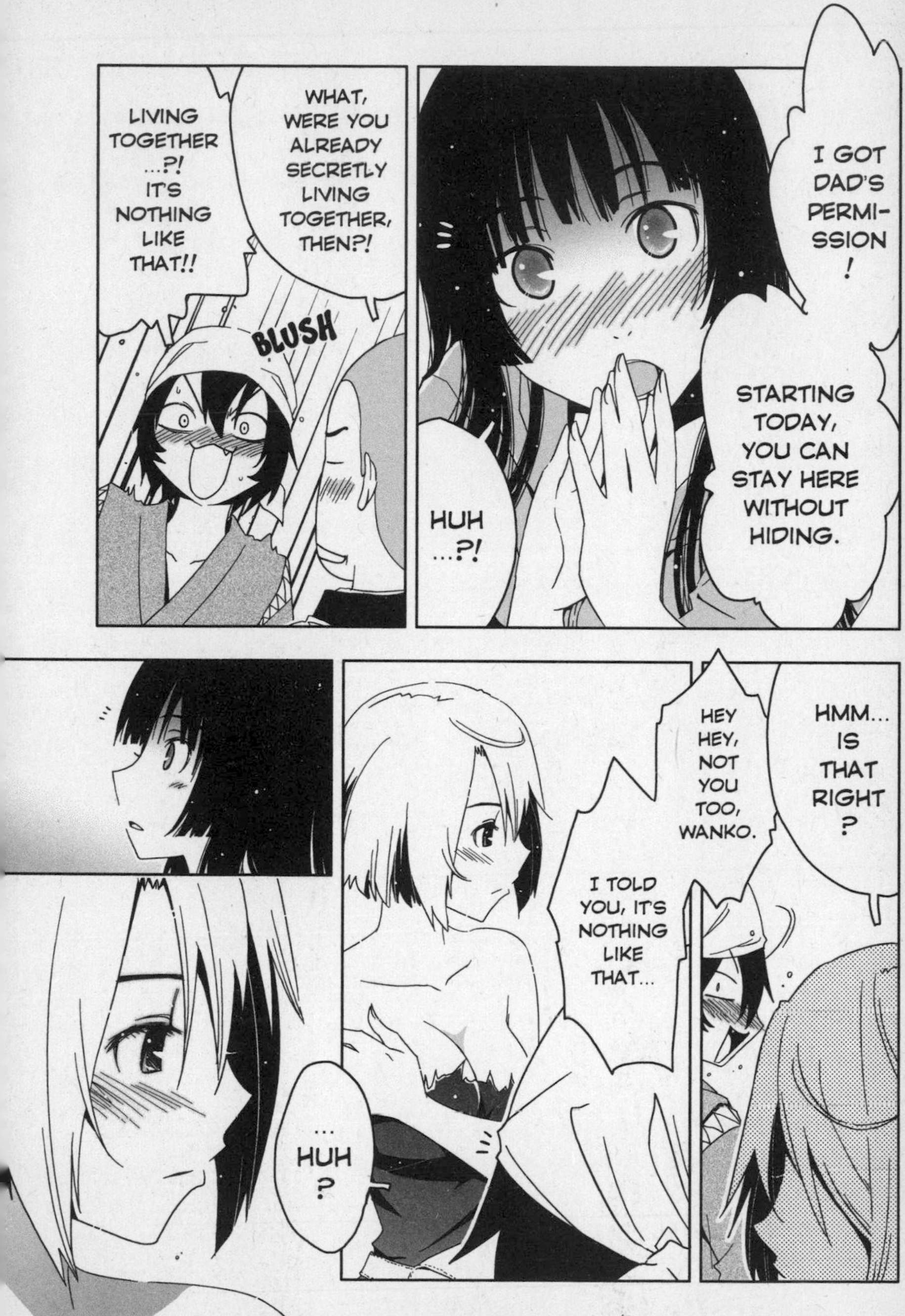
I GOT DAD'S PERMI-SSION!
STARTING TODAY, YOU CAN STAY HERE WITHOUT HIDING.
HUH ...?!
WHAT, WERE YOU ALREADY SECRETLY LIVING TOGETHER, THEN?!
LIVING TOGETHER ...?! IT'S NOTHING LIKE THAT!!
BLUSH
HMM... IS THAT RIGHT?
HEY HEY, NOT YOU TOO, WANKO.
I TOLD YOU, IT'S NOTHING LIKE THAT...
... HUH?

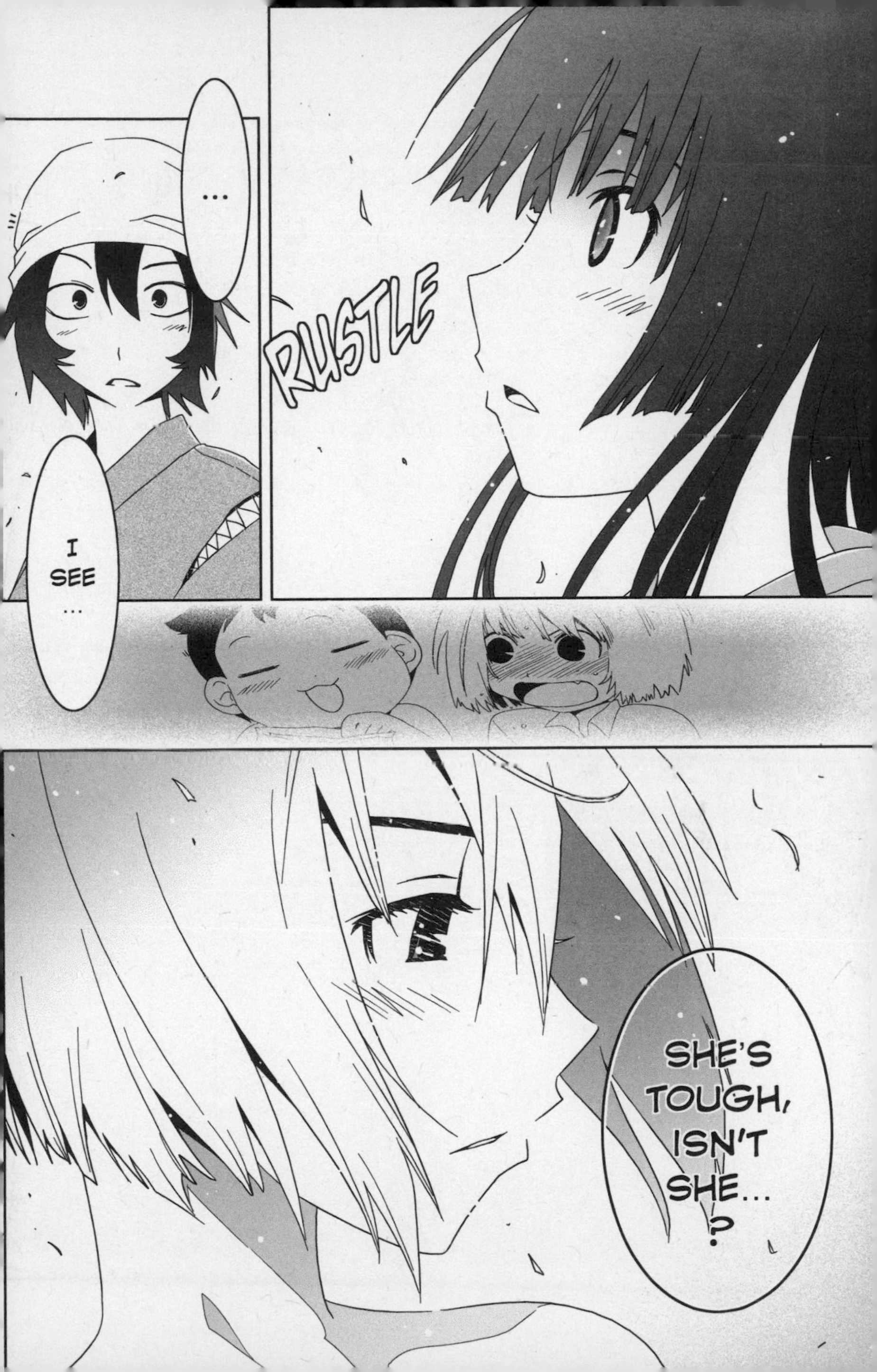
RUSTLE
...
I SEE...
SHE'S TOUGH, ISN'T SHE...?

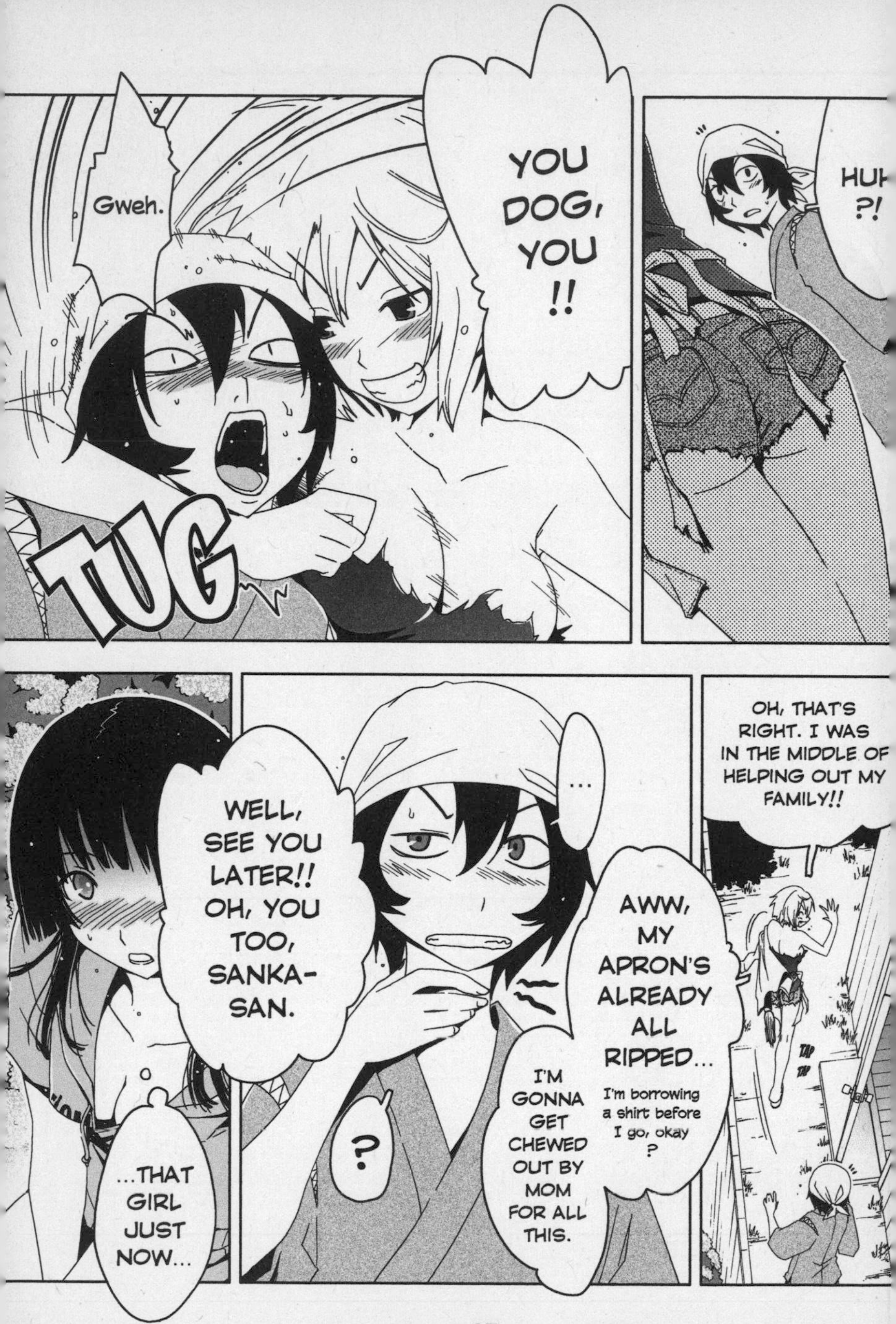
HUH ?!
YOU DOG, YOU !!
Gweh.
TUG
OH, THAT'S RIGHT. I WAS IN THE MIDDLE OF HELPING OUT MY FAMILY!!
TAP TAP
WELL, SEE YOU LATER!! OH, YOU TOO, SANKA-SAN.
...
AWW, MY APRON'S ALREADY ALL RIPPED...
I'm borrowing a shirt before I go, okay ?
I'M GONNA GET CHEWED OUT BY MOM FOR ALL THIS.
?
...THAT GIRL JUST NOW...

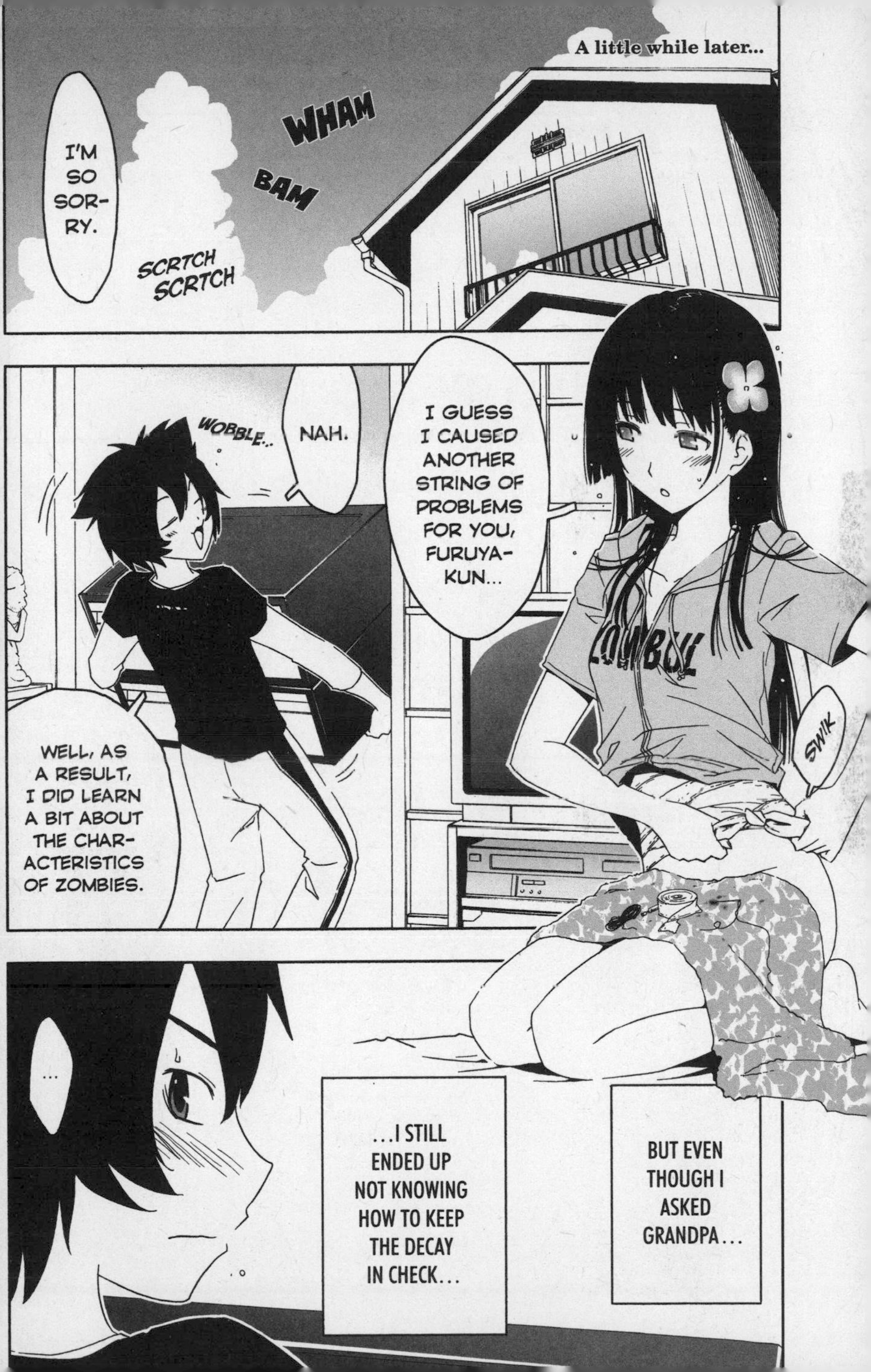
A little while later...
WHAM
BAM
I'M SO SOR-RY.
SCRTCH SCRTCH
I GUESS I CAUSED ANOTHER STRING OF PROBLEMS FOR YOU, FURUYA-KUN...
SWIK
NAH.
WOBBLE...
WELL, AS A RESULT, I DID LEARN A BIT ABOUT THE CHAR-ACTERISTICS OF ZOMBIES.
BUT EVEN THOUGH I ASKED GRANDPA...
...I STILL ENDED UP NOT KNOWING HOW TO KEEP THE DECAY IN CHECK...
...

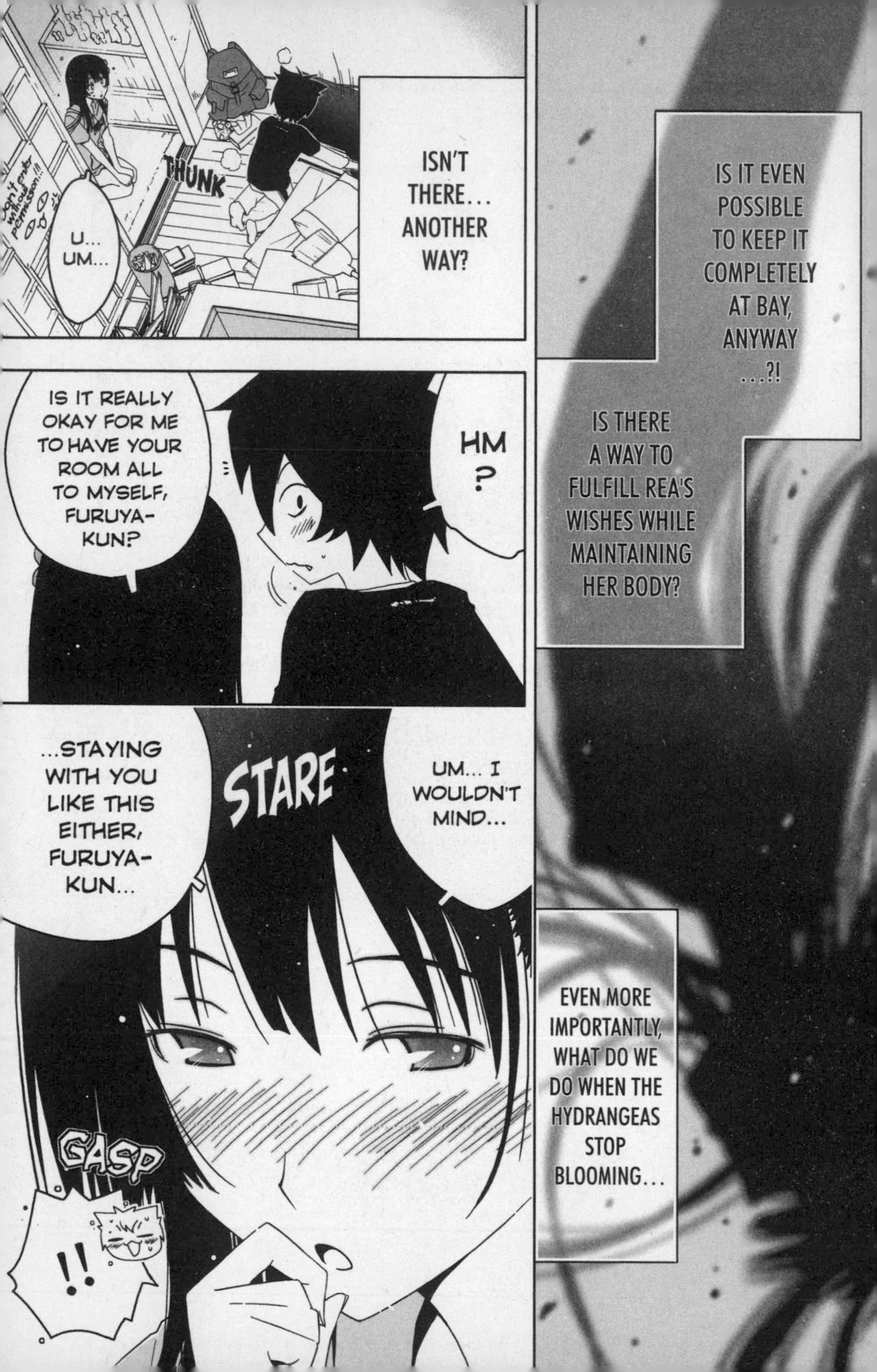
IS IT EVEN POSSIBLE TO KEEP IT COMPLETELY AT BAY, ANYWAY ...?!
IS THERE A WAY TO FULFILL REA'S WISHES WHILE MAINTAINING HER BODY?
EVEN MORE IMPORTANTLY, WHAT DO WE DO WHEN THE HYDRANGEAS STOP BLOOMING...
ISN'T THERE... ANOTHER WAY?
THUNK
U... UM...
HM ?
IS IT REALLY OKAY FOR ME TO HAVE YOUR ROOM ALL TO MYSELF, FURUYA-KUN?
UM... I WOULDN'T MIND...
STARE
...STAYING WITH YOU LIKE THIS EITHER, FURUYA-KUN...
GASP
!!

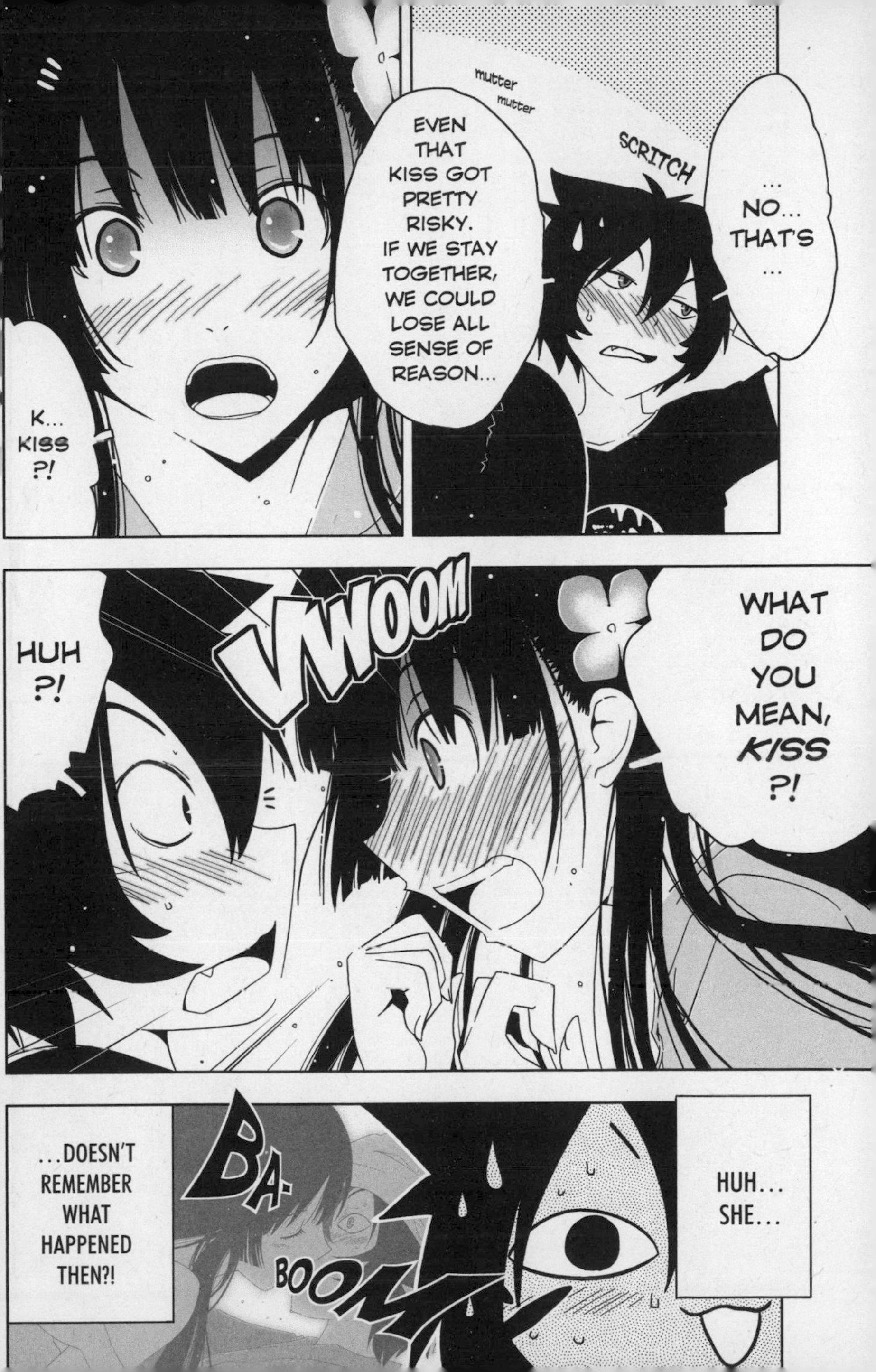
... NO... THAT'S ...
SCRITCH
mutter mutter
EVEN THAT KISS GOT PRETTY RISKY. IF WE STAY TOGETHER, WE COULD LOSE ALL SENSE OF REASON...
K... KISS ?!
WHAT DO YOU MEAN, *KISS* ?!
VWOOM
HUH ?!
HUH... SHE...
BA-BOOM
...DOESN'T REMEMBER WHAT HAPPENED THEN?!

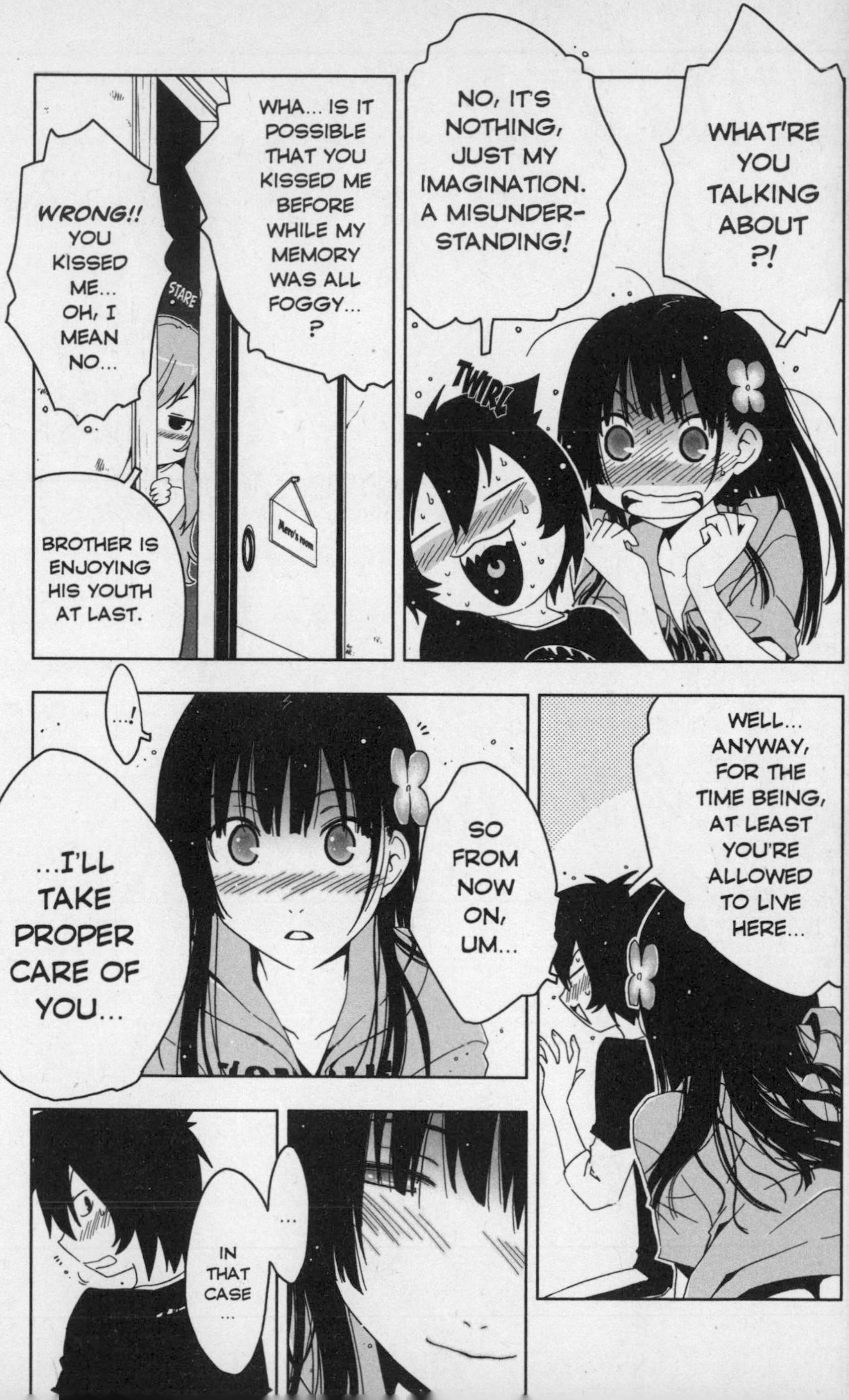
WHAT'RE YOU TALKING ABOUT ?!
NO, IT'S NOTHING, JUST MY IMAGINATION. A MISUNDER-STANDING!
TWIRL
WHA... IS IT POSSIBLE THAT YOU KISSED ME BEFORE WHILE MY MEMORY WAS ALL FOGGY... ?
WRONG!! YOU KISSED ME... OH, I MEAN NO...
STARE
BROTHER IS ENJOYING HIS YOUTH AT LAST.
Mero's room
WELL... ANYWAY, FOR THE TIME BEING, AT LEAST YOU'RE ALLOWED TO LIVE HERE...
SO FROM NOW ON, UM...
...!
...I'LL TAKE PROPER CARE OF YOU...
...
IN THAT CASE ...

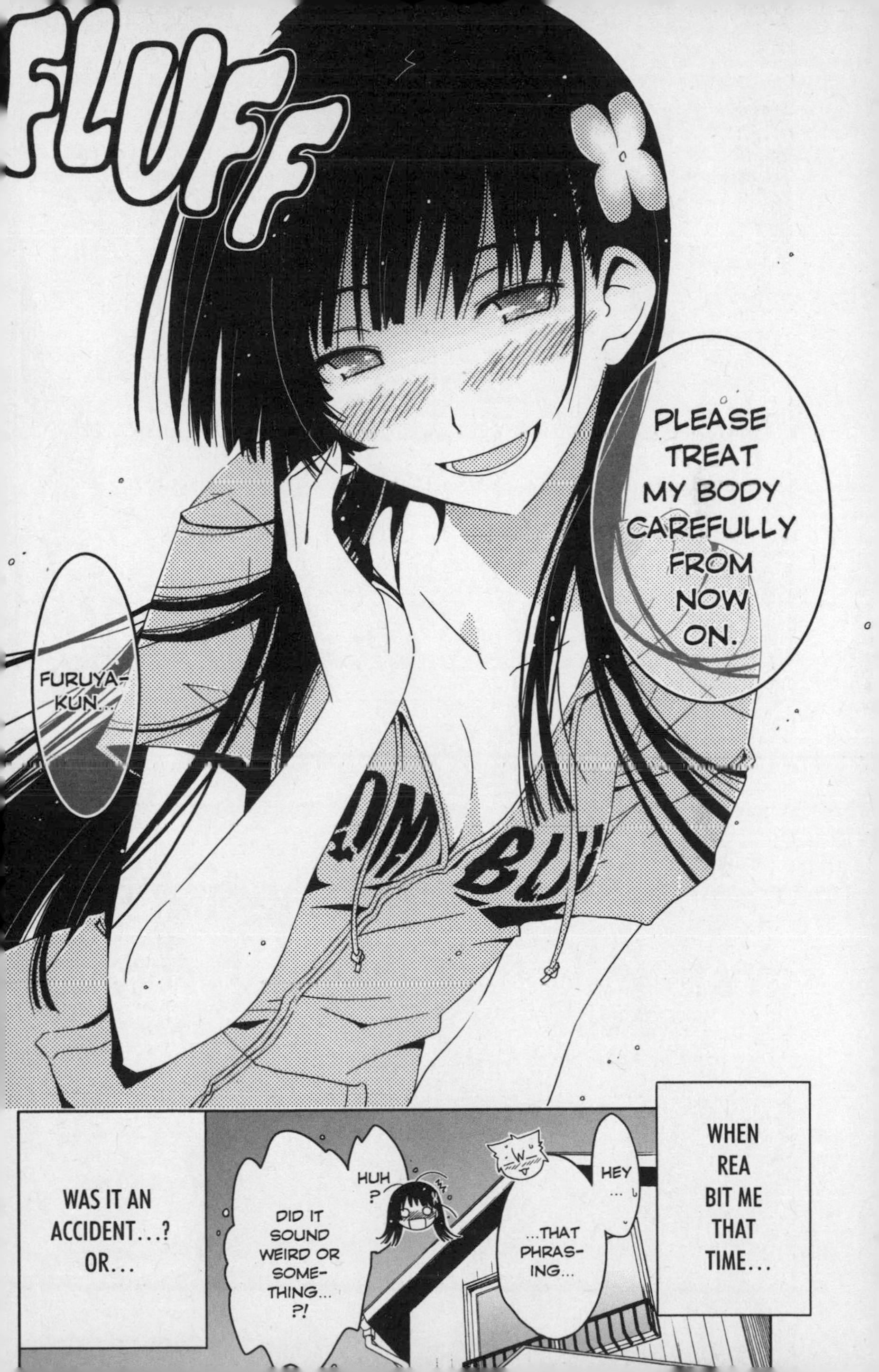
FLUFF
PLEASE TREAT MY BODY CAREFULLY FROM NOW ON.
FURUYA-KUN...
WHEN REA BIT ME THAT TIME...
HEY...
...THAT PHRAS-ING...
HUH?
DID IT SOUND WEIRD OR SOME-THING...?!
WAS IT AN ACCIDENT...? OR...

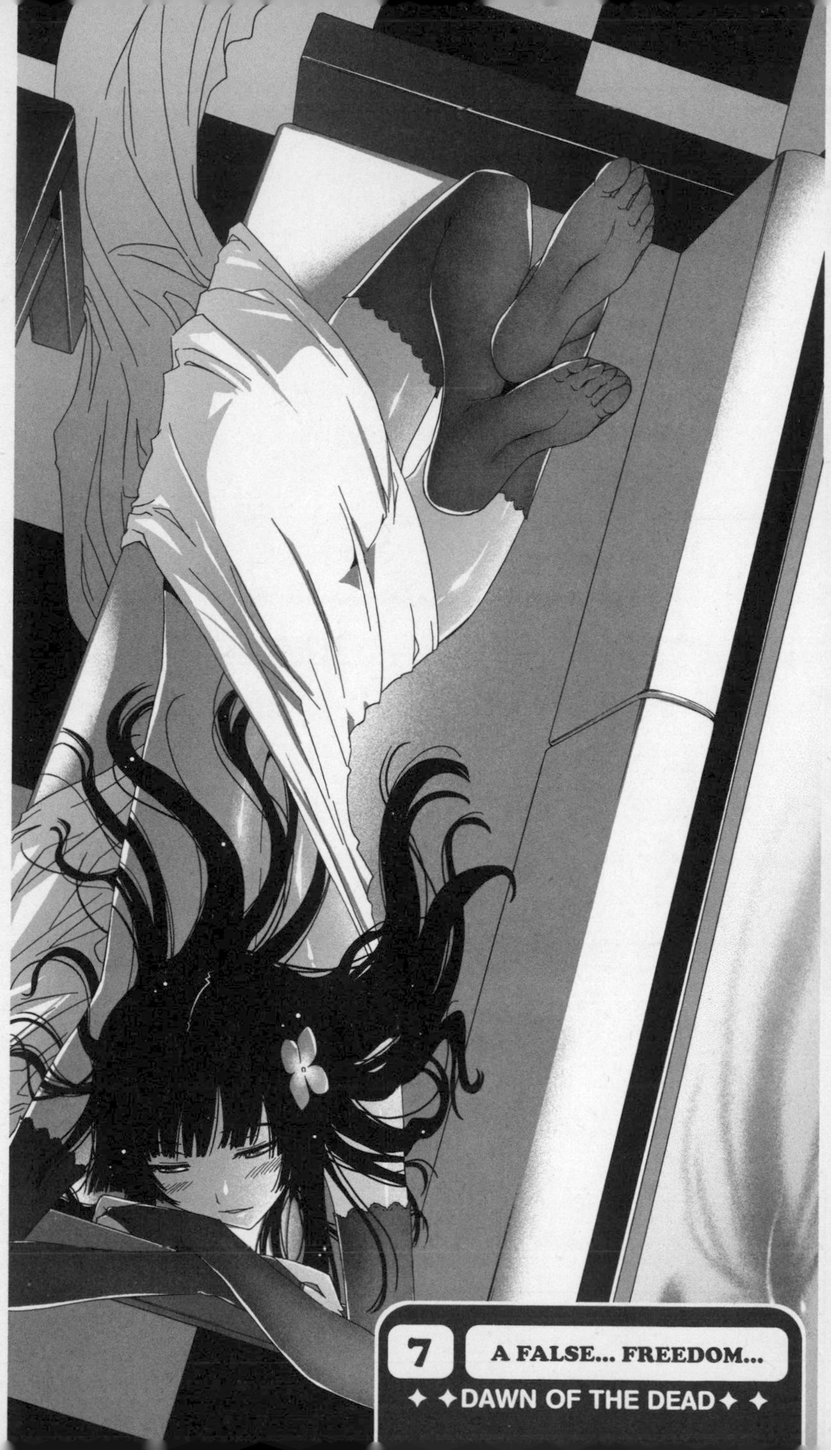
7
A FALSE... FREEDOM...
✦ ✦DAWN OF THE DEAD✦ ✦

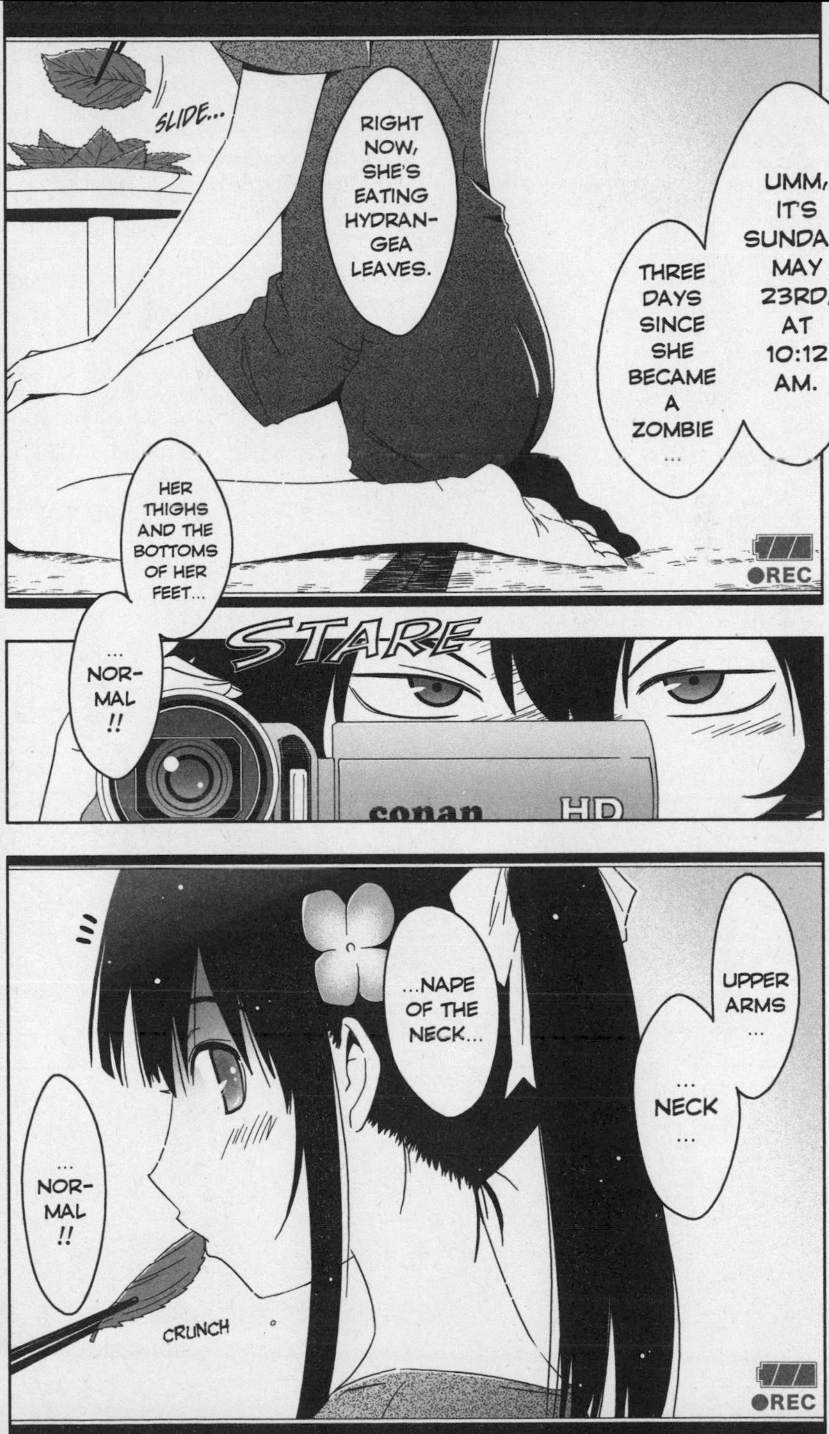
UMM, IT'S SUNDAY, MAY 23RD, AT 10:12 AM.
THREE DAYS SINCE SHE BECAME A ZOMBIE...
RIGHT NOW, SHE'S EATING HYDRAN-GEA LEAVES.
SLIDE...
REC
HER THIGHS AND THE BOTTOMS OF HER FEET...
STARE
... NOR-MAL !!
conan HD
UPPER ARMS ...
... NECK ...
...NAPE OF THE NECK...
!!!
... NOR-MAL !!
CRUNCH
REC

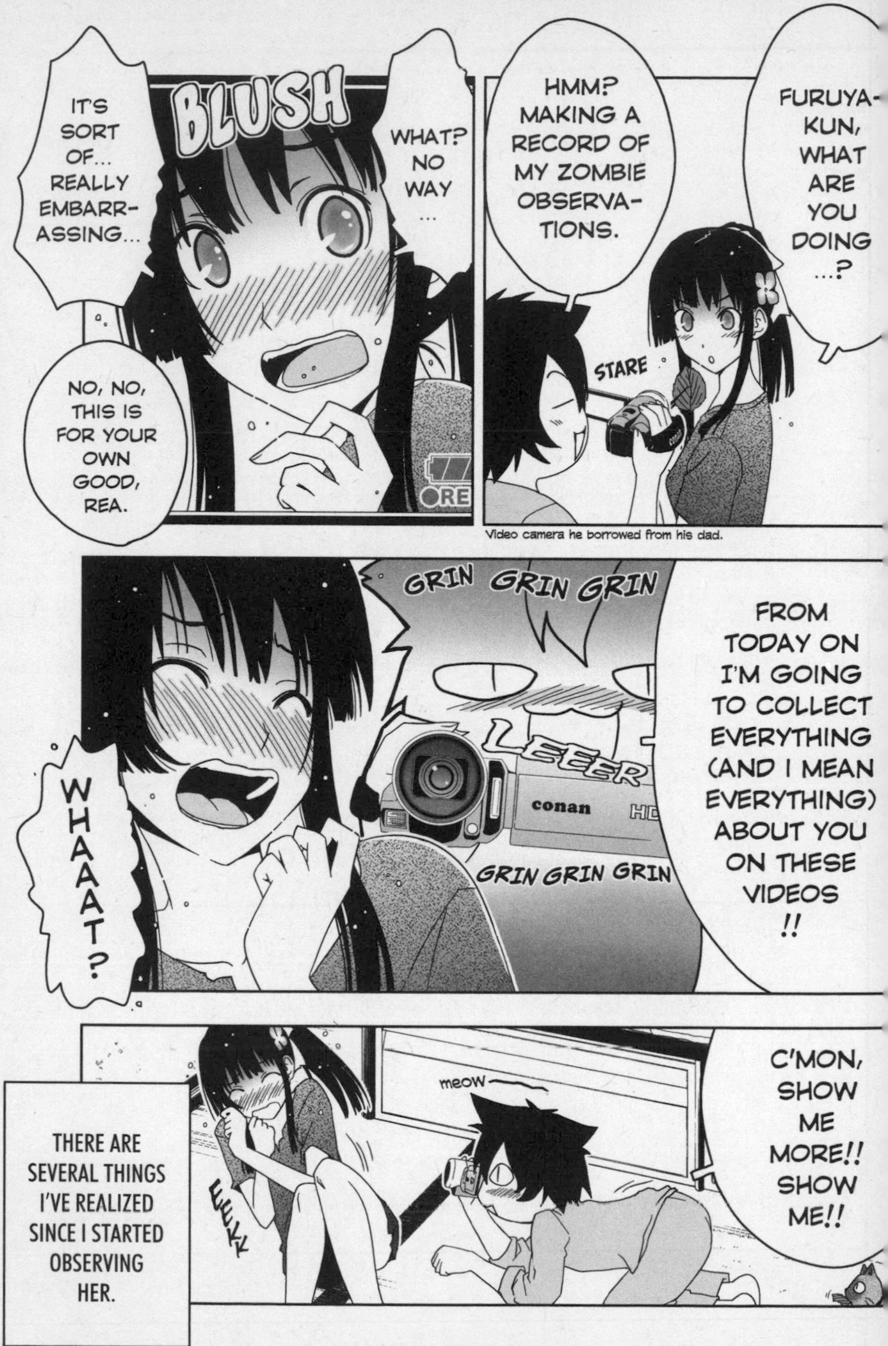
FURUYA-KUN, WHAT ARE YOU DOING ...?
HMM? MAKING A RECORD OF MY ZOMBIE OBSERVATIONS.
STARE
Video camera he borrowed from his dad.
WHAT? NO WAY ...
BLUSH
IT'S SORT OF... REALLY EMBARRASSING...
NO, NO, THIS IS FOR YOUR OWN GOOD, REA.
FROM TODAY ON I'M GOING TO COLLECT EVERYTHING (AND I MEAN EVERYTHING) ABOUT YOU ON THESE VIDEOS !!
GRIN GRIN GRIN
LEEER
conan HD
GRIN GRIN GRIN
WHAAAT?
C'MON, SHOW ME MORE!! SHOW ME!!
meow
EEEK
THERE ARE SEVERAL THINGS I'VE REALIZED SINCE I STARTED OBSERVING HER.

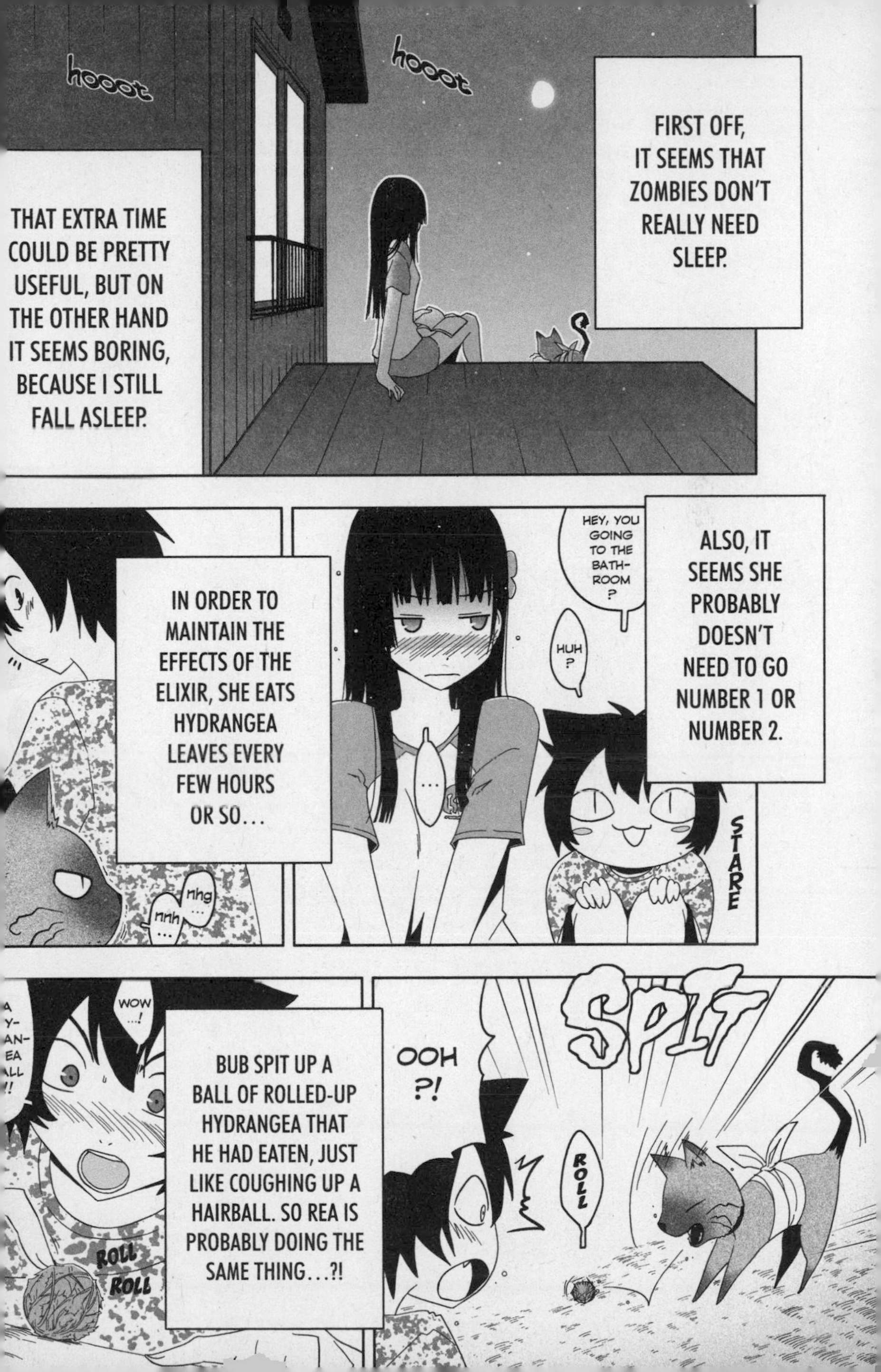
hoooot
FIRST OFF, IT SEEMS THAT ZOMBIES DON'T REALLY NEED SLEEP.
THAT EXTRA TIME COULD BE PRETTY USEFUL, BUT ON THE OTHER HAND IT SEEMS BORING, BECAUSE I STILL FALL ASLEEP.
hoooot
ALSO, IT SEEMS SHE PROBABLY DOESN'T NEED TO GO NUMBER 1 OR NUMBER 2.
HEY, YOU GOING TO THE BATH-ROOM?
HUH?
...
STARE
IN ORDER TO MAINTAIN THE EFFECTS OF THE ELIXIR, SHE EATS HYDRANGEA LEAVES EVERY FEW HOURS OR SO…
nhg...
nnh...
SPIT
OOH?!
ROLL
BUB SPIT UP A BALL OF ROLLED-UP HYDRANGEA THAT HE HAD EATEN, JUST LIKE COUGHING UP A HAIRBALL. SO REA IS PROBABLY DOING THE SAME THING…?!
WOW...!
ROLL ROLL

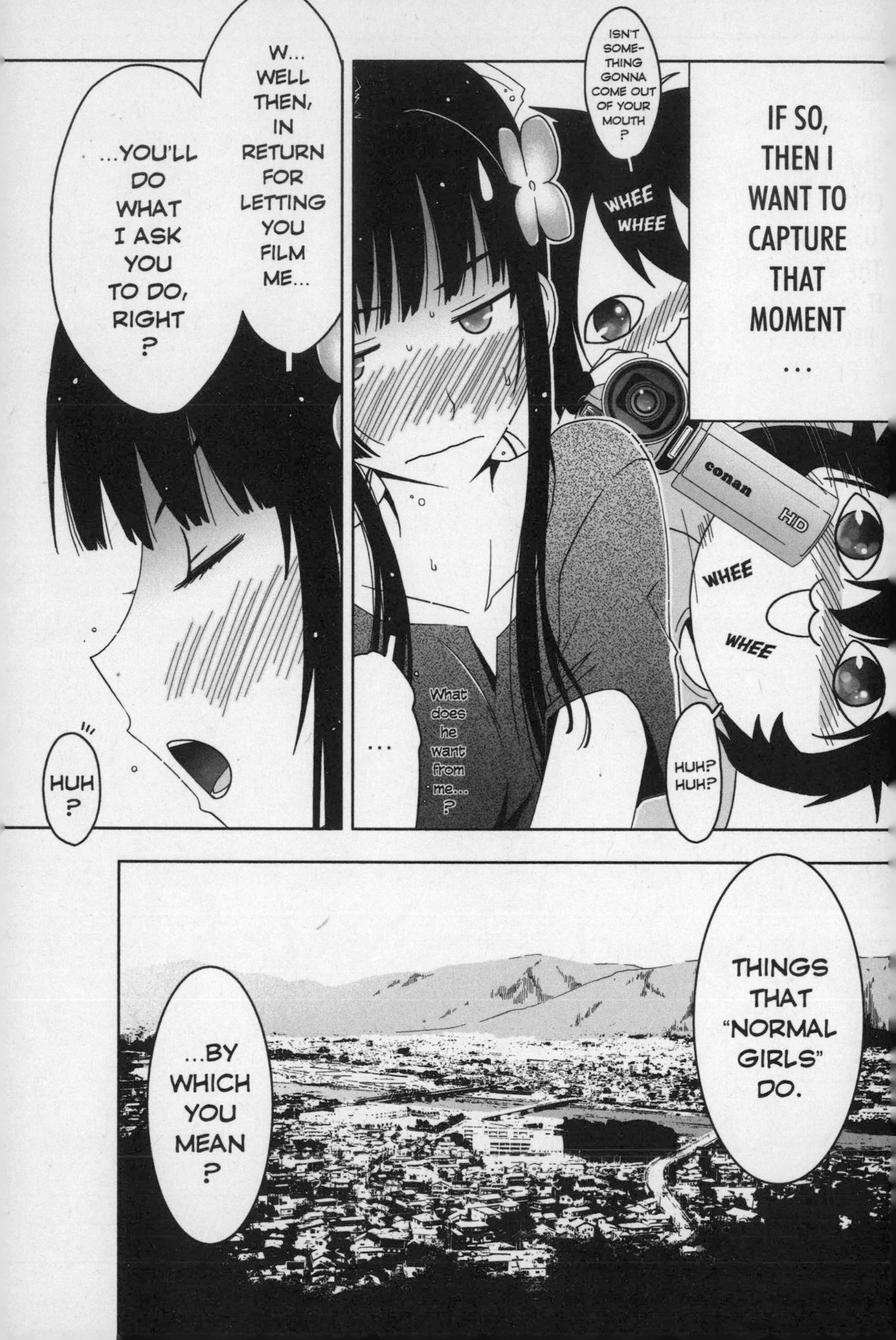
IF SO, THEN I WANT TO CAPTURE THAT MOMENT...
ISN'T SOME-THING GONNA COME OUT OF YOUR MOUTH?
WHEE WHEE
conan HD
WHEE
WHEE
HUH? HUH?
...
What does he want from me...?
W... WELL THEN, IN RETURN FOR LETTING YOU FILM ME...
...YOU'LL DO WHAT I ASK YOU TO DO, RIGHT?
HUH?
THINGS THAT "NORMAL GIRLS" DO.
...BY WHICH YOU MEAN?

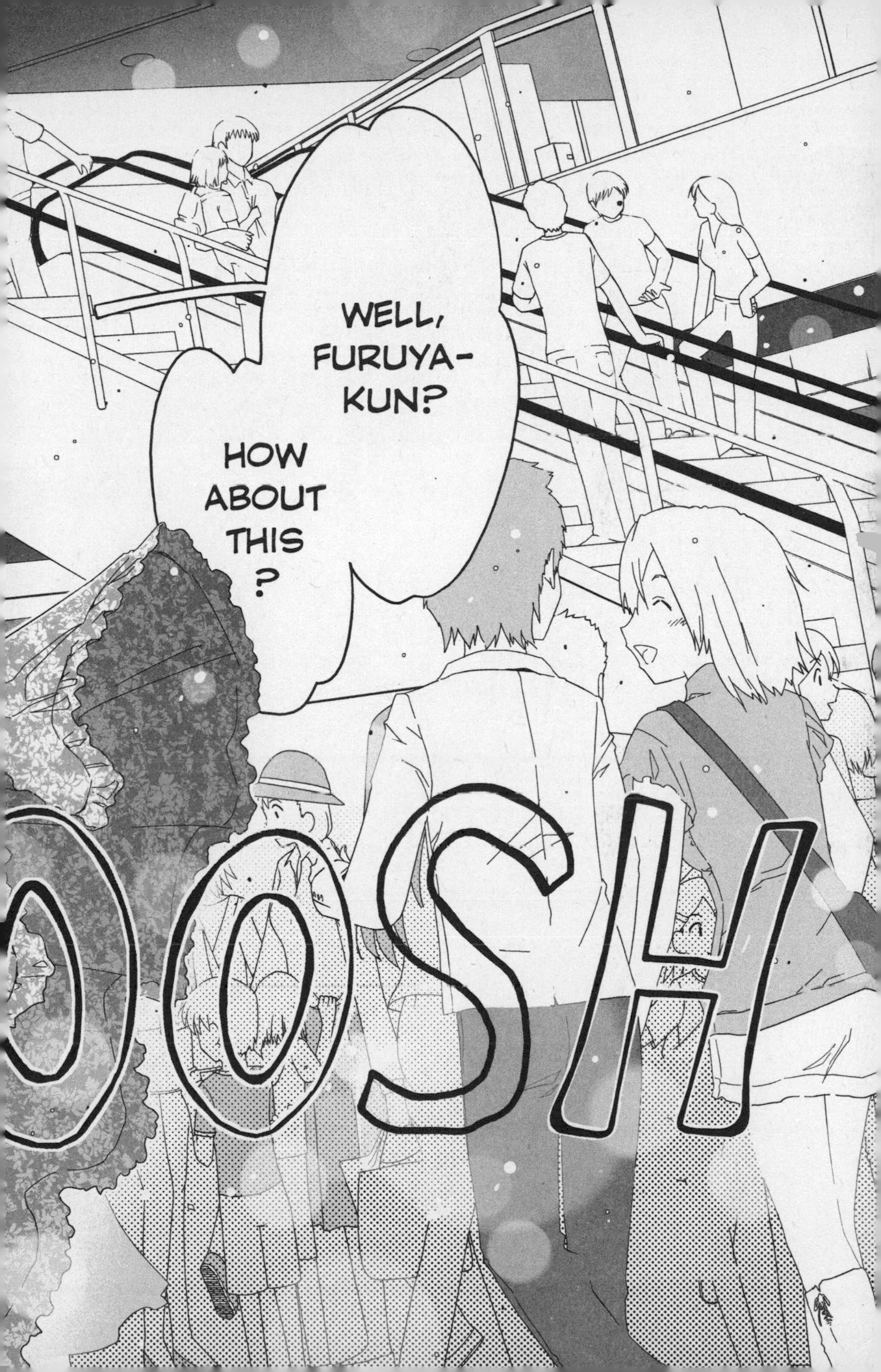
WELL, FURUYA-KUN?
HOW ABOUT THIS?
OOSH

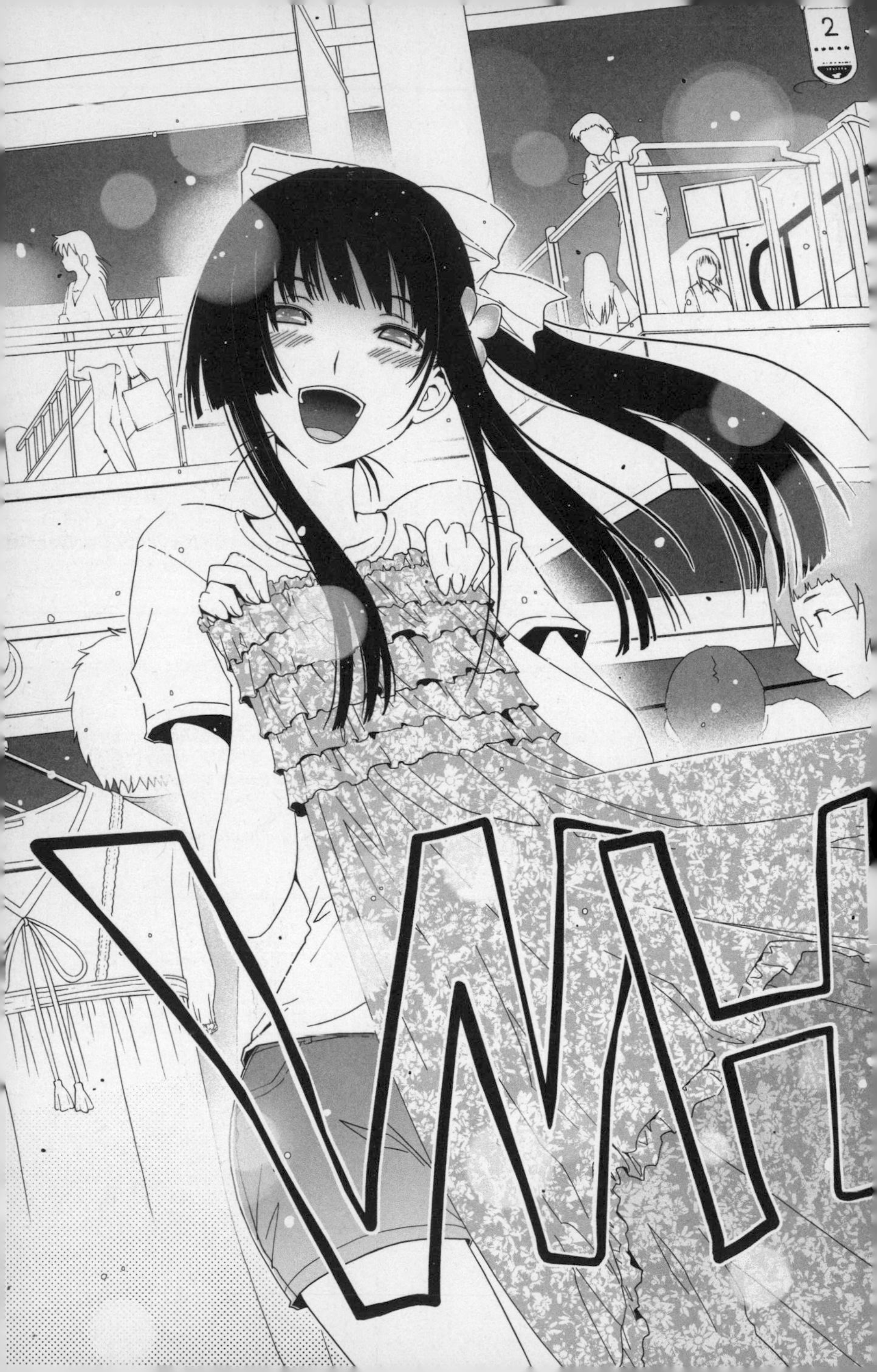
WH

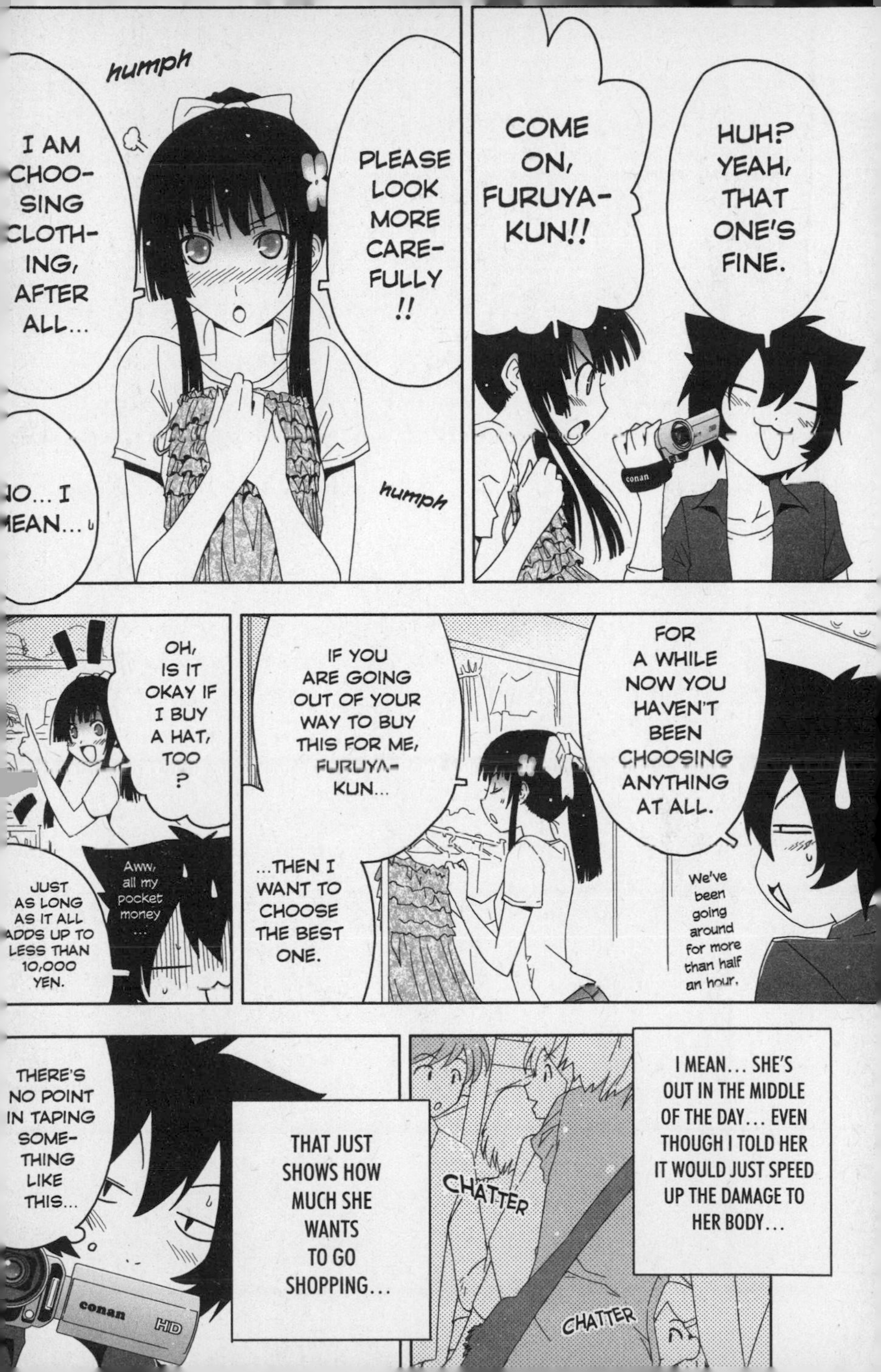
HUH? YEAH, THAT ONE'S FINE.
COME ON, FURUYA-KUN!!
conan
PLEASE LOOK MORE CAREFULLY!!
humph
I AM CHOOSING CLOTHING, AFTER ALL...
humph
O... I EAN...
FOR A WHILE NOW YOU HAVEN'T BEEN CHOOSING ANYTHING AT ALL.
We've been going around for more than half an hour.
IF YOU ARE GOING OUT OF YOUR WAY TO BUY THIS FOR ME, FURUYA-KUN...
...THEN I WANT TO CHOOSE THE BEST ONE.
OH, IS IT OKAY IF I BUY A HAT, TOO?
Aww, all my pocket money ...
JUST AS LONG AS IT ALL ADDS UP TO LESS THAN 10,000 YEN.
I MEAN... SHE'S OUT IN THE MIDDLE OF THE DAY... EVEN THOUGH I TOLD HER IT WOULD JUST SPEED UP THE DAMAGE TO HER BODY...
CHATTER
CHATTER
THAT JUST SHOWS HOW MUCH SHE WANTS TO GO SHOPPING...
THERE'S NO POINT IN TAPING SOMETHING LIKE THIS...
conan
HD

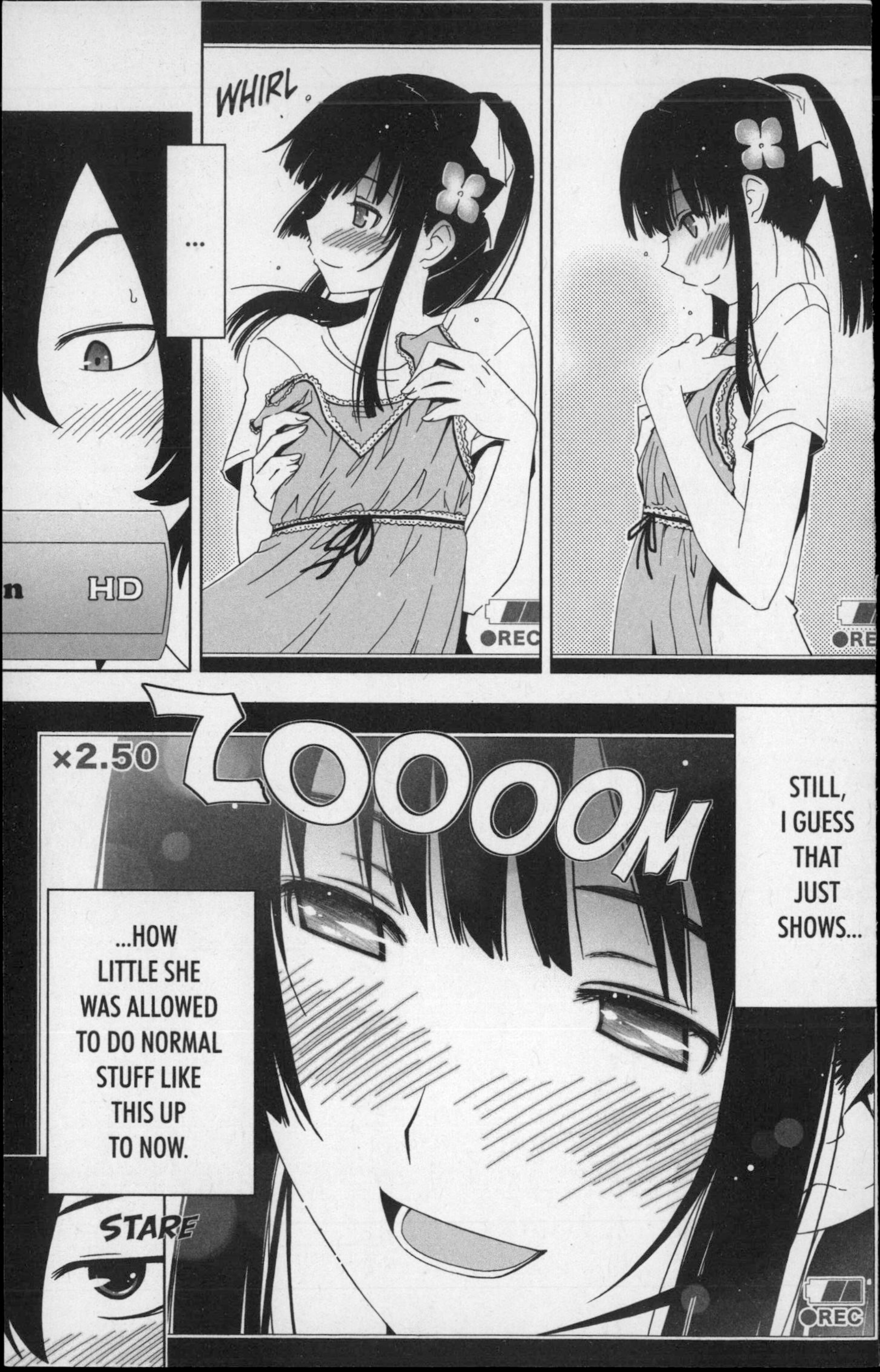
WHIRL
REC
...
HD
STILL, I GUESS THAT JUST SHOWS...
ZOOOOM
×2.50
...HOW LITTLE SHE WAS ALLOWED TO DO NORMAL STUFF LIKE THIS UP TO NOW.
STARE
REC

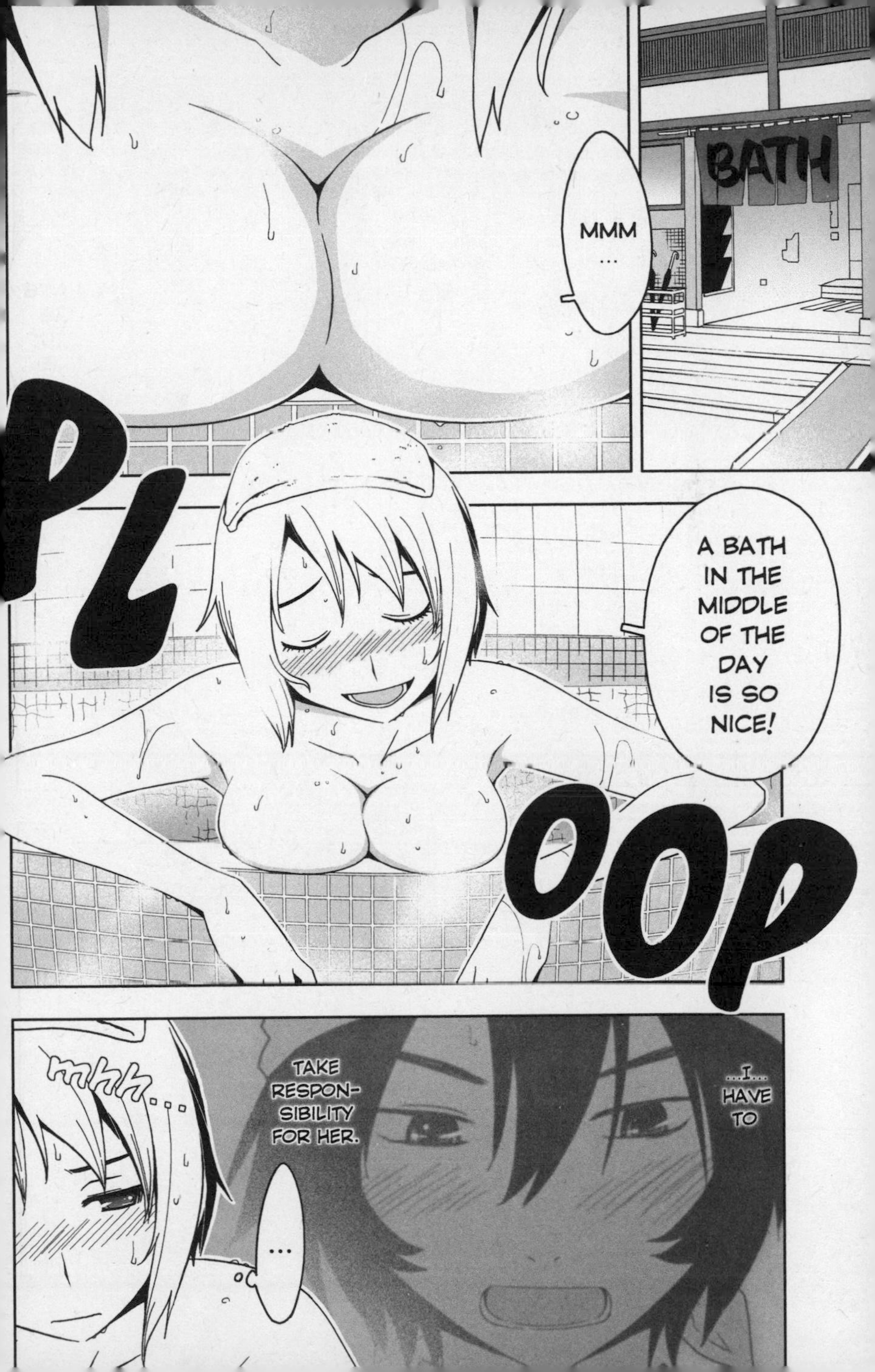
BATH
MMM ...
PLOOP
A BATH IN THE MIDDLE OF THE DAY IS SO NICE!
...I... HAVE TO
TAKE RESPON-SIBILITY FOR HER.
...
mhh...

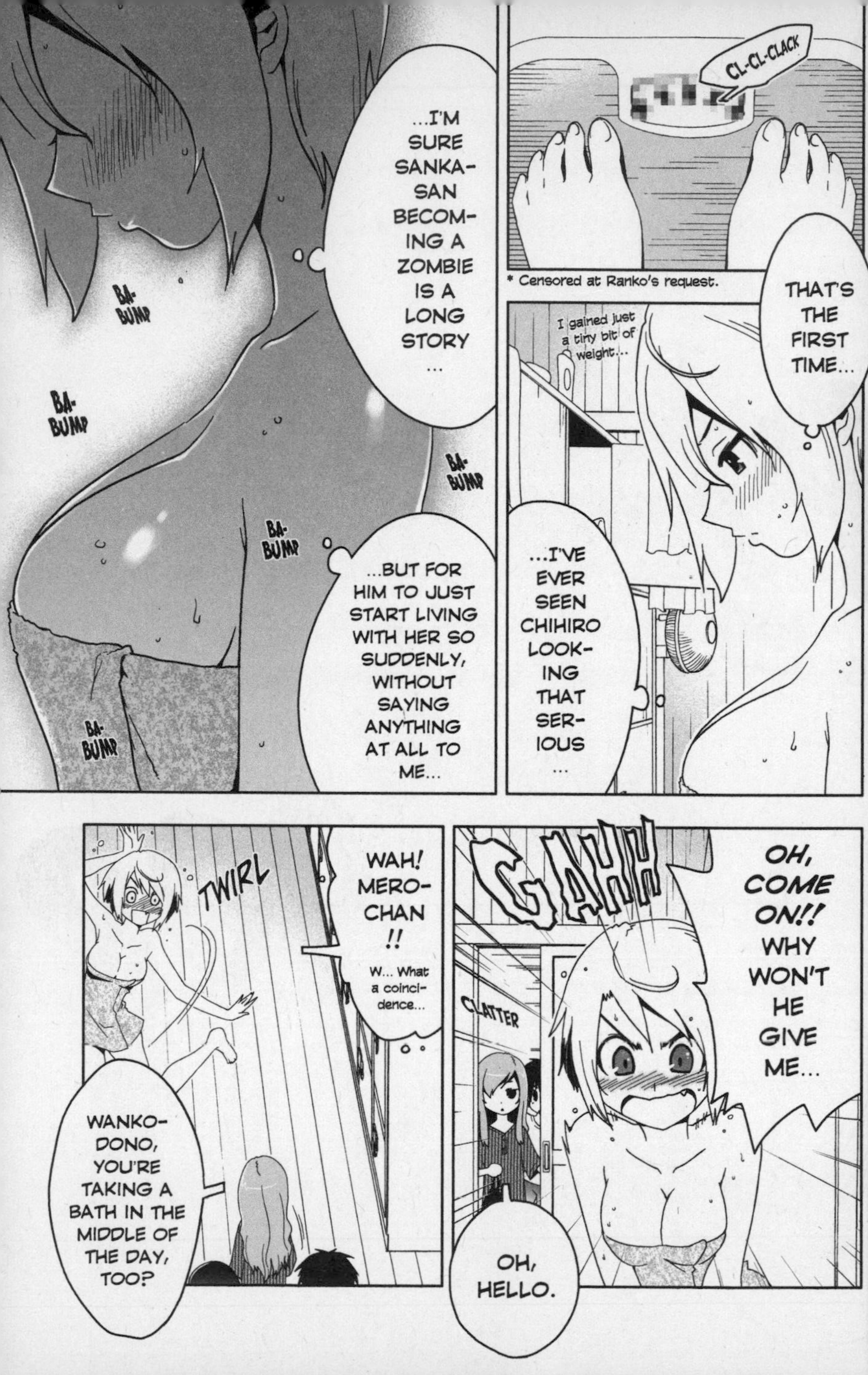
CL-CL-CLACK
* Censored at Ranko's request.
THAT'S THE FIRST TIME...
I gained just a tiny bit of weight...
...I'VE EVER SEEN CHIHIRO LOOKING THAT SERIOUS...
...I'M SURE SANKA-SAN BECOMING A ZOMBIE IS A LONG STORY...
BA-BUMP
BA-BUMP
BA-BUMP
BA-BUMP
BA-BUMP
...BUT FOR HIM TO JUST START LIVING WITH HER SO SUDDENLY, WITHOUT SAYING ANYTHING AT ALL TO ME...
GAHH
OH, COME ON!! WHY WON'T HE GIVE ME...
CLATTER
OH, HELLO.
WAH! MERO-CHAN!!
W... What a coincidence...
TWIRL
WANKO-DONO, YOU'RE TAKING A BATH IN THE MIDDLE OF THE DAY, TOO?

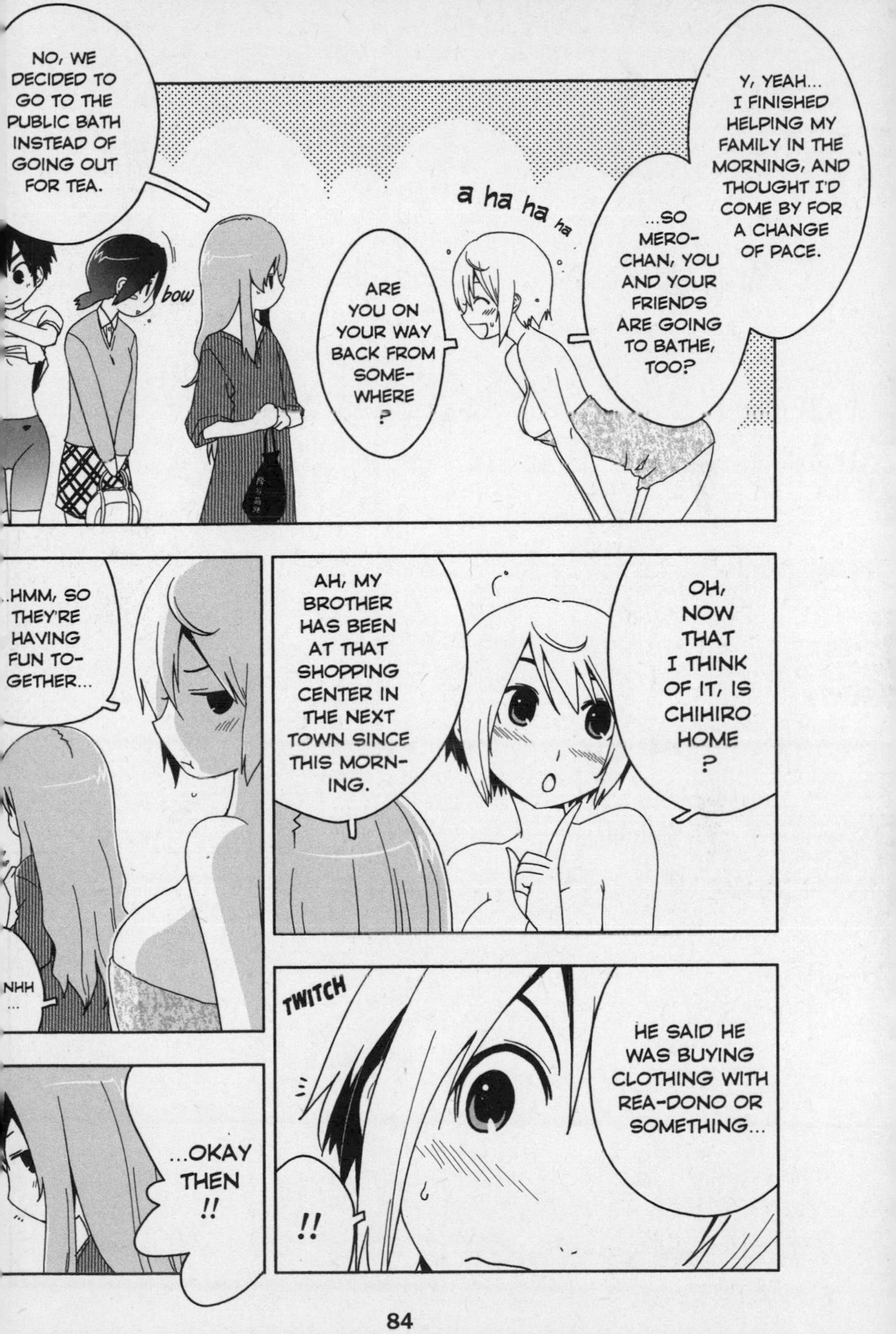
Y, YEAH... I FINISHED HELPING MY FAMILY IN THE MORNING, AND THOUGHT I'D COME BY FOR A CHANGE OF PACE.
...SO MERO-CHAN, YOU AND YOUR FRIENDS ARE GOING TO BATHE, TOO?
a ha ha ha
ARE YOU ON YOUR WAY BACK FROM SOME-WHERE?
bow
NO, WE DECIDED TO GO TO THE PUBLIC BATH INSTEAD OF GOING OUT FOR TEA.
OH, NOW THAT I THINK OF IT, IS CHIHIRO HOME?
AH, MY BROTHER HAS BEEN AT THAT SHOPPING CENTER IN THE NEXT TOWN SINCE THIS MORN-ING.
.HMM, SO THEY'RE HAVING FUN TO-GETHER...
NHH ...
TWITCH
HE SAID HE WAS BUYING CLOTHING WITH REA-DONO OR SOMETHING...
!!
...OKAY THEN !!

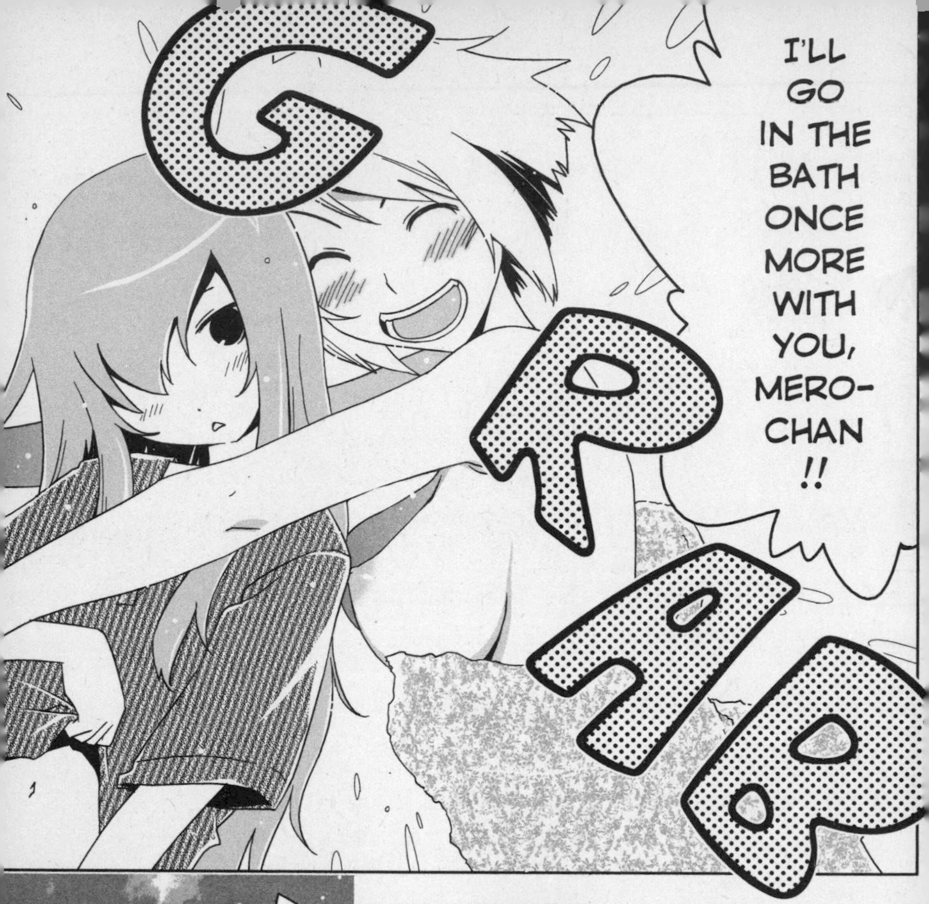
I'LL GO IN THE BATH ONCE MORE WITH YOU, MERO-CHAN!!
GRAB

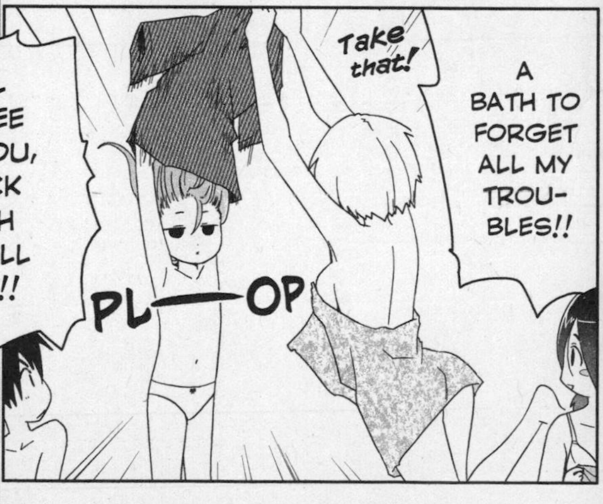
A BATH TO FORGET ALL MY TROUBLES!!
Take that!
PL—OP
ALL THREE OF YOU, STICK WITH ME ALL DAY!!

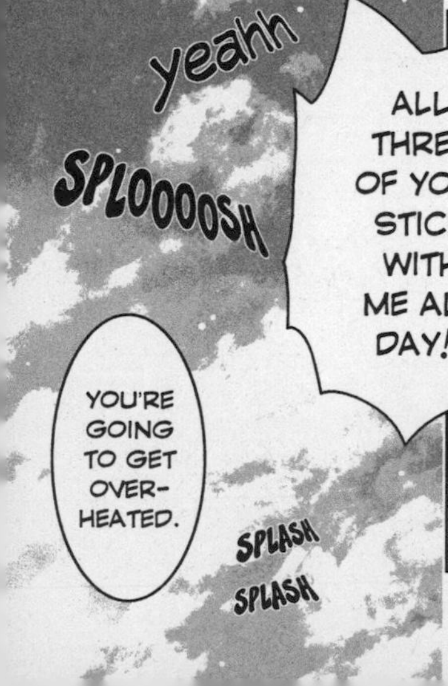
yeahh
SPLOOOOSH
YOU'RE GOING TO GET OVERHEATED.
SPLASH
SPLASH

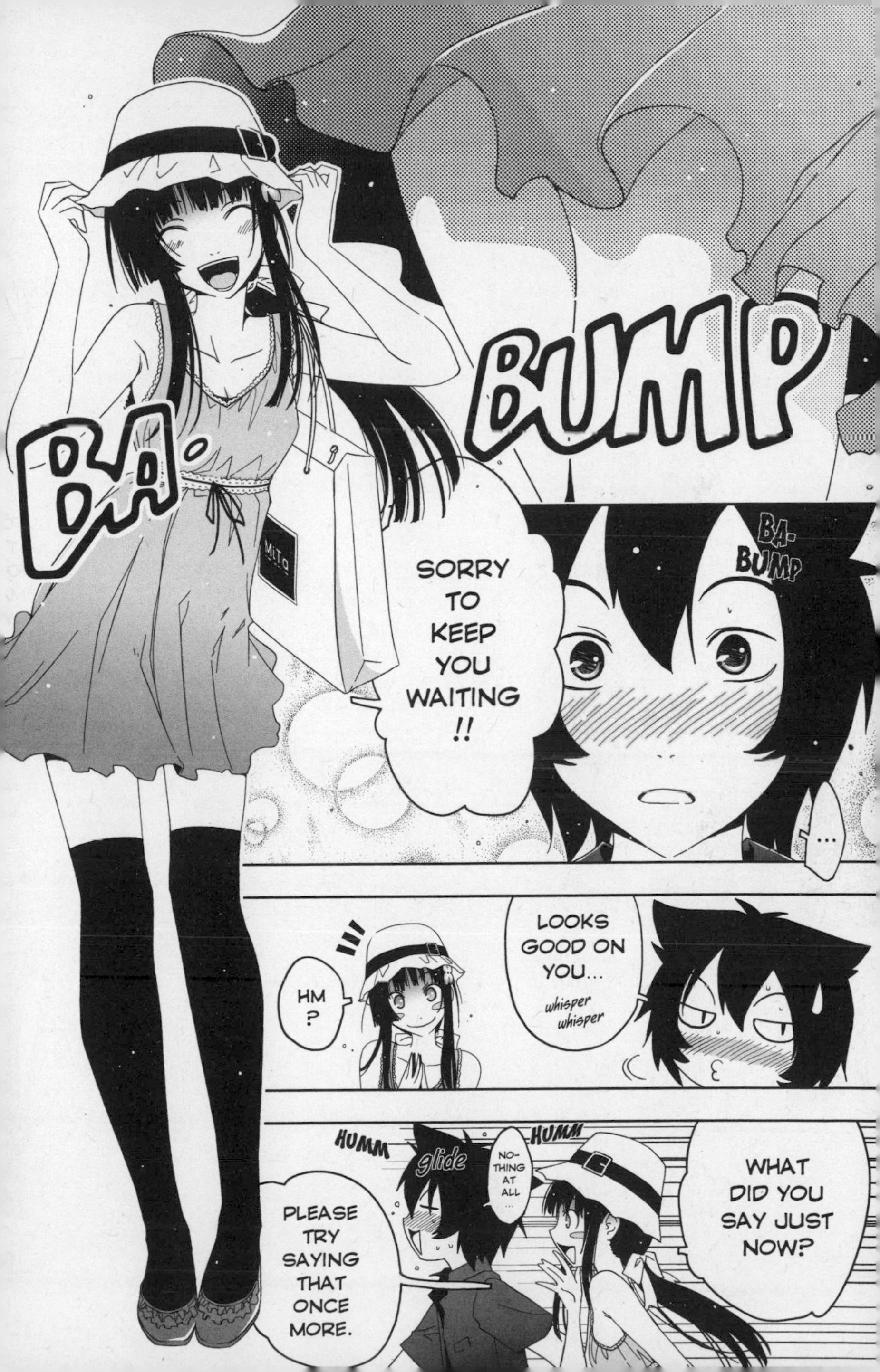
BUMP
BA-
BUMP
SORRY TO KEEP YOU WAITING!!
...
LOOKS GOOD ON YOU...
whisper whisper
!!!
HM ?
WHAT DID YOU SAY JUST NOW?
HUMM
NO-THING AT ALL ...
glide
HUMM
PLEASE TRY SAYING THAT ONCE MORE.
BA-

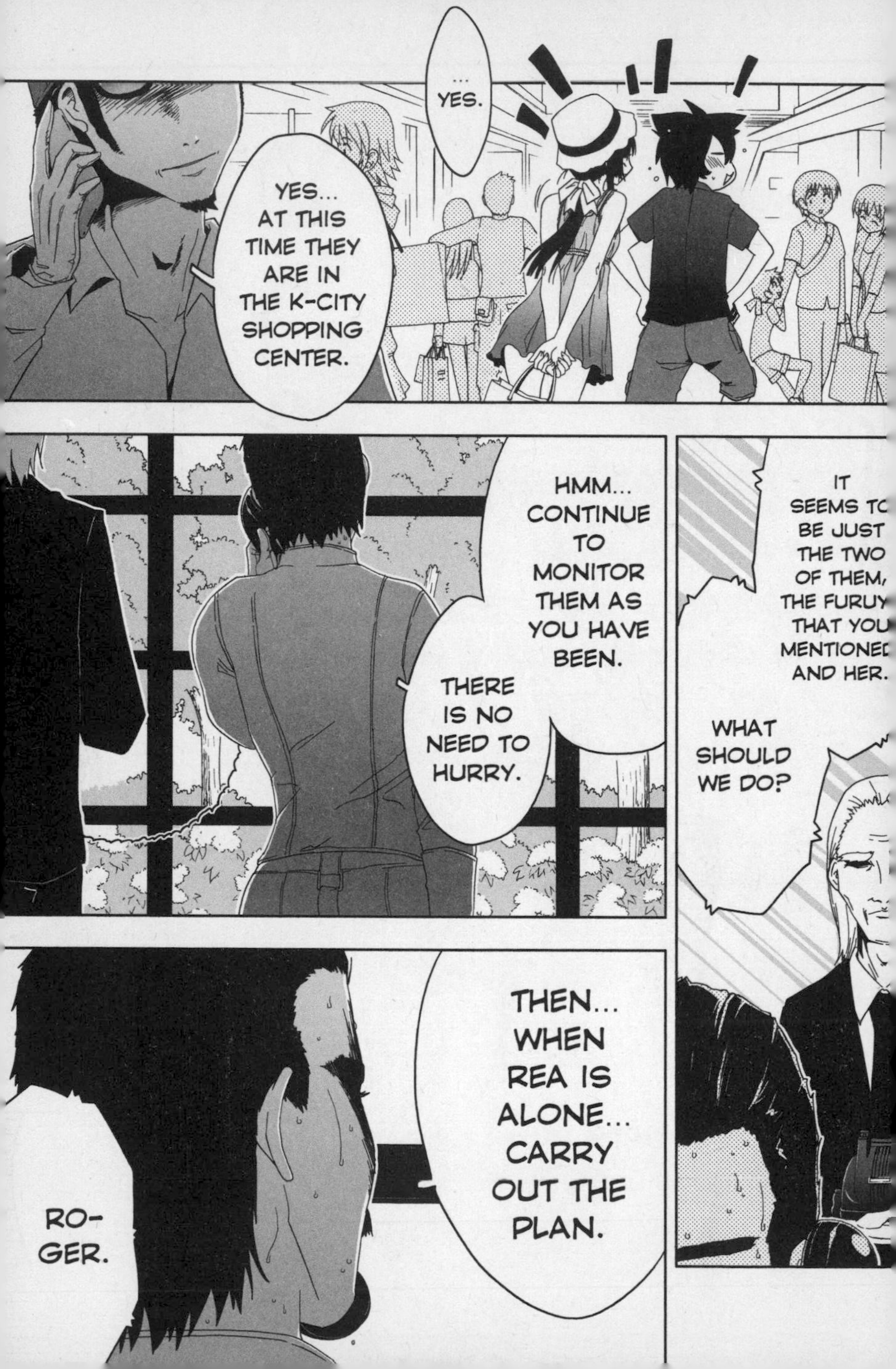
... YES.
YES... AT THIS TIME THEY ARE IN THE K-CITY SHOPPING CENTER.
IT SEEMS TO BE JUST THE TWO OF THEM, THE FURUY THAT YOU MENTIONED AND HER.
WHAT SHOULD WE DO?
HMM... CONTINUE TO MONITOR THEM AS YOU HAVE BEEN.
THERE IS NO NEED TO HURRY.
THEN... WHEN REA IS ALONE... CARRY OUT THE PLAN.
RO-GER.

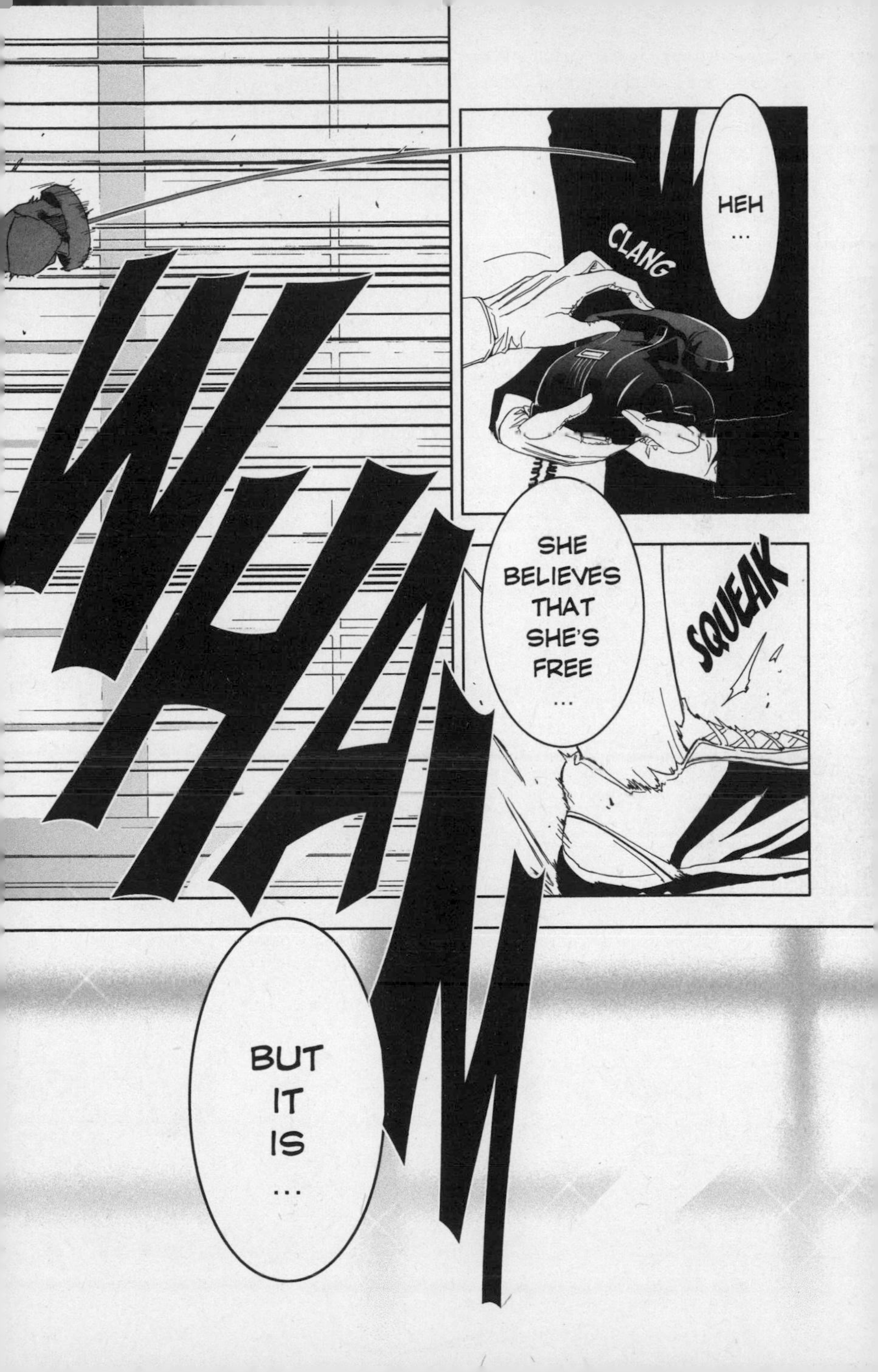
HEH ...
CLANG
SQUEAK
SHE BELIEVES THAT SHE'S FREE ...
WHAM
BUT IT IS ...

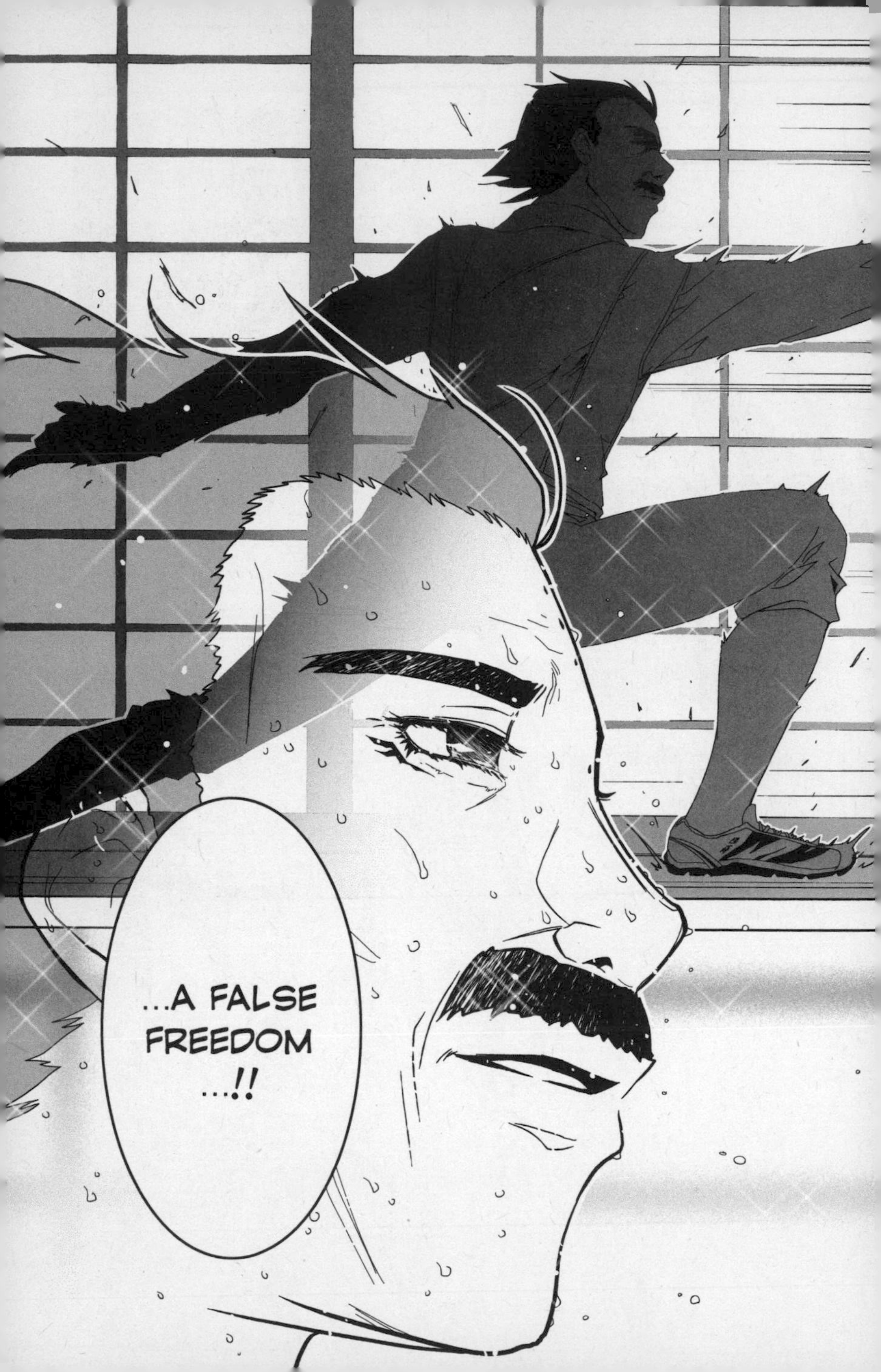
...A FALSE FREEDOM ...!!

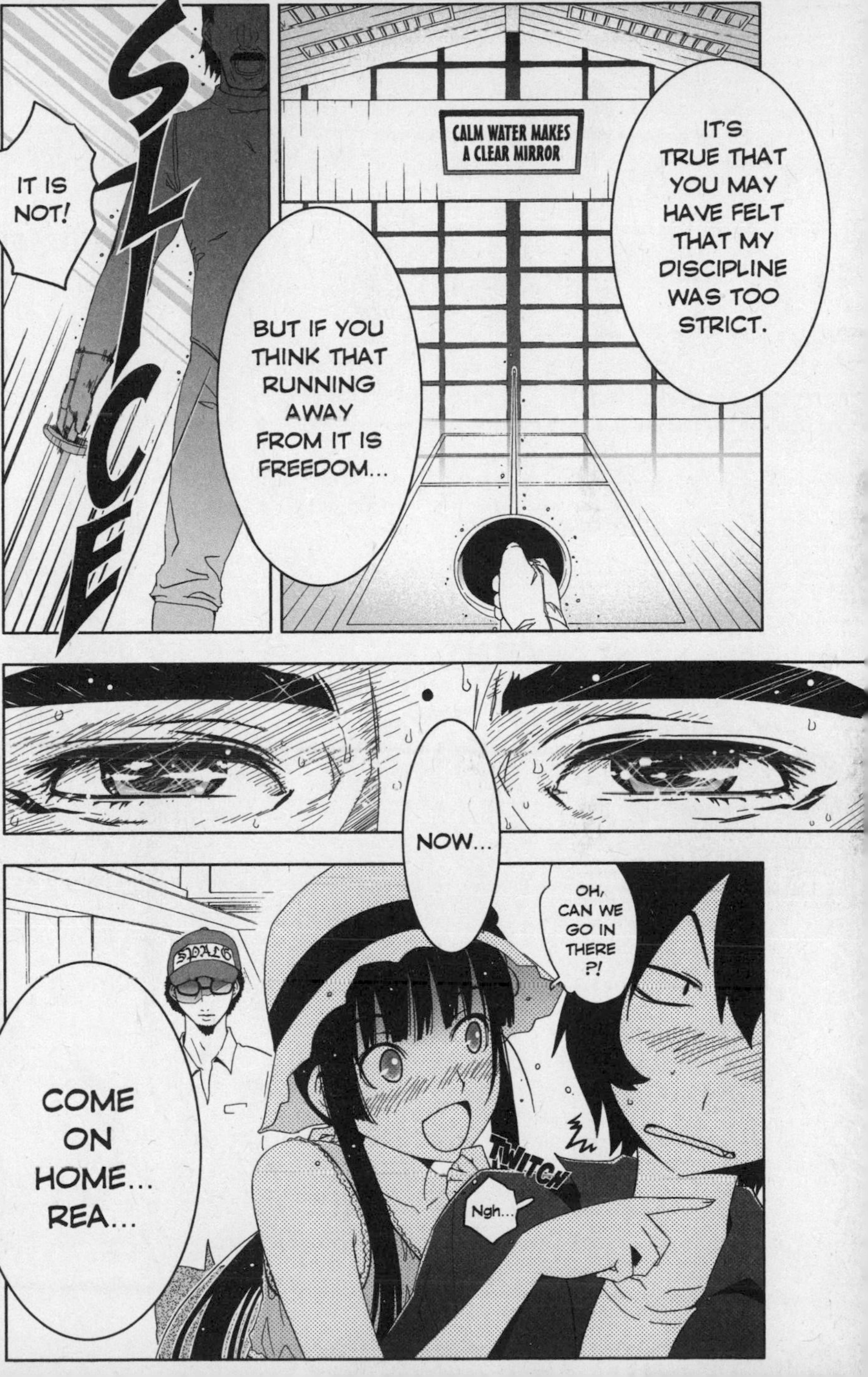
IT'S TRUE THAT YOU MAY HAVE FELT THAT MY DISCIPLINE WAS TOO STRICT.
CALM WATER MAKES A CLEAR MIRROR
BUT IF YOU THINK THAT RUNNING AWAY FROM IT IS FREEDOM...
SLICE
IT IS NOT!
NOW...
OH, CAN WE GO IN THERE?!
TWITCH
Ngh...
COME ON HOME... REA...

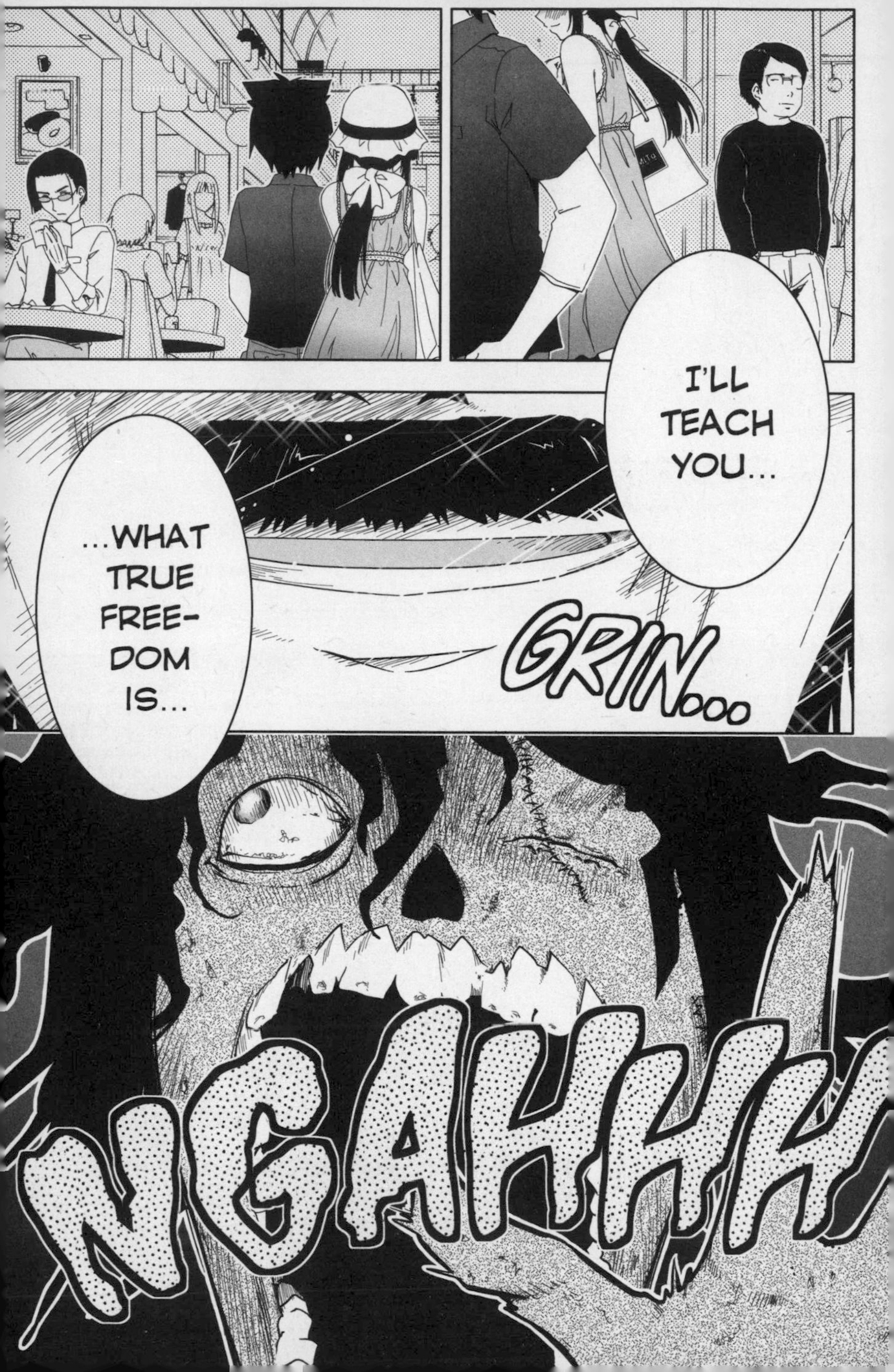
I'LL TEACH YOU...
...WHAT TRUE FREE-DOM IS...
GRIN...
NGAHHH

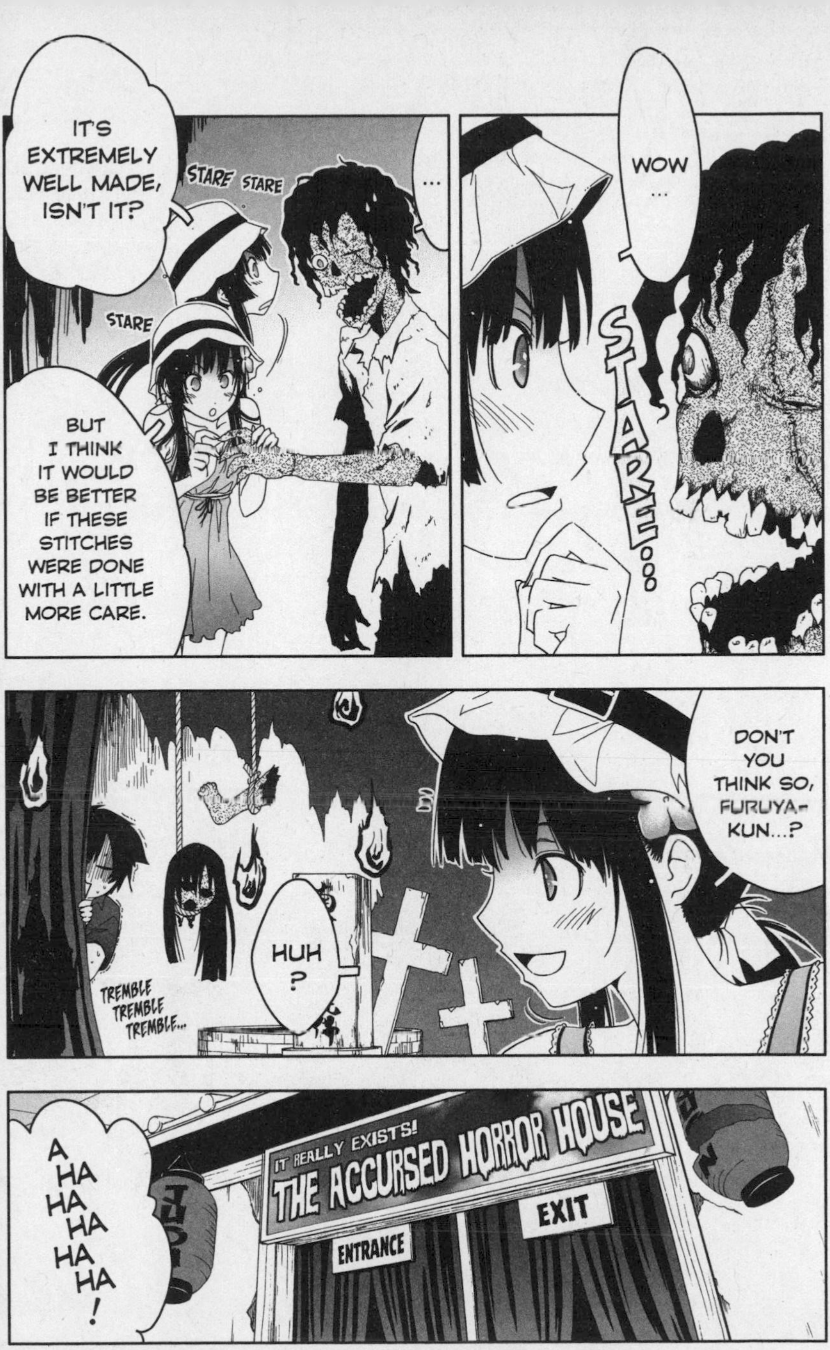
WOW ...
STARE...
...
STARE STARE
IT'S EXTREMELY WELL MADE, ISN'T IT?
STARE
BUT I THINK IT WOULD BE BETTER IF THESE STITCHES WERE DONE WITH A LITTLE MORE CARE.
DON'T YOU THINK SO, FURUYA-KUN...?
HUH?
TREMBLE TREMBLE TREMBLE...
IT REALLY EXISTS!
THE ACCURSED HORROR HOUSE
EXIT
ENTRANCE
A HA HA HA HA HA HA!

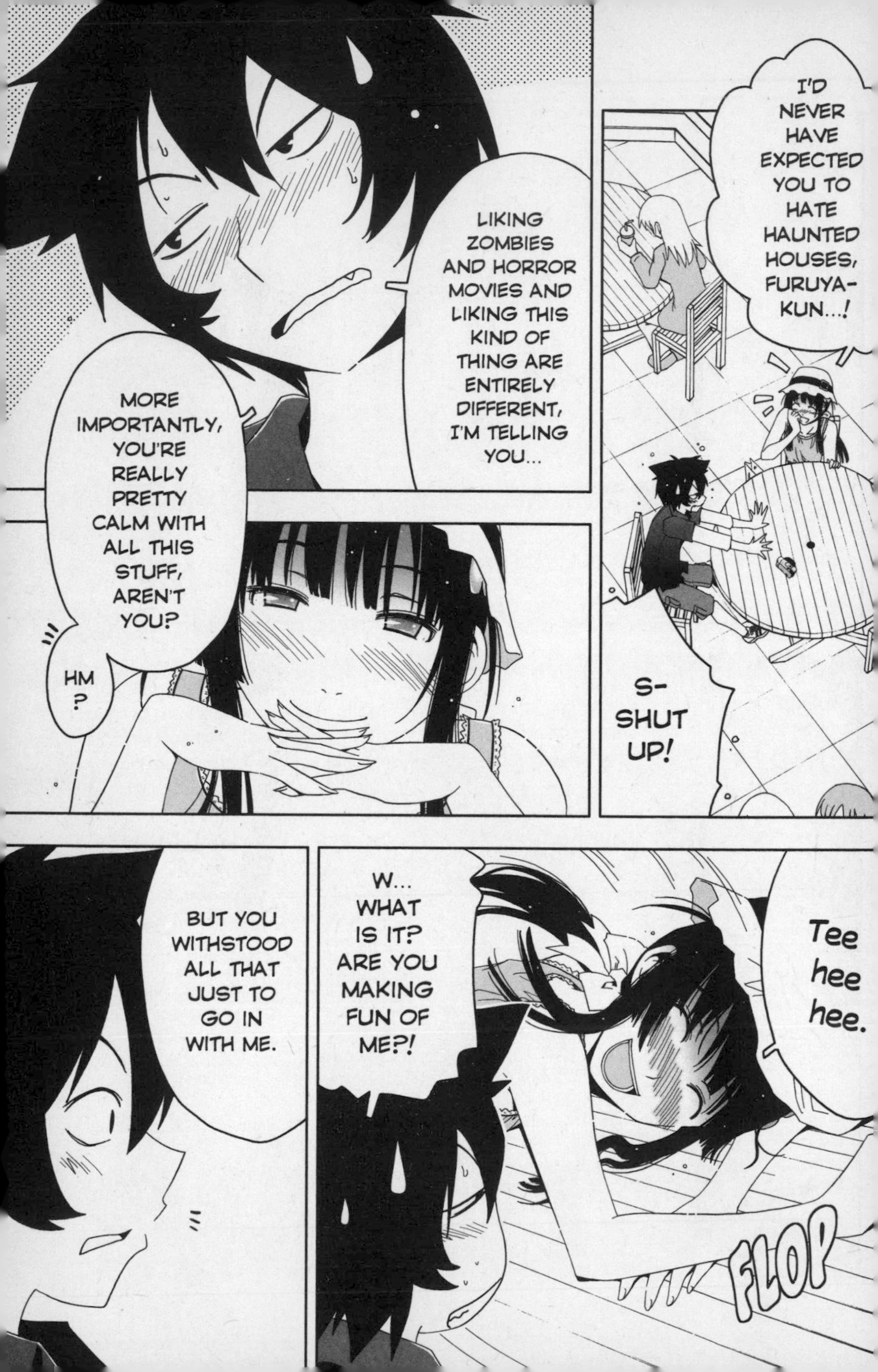
I'D NEVER HAVE EXPECTED YOU TO HATE HAUNTED HOUSES, FURUYA-KUN...!
S-SHUT UP!
LIKING ZOMBIES AND HORROR MOVIES AND LIKING THIS KIND OF THING ARE ENTIRELY DIFFERENT, I'M TELLING YOU...
MORE IMPORTANTLY, YOU'RE REALLY PRETTY CALM WITH ALL THIS STUFF, AREN'T YOU?
HM?
Tee hee hee.
FLOP
W... WHAT IS IT? ARE YOU MAKING FUN OF ME?!
BUT YOU WITHSTOOD ALL THAT JUST TO GO IN WITH ME.

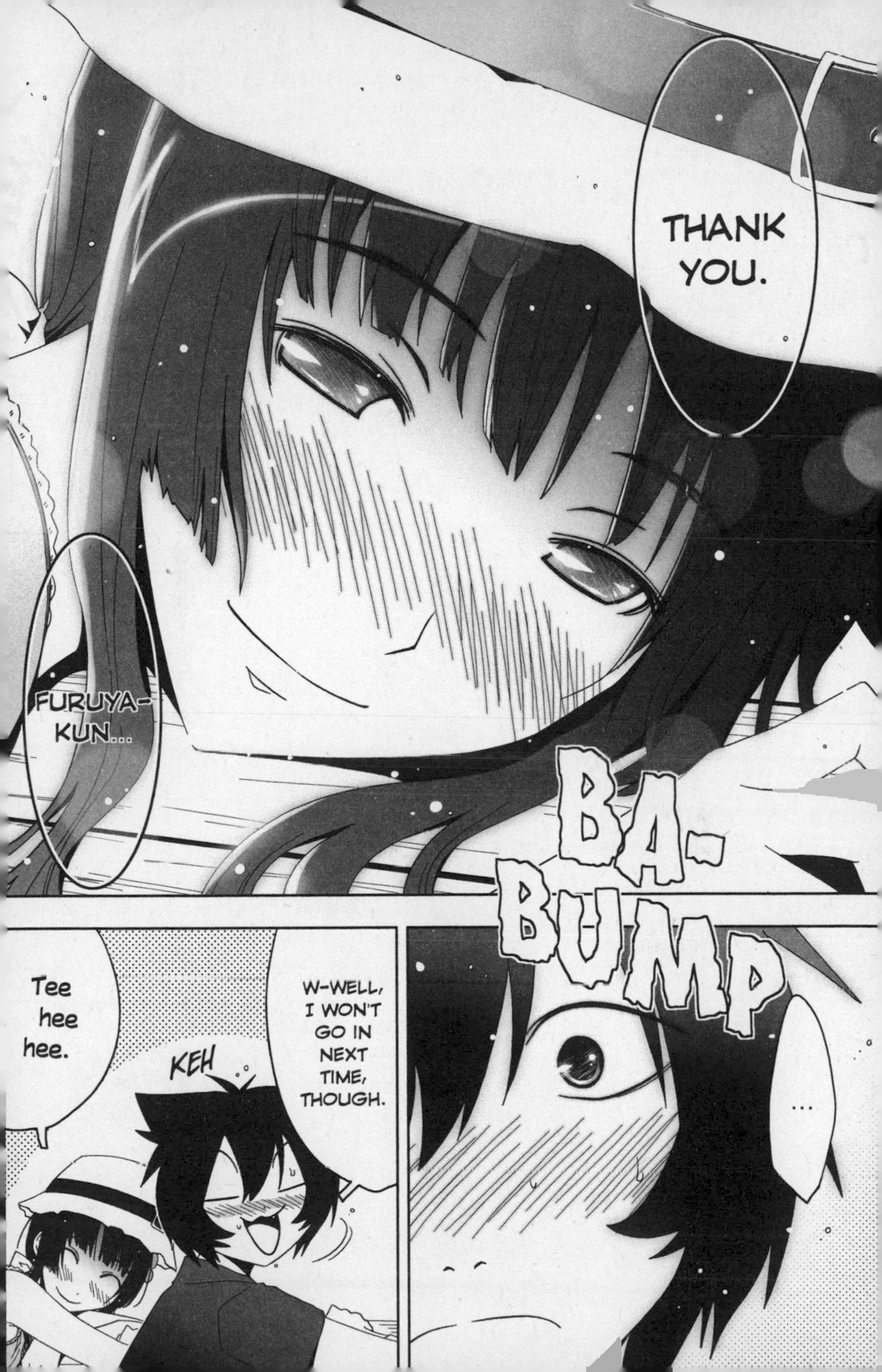
THANK YOU.
FURUYA-KUN...
BA-BUMP
...
W-WELL, I WON'T GO IN NEXT TIME, THOUGH.
KEH
Tee hee hee.

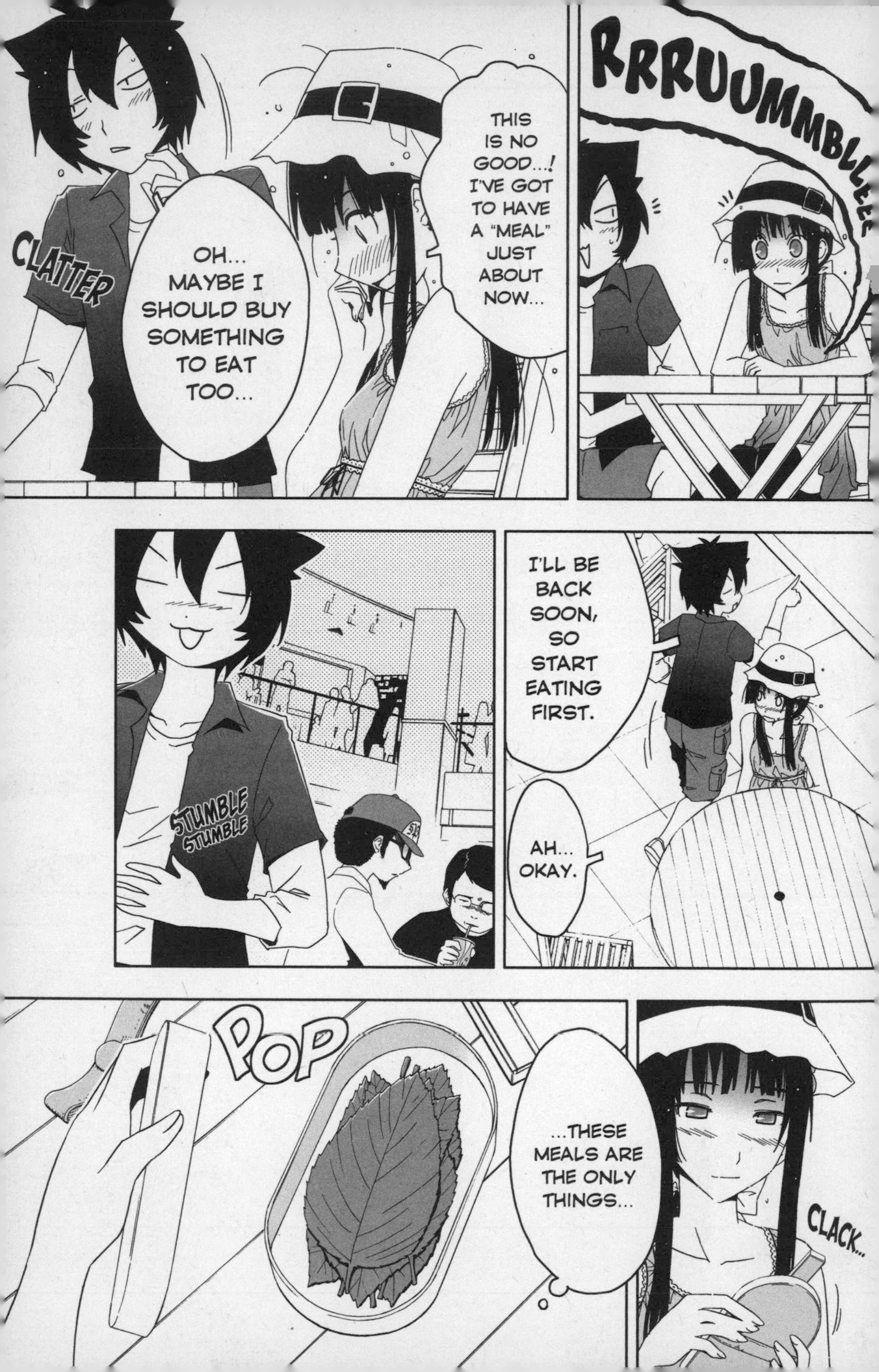
RRRUUMMBLLEEE
THIS IS NO GOOD...! I'VE GOT TO HAVE A "MEAL" JUST ABOUT NOW...
OH... MAYBE I SHOULD BUY SOMETHING TO EAT TOO...
CLATTER
I'LL BE BACK SOON, SO START EATING FIRST.
AH... OKAY.
STUMBLE STUMBLE
...THESE MEALS ARE THE ONLY THINGS...
CLACK...
POP

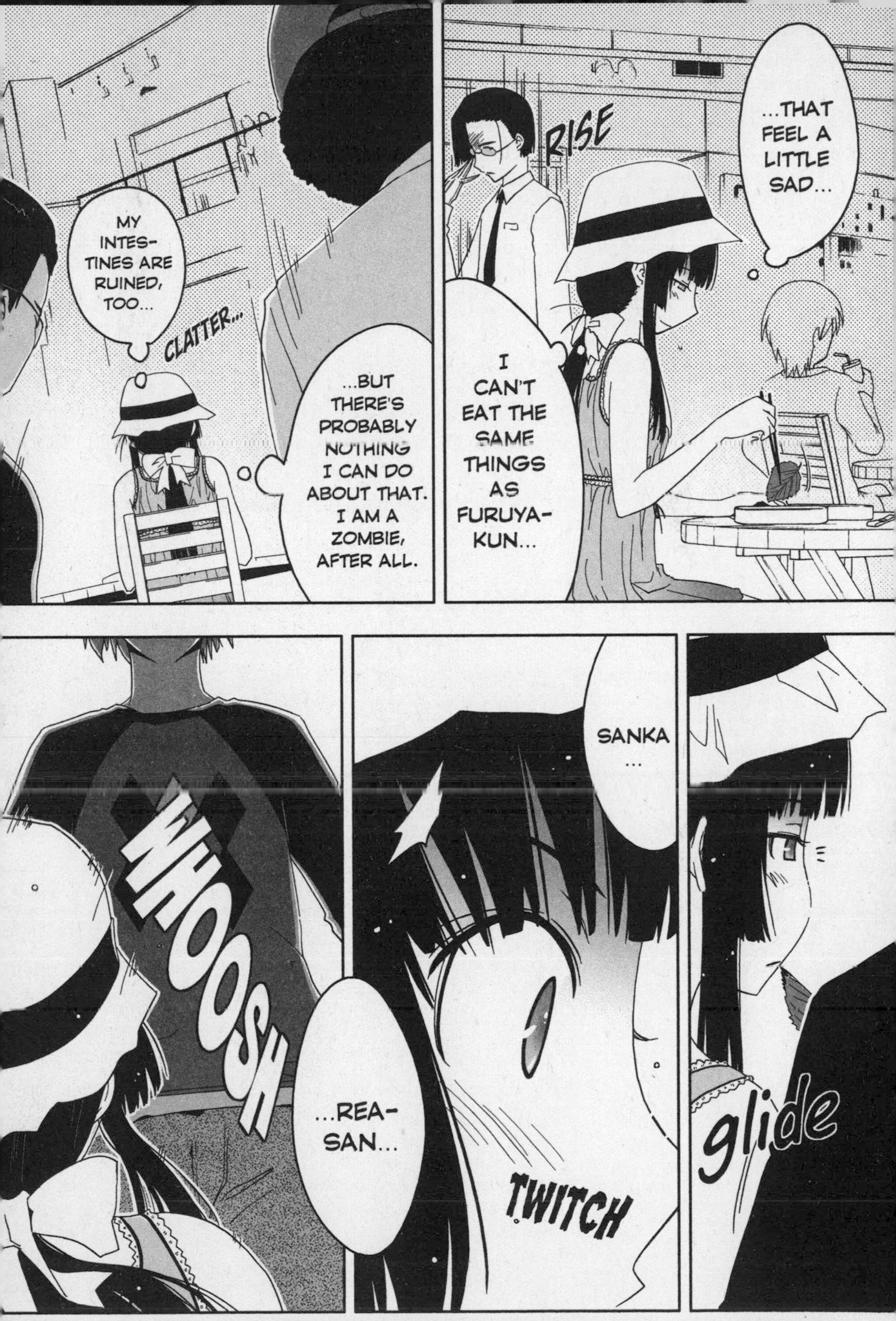
I CAN'T EAT THE SAME THINGS AS FURUYA-KUN...
RISE
...THAT FEEL A LITTLE SAD...
MY INTES-TINES ARE RUINED, TOO...
CLATTER...
...BUT THERE'S PROBABLY NOTHING I CAN DO ABOUT THAT. I AM A ZOMBIE, AFTER ALL.
glide
SANKA ...
...REA-SAN...
TWITCH
WHOOSH

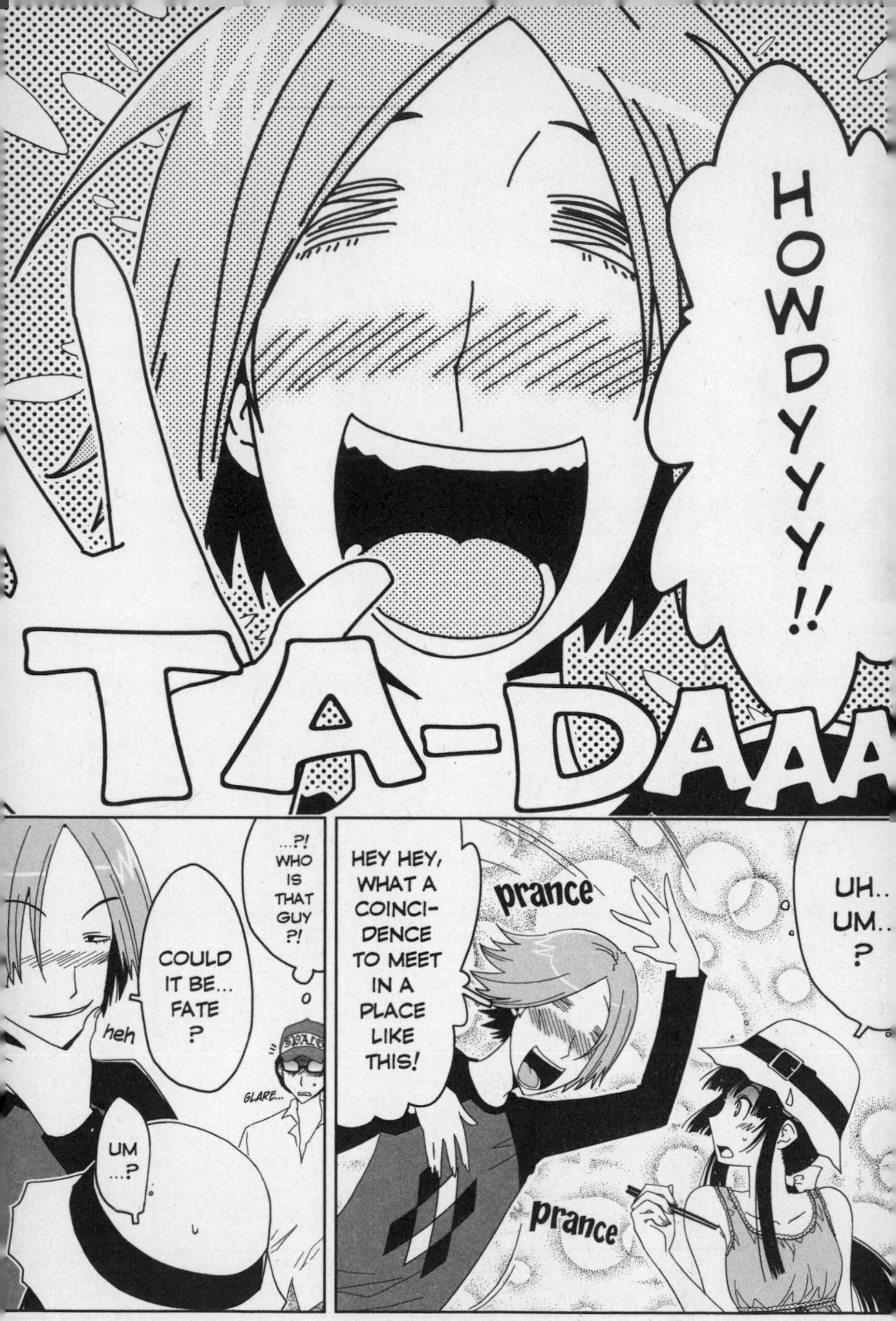
HOWDYYY!!
TA-DAAA
UH... UM...?
HEY HEY, WHAT A COINCIDENCE TO MEET IN A PLACE LIKE THIS!
prance
prance
...?! WHO IS THAT GUY?!
COULD IT BE... FATE?
heh
GLARE...
UM...?

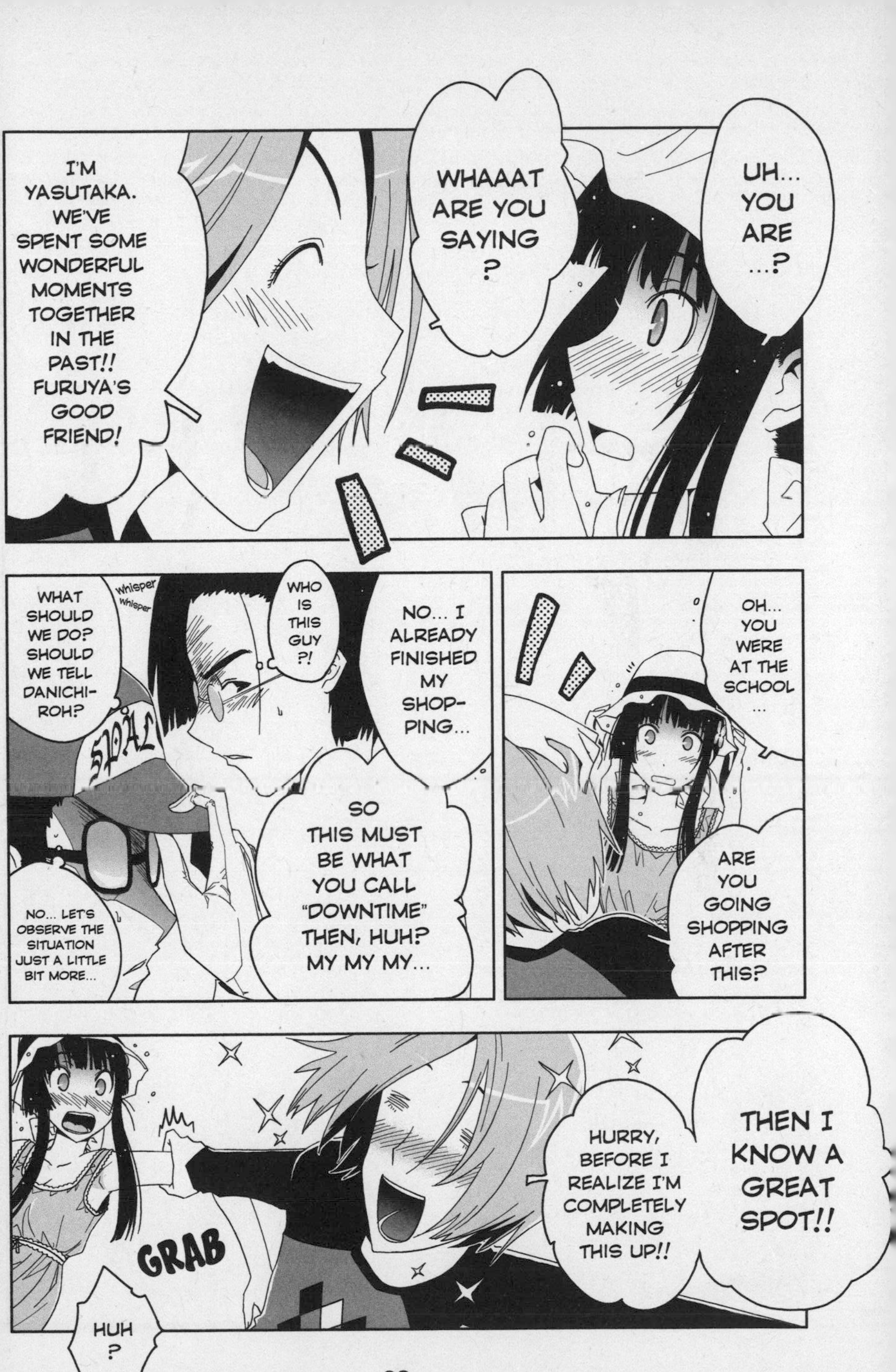
UH... YOU ARE ...?
WHAAAT ARE YOU SAYING?
I'M YASUTAKA. WE'VE SPENT SOME WONDERFUL MOMENTS TOGETHER IN THE PAST!! FURUYA'S GOOD FRIEND!
OH... YOU WERE AT THE SCHOOL...
ARE YOU GOING SHOPPING AFTER THIS?
NO... I ALREADY FINISHED MY SHOP-PING...
WHO IS THIS GUY?!
Whisper Whisper
WHAT SHOULD WE DO? SHOULD WE TELL DANICHI-ROH?
SO THIS MUST BE WHAT YOU CALL "DOWNTIME" THEN, HUH? MY MY MY...
NO... LET'S OBSERVE THE SITUATION JUST A LITTLE BIT MORE...
THEN I KNOW A GREAT SPOT!!
HURRY, BEFORE I REALIZE I'M COMPLETELY MAKING THIS UP!!
GRAB
HUH?

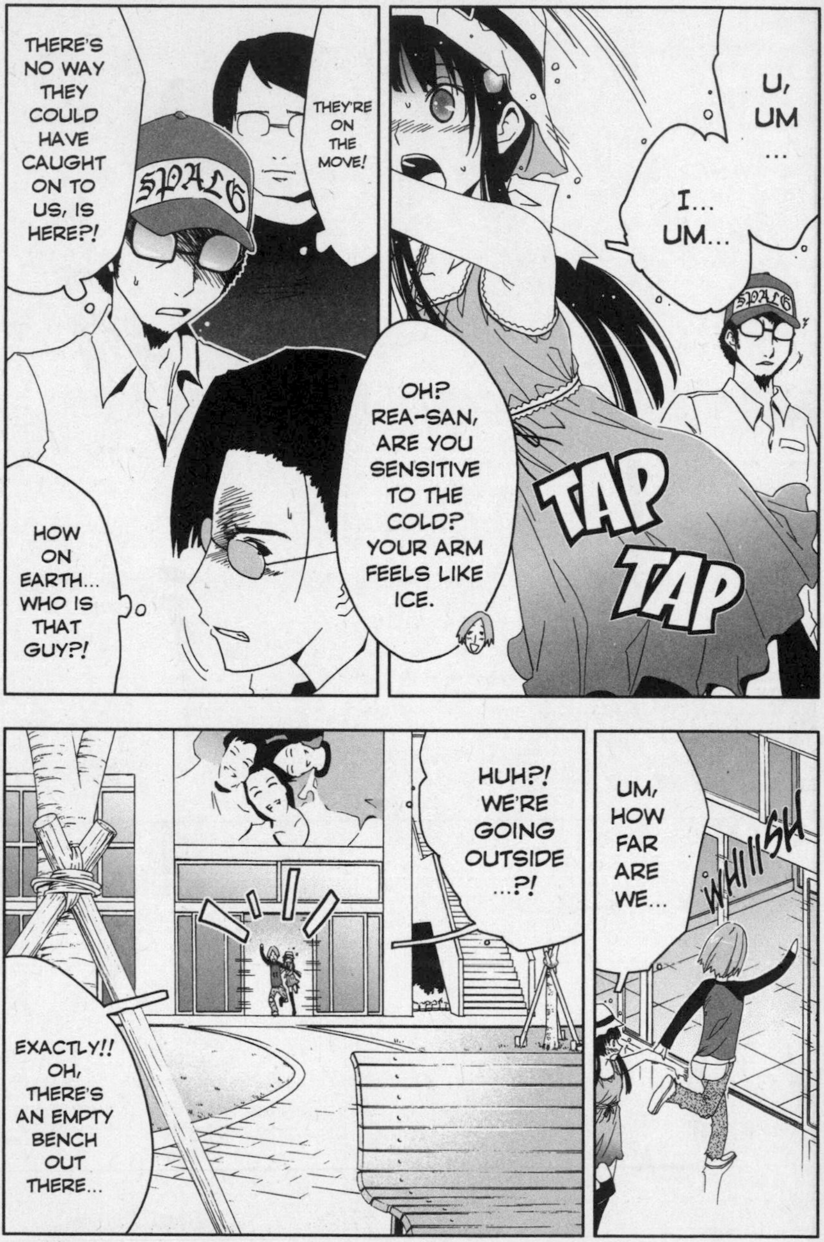
U, UM ...
I... UM...
OH? REA-SAN, ARE YOU SENSITIVE TO THE COLD? YOUR ARM FEELS LIKE ICE.
TAP TAP
THEY'RE ON THE MOVE!
THERE'S NO WAY THEY COULD HAVE CAUGHT ON TO US, IS HERE?!
HOW ON EARTH... WHO IS THAT GUY?!
UM, HOW FAR ARE WE...
WHIISH
HUH?! WE'RE GOING OUTSIDE ...?!
EXACTLY!! OH, THERE'S AN EMPTY BENCH OUT THERE...

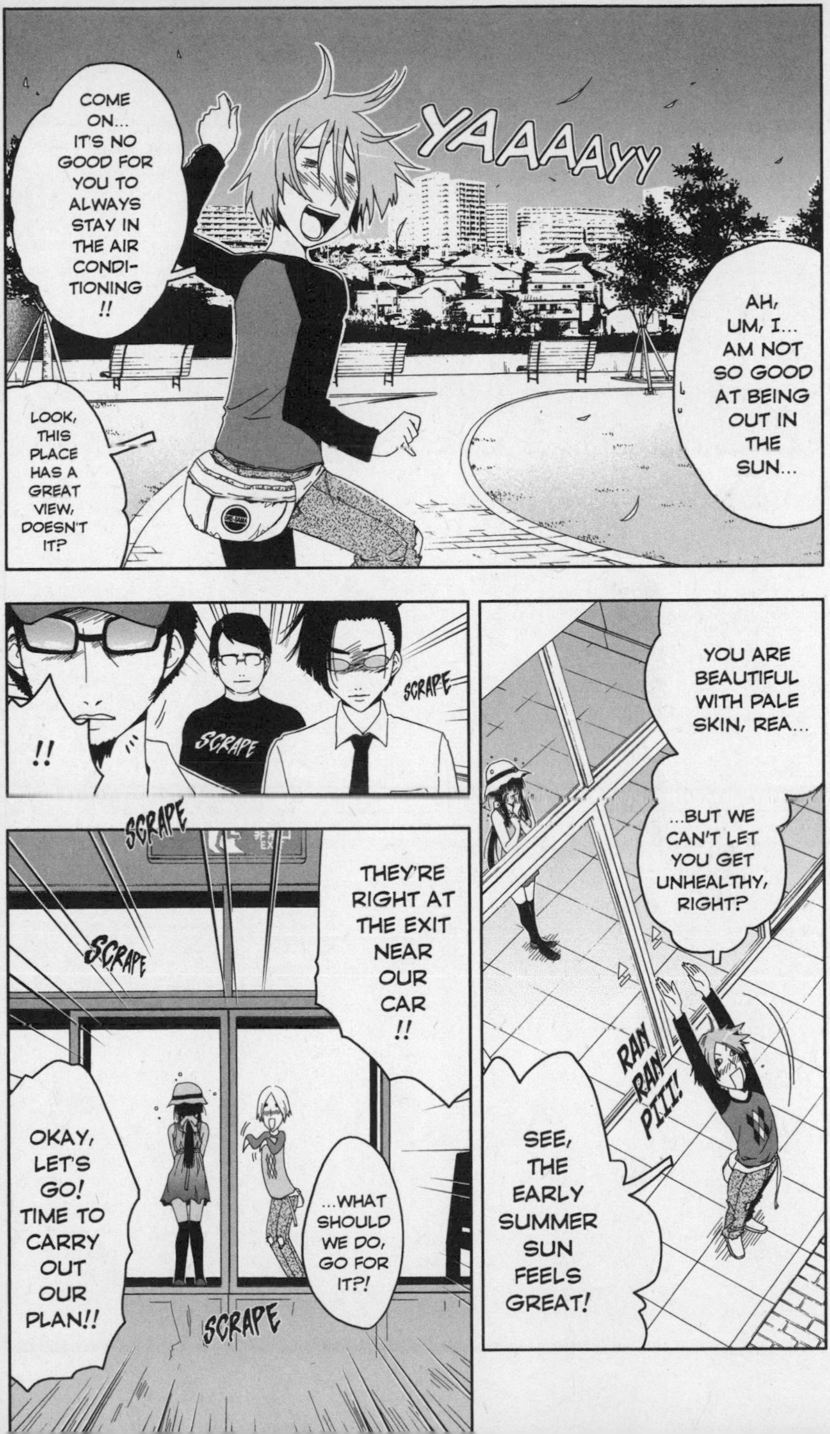
AH, UM, I... AM NOT SO GOOD AT BEING OUT IN THE SUN...
YAAAAAYY
COME ON... IT'S NO GOOD FOR YOU TO ALWAYS STAY IN THE AIR CONDI-TIONING!!
LOOK, THIS PLACE HAS A GREAT VIEW, DOESN'T IT?
YOU ARE BEAUTIFUL WITH PALE SKIN, REA...
...BUT WE CAN'T LET YOU GET UNHEALTHY, RIGHT?
RAN RAN PIII!
SEE, THE EARLY SUMMER SUN FEELS GREAT!
SCRAPE
SCRAPE
!!
SCRAPE
THEY'RE RIGHT AT THE EXIT NEAR OUR CAR!!
SCRAPE
...WHAT SHOULD WE DO, GO FOR IT?!
OKAY, LET'S GO! TIME TO CARRY OUT OUR PLAN!!
SCRAPE

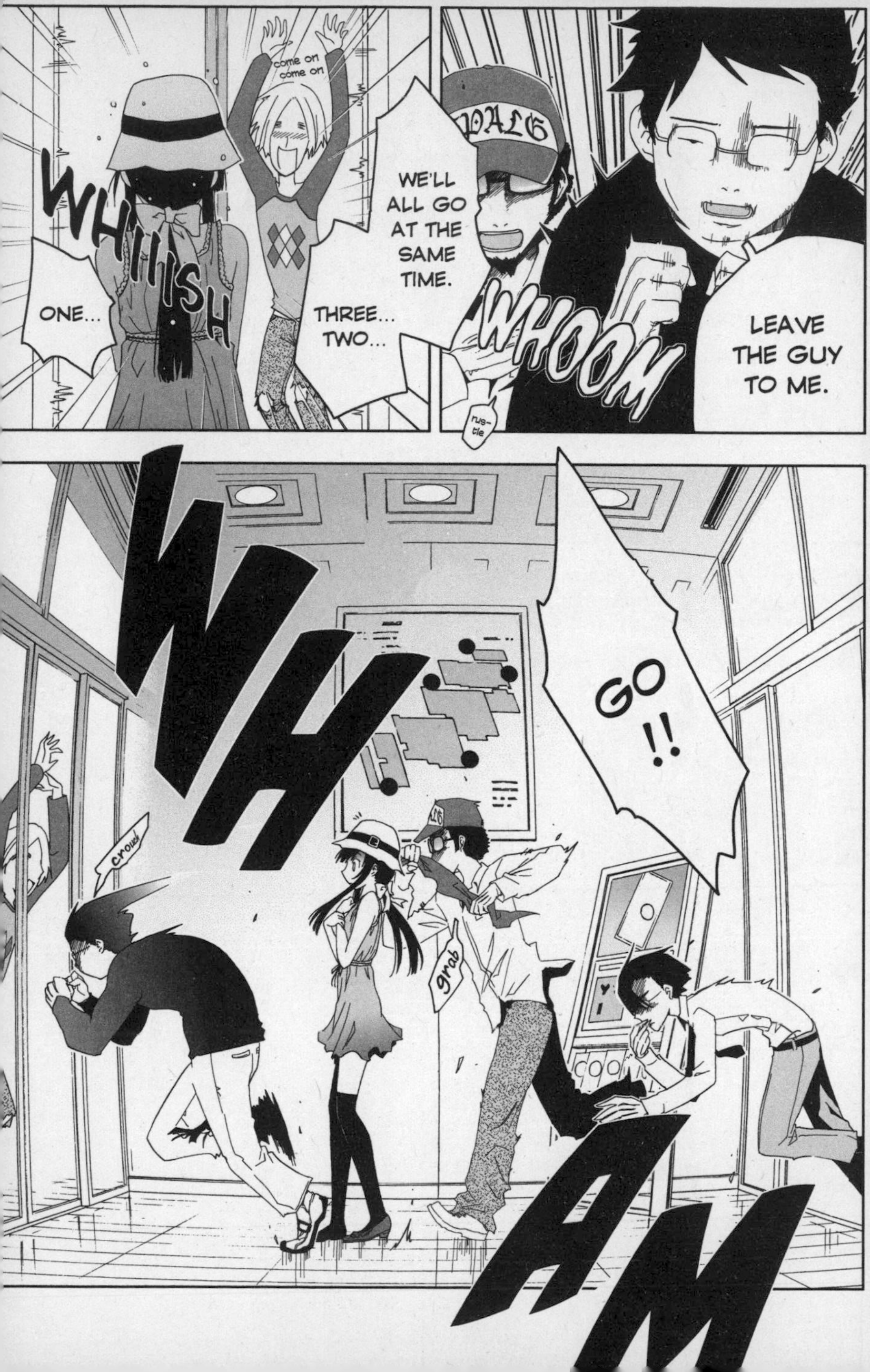
LEAVE THE GUY TO ME.
WHOOM
WE'LL ALL GO AT THE SAME TIME.
rustle
come on come on
THREE... TWO...
WHIIISH
ONE...
GO !!
WHAM
grab
crouch

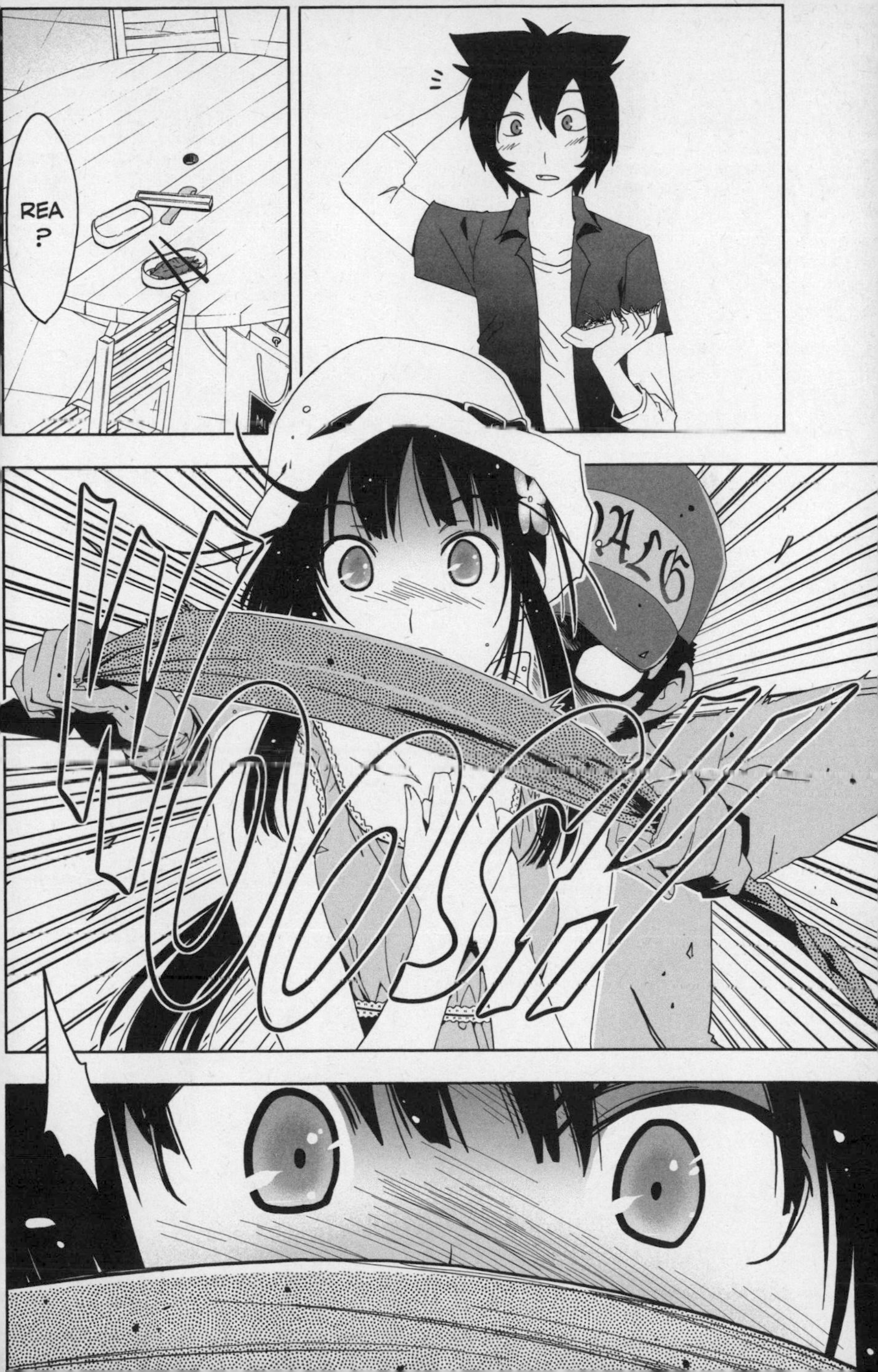
REA
?
WOOSH

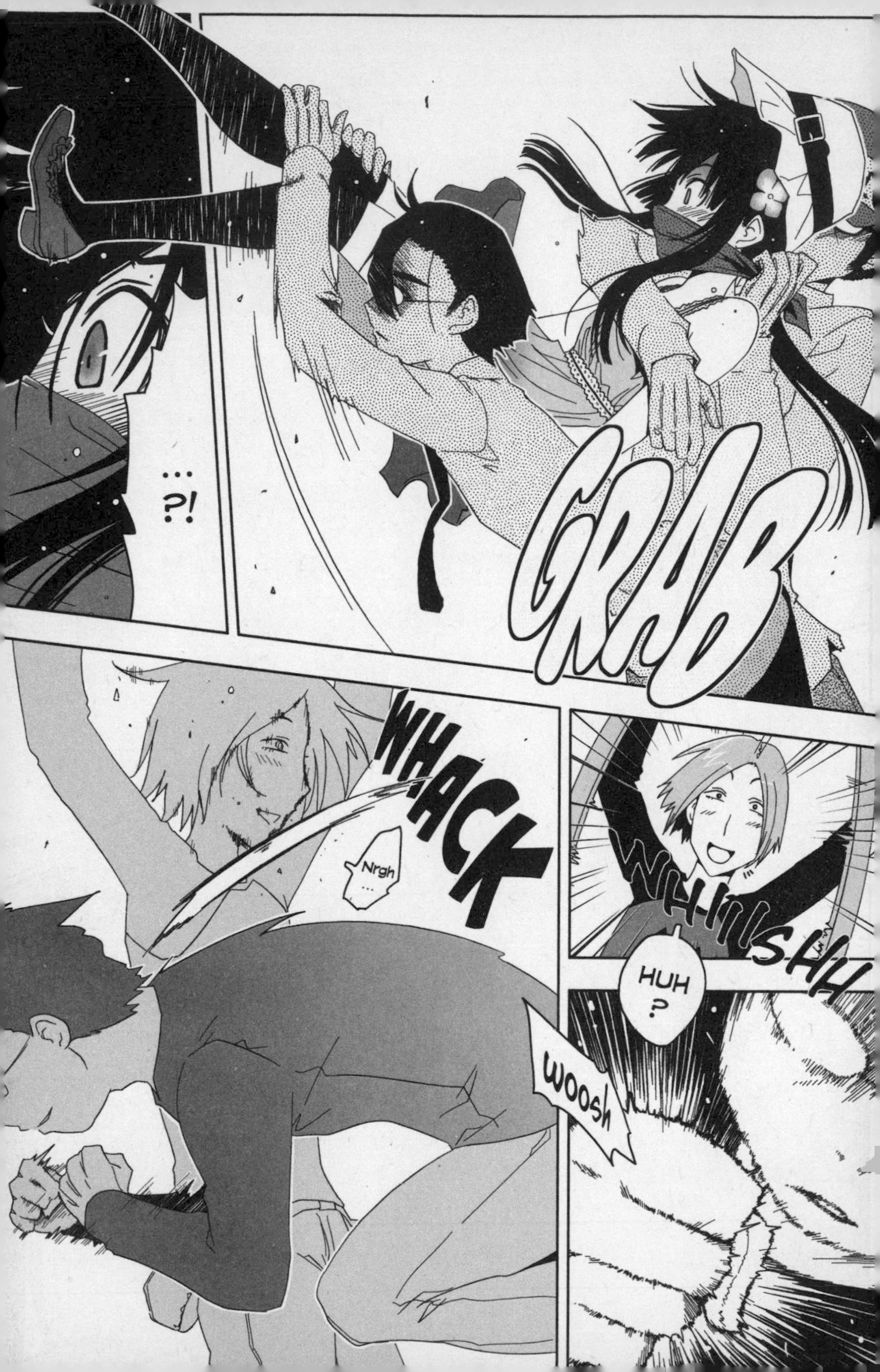
GRAB
...
?!
WHIIISHH
HUH?
WOOSH
WHACK
Nrgh...

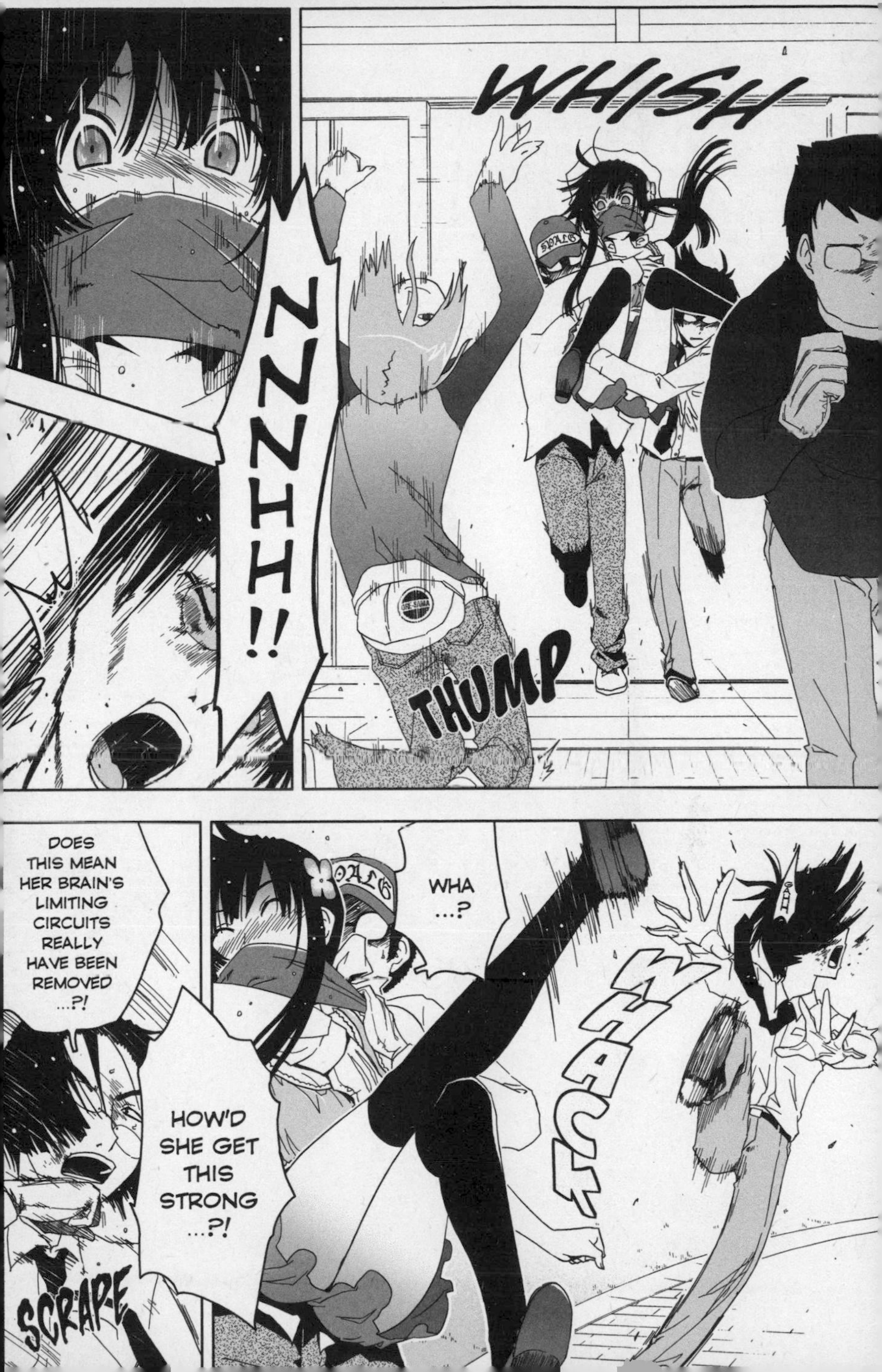
WHISH
THUMP
NNNHH!!
WHA ...?
WHACK
DOES THIS MEAN HER BRAIN'S LIMITING CIRCUITS REALLY HAVE BEEN REMOVED ...?!
HOW'D SHE GET THIS STRONG ...?!
SCRAPE

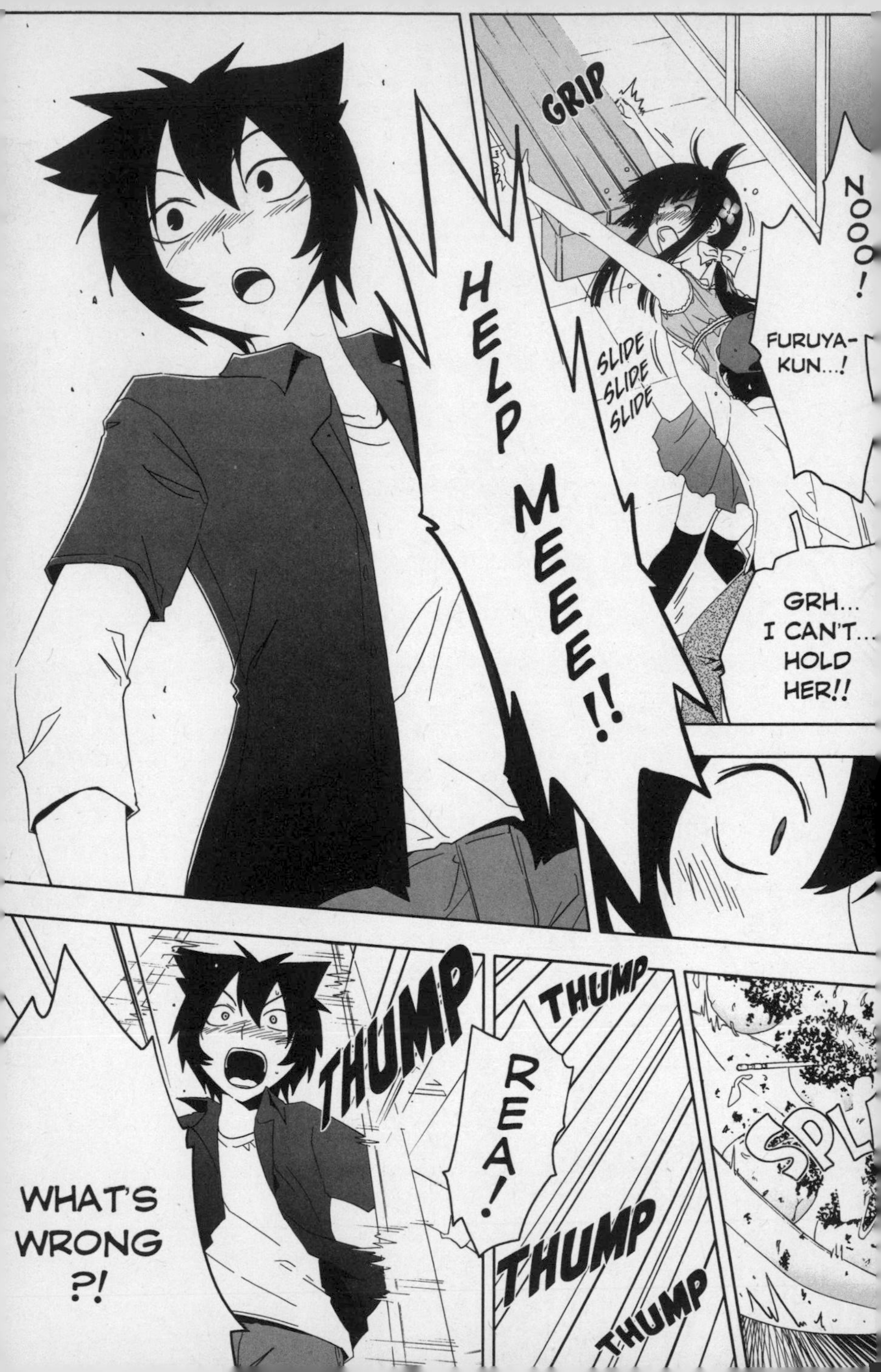
GRIP
NOOO!
FURUYA-KUN...!
SLIDE SLIDE SLIDE
GRH... I CAN'T... HOLD HER!!
HELP MEEE!!
SPL
THUMP
REA!
THUMP
THUMP
THUMP
WHAT'S WRONG?!
THUMP

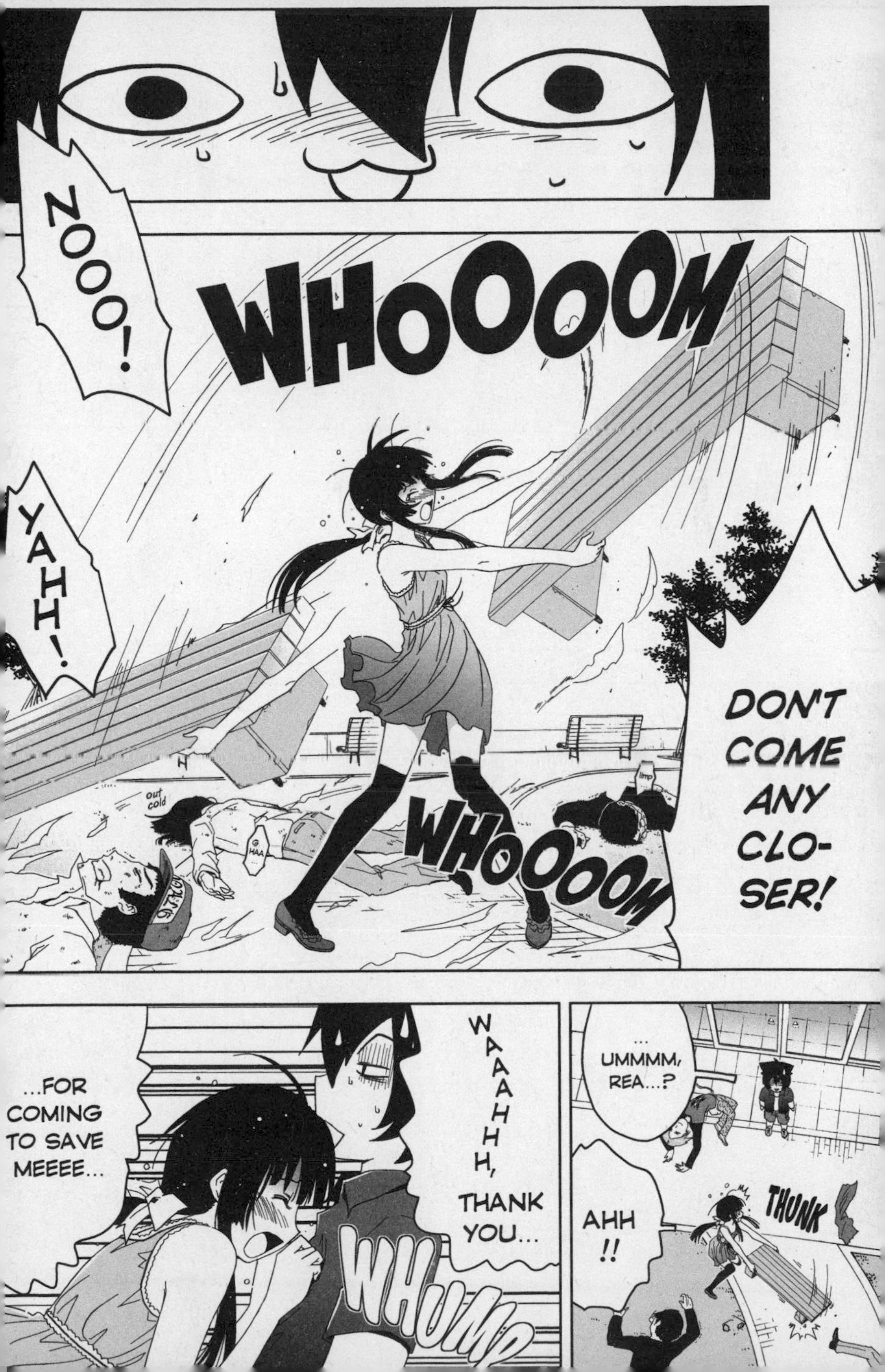
DON'T COME ANY CLO- SER!
WHOOOOM
NOOOO!
YAHH!
limp
out cold
G HAA
WHOOOOM
... UMMMM, REA...?
THUNK
AHH !!
WAAAAHHHH, THANK YOU...
...FOR COMING TO SAVE MEEEE...
WHUM

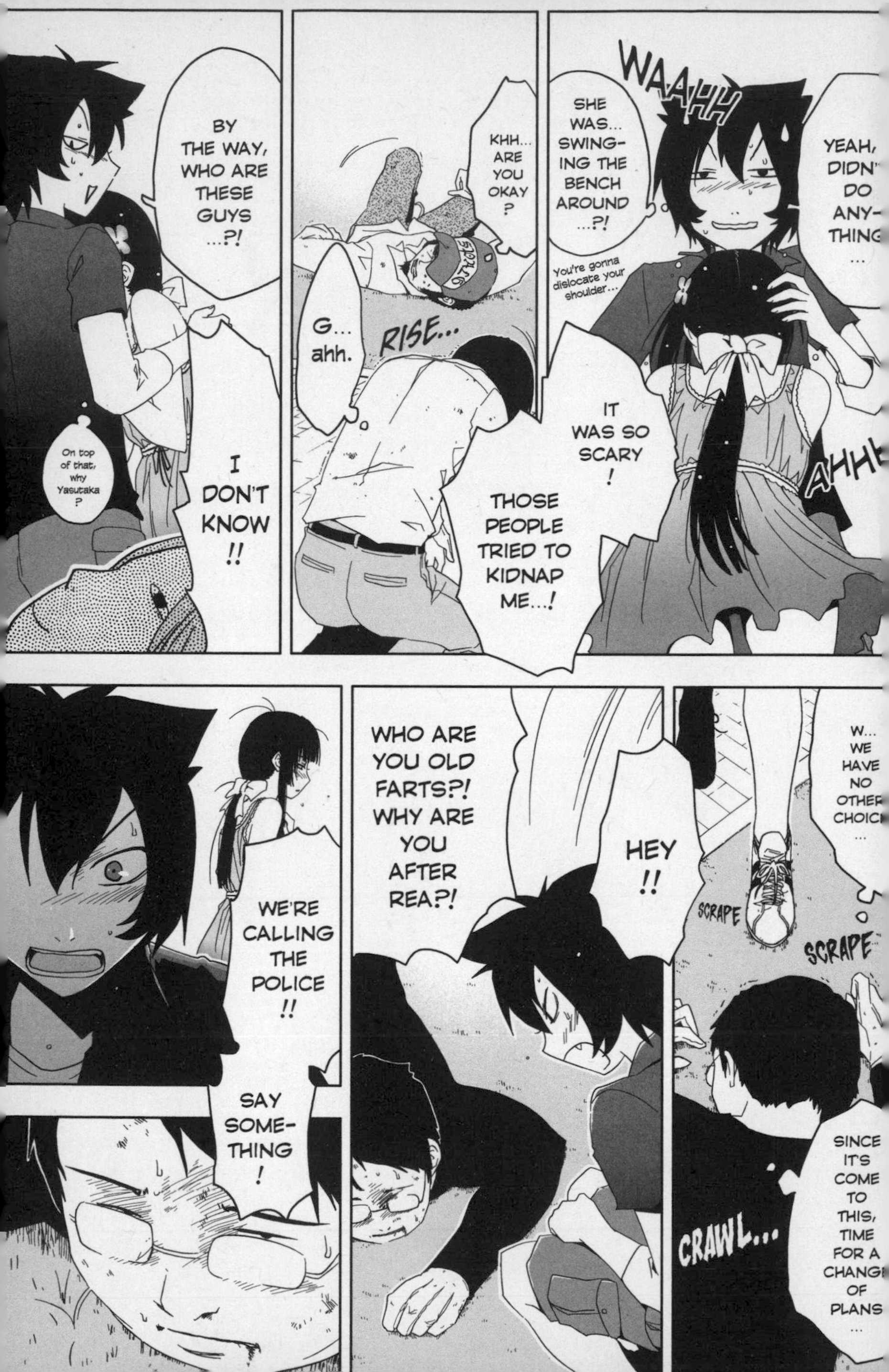
YEAH, DIDN' DO ANYTHING...
WAAHH
SHE WAS... SWING-ING THE BENCH AROUND...?!
You're gonna dislocate your shoulder...
AHH
IT WAS SO SCARY!
THOSE PEOPLE TRIED TO KIDNAP ME...!
KHH... ARE YOU OKAY?
G... ahh.
RISE...
BY THE WAY, WHO ARE THESE GUYS...?!
I DON'T KNOW!!
On top of that, why Yasutaka?
W... WE HAVE NO OTHER CHOIC...
SCRAPE
SCRAPE
SINCE IT'S COME TO THIS, TIME FOR A CHANG OF PLANS...
CRAWL...
HEY!!
WHO ARE YOU OLD FARTS?! WHY ARE YOU AFTER REA?!
WE'RE CALLING THE POLICE!!
SAY SOME-THING!

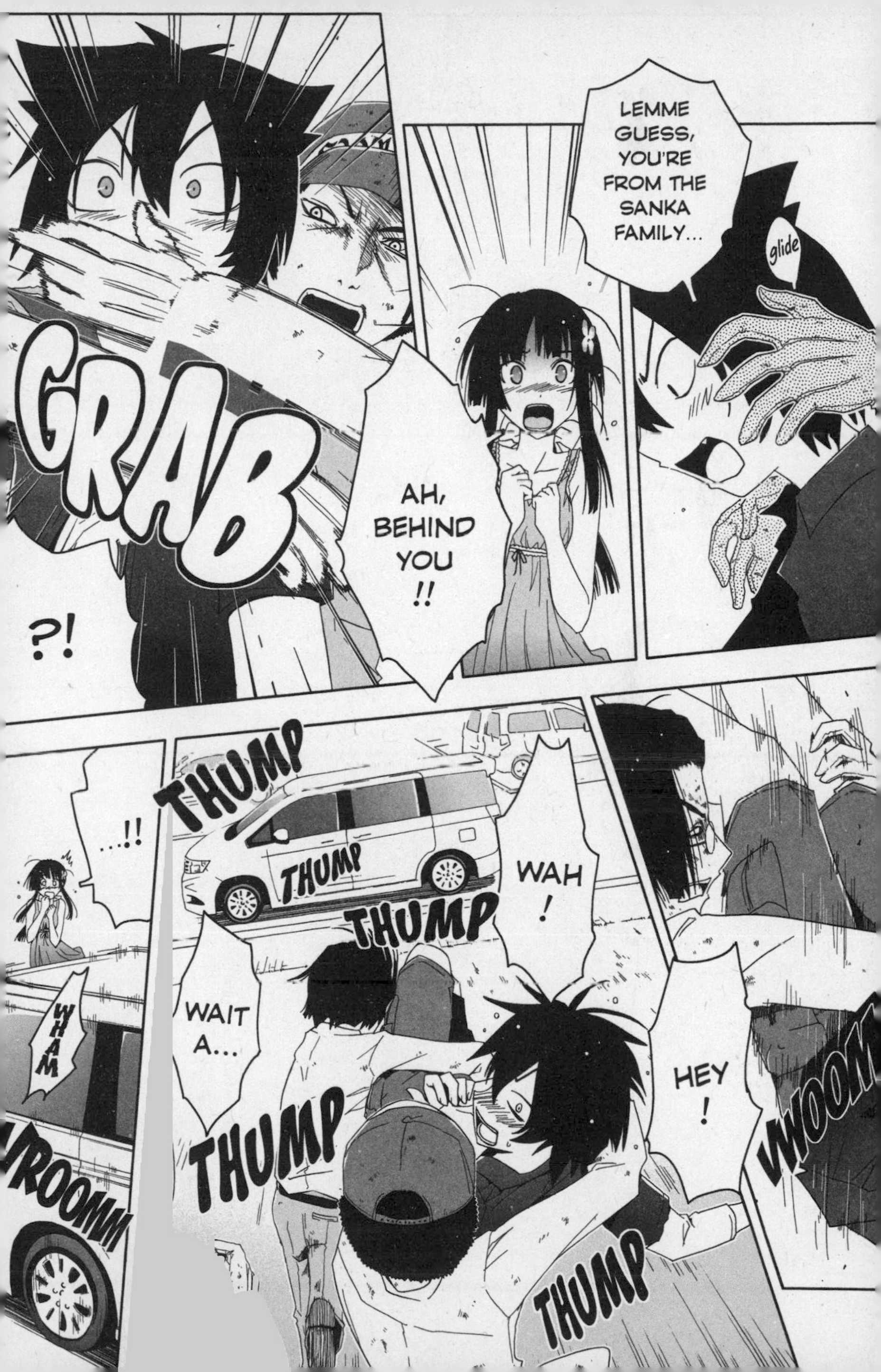
LEMME GUESS, YOU'RE FROM THE SANKA FAMILY...
glide
AH, BEHIND YOU !!
GRAB
?!
VWOOM
HEY !
WAH !
THUMP
THUMP
THUMP
WAIT A...
THUMP
THUMP
...!!
WHAM
VROOMM

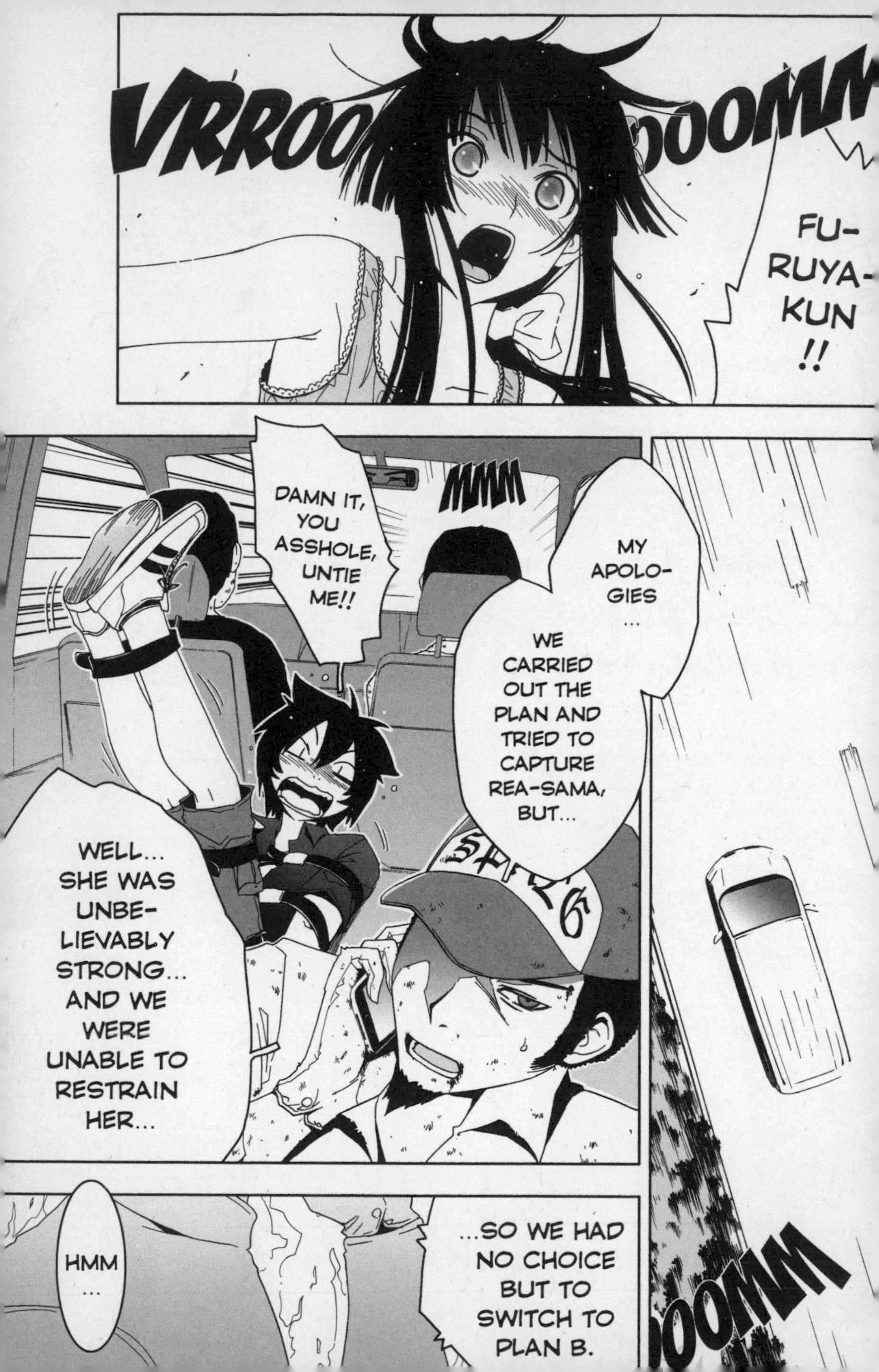
VRROOOOMM
FU-RUYA-KUN!!
DOOMM
MMM
DAMN IT, YOU ASSHOLE, UNTIE ME!!
MY APOLOGIES...
WE CARRIED OUT THE PLAN AND TRIED TO CAPTURE REA-SAMA, BUT...
WELL... SHE WAS UNBELIEVABLY STRONG... AND WE WERE UNABLE TO RESTRAIN HER...
...SO WE HAD NO CHOICE BUT TO SWITCH TO PLAN B.
HMM...

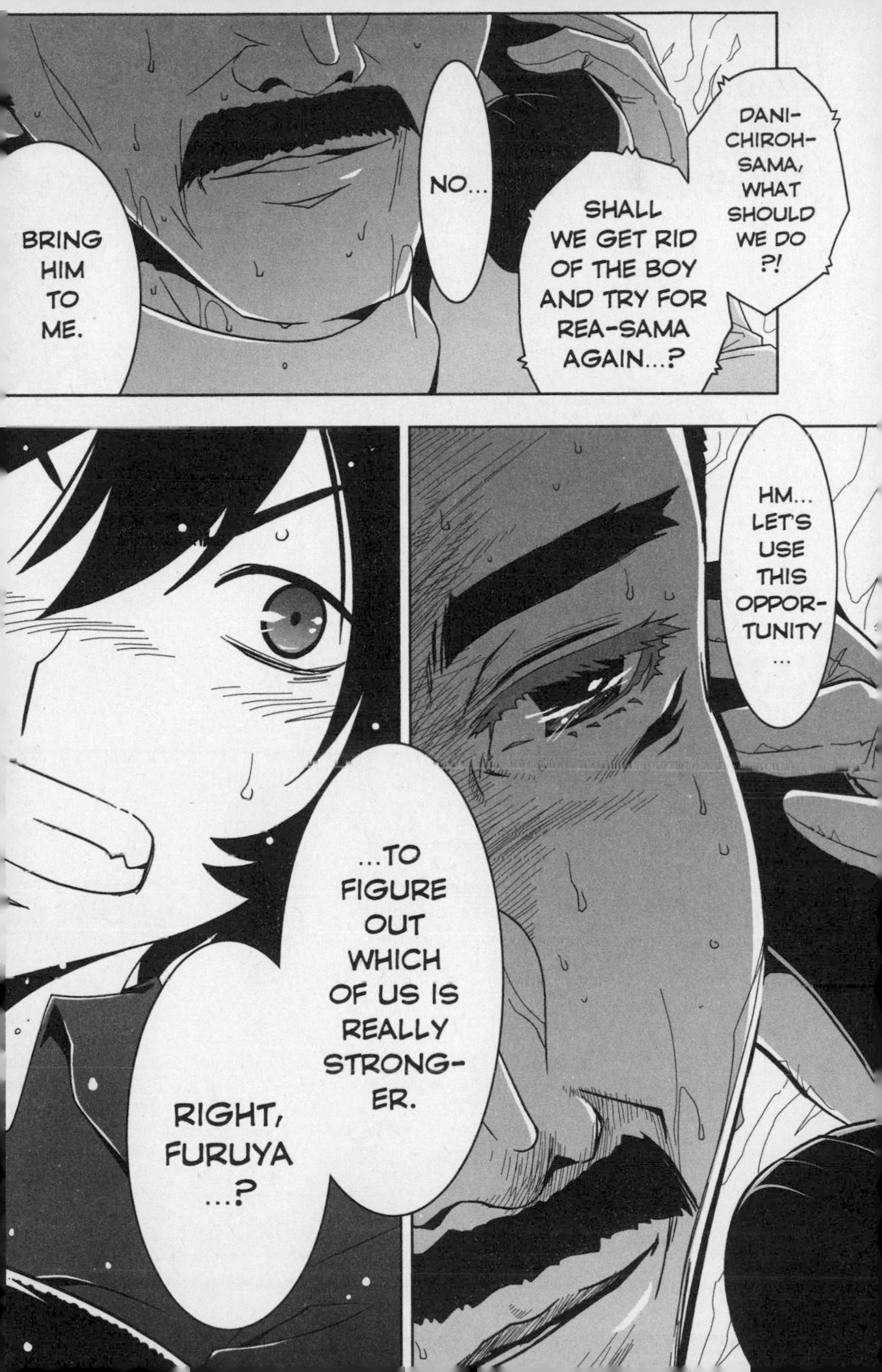
DANI-CHIROH-SAMA, WHAT SHOULD WE DO?!
SHALL WE GET RID OF THE BOY AND TRY FOR REA-SAMA AGAIN...?
NO...
BRING HIM TO ME.
HM... LET'S USE THIS OPPOR-TUNITY...
...TO FIGURE OUT WHICH OF US IS REALLY STRONG-ER.
RIGHT, FURUYA...?

SANKAREA ANECDOTES

About the Setting

2

This time I'll talk about the setting of this story, the town of Shiyoh.
Even outside of "Sankarea," I always base the settings of my published works on actual locales (though the names and the details of the terrain are made up). Just as with my previous works, this time around I used a real place as a model for the setting again.

The chance for this occurred when I was on vacation, traveling. I happened to pass this place by train and thought, "Wow." It's not that it had any particular characteristics, but for some reason the place had something that stayed inside of me.

A while later, it came time for me to begin a new comic about zombies. Though I considered a lot of different ideas, none of them really took shape, and I nearly decided to give up on the subject.

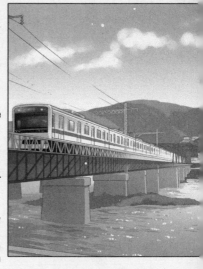

It was then that I suddenly remembered the area I just mentioned. I had a vague thought, like, "I don't know if I can gain something from this, but let's go there, and I can take a breather, too!" Without any concrete plans, I left suddenly on the first train towards the place.

Anyway, while taking pictures, I hung around the area with no real purpose at all. I'm the type who enjoys just walking around an area I don't know, and it felt good to take a break from work. The town, the nature, the lives of the local people...

While looking at all sorts of things, I started to feel more and more like, "Oh, I think I can use this," "That place is great, huh." All kinds of ideas came bubbling up, and just as though my writer's block had never happened, I was completely ready to go as soon as I got home!! Ah, it's the first time I've gotten so much out of location hunting. (Heh!)

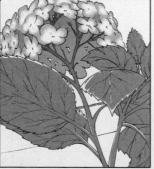

Hydrangeas are so connected to this story because when I went, they just happened to be having a hydrangea festival nearby, and so I ended up thinking that having zombies made from hydrangea toxins was a surprisingly weird b possibly good idea. When I looked down at the town from an herb garden on top of the mountain, the character of a daughter of a famous family living in mansion on the mountain, semi-isolated from the outside world, who dies an becomes a zombie because she wants to be free came bubbling up.

So that place that became the setting for "Sankarea"... any bored people ou there, why not try to investigate where it is? Though I think if you search a litt you'll find it right away. (Heh.)

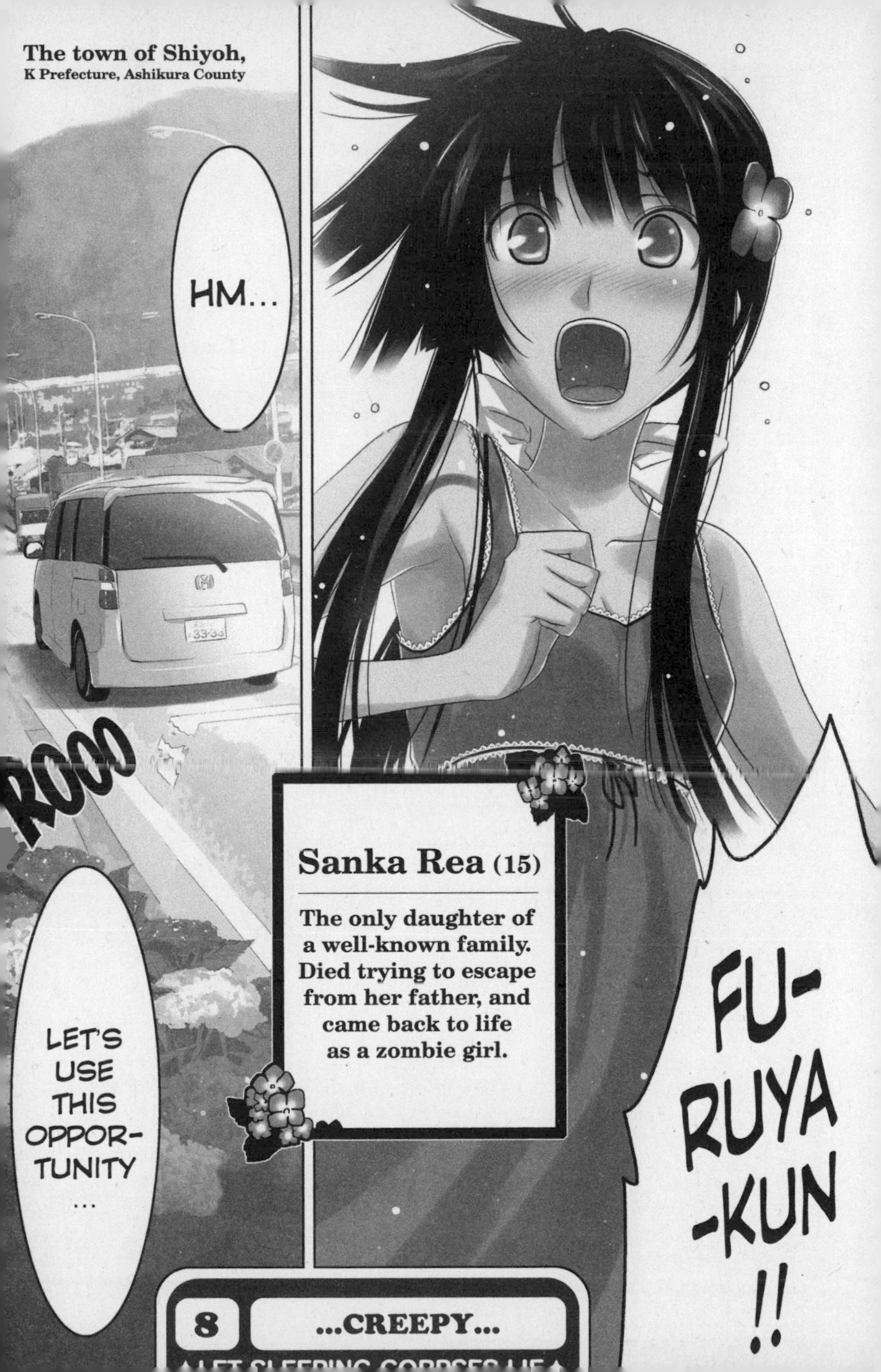

Sanka Rea (15)
The only daughter of a well-known family. Died trying to escape from her father, and came back to life as a zombie girl.
FU-RUYA-KUN!!
The town of Shiyoh, K Prefecture, Ashikura County
HM...
ROOO
LET'S USE THIS OPPORTUNITY...
8 ...CREEPY...

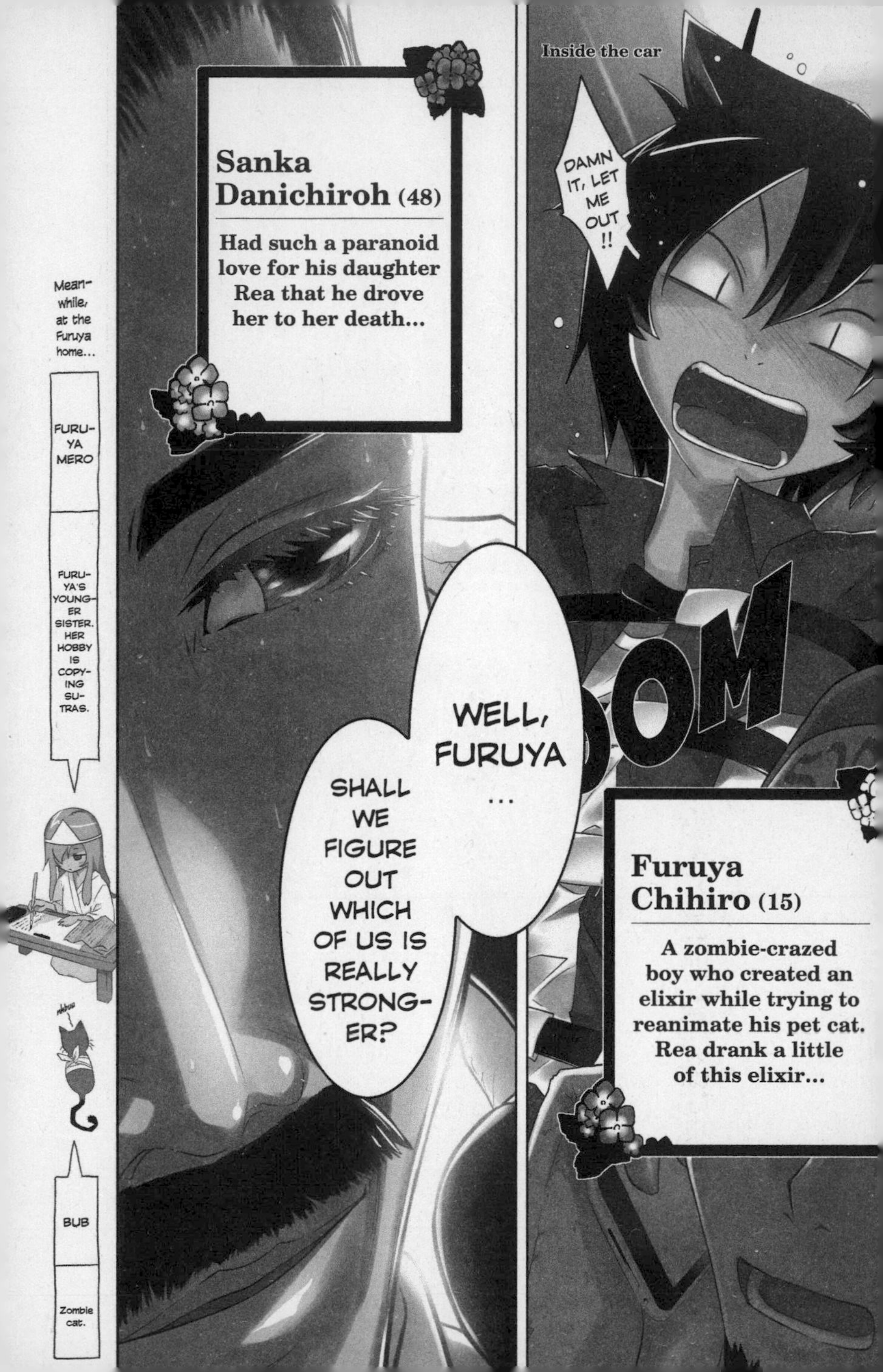
Inside the car
DAMN IT, LET ME OUT !!
OOM
Furuya Chihiro (15)
A zombie-crazed boy who created an elixir while trying to reanimate his pet cat. Rea drank a little of this elixir...
Sanka Danichiroh (48)
Had such a paranoid love for his daughter Rea that he drove her to her death...
WELL, FURUYA ...
SHALL WE FIGURE OUT WHICH OF US IS REALLY STRONGER?
Mean-while, at the Furuya home...
FURU-YA MERO
FURU-YA'S YOUNG-ER SISTER. HER HOBBY IS COPY-ING SU-TRAS.
BUB
Zombie cat.

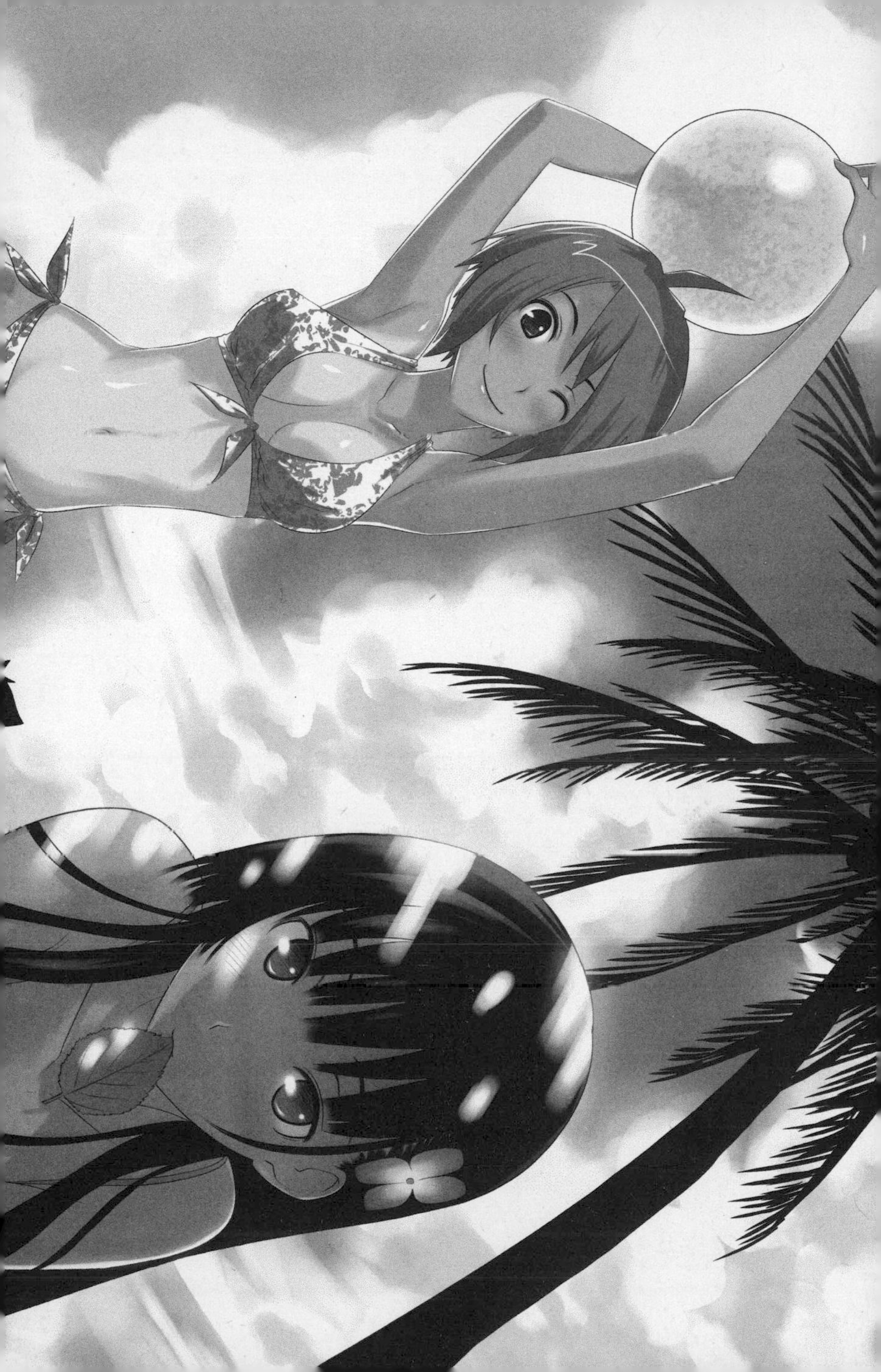

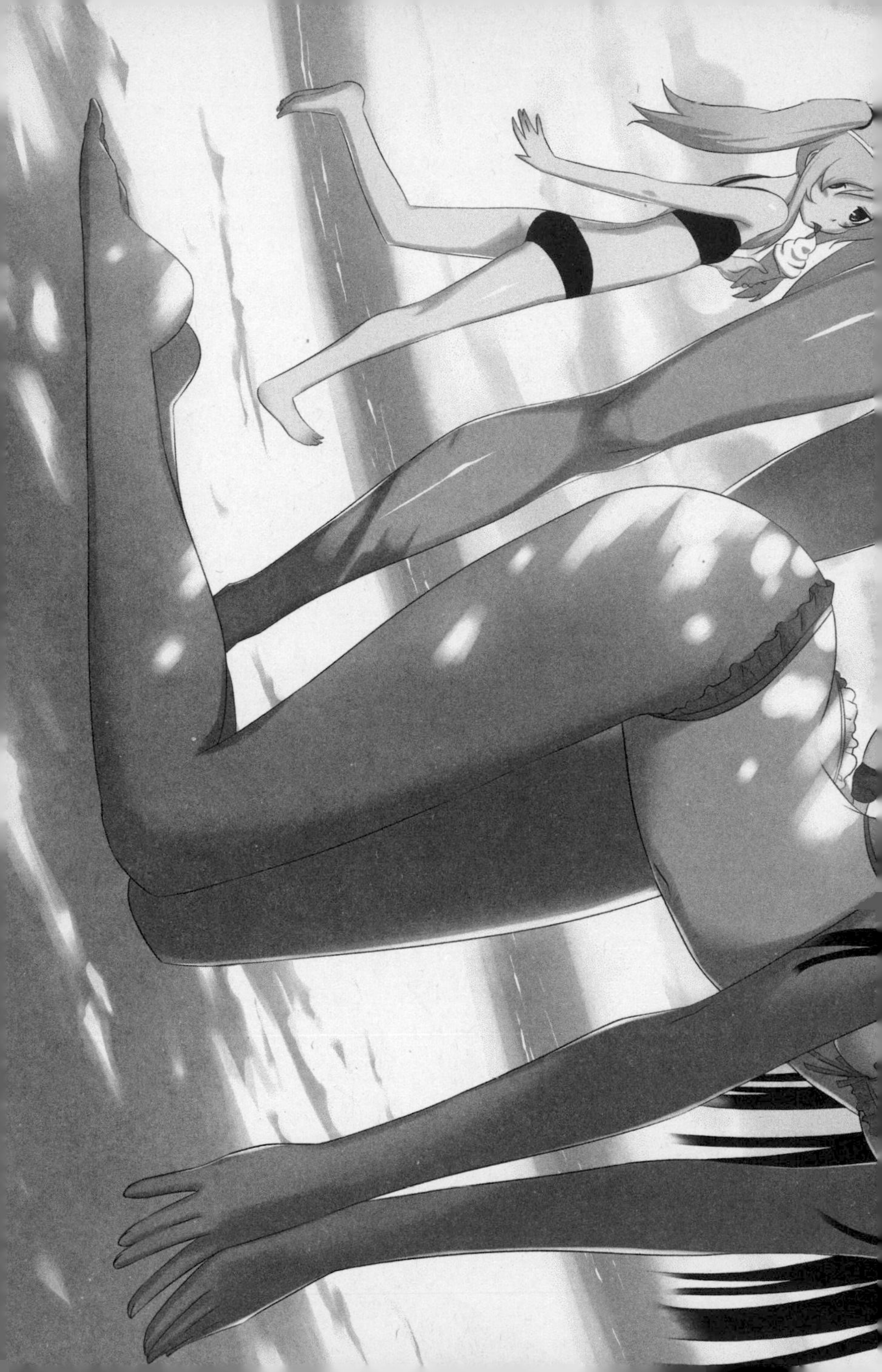

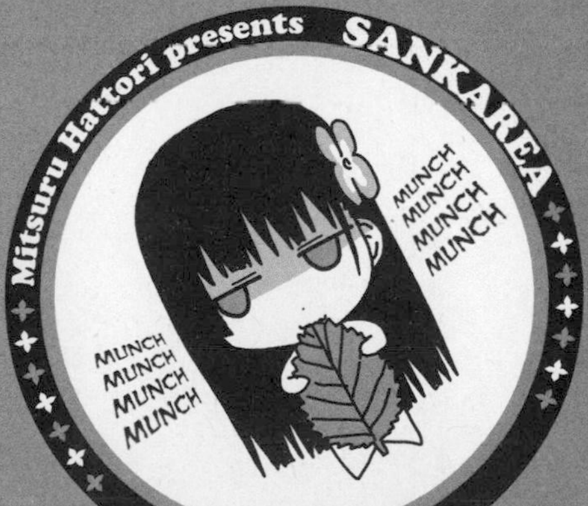
Mitsuru Hattori presents SANKAREA
MUNCH MUNCH MUNCH MUNCH
MUNCH MUNCH MUNCH MUNCH

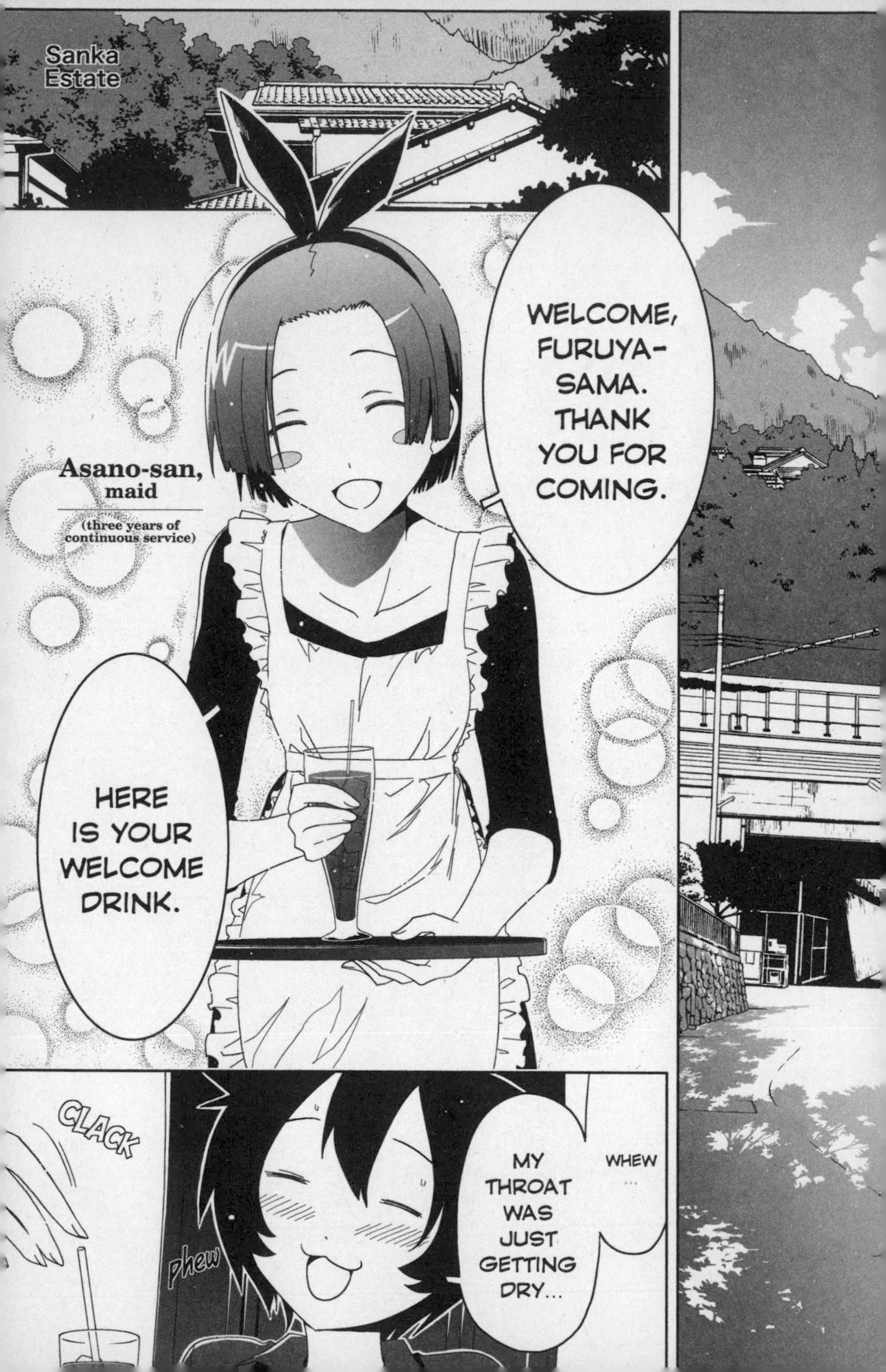
Sanka Estate
WELCOME, FURUYA-SAMA. THANK YOU FOR COMING.
Asano-san, maid
(three years of continuous service)
HERE IS YOUR WELCOME DRINK.
WHEW...
MY THROAT WAS JUST GETTING DRY...
phew
CLACK

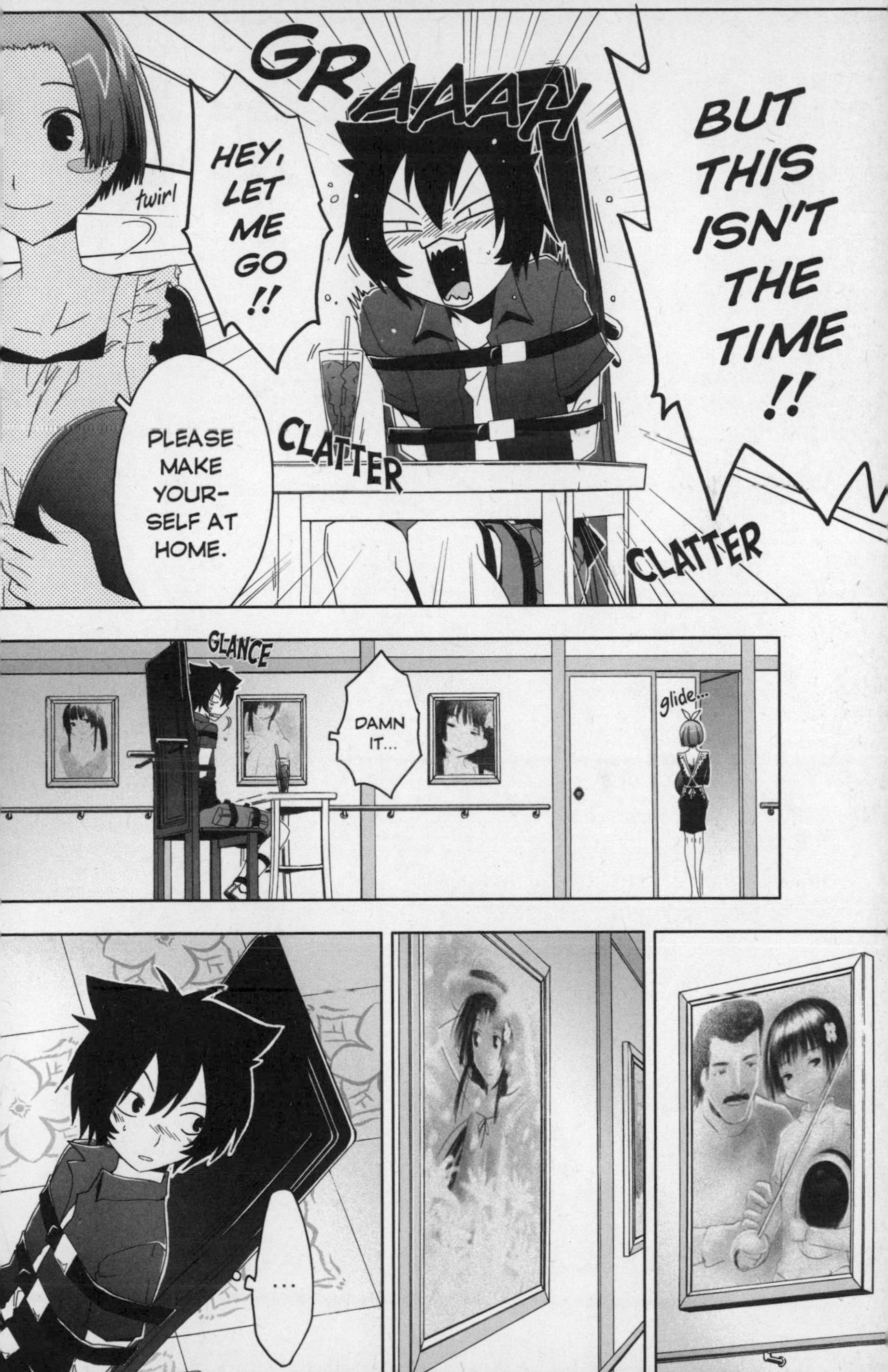
BUT THIS ISN'T THE TIME!!
GRAAAH
HEY, LET ME GO!!
twirl
CLATTER
CLATTER
PLEASE MAKE YOURSELF AT HOME.
glide...
DAMN IT...
GLANCE
...

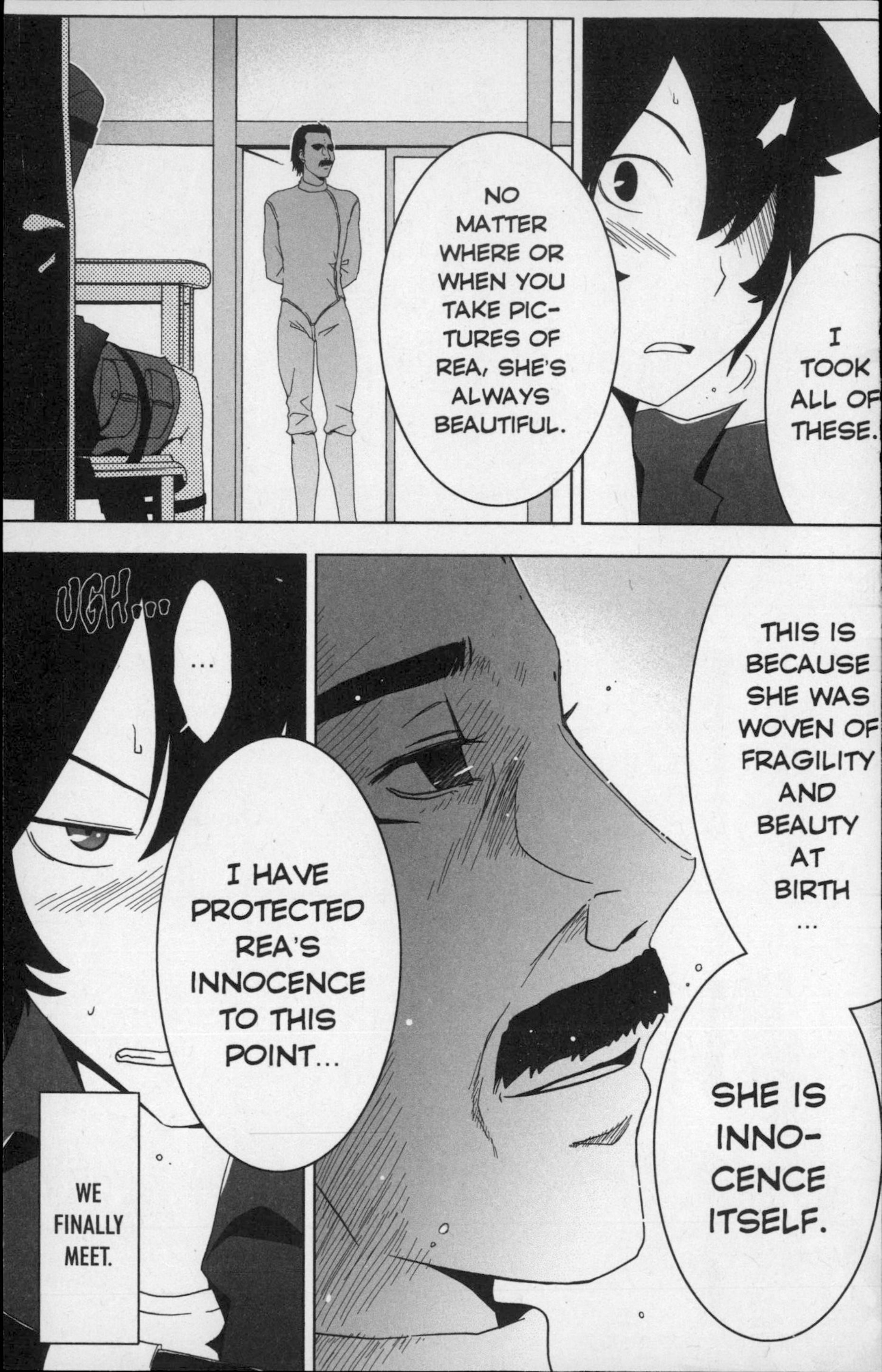
I TOOK ALL OF THESE.
NO MATTER WHERE OR WHEN YOU TAKE PICTURES OF REA, SHE'S ALWAYS BEAUTIFUL.
THIS IS BECAUSE SHE WAS WOVEN OF FRAGILITY AND BEAUTY AT BIRTH ...
SHE IS INNOCENCE ITSELF.
I HAVE PROTECTED REA'S INNOCENCE TO THIS POINT...
UGH...
...
WE FINALLY MEET.

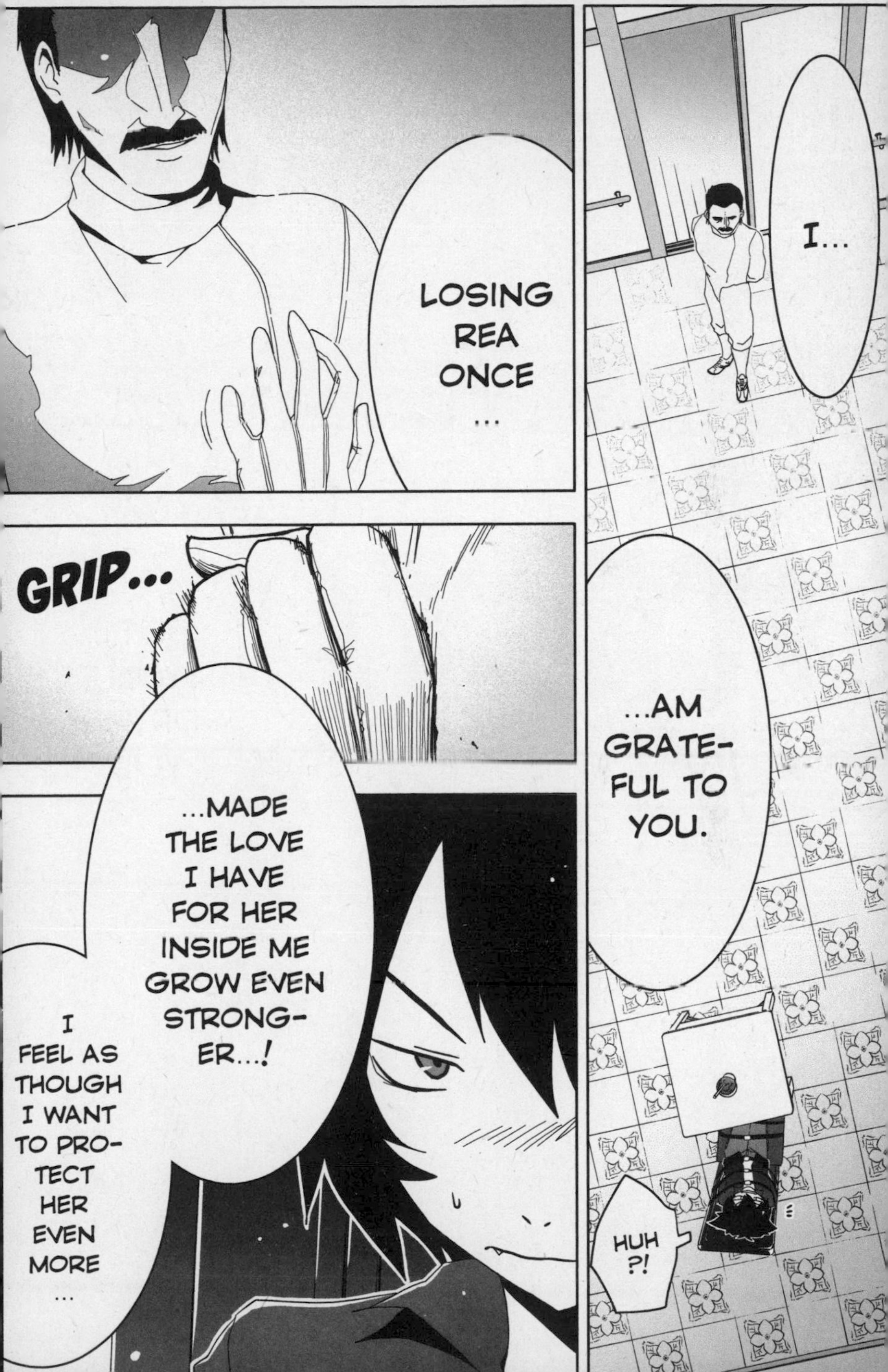
I...
...AM GRATE-FUL TO YOU.
HUH ?!
LOSING REA ONCE ...
GRIP...
...MADE THE LOVE I HAVE FOR HER INSIDE ME GROW EVEN STRONG-ER...!
I FEEL AS THOUGH I WANT TO PRO-TECT HER EVEN MORE ...

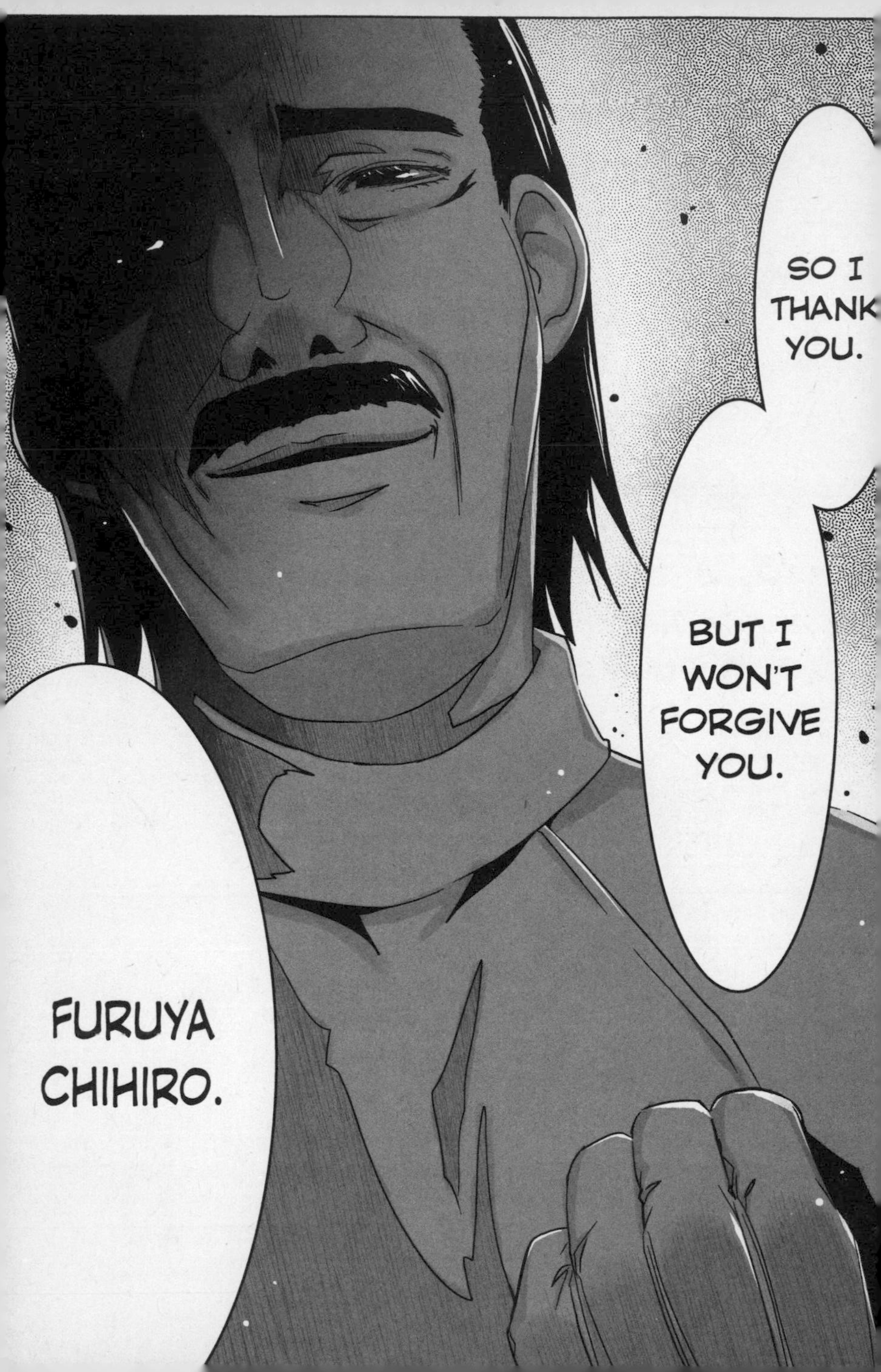
SO I THANK YOU.
BUT I WON'T FORGIVE YOU.
FURUYA CHIHIRO.

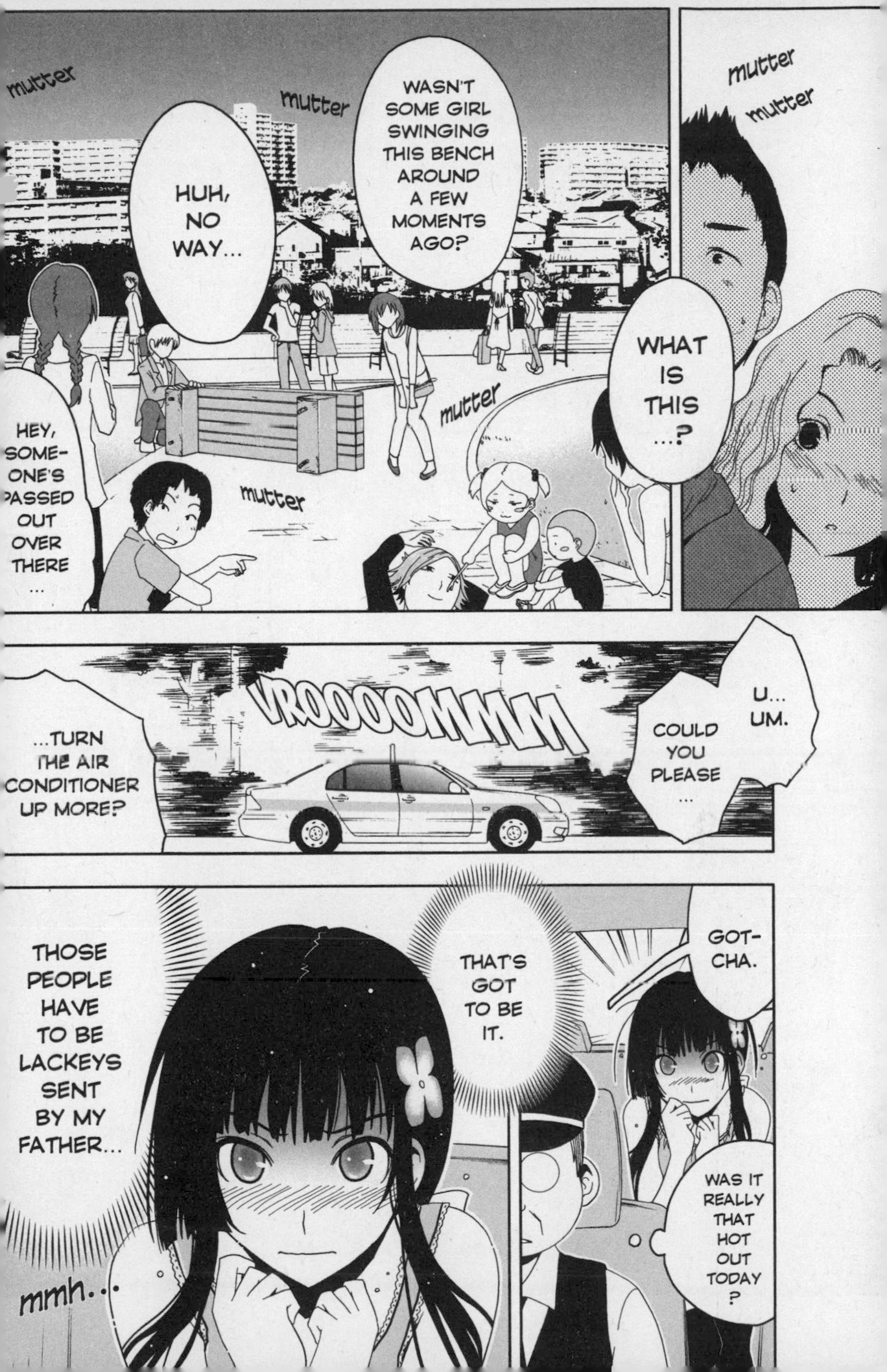
mutter
mutter
WHAT IS THIS ...?
WASN'T SOME GIRL SWINGING THIS BENCH AROUND A FEW MOMENTS AGO?
mutter
HUH, NO WAY...
mutter
mutter
mutter
HEY, SOME-ONE'S PASSED OUT OVER THERE ...
U... UM.
COULD YOU PLEASE ...
VROOOOMMMM
...TURN THE AIR CONDITIONER UP MORE?
GOT-CHA.
WAS IT REALLY THAT HOT OUT TODAY?
THAT'S GOT TO BE IT.
THOSE PEOPLE HAVE TO BE LACKEYS SENT BY MY FATHER...
mmh...

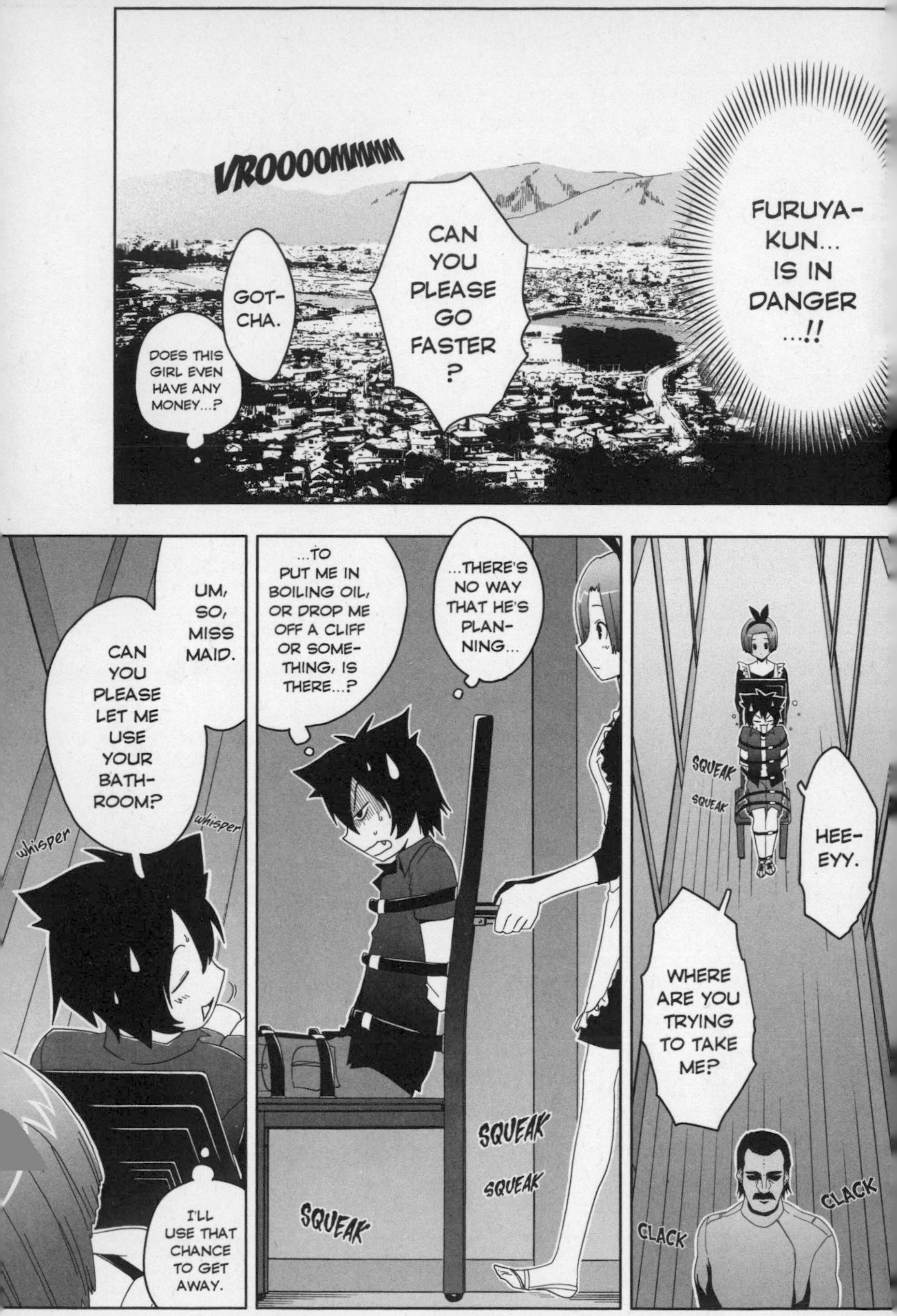
FURUYA-KUN... IS IN DANGER ...!!
VROOOOMMMM
CAN YOU PLEASE GO FASTER?
GOT-CHA.
DOES THIS GIRL EVEN HAVE ANY MONEY...?
HEE-EYY.
WHERE ARE YOU TRYING TO TAKE ME?
SQUEAK
SQUEAK
CLACK
CLACK
...THERE'S NO WAY THAT HE'S PLAN-NING...
...TO PUT ME IN BOILING OIL, OR DROP ME OFF A CLIFF OR SOME-THING, IS THERE...?
SQUEAK
SQUEAK
SQUEAK
UM, SO, MISS MAID.
CAN YOU PLEASE LET ME USE YOUR BATH-ROOM?
whisper
whisper
I'LL USE THAT CHANCE TO GET AWAY.

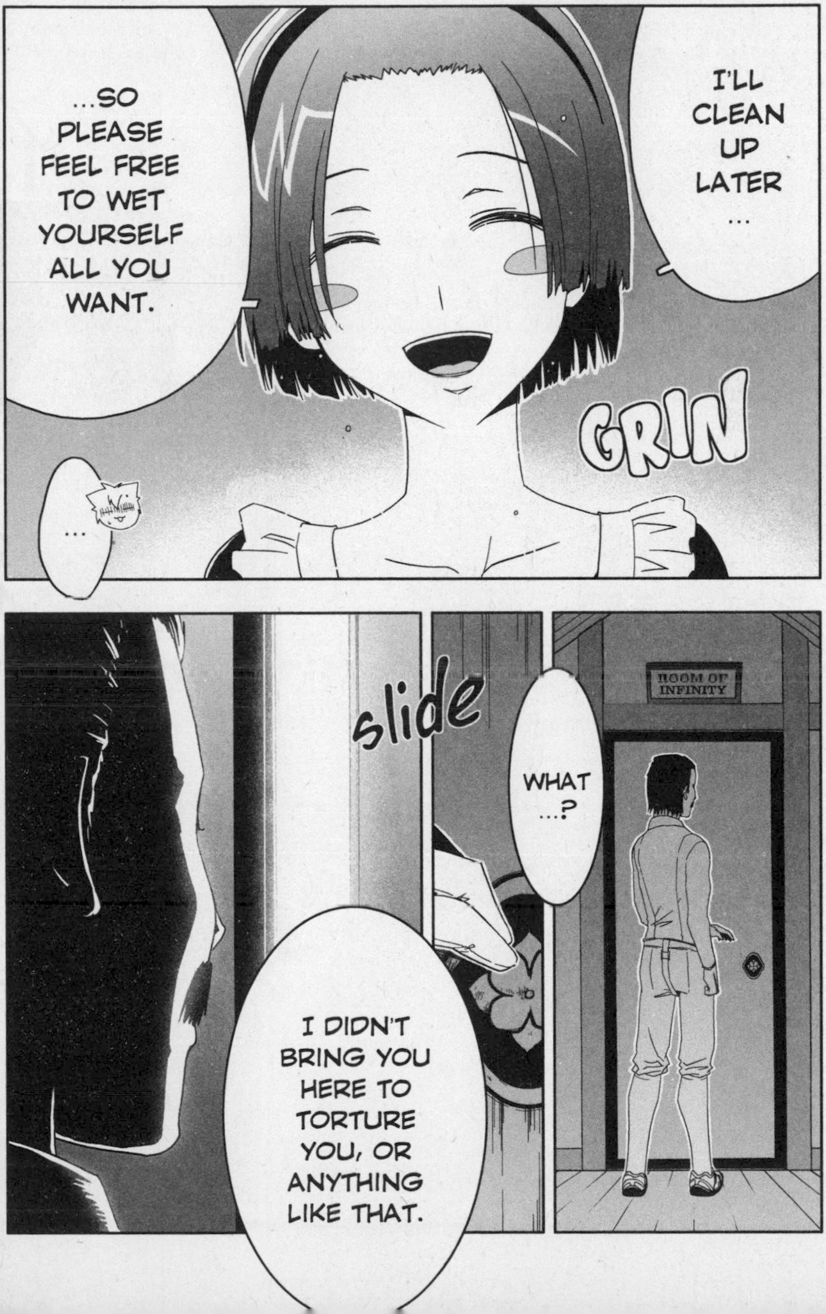
I'LL CLEAN UP LATER ...
...SO PLEASE FEEL FREE TO WET YOURSELF ALL YOU WANT.
GRIN
...
ROOM OF INFINITY
WHAT ...?
slide
I DIDN'T BRING YOU HERE TO TORTURE YOU, OR ANYTHING LIKE THAT.

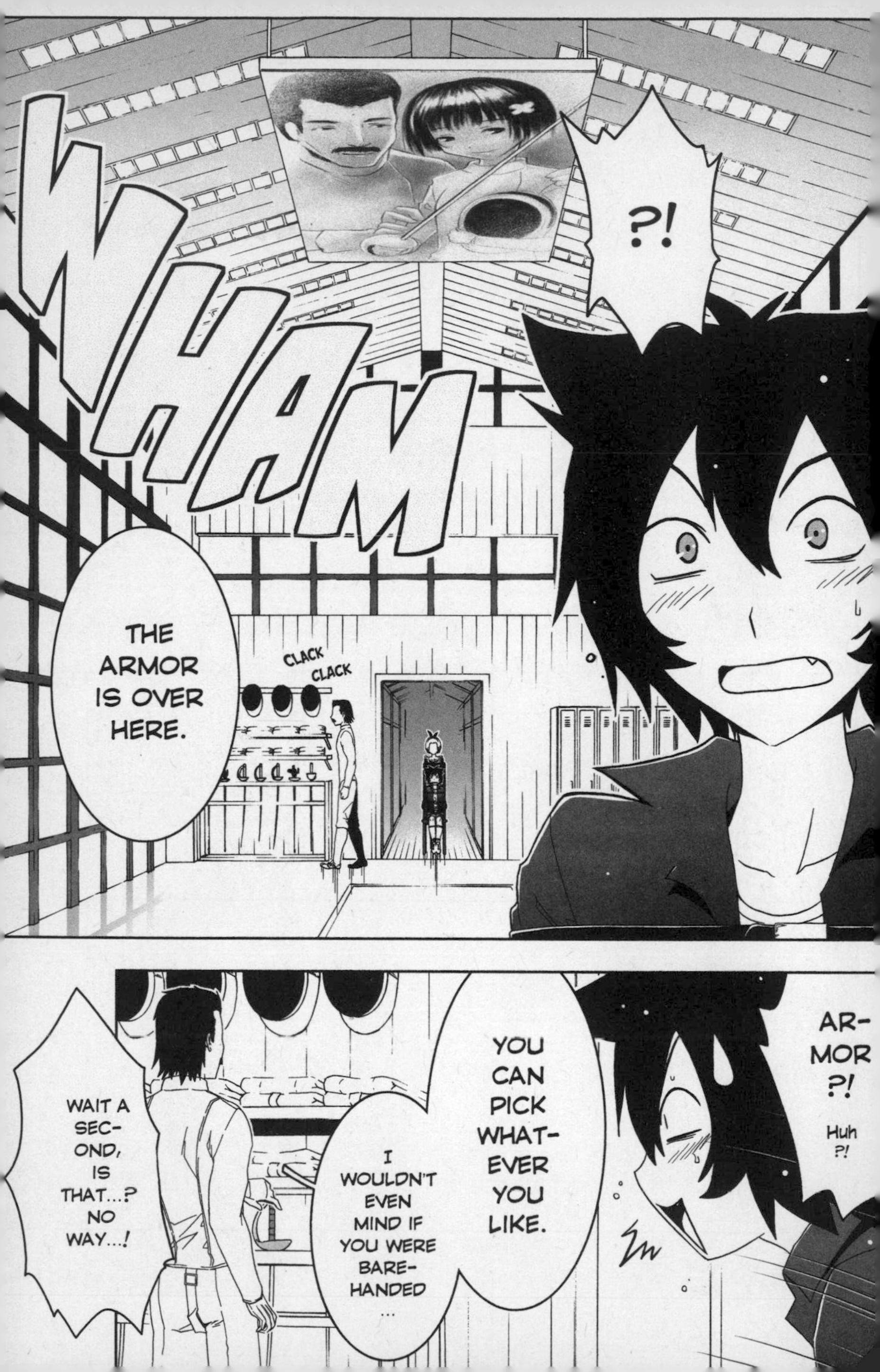
?!
WHAM
CLACK CLACK
THE ARMOR IS OVER HERE.
AR-MOR?!
Huh?!
YOU CAN PICK WHAT-EVER YOU LIKE.
I WOULDN'T EVEN MIND IF YOU WERE BARE-HANDED...
WAIT A SEC-OND, IS THAT...? NO WAY...!

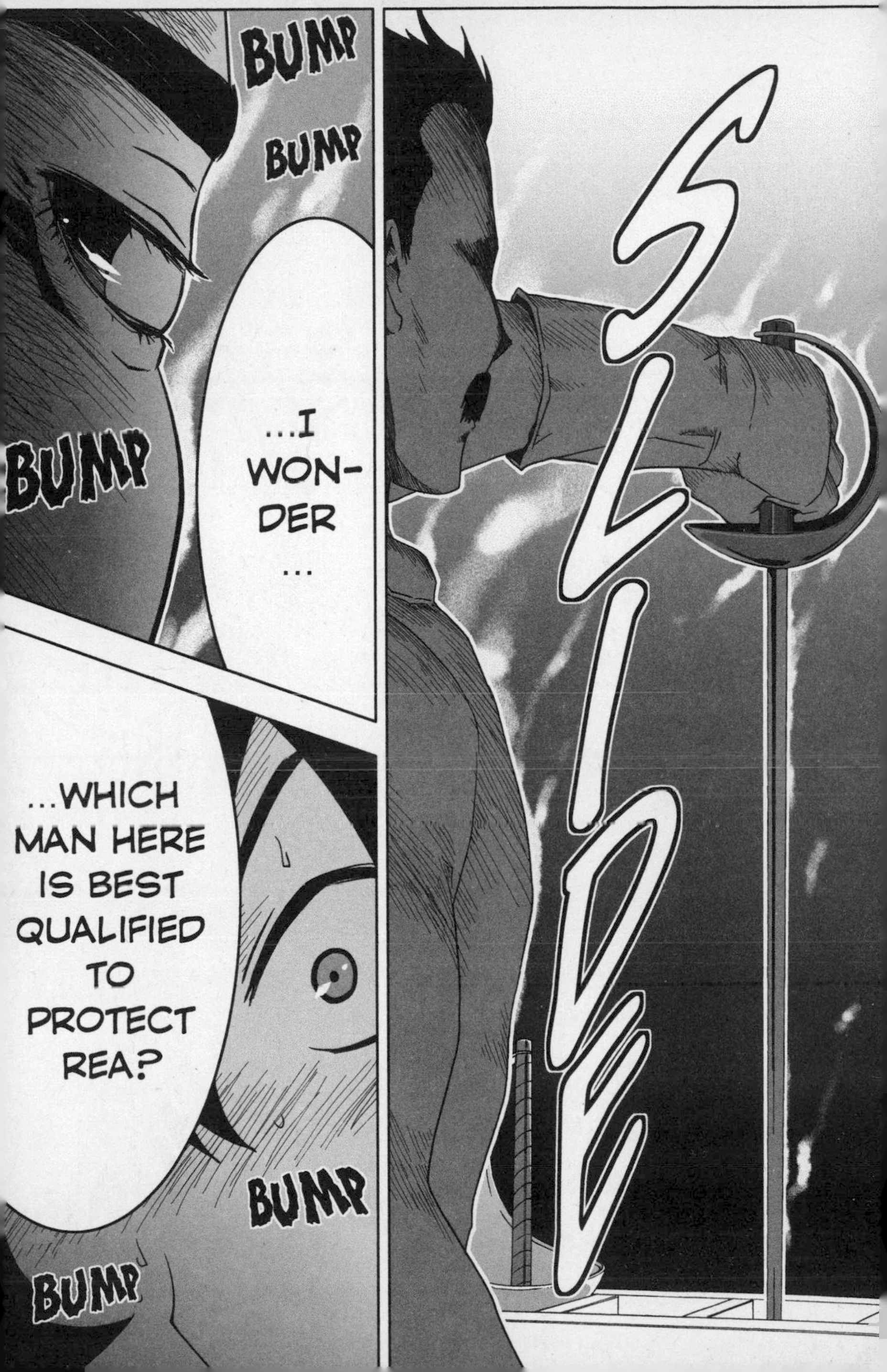
SLIDE
BUMP
BUMP
...I WONDER...
BUMP
...WHICH MAN HERE IS BEST QUALIFIED TO PROTECT REA?
BUMP
BUMP

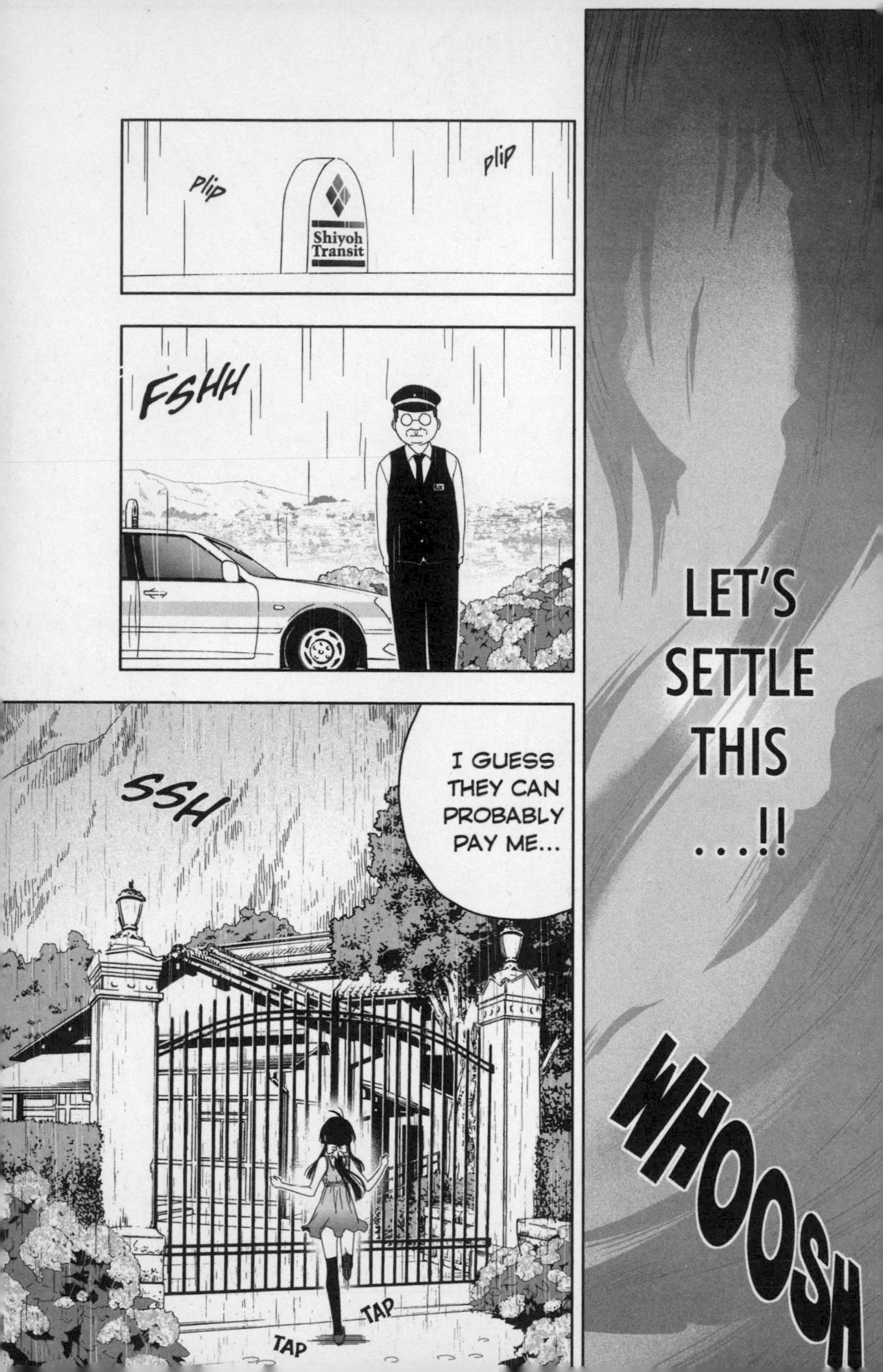
LET'S SETTLE THIS ...!!
WHOOSH
plip
plip
Shiyoh Transit
FSHH
SSH
I GUESS THEY CAN PROBABLY PAY ME...
TAP
TAP

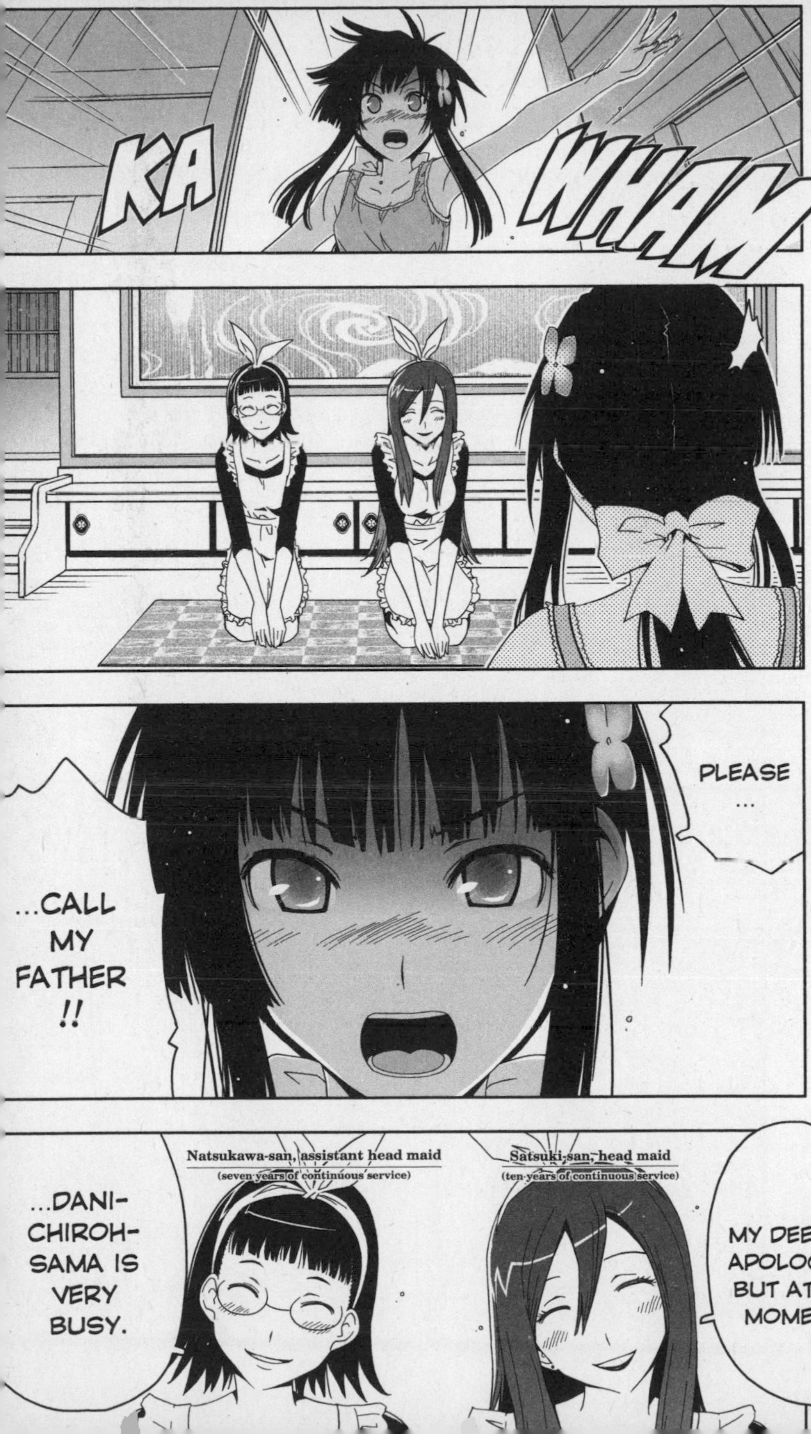
KA WHAM
PLEASE ...
...CALL MY FATHER !!
MY DEEPEST APOLOGIES, BUT AT THE MOMENT...
Satsuki-san, head maid
(ten years of continuous service)
Natsukawa-san, assistant head maid
(seven years of continuous service)
...DANI-CHIROH-SAMA IS VERY BUSY.

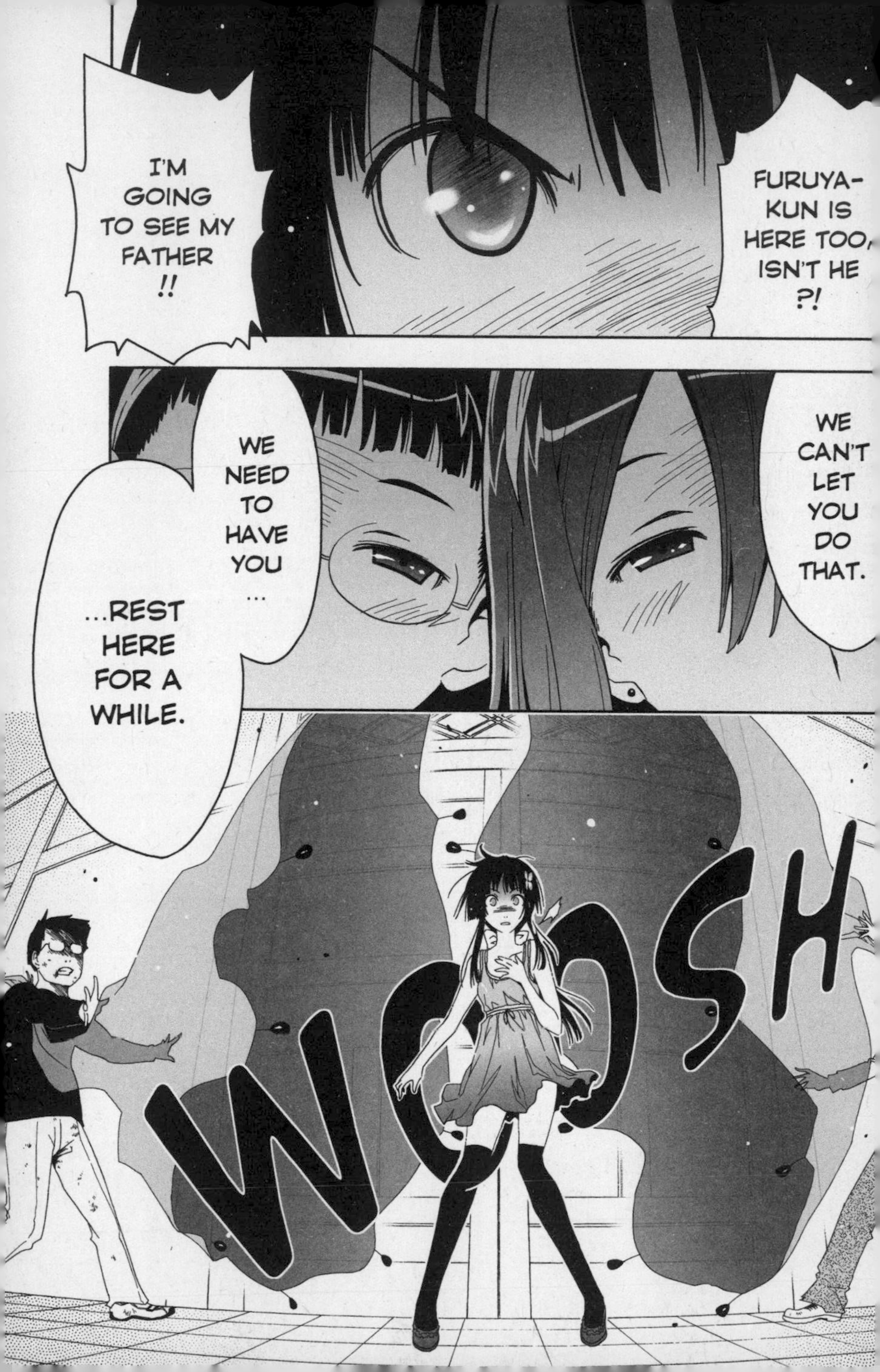
FURUYA-KUN IS HERE TOO, ISN'T HE ?!
I'M GOING TO SEE MY FATHER !!
WE CAN'T LET YOU DO THAT.
WE NEED TO HAVE YOU ...
...REST HERE FOR A WHILE.
WOOSH

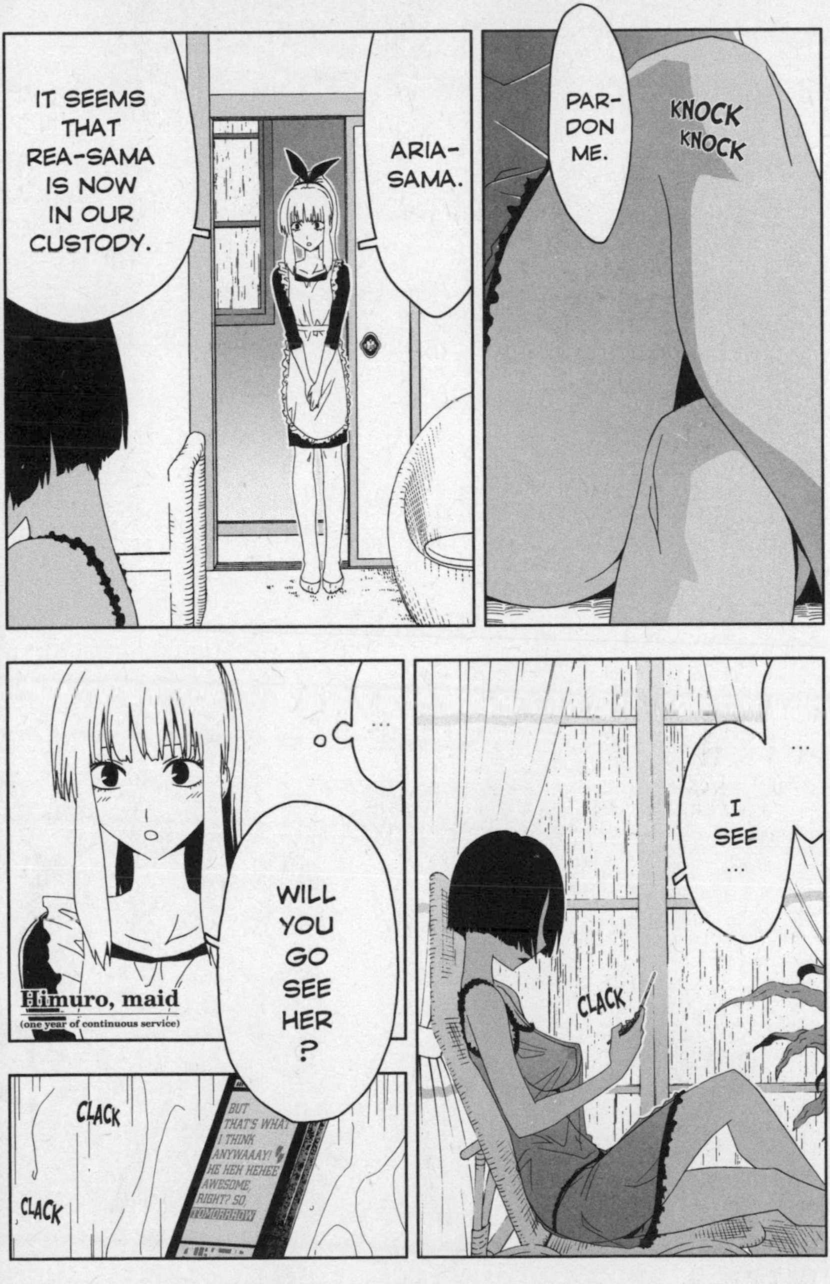
PARDON ME.
KNOCK KNOCK
ARIA-SAMA.
IT SEEMS THAT REA-SAMA IS NOW IN OUR CUSTODY.
... I SEE ...
CLACK
...
WILL YOU GO SEE HER?
Himuro, maid
(one year of continuous service)
CLACK
BUT THAT'S WHAT I THINK ANYWAAAY! HE HEH HEHEE AWESOME, RIGHT? SO, TOMORROW
CLACK

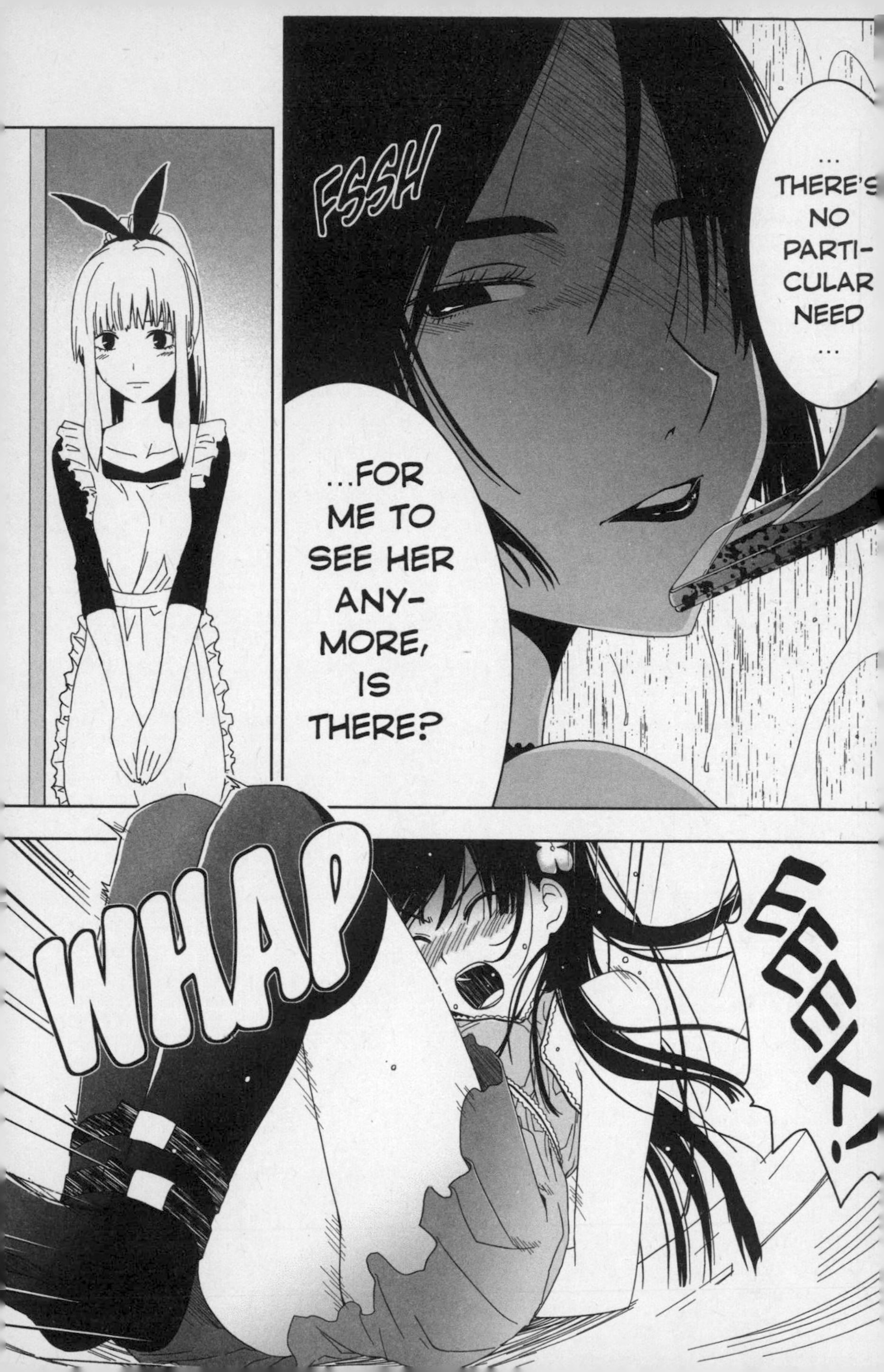

... THERE'S NO PARTI- CULAR NEED ...
FSSH
...FOR ME TO SEE HER ANY- MORE, IS THERE?
EEEEK!
WHAP

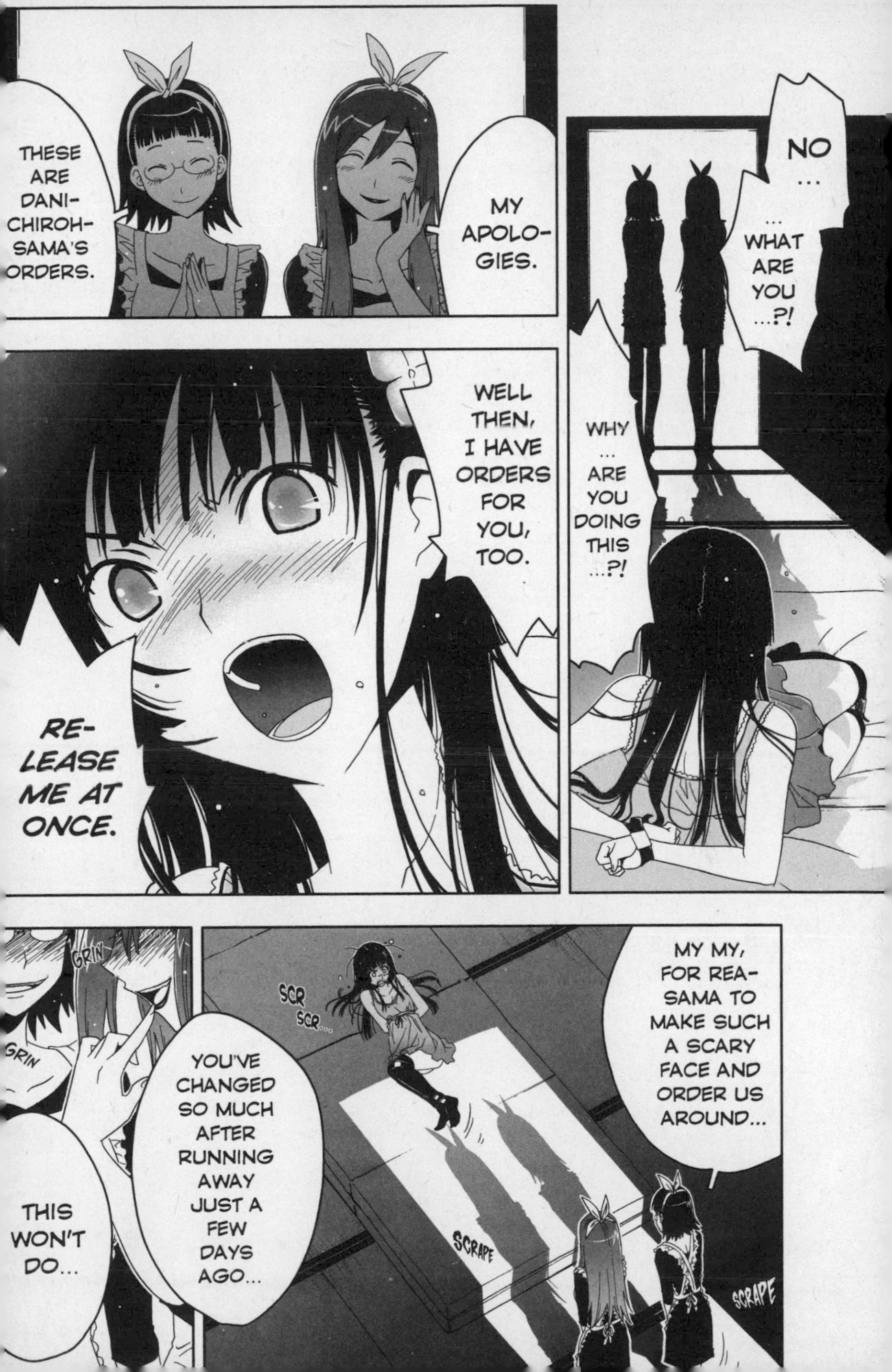
NO ...
... WHAT ARE YOU ...?!
WHY ... ARE YOU DOING THIS ...?!
MY APOLO-GIES.
THESE ARE DANI-CHIROH-SAMA'S ORDERS.
WELL THEN, I HAVE ORDERS FOR YOU, TOO.
RE-LEASE ME AT ONCE.
MY MY, FOR REA-SAMA TO MAKE SUCH A SCARY FACE AND ORDER US AROUND...
SCR SCR...
SCRAPE
SCRAPE
YOU'VE CHANGED SO MUCH AFTER RUNNING AWAY JUST A FEW DAYS AGO...
GRIN
GRIN
THIS WON'T DO...

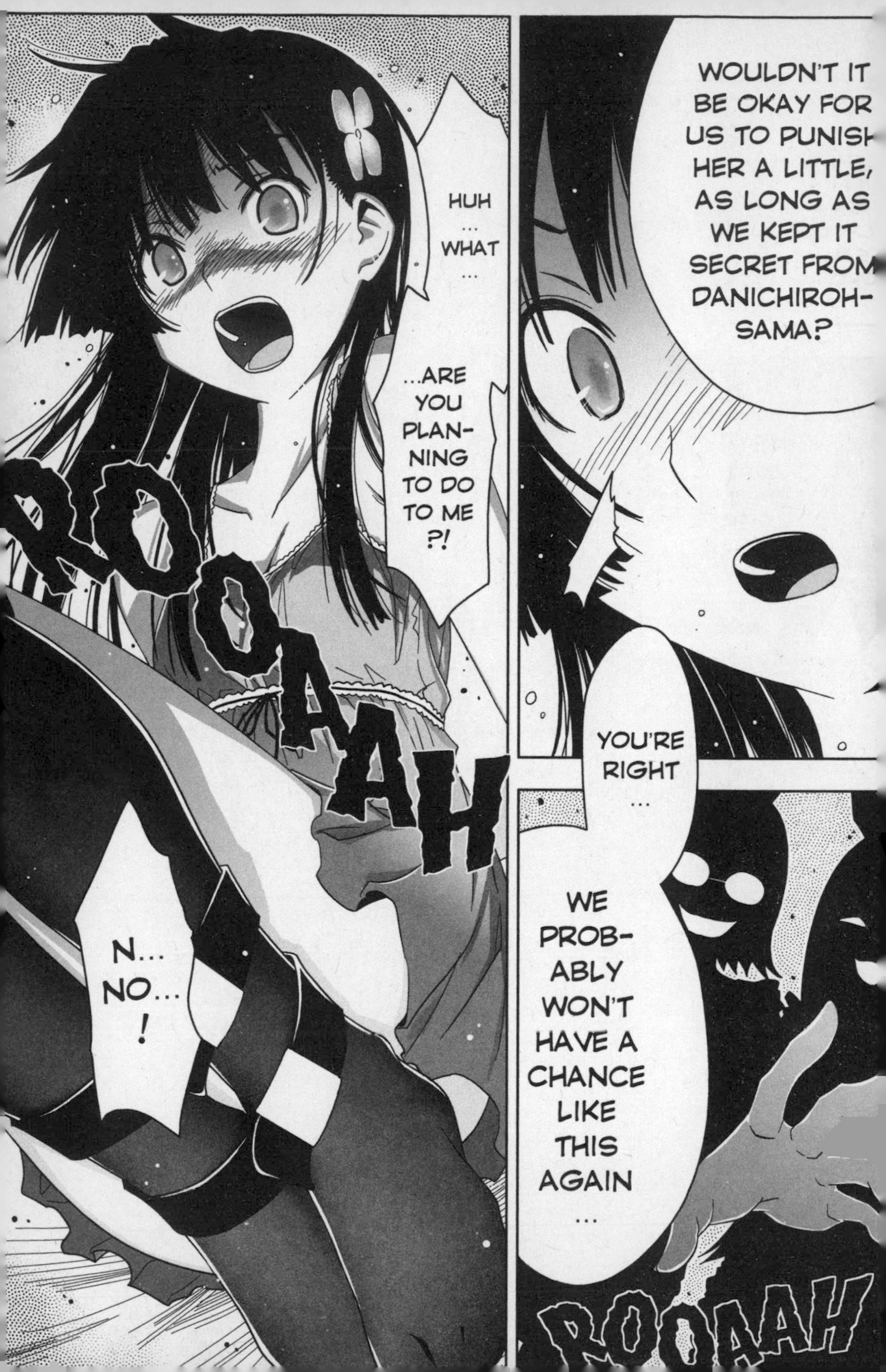
WOULDN'T IT BE OKAY FOR US TO PUNISH HER A LITTLE, AS LONG AS WE KEPT IT SECRET FROM DANICHIROH-SAMA?
YOU'RE RIGHT ...
WE PROBABLY WON'T HAVE A CHANCE LIKE THIS AGAIN ...
ROOAAH
HUH ... WHAT ...
...ARE YOU PLANNING TO DO TO ME ?!
ROOOAAH
N... NO... !

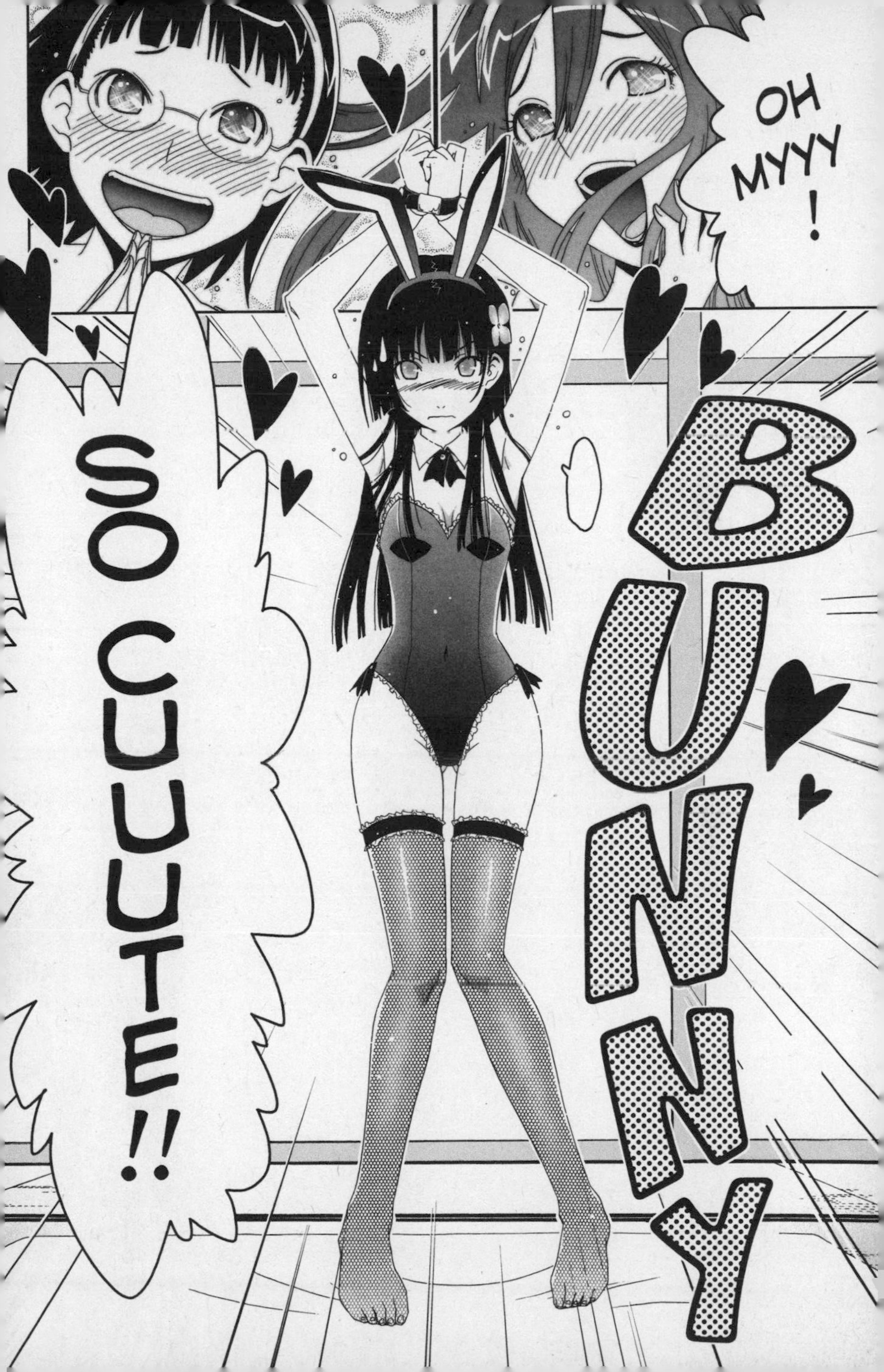
OH MYYY!
BUNNY
SO CUUUTE!!

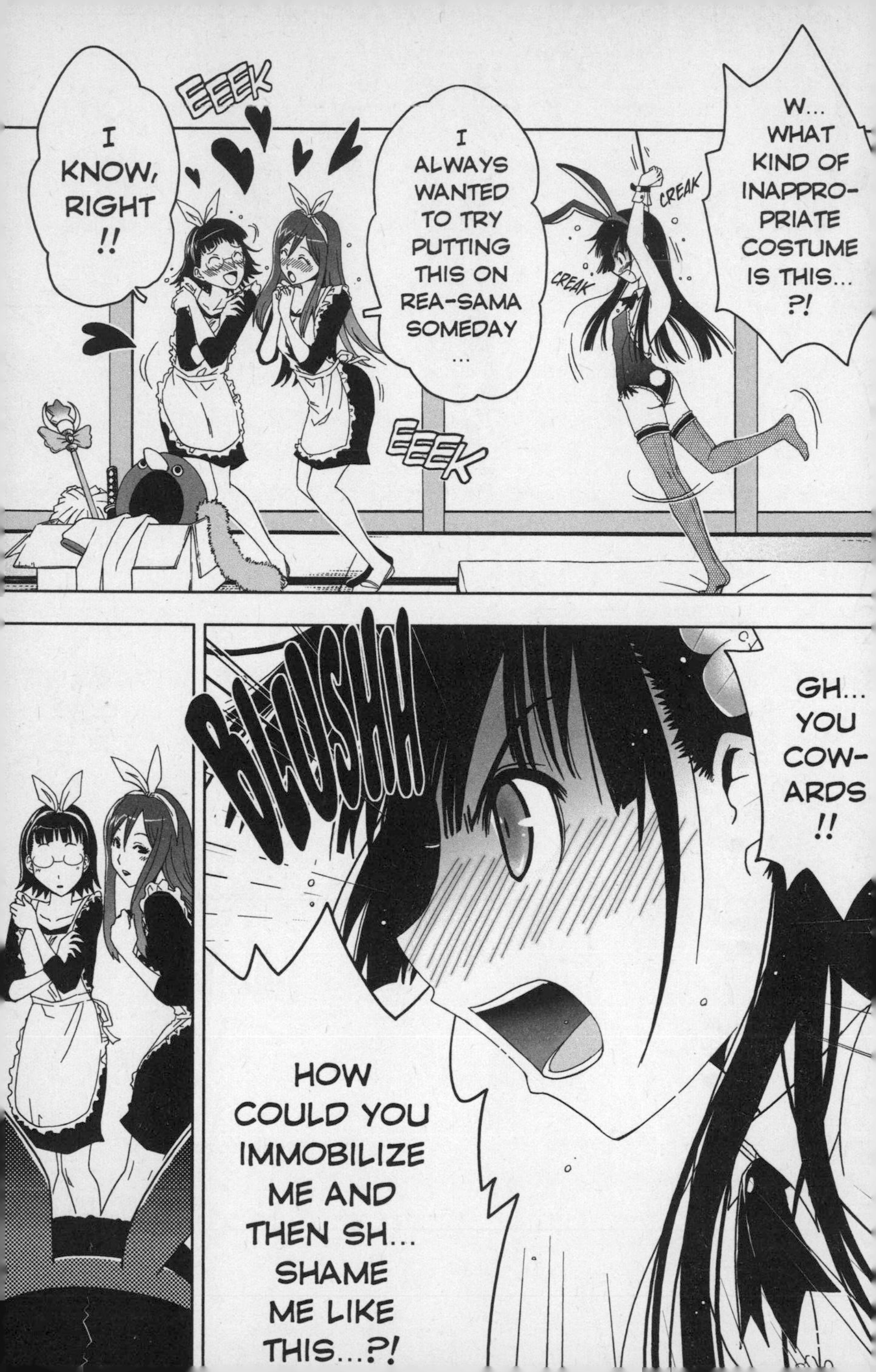
W... WHAT KIND OF INAPPROPRIATE COSTUME IS THIS...?!
CREAK
CREAK
I ALWAYS WANTED TO TRY PUTTING THIS ON REA-SAMA SOMEDAY...
EEEK
I KNOW, RIGHT!!
EEEK
GH... YOU COWARDS!!
BLUSHH
HOW COULD YOU IMMOBILIZE ME AND THEN SH... SHAME ME LIKE THIS...?!

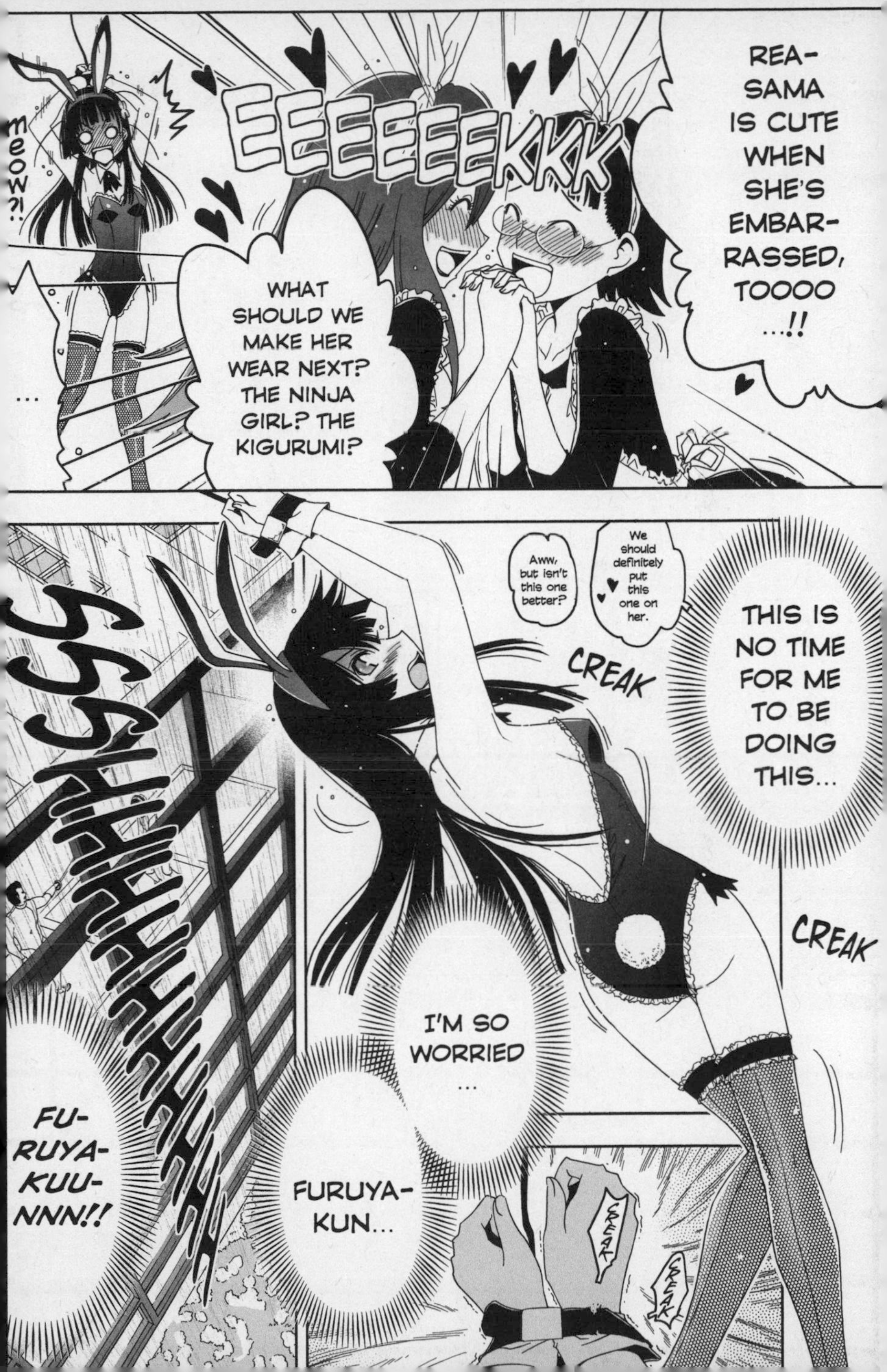
REA-SAMA IS CUTE WHEN SHE'S EMBARRASSED, TOOOO ...!!
EEEEEEEKKK
WHAT SHOULD WE MAKE HER WEAR NEXT? THE NINJA GIRL? THE KIGURUMI?
meow?!
...
We should definitely put this one on her.
Aww, but isn't this one better?
THIS IS NO TIME FOR ME TO BE DOING THIS...
CREAK
CREAK
I'M SO WORRIED ...
FURUYA-KUN...
CREAK
CREAK
SSSHHHHHHHHHHH
FU-RUYA-KUUN-NNN!!

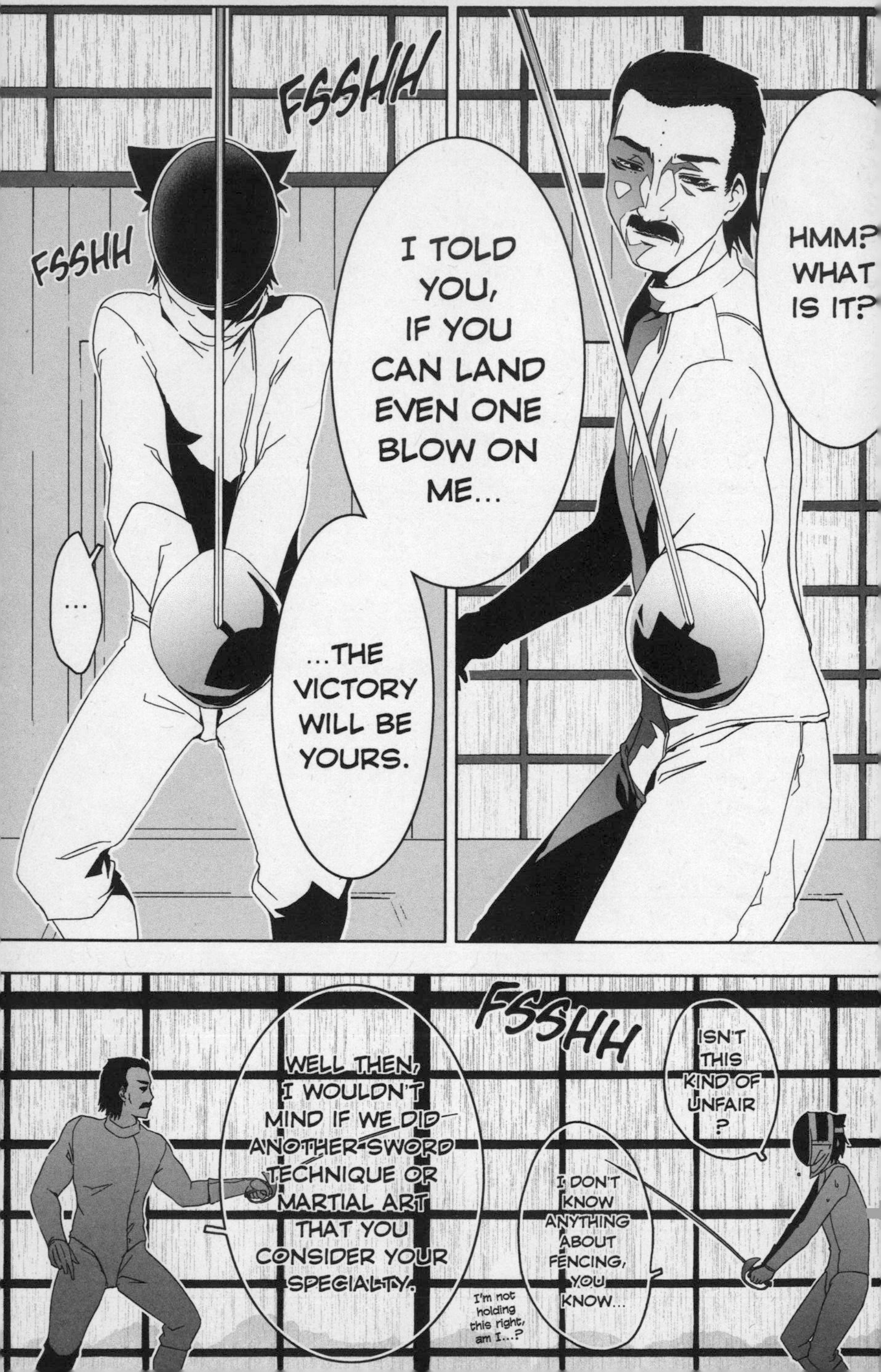
HMM? WHAT IS IT?
I TOLD YOU, IF YOU CAN LAND EVEN ONE BLOW ON ME...
FSSHH
FSSHH
...THE VICTORY WILL BE YOURS.
...
FSSHH
ISN'T THIS KIND OF UNFAIR ?
I DON'T KNOW ANYTHING ABOUT FENCING, YOU KNOW...
I'm not holding this right, am I...?
WELL THEN, I WOULDN'T MIND IF WE DID ANOTHER SWORD TECHNIQUE OR MARTIAL ART THAT YOU CONSIDER YOUR SPECIALTY.

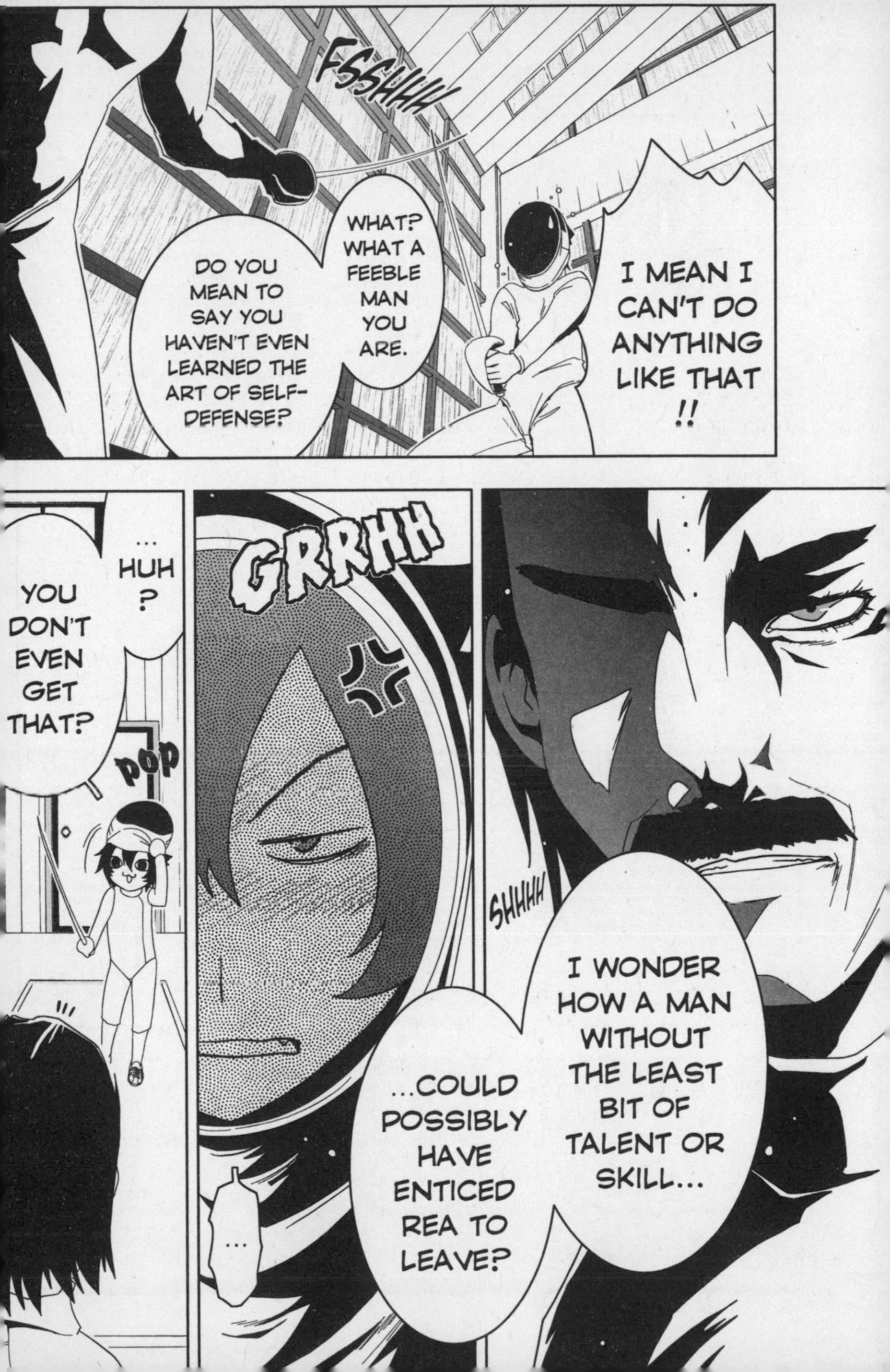
I MEAN I CAN'T DO ANYTHING LIKE THAT!!
FSSHHH
WHAT? WHAT A FEEBLE MAN YOU ARE.
DO YOU MEAN TO SAY YOU HAVEN'T EVEN LEARNED THE ART OF SELF-DEFENSE?
I WONDER HOW A MAN WITHOUT THE LEAST BIT OF TALENT OR SKILL...
...COULD POSSIBLY HAVE ENTICED REA TO LEAVE?
SHHHH
GRRHH
...
...HUH?
YOU DON'T EVEN GET THAT?
POP

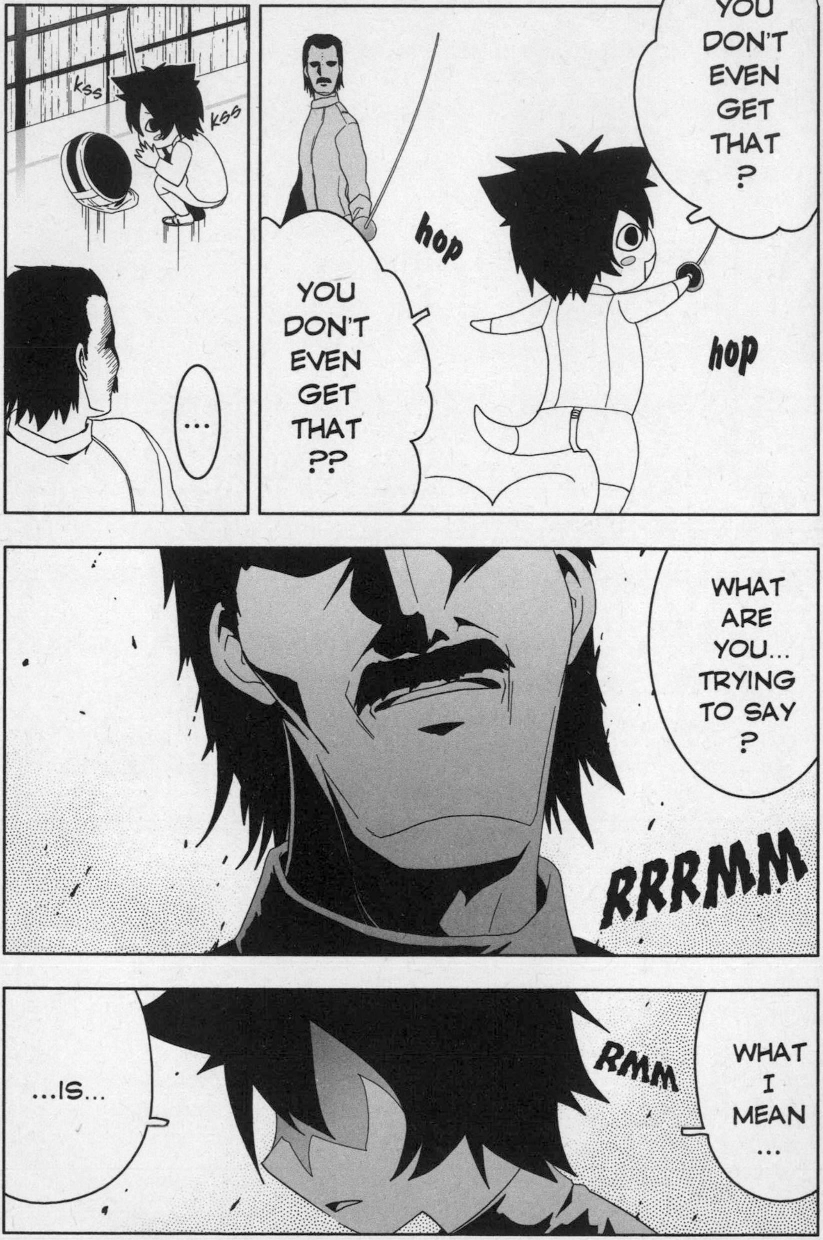
YOU DON'T EVEN GET THAT?
hop
YOU DON'T EVEN GET THAT??
hop
kss
kss
...
WHAT ARE YOU... TRYING TO SAY?
RRRMM
WHAT I MEAN...
RMM
...IS...

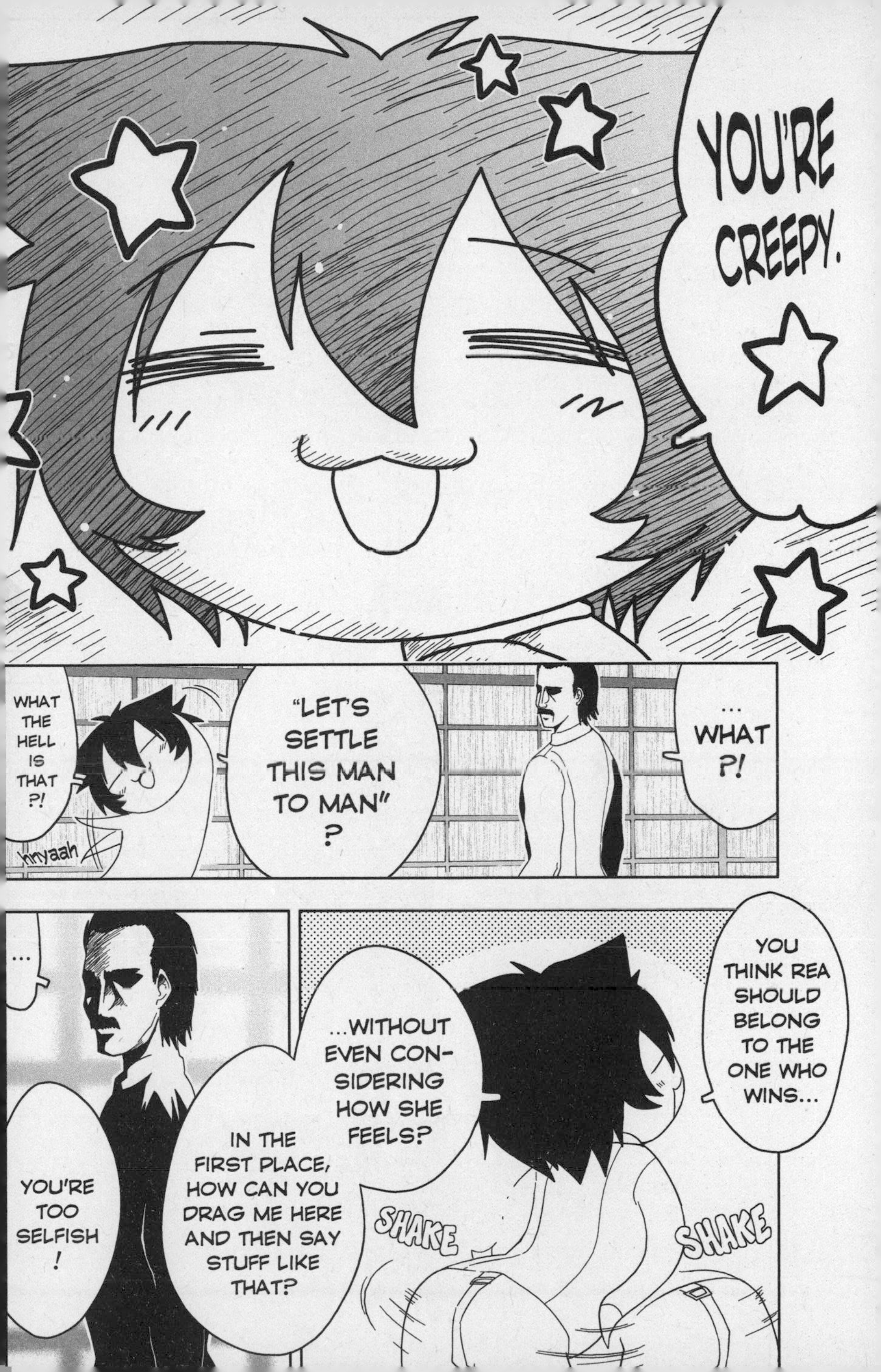
YOU'RE CREEPY.
... WHAT?!
"LET'S SETTLE THIS MAN TO MAN"?
WHAT THE HELL IS THAT?!
hnyaah
YOU THINK REA SHOULD BELONG TO THE ONE WHO WINS...
...WITHOUT EVEN CON-SIDERING HOW SHE FEELS?
IN THE FIRST PLACE, HOW CAN YOU DRAG ME HERE AND THEN SAY STUFF LIKE THAT?
SHAKE
SHAKE
...
YOU'RE TOO SELFISH!

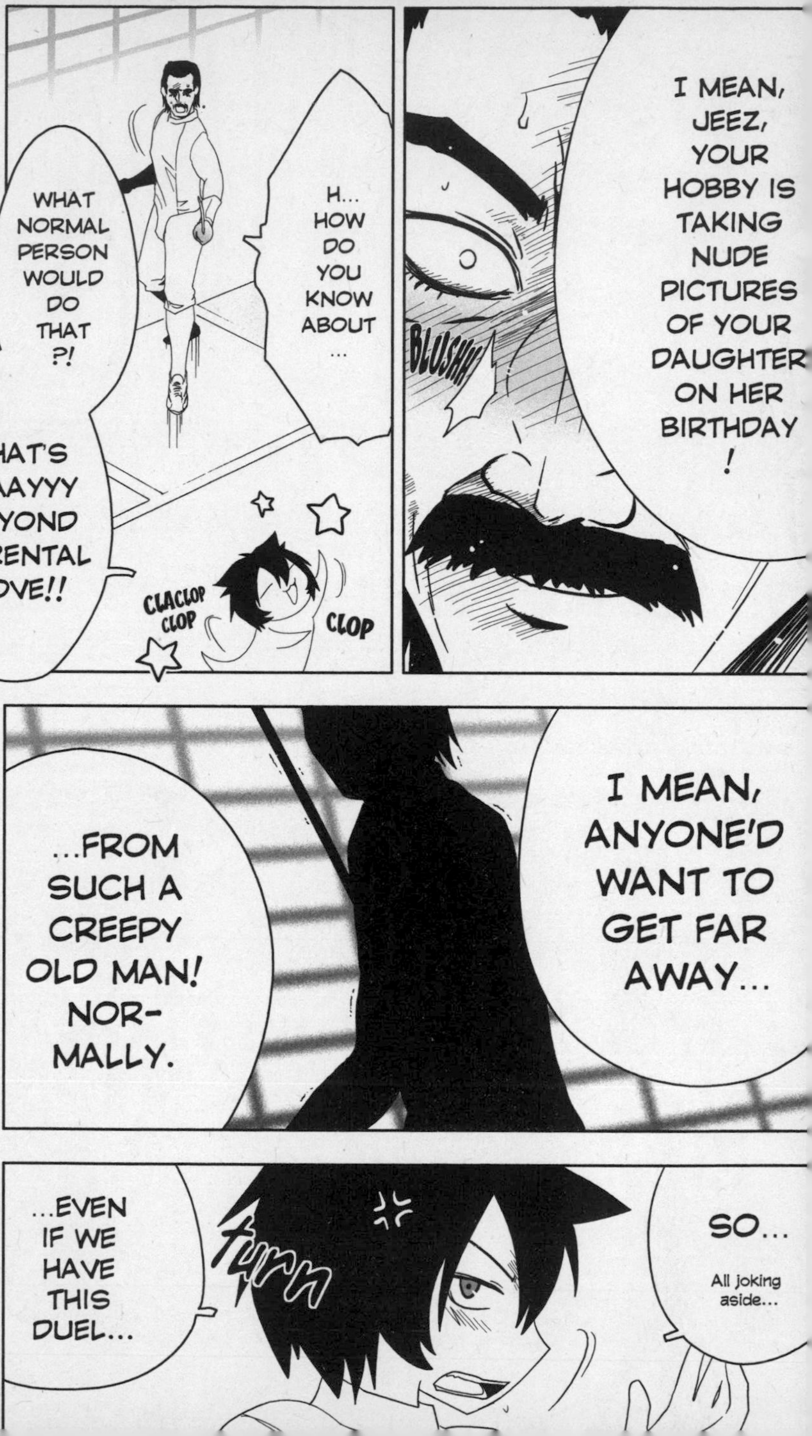
I MEAN, JEEZ, YOUR HOBBY IS TAKING NUDE PICTURES OF YOUR DAUGHTER ON HER BIRTHDAY!
BLUSH
H... HOW DO YOU KNOW ABOUT...
WHAT NORMAL PERSON WOULD DO THAT?!
THAT'S WAAYYY BEYOND PARENTAL LOVE!!
CLOP
CLACLOP CLOP
I MEAN, ANYONE'D WANT TO GET FAR AWAY...
...FROM SUCH A CREEPY OLD MAN! NOR-MALLY.
SO...
All joking aside...
turn
...EVEN IF WE HAVE THIS DUEL...

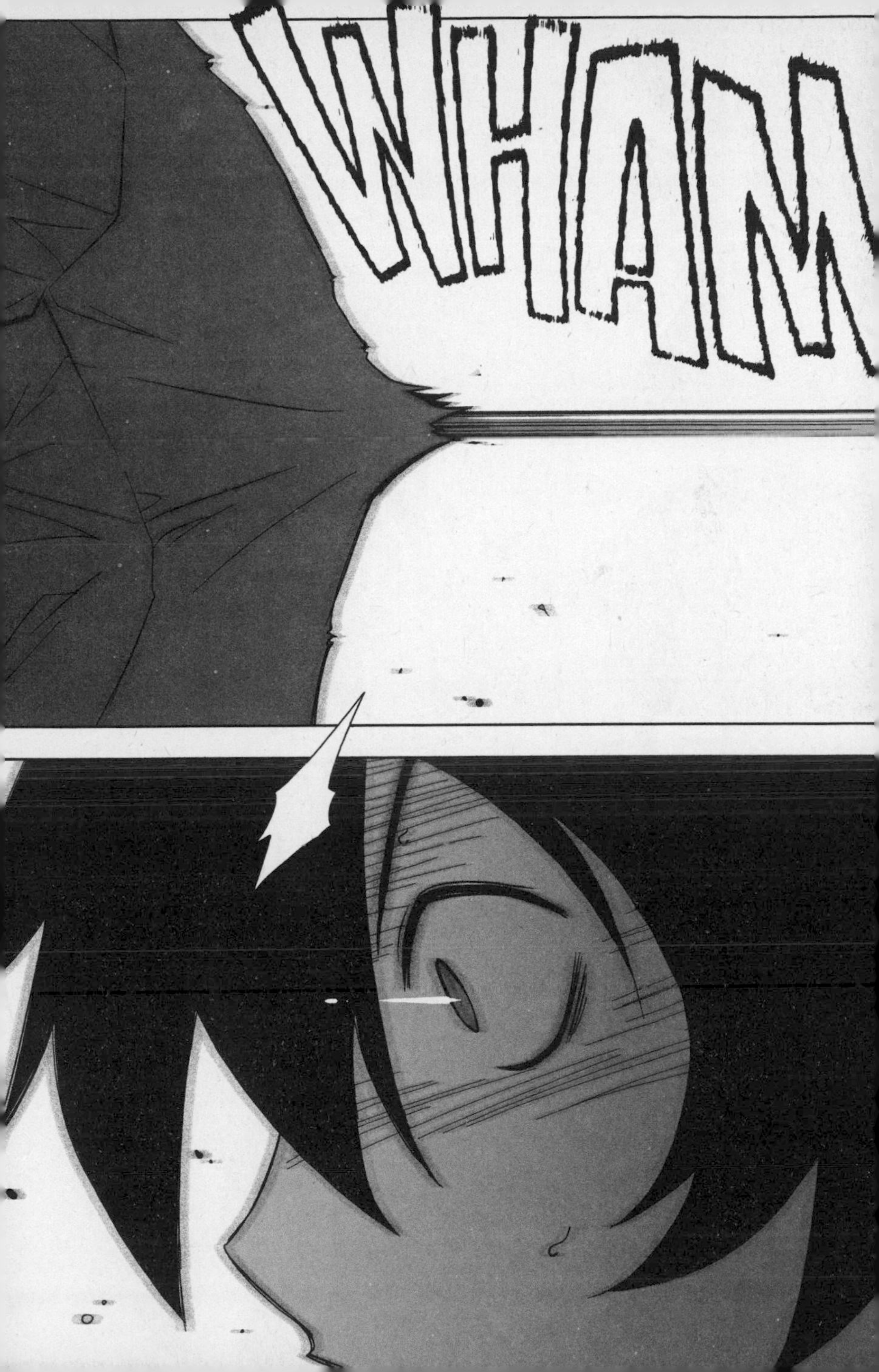
WHAM

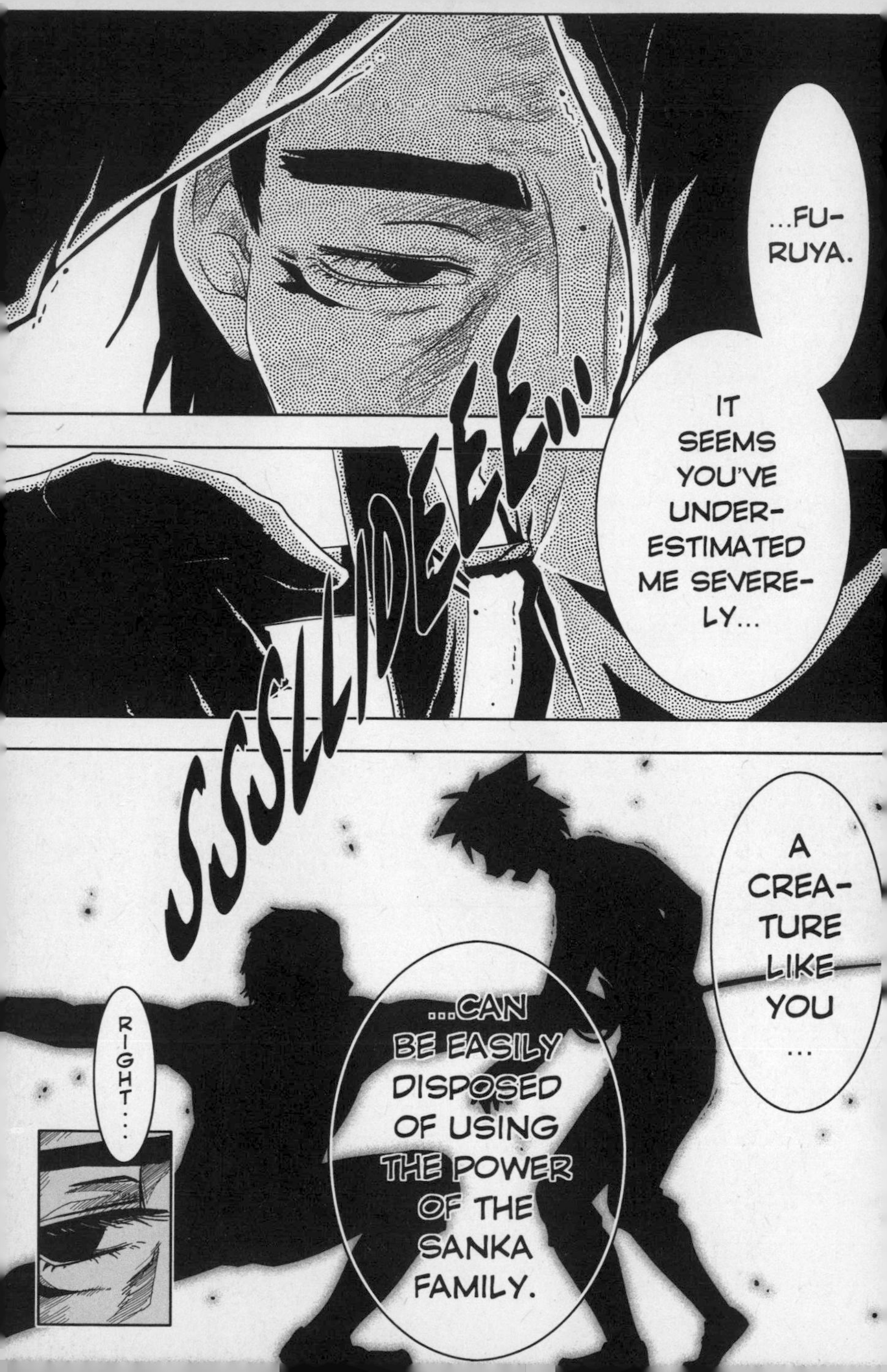
...FU-RUYA.
IT SEEMS YOU'VE UNDER-ESTIMATED ME SEVERE-LY...
SSSLIDEEE...
A CREA-TURE LIKE YOU...
...CAN BE EASILY DISPOSED OF USING THE POWER OF THE SANKA FAMILY.
RIGHT...

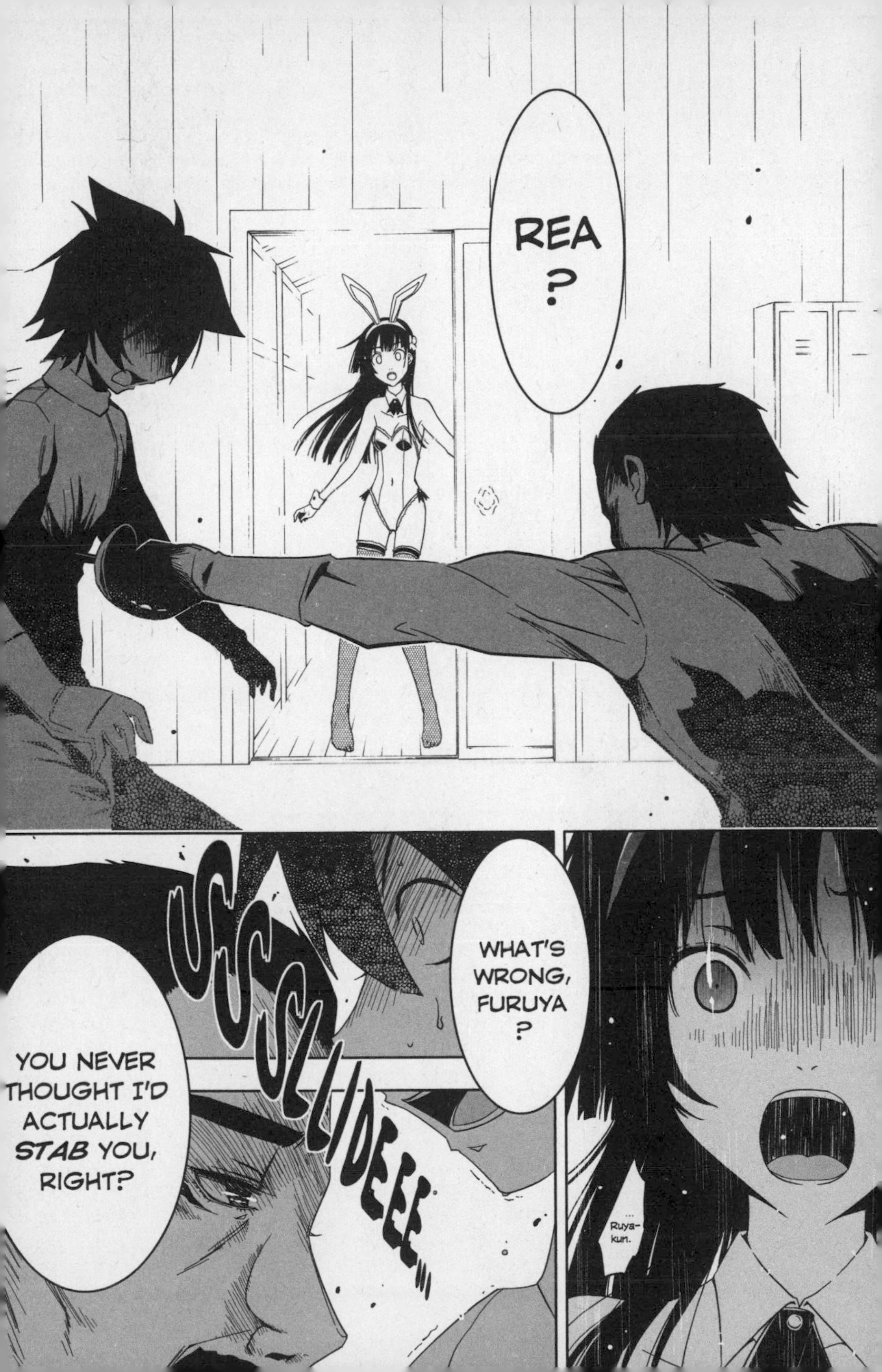
REA?
... Ruya-kun.
WHAT'S WRONG, FURUYA?
SSSLIDEEE...
YOU NEVER THOUGHT I'D ACTUALLY *STAB* YOU, RIGHT?

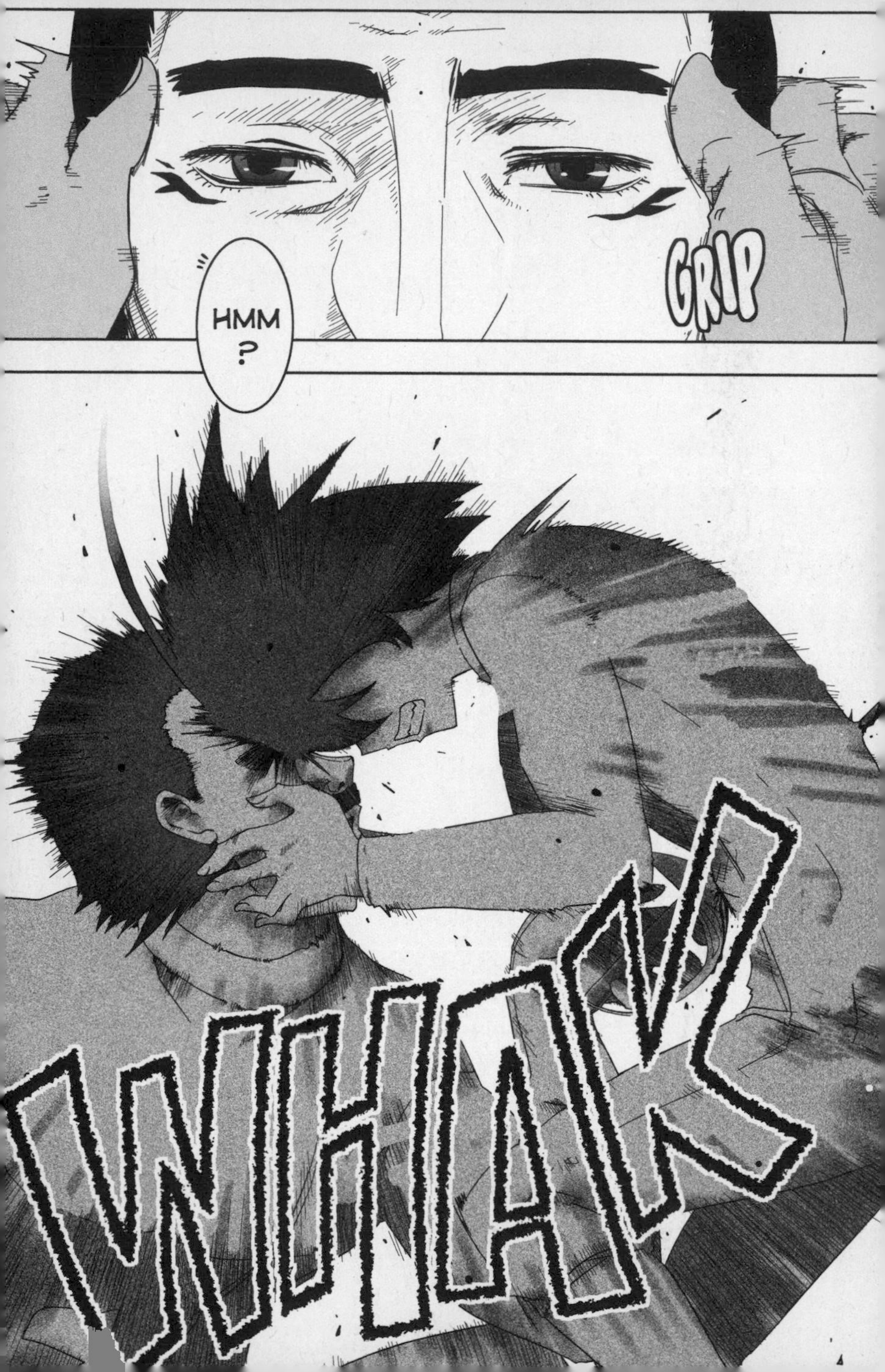
GRIP
HMM ?
WHAK

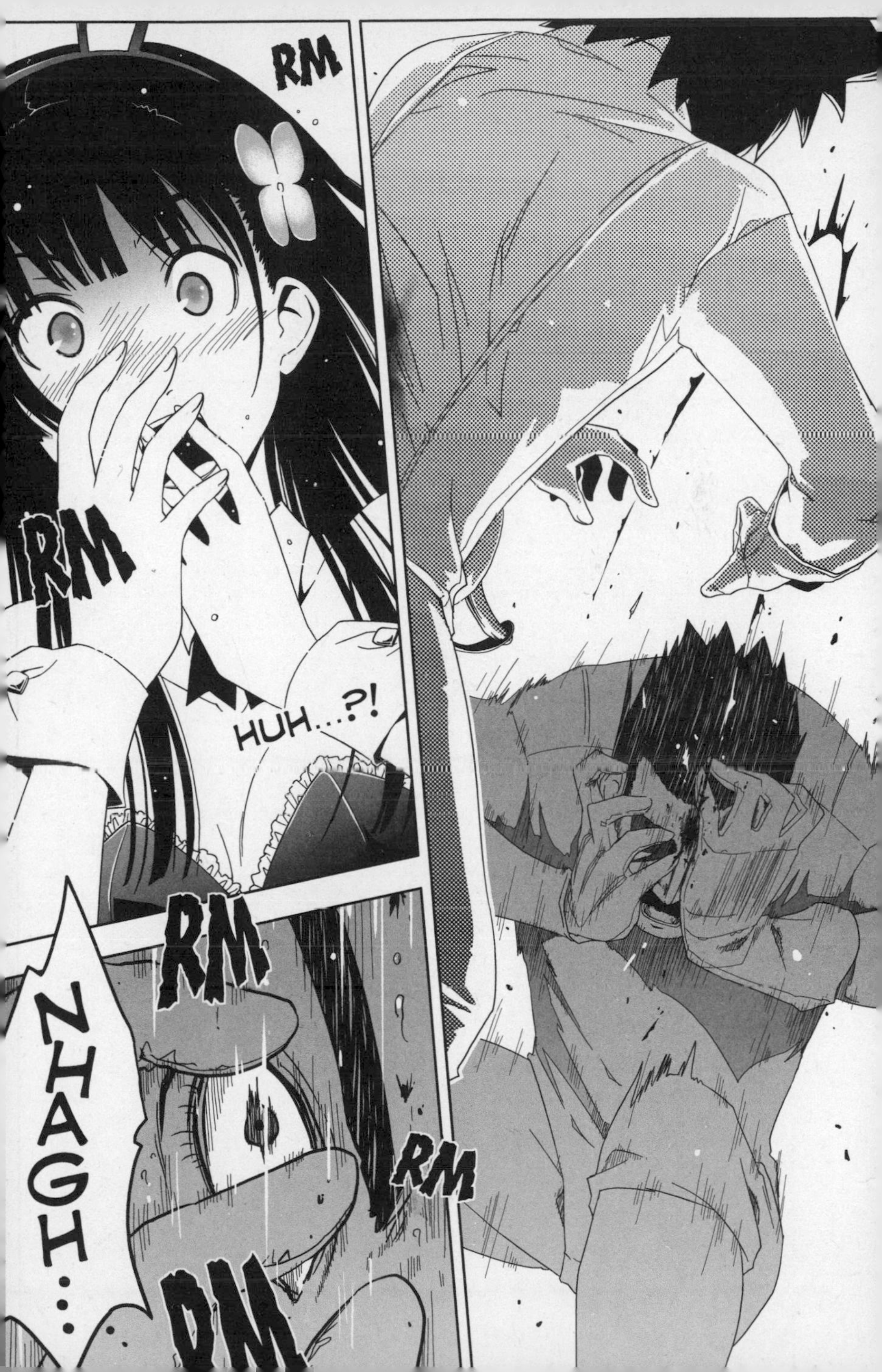
RM
RM
HUH...?!
RM
NHAGH...
RM
RM

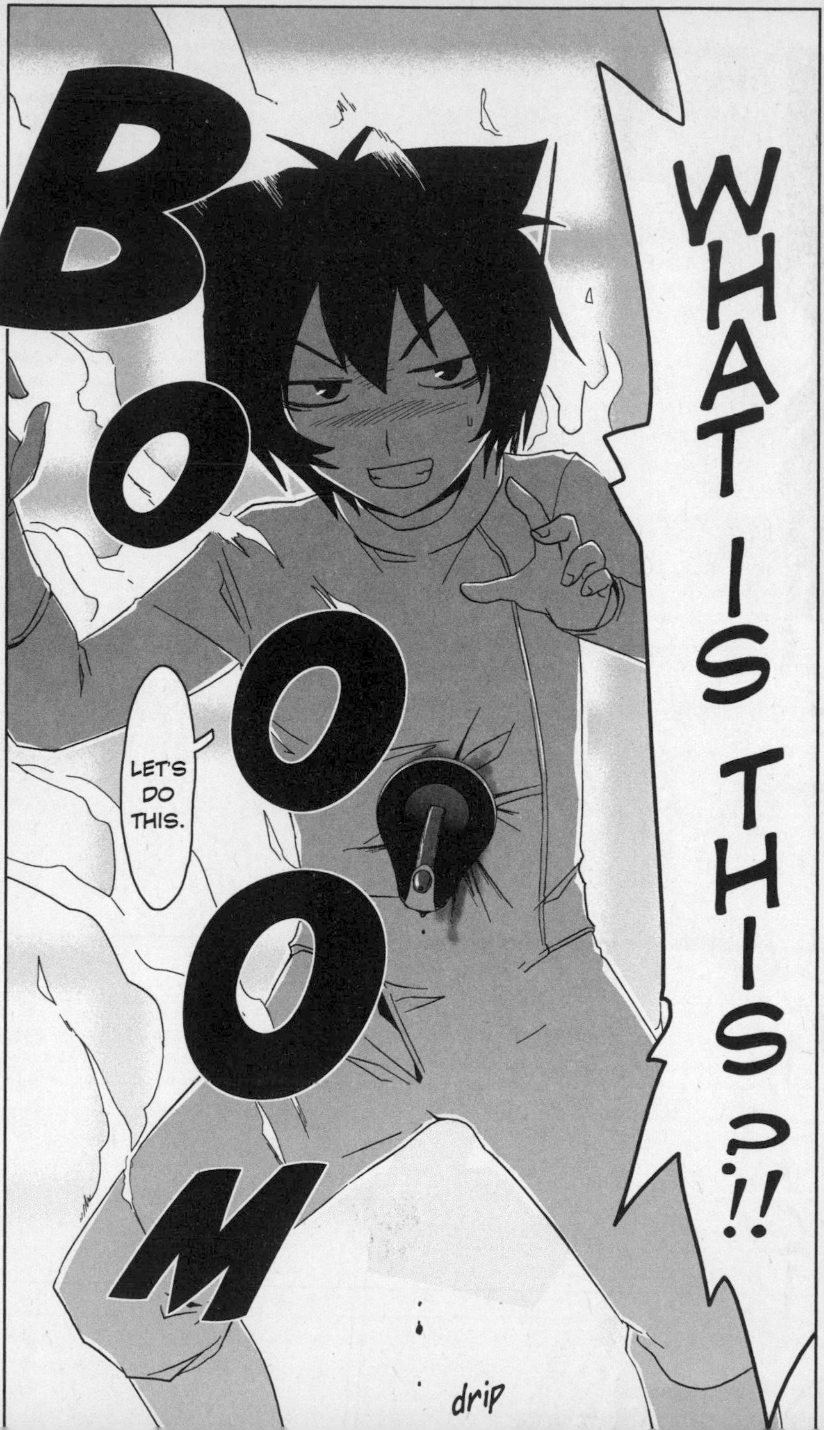
WHAT IS THIS?!!
BOOOOM
LET'S DO THIS.
drip

SANKAREA ANECDOTES 3

About Rea and the story

Vhen you take off the cover of volume one (the Japanese edition), the initial haracter settings are printed there, but actually that Rea was from when the story and irection of the character were already rather solidified. It took quite a while to get to that oint! And so here I'd like to present to everyone, in rough form, the changes both Rea and the story vent through. They're completely different, and it's rather interesting. (Heh!)

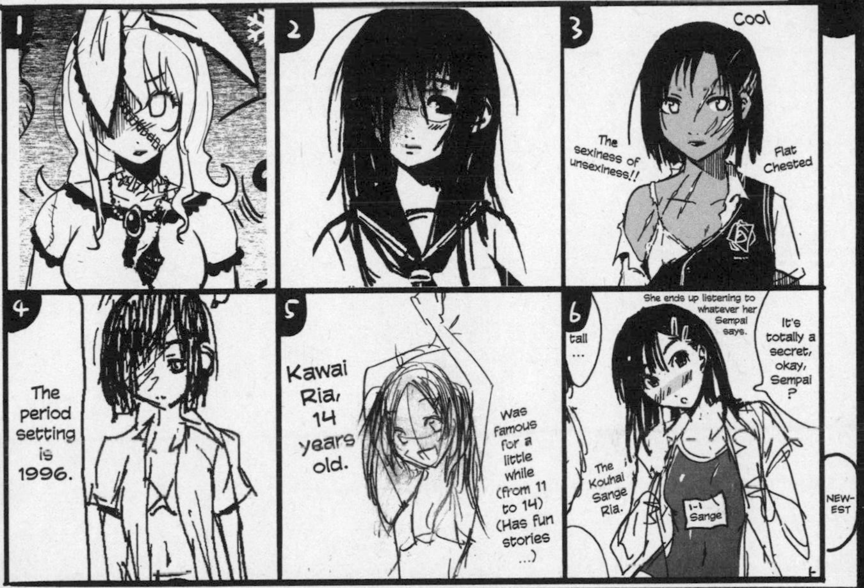
1
2
3
Cool
The sexiness of unsexiness!!
Flat Chested
4
The period setting is 1996.
5
Kawai Ria, 14 years old.
Was famous for a little while (from 11 to 14) (Has fun stories ...)
6
She ends up listening to whatever her Sempai says.
tall ...
It's totally a secret, okay, Sempai?
The Kouhai Sange Ria.
1-1 Sange
NEW-EST

1: The very first design. At this time I was still trying to create a work along the lines of a "zombie fairytale." I do like his one as it is.

2: When I gave up the zombie fairytale and decided to set it in the modern era, I drew this without any real ideas. Anyway, I decided on black hair here.

3: Um... I was trying to make this a battle action story? (Heh.)

4: The basic plot is that due to a natural disaster, a certain city within the Tokyo region becomes a separate island. While exploring the ruins there, the characters happen to meet zombies. The female friend gets bitten. The city is soon overrun by zombies... it was a story with kind of a classic feeling. I thought, "What's the point of even writing something like this nowadays?"... and so I dropped it.

5: A girl who used to be a wild junior idol hides that fact and goes to school, but the main character finds her out... and that was the setting. Huh? What happened to the zombies?

6: Finally you can begin to see a hint of Rea... but I was concerned about how to involve the zombie aspect of the story, so I got stuck. Then, as I wrote in the prior anecdote, I finally arrived at the initial setting from Volume 1 because I went on that spontaneous trip.

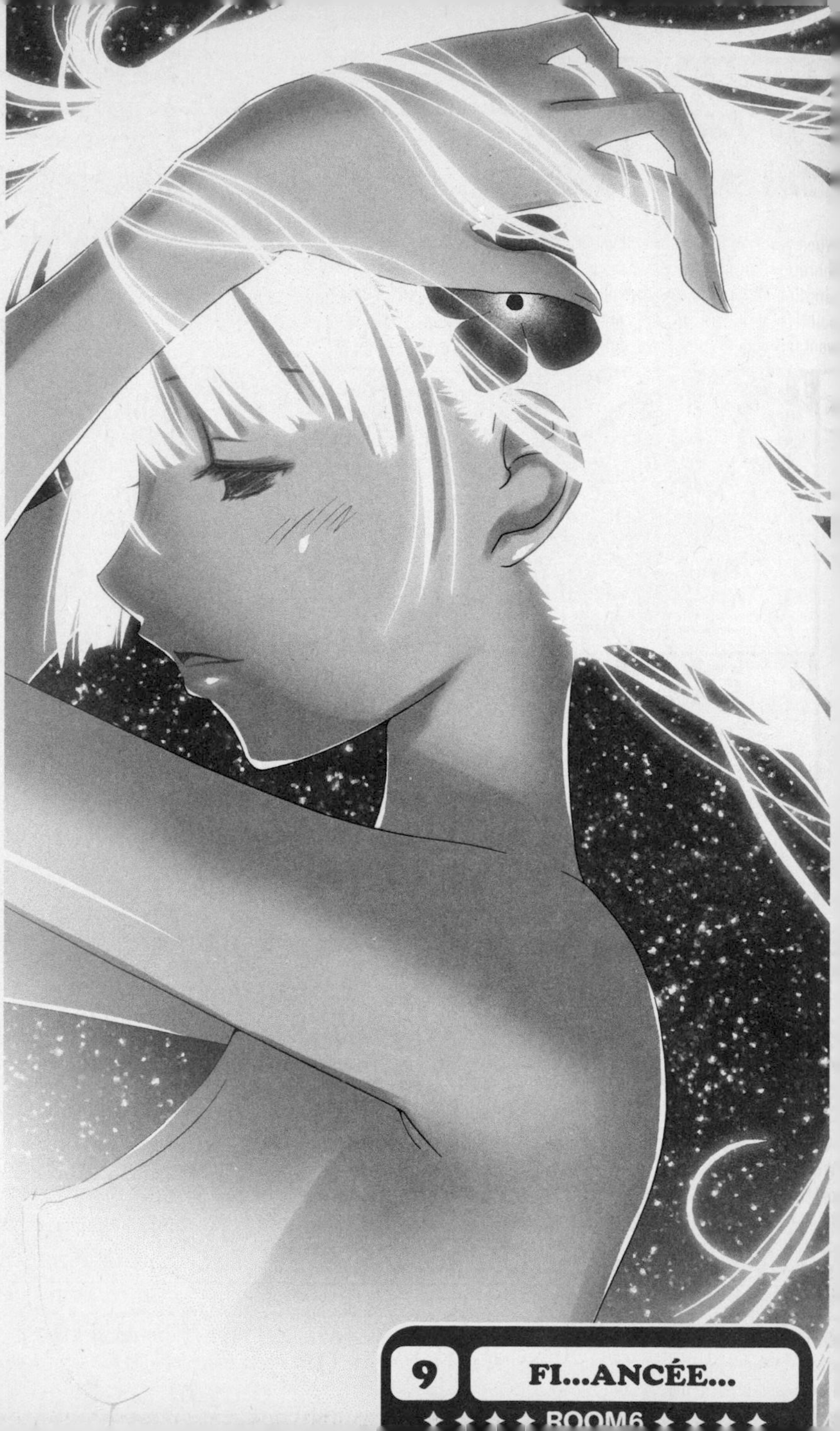

9 FI...ANCÉE...

ROOM6

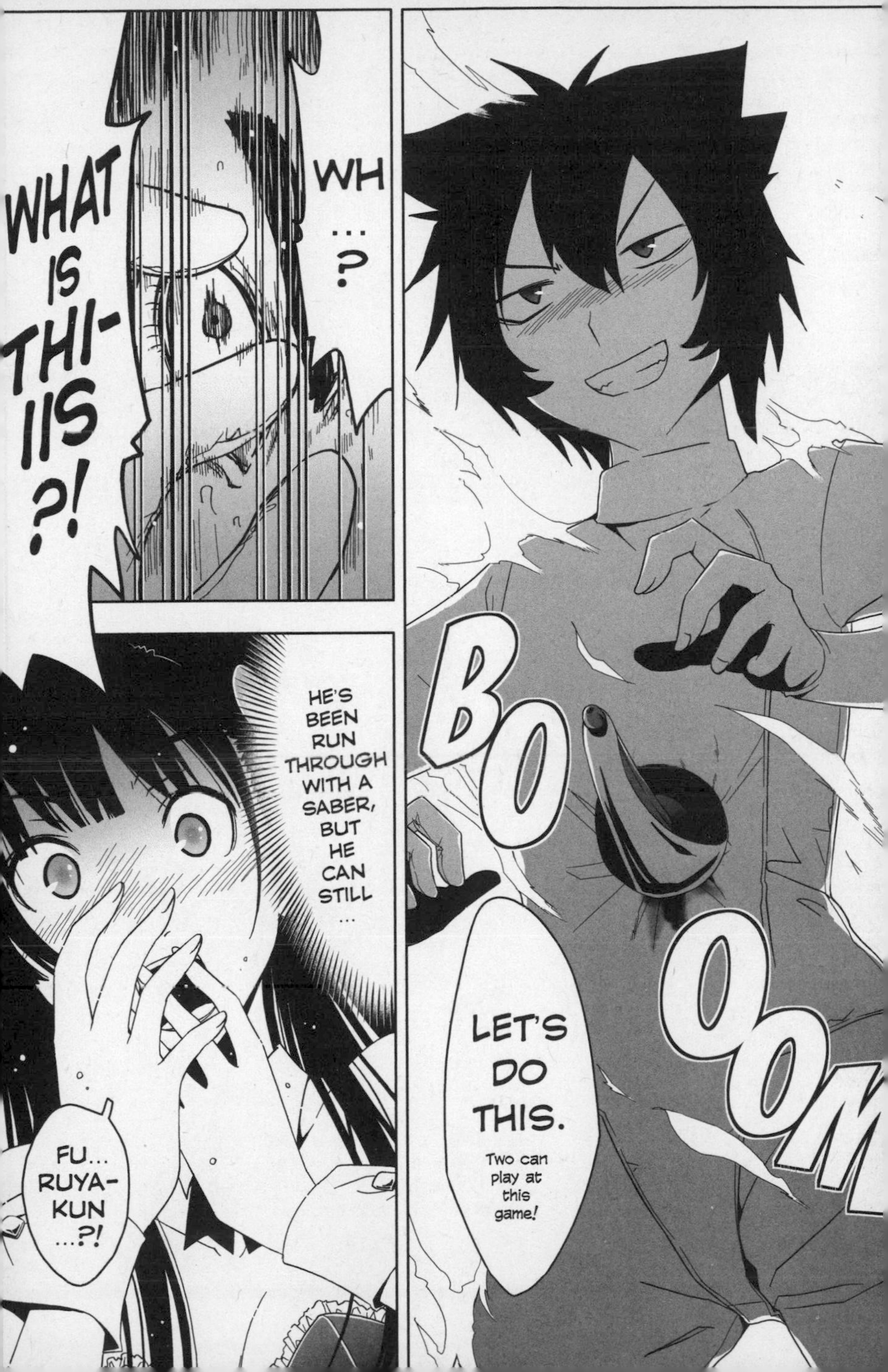
BOOOM
LET'S DO THIS.
Two can play at this game!
WH ... ?
WHAT IS THI-IIS ?!
HE'S BEEN RUN THROUGH WITH A SABER, BUT HE CAN STILL ...
FU... RUYA-KUN ...?!

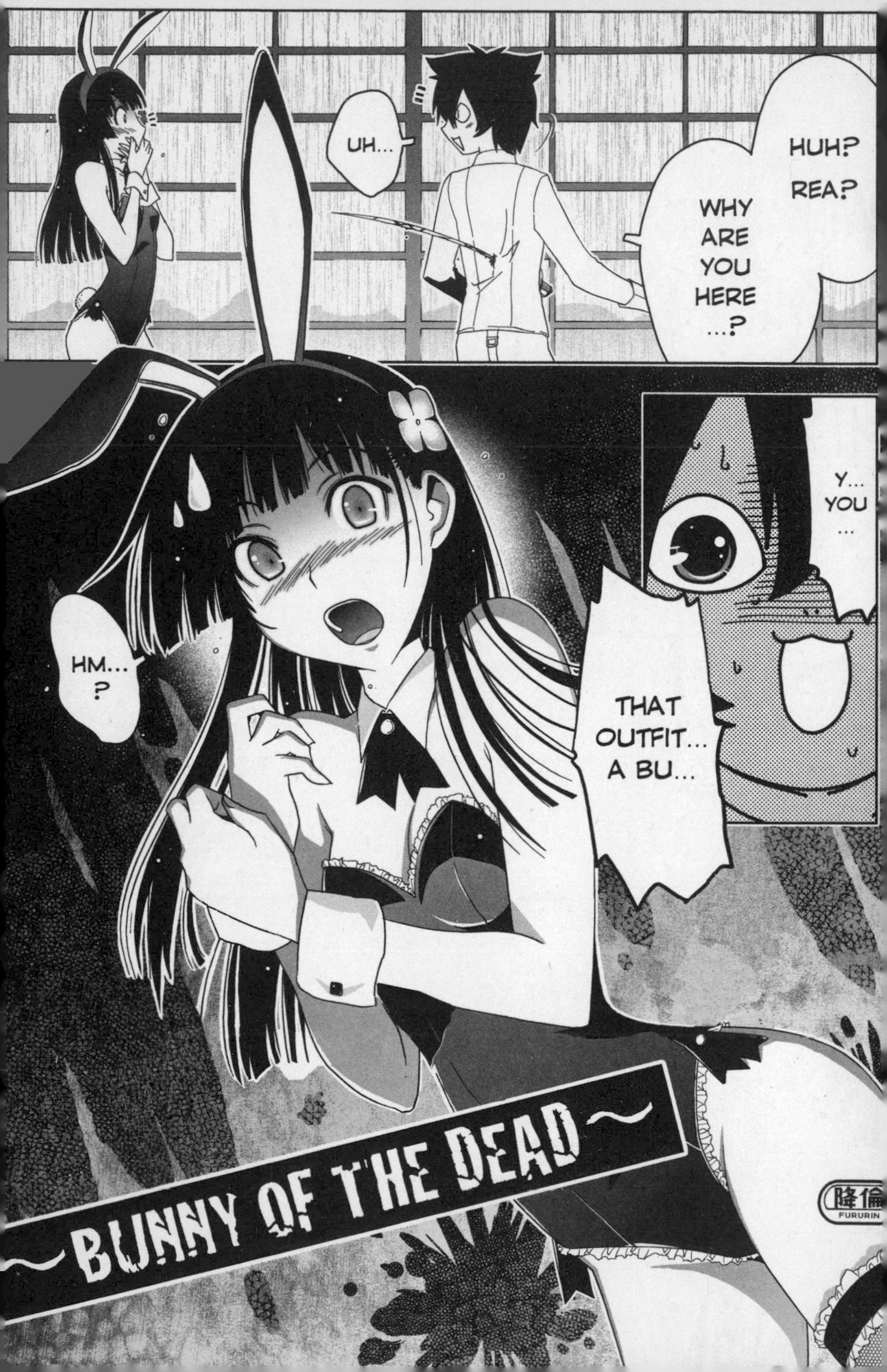
HUH? REA? WHY ARE YOU HERE ...?
UH...
Y... YOU ...
THAT OUTFIT... A BU...
HM... ?
降倫 FURURIN
~BUNNY OF THE DEAD~

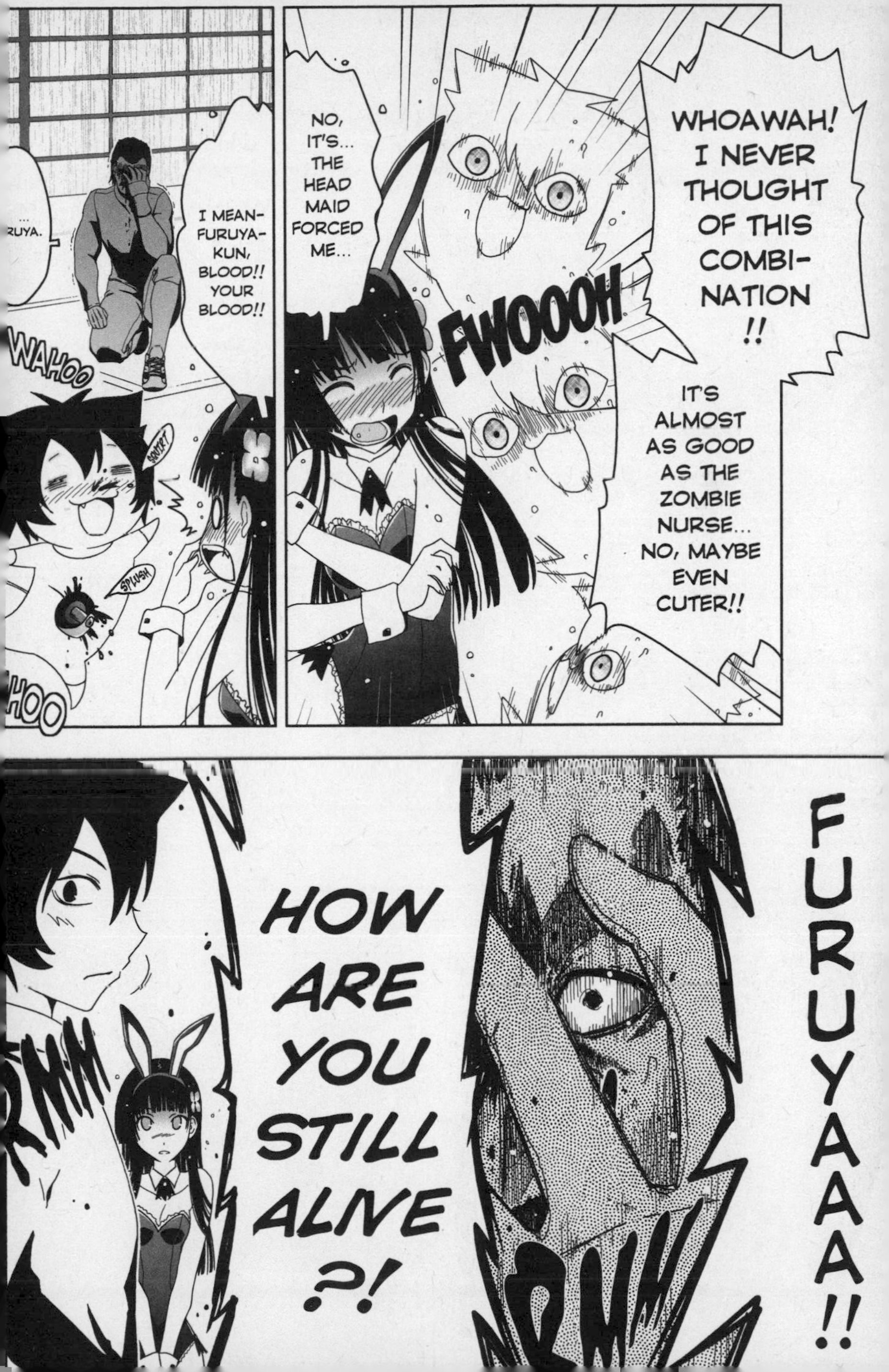
WHOAWAH! I NEVER THOUGHT OF THIS COMBI-NATION!!
IT'S ALMOST AS GOOD AS THE ZOMBIE NURSE... NO, MAYBE EVEN CUTER!!
FWOOOH
NO, IT'S... THE HEAD MAID FORCED ME...
I MEAN-FURUYA-KUN, BLOOD!! YOUR BLOOD!!
WAHOO
SQUIRT
SPLUSH
FURUYAAA!!
HOW ARE YOU STILL ALIVE?!

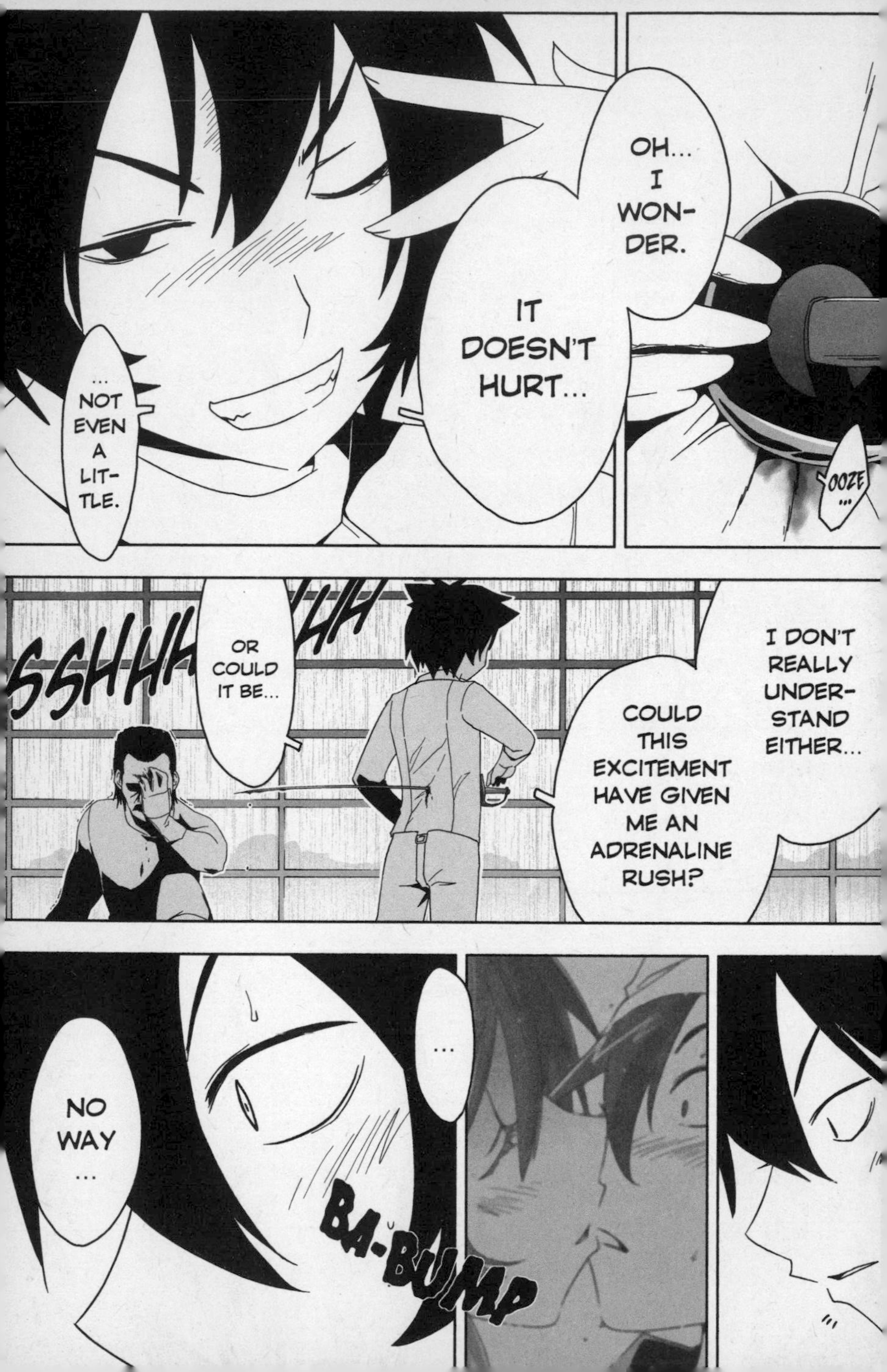
OOZE...
OH... I WONDER.
IT DOESN'T HURT...
...NOT EVEN A LITTLE.
I DON'T REALLY UNDERSTAND EITHER...
COULD THIS EXCITEMENT HAVE GIVEN ME AN ADRENALINE RUSH?
OR COULD IT BE...
SSHHHHHH
...
NO WAY...
BA-BUMP

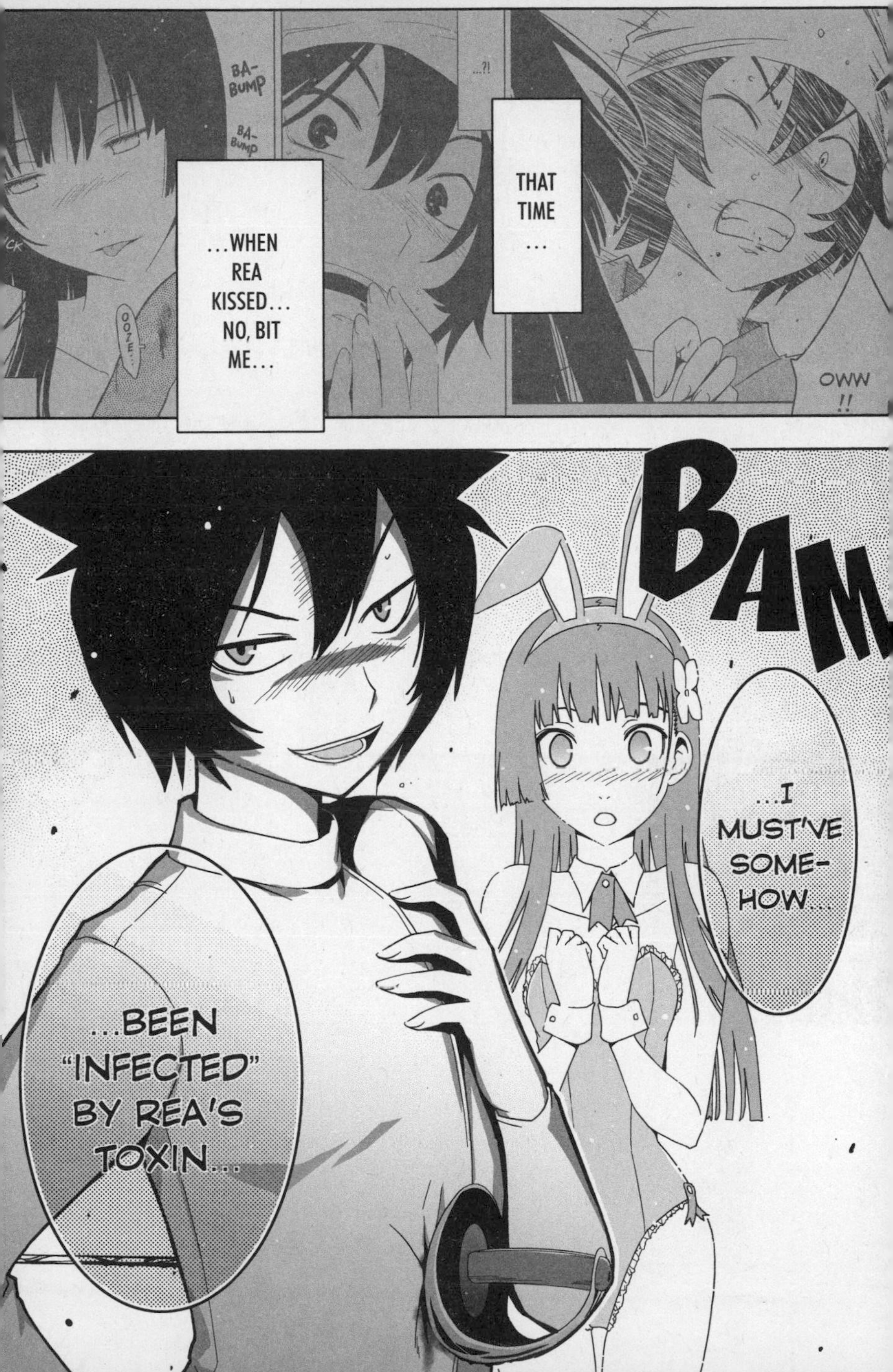
OWW!!
THAT TIME...
...?!
...WHEN REA KISSED... NO, BIT ME...
BA-BUMP
BA-BUMP
OOZE...
BAM
...I MUST'VE SOME-HOW...
...BEEN "INFECTED" BY REA'S TOXIN...

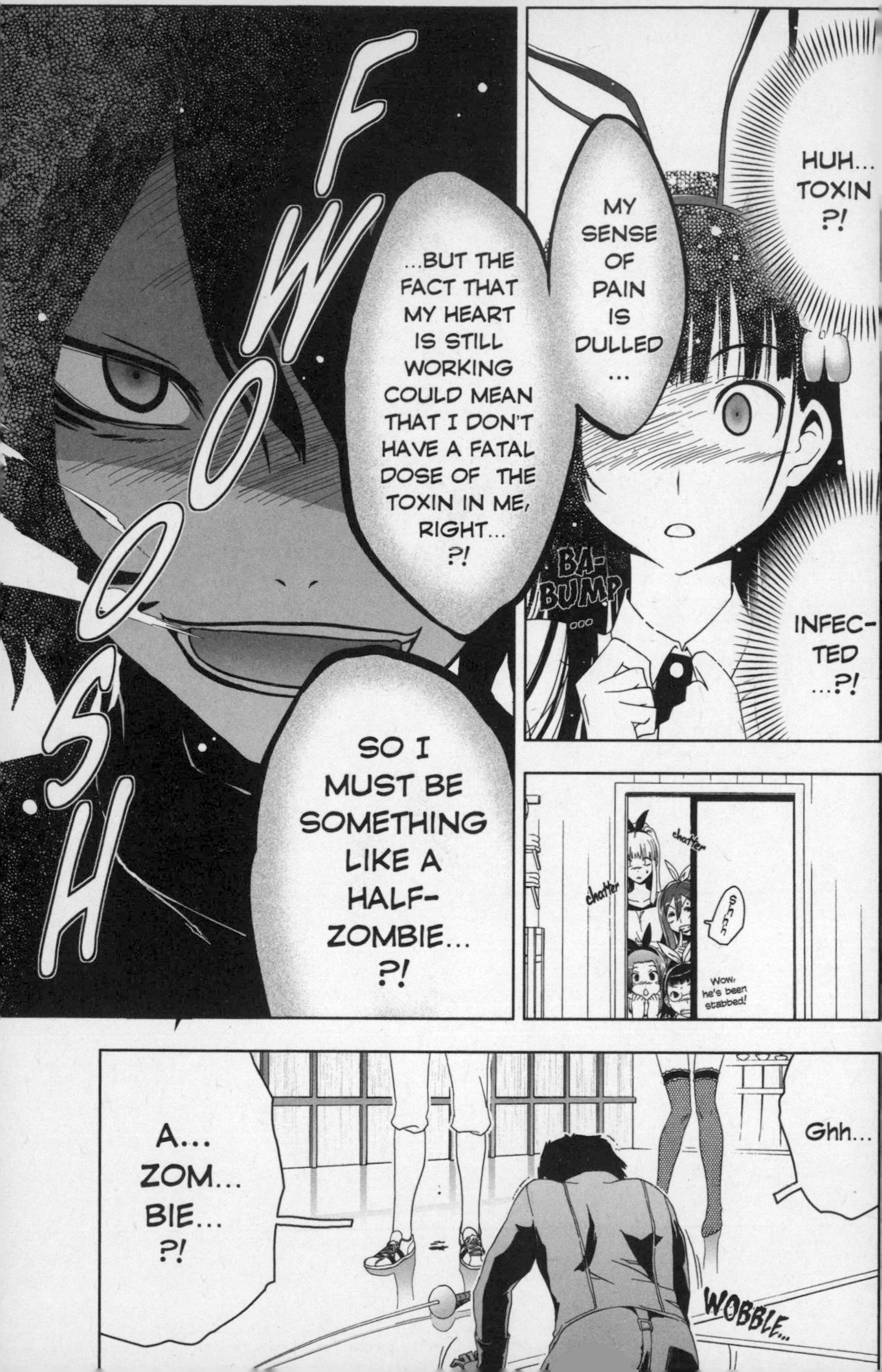
HUH... TOXIN ?!
MY SENSE OF PAIN IS DULLED ...
BA-BUMP
INFECTED ...?!
chatter
Shhh
chatter
Wow, he's been stabbed!
...BUT THE FACT THAT MY HEART IS STILL WORKING COULD MEAN THAT I DON'T HAVE A FATAL DOSE OF THE TOXIN IN ME, RIGHT... ?!
SO I MUST BE SOMETHING LIKE A HALF-ZOMBIE... ?!
FWOOOOSH
Ghh...
A... ZOM... BIE... ?!
WOBBLE...

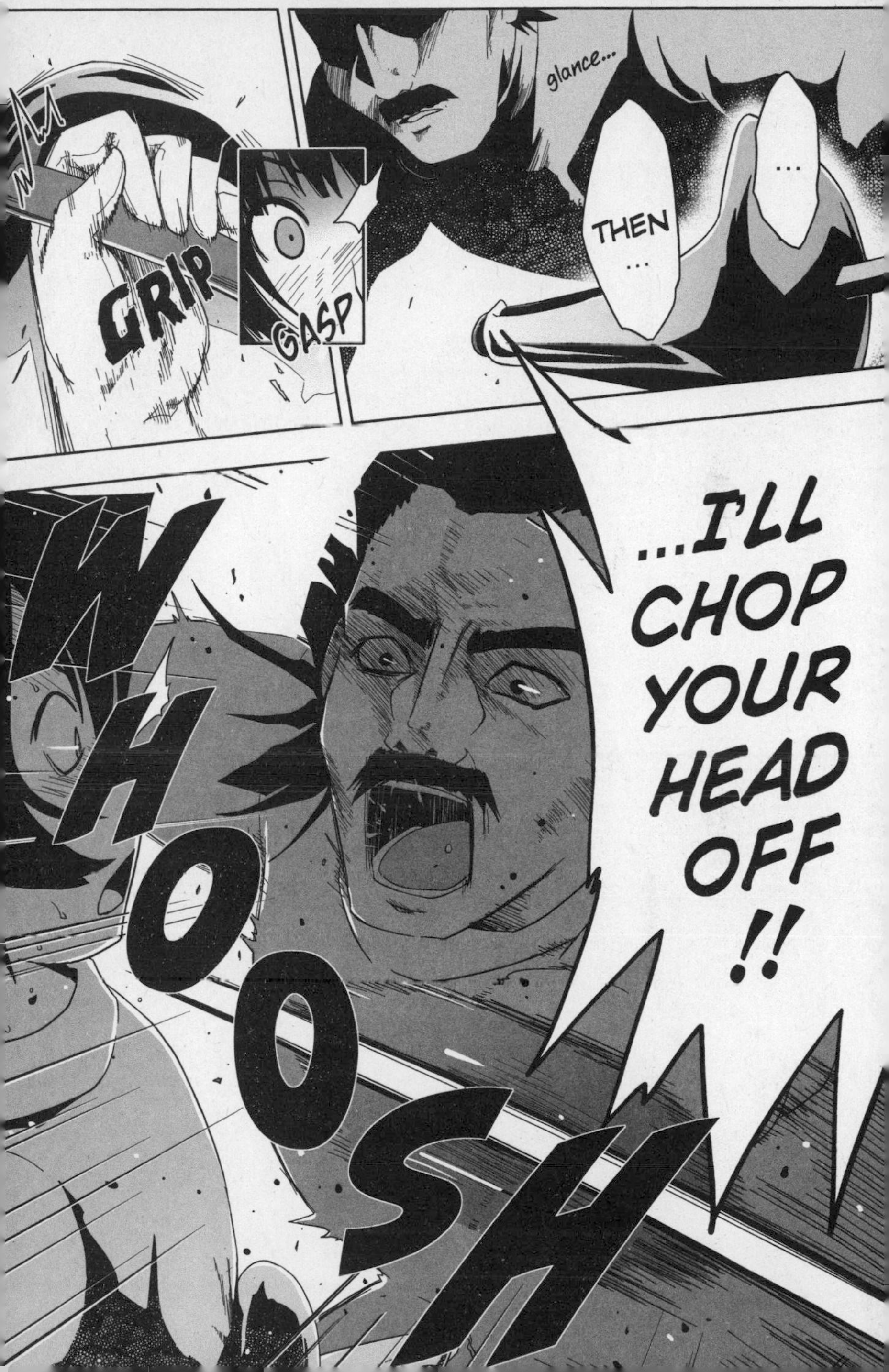
glance...
...
THEN ...
GASP
GRIP
...I'LL CHOP YOUR HEAD OFF!!
WHOOSH

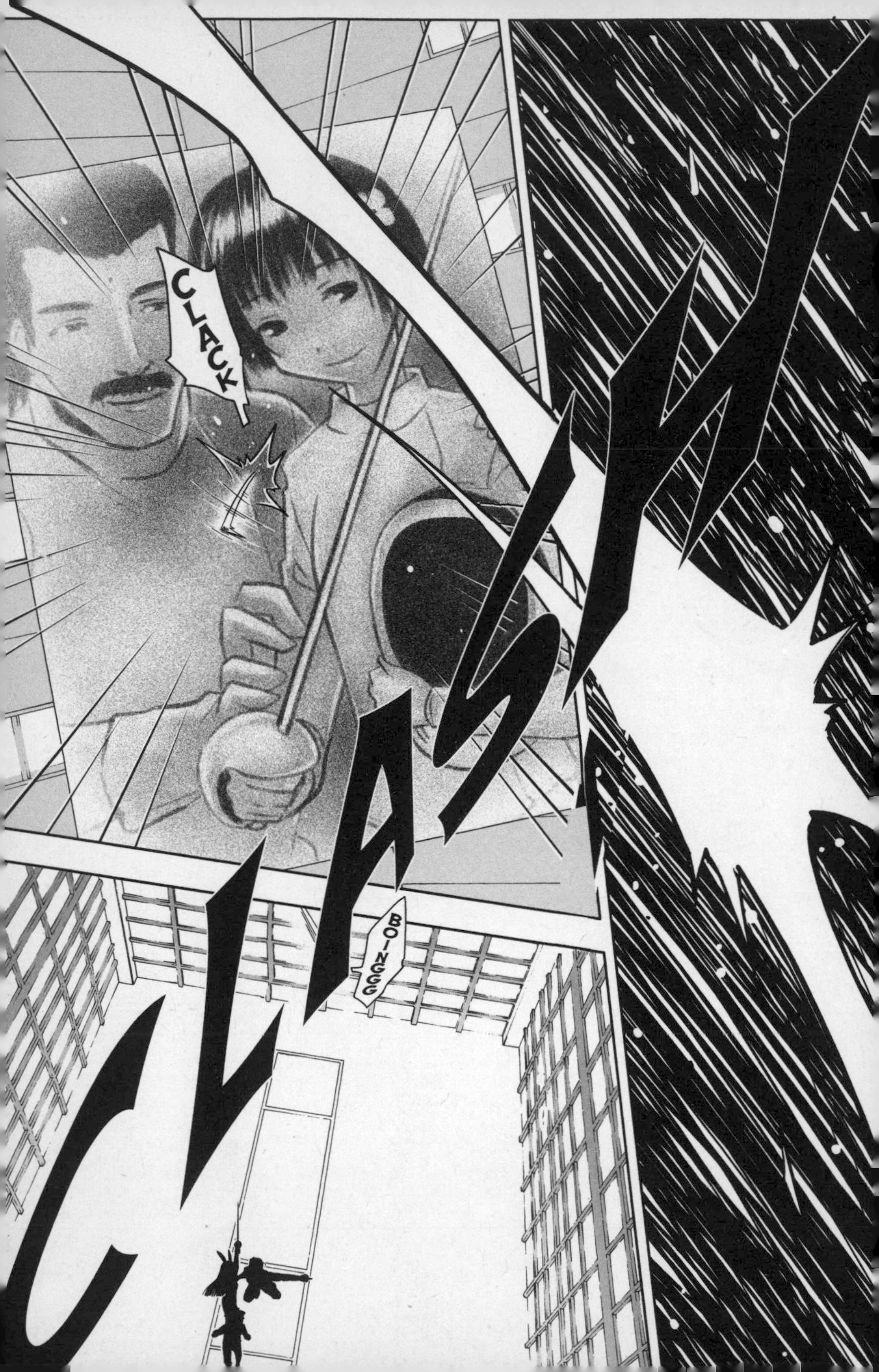
CLASH
CLACK
BOINGGG

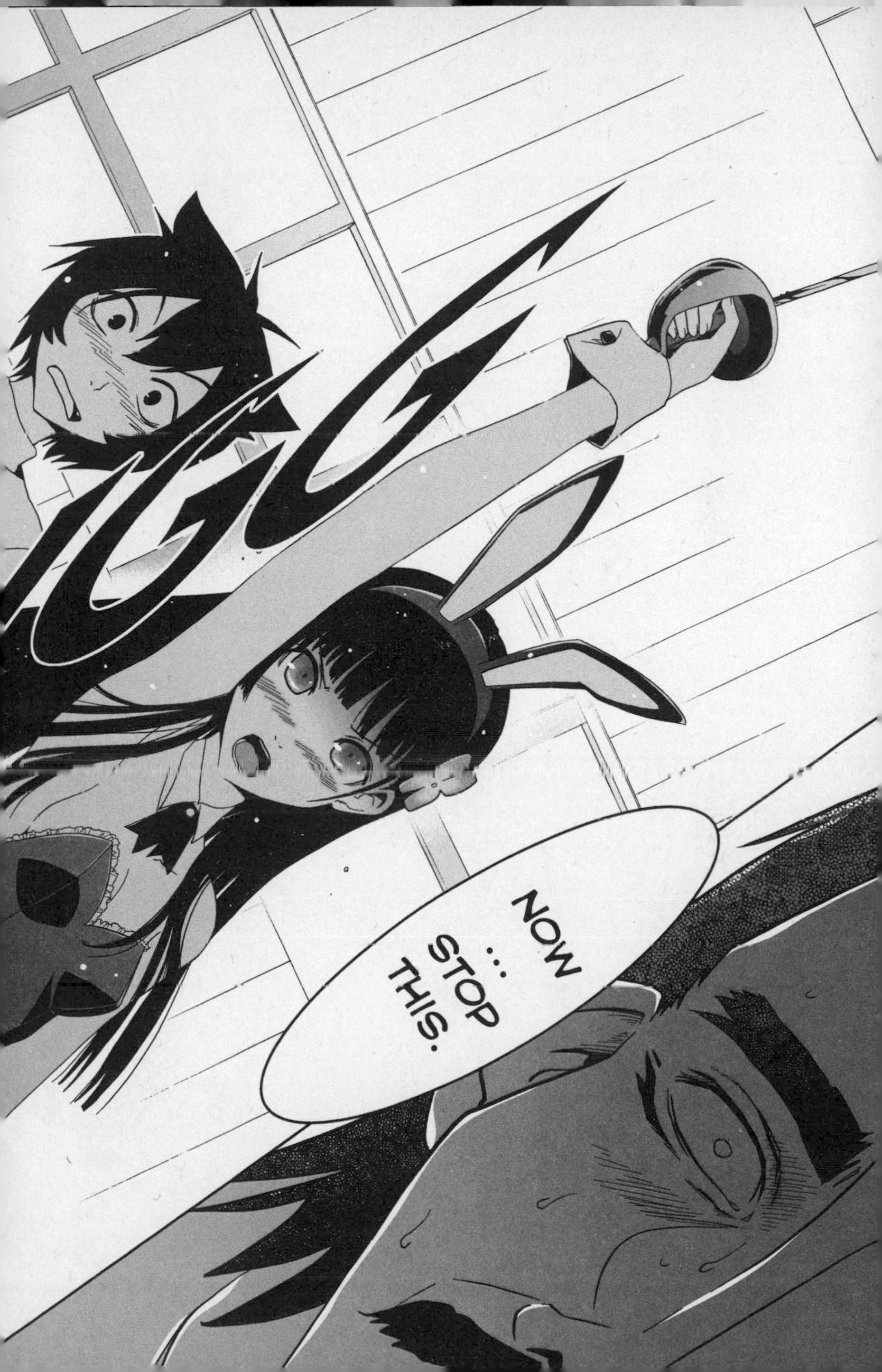
NOW... STOP THIS.

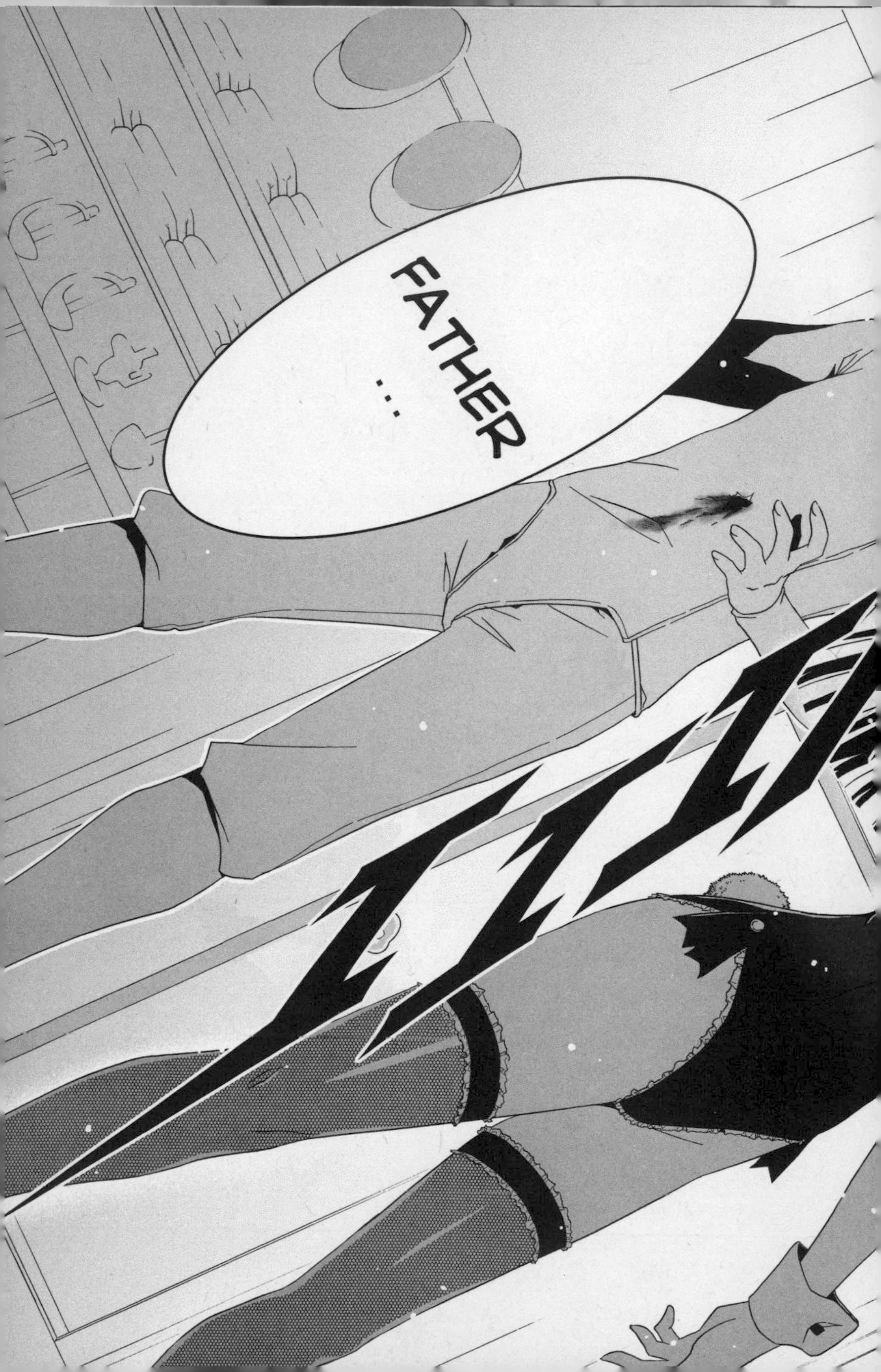
FATHER ...

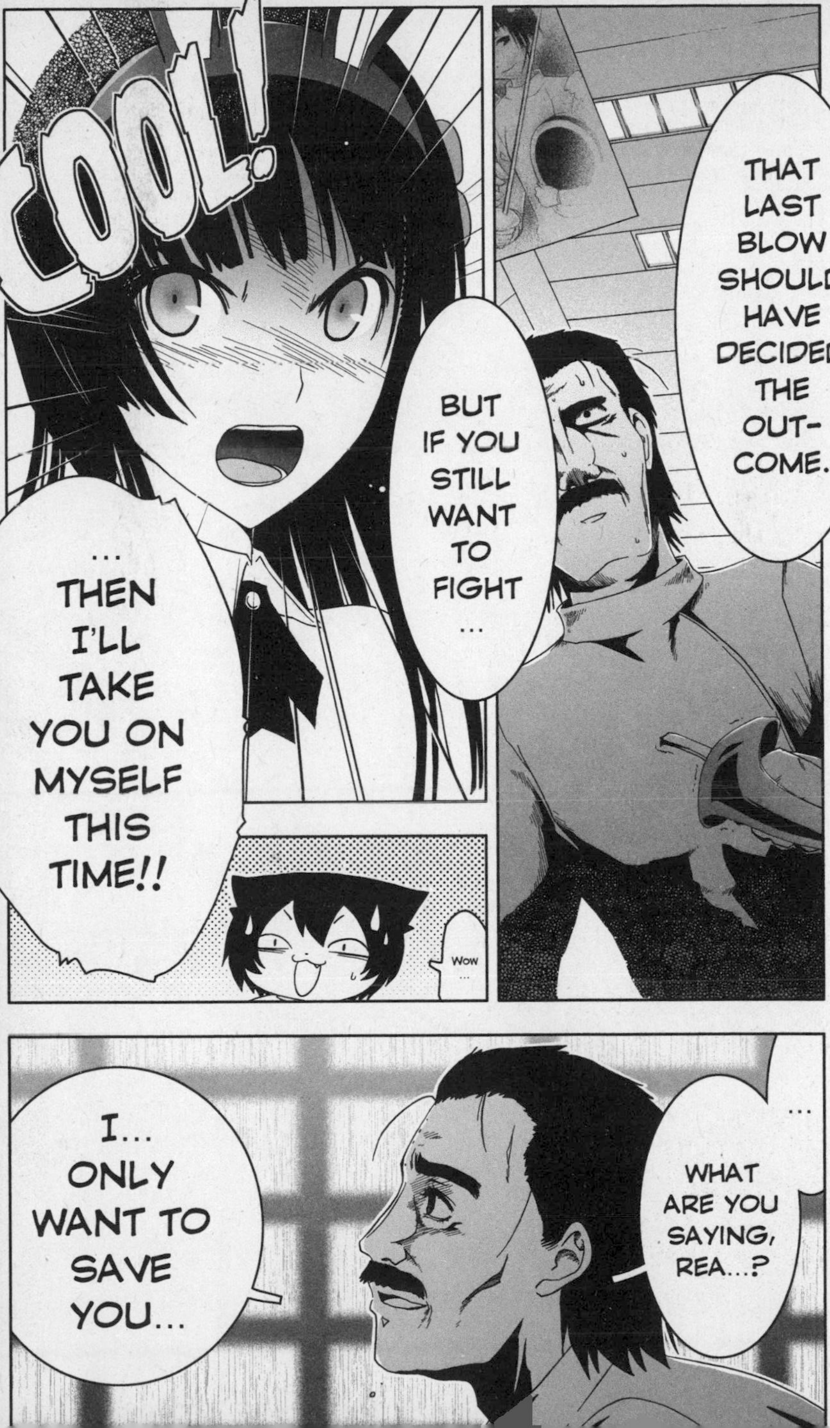
THAT LAST BLOW SHOULD HAVE DECIDED THE OUT-COME.
BUT IF YOU STILL WANT TO FIGHT ...
COOL!
... THEN I'LL TAKE YOU ON MYSELF THIS TIME!!
Wow ...
... WHAT ARE YOU SAYING, REA...?
I... ONLY WANT TO SAVE YOU...

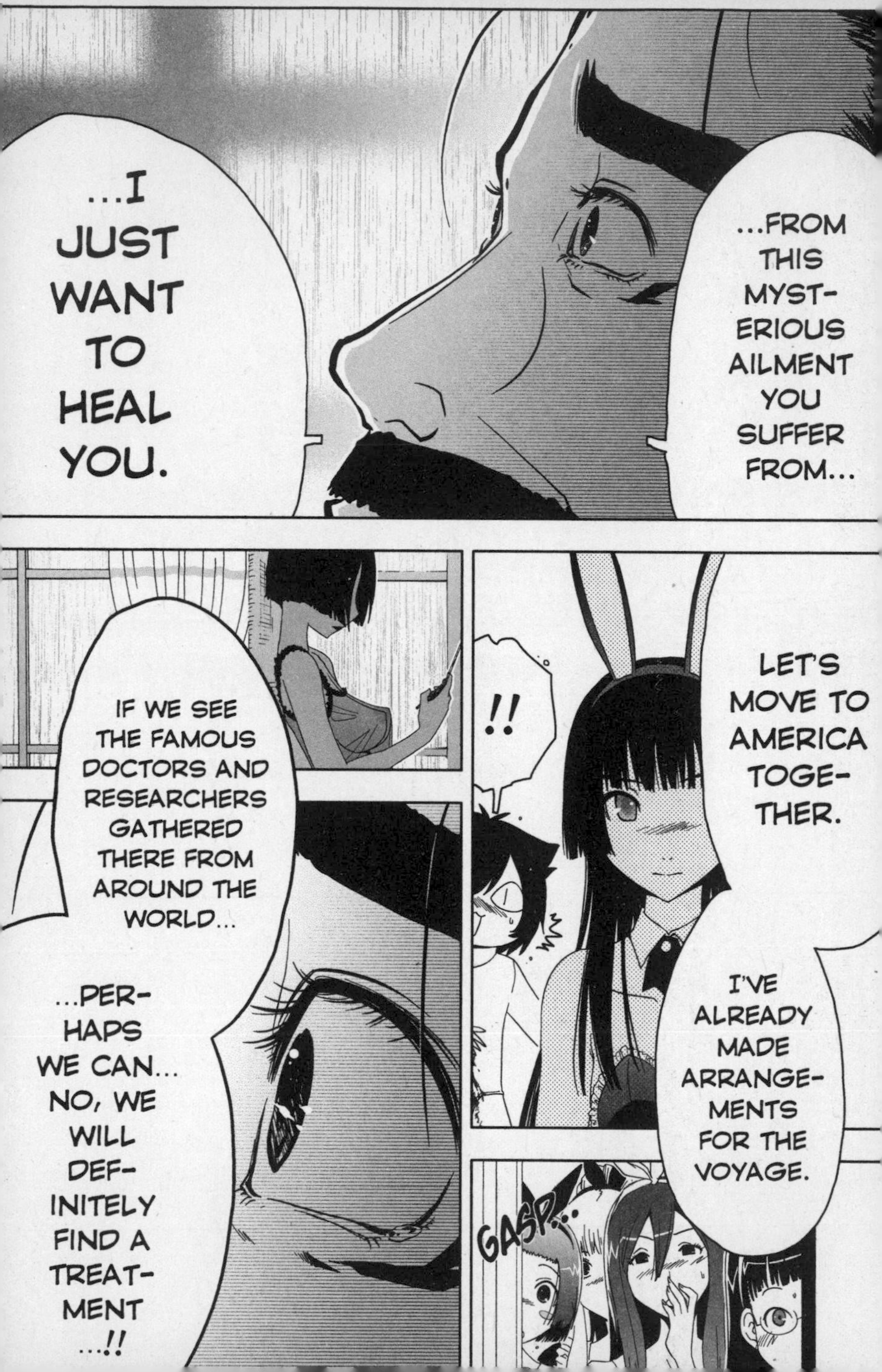
...FROM THIS MYST-ERIOUS AILMENT YOU SUFFER FROM...
...I JUST WANT TO HEAL YOU.
LET'S MOVE TO AMERICA TOGE-THER.
!!
I'VE ALREADY MADE ARRANGE-MENTS FOR THE VOYAGE.
GASP...
IF WE SEE THE FAMOUS DOCTORS AND RESEARCHERS GATHERED THERE FROM AROUND THE WORLD...
...PER-HAPS WE CAN... NO, WE WILL DEF-INITELY FIND A TREAT-MENT ...!!

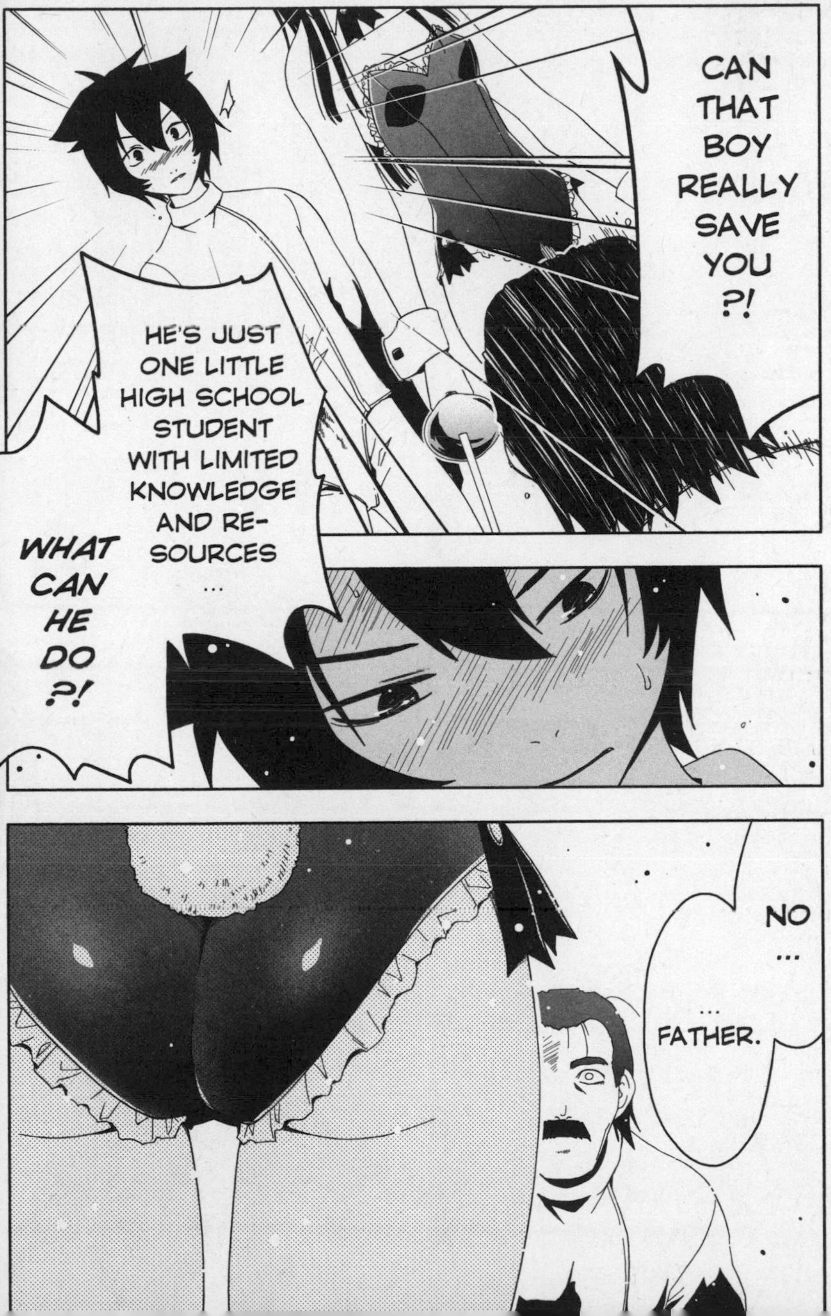
CAN THAT BOY REALLY SAVE YOU ?!
HE'S JUST ONE LITTLE HIGH SCHOOL STUDENT WITH LIMITED KNOWLEDGE AND RE-SOURCES ...
WHAT CAN HE DO ?!
NO ... ... FATHER.

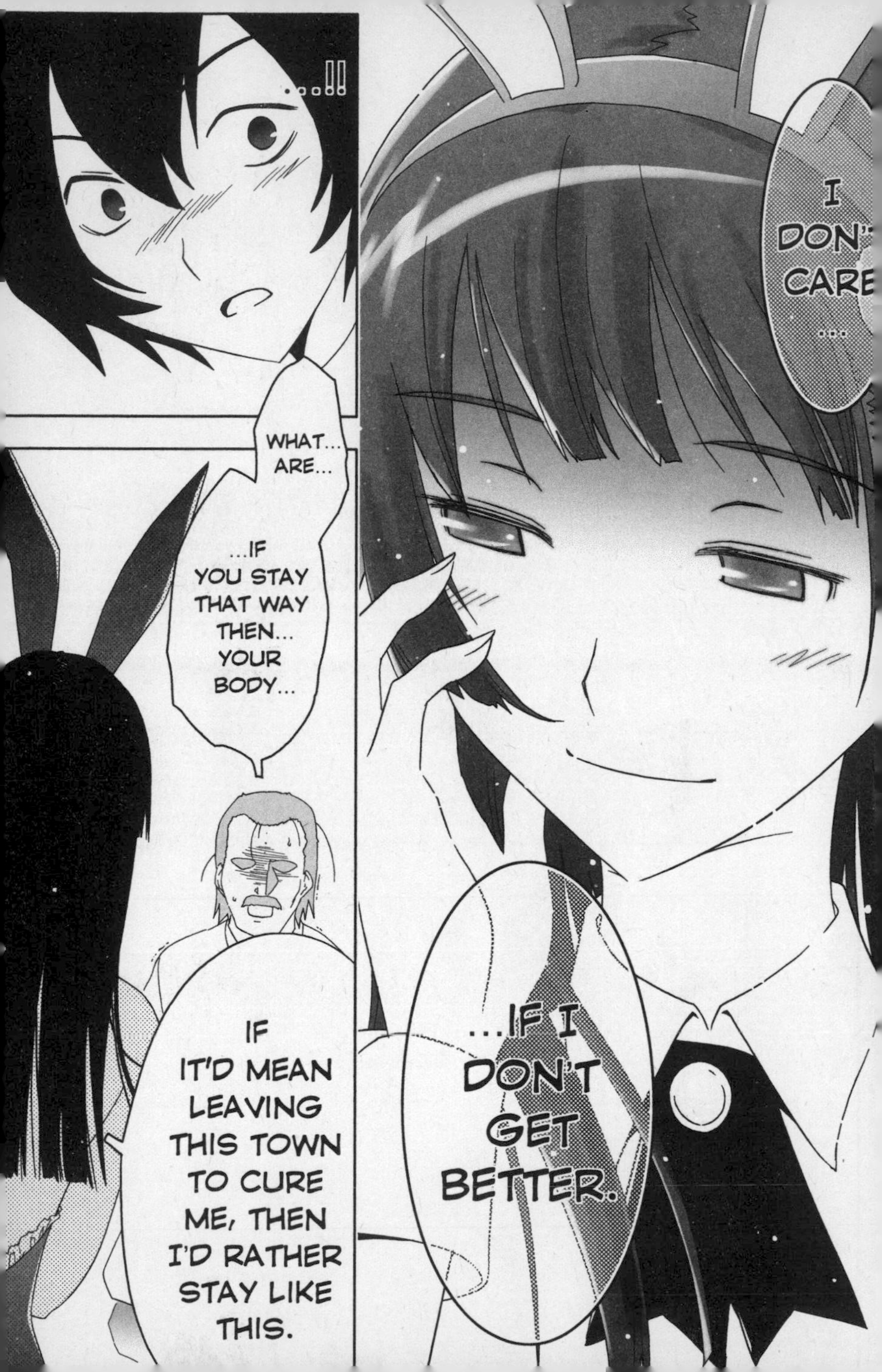
I DON'T CARE...
...IF I DON'T GET BETTER.
...!!
WHAT... ARE... ...IF YOU STAY THAT WAY THEN... YOUR BODY...
IF IT'D MEAN LEAVING THIS TOWN TO CURE ME, THEN I'D RATHER STAY LIKE THIS.

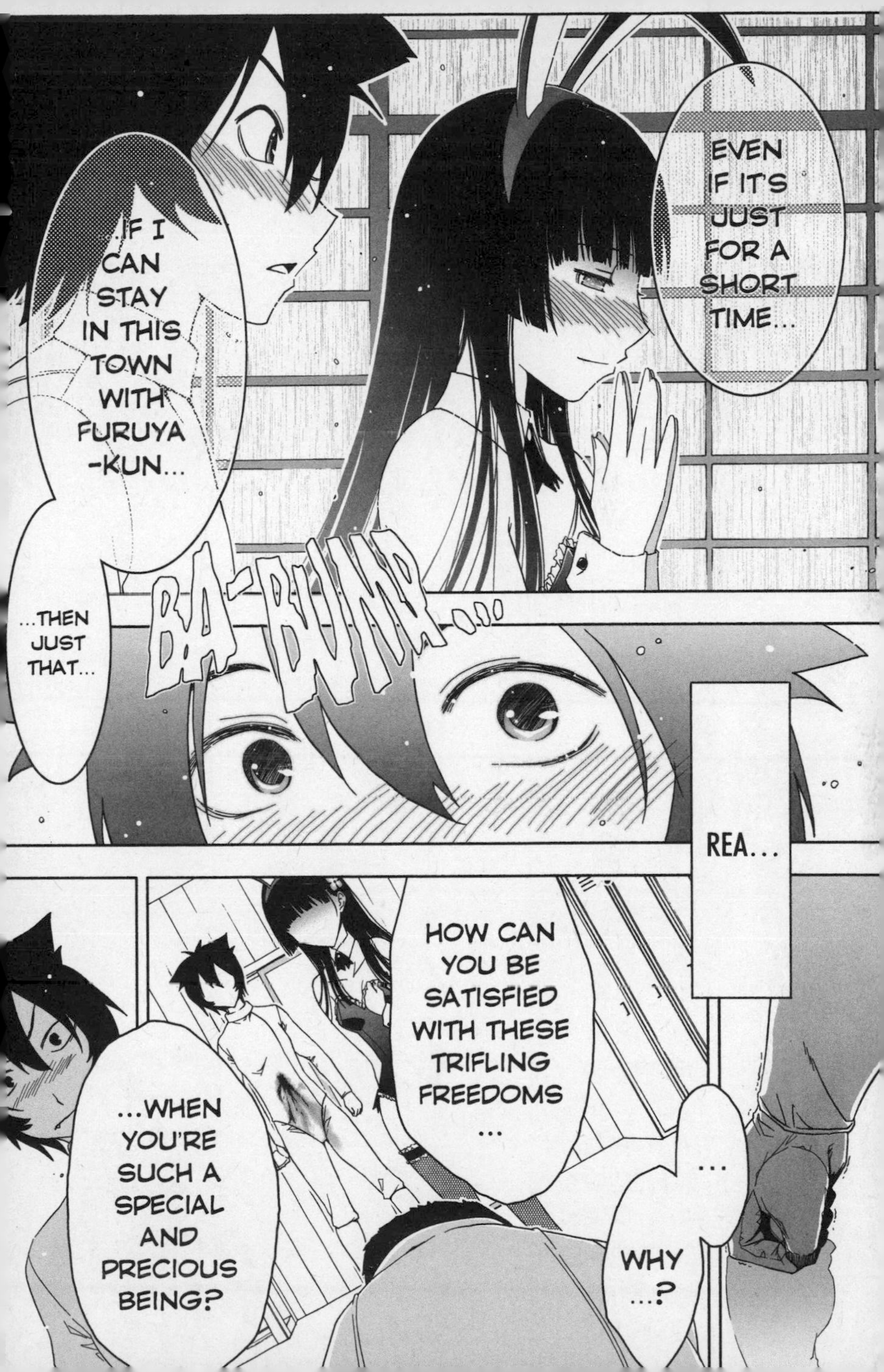
EVEN IF IT'S JUST FOR A SHORT TIME...
...IF I CAN STAY IN THIS TOWN WITH FURUYA-KUN...
...THEN JUST THAT...
BA-BUMP...
REA...
...
WHY ...?
HOW CAN YOU BE SATISFIED WITH THESE TRIFLING FREEDOMS ...
...WHEN YOU'RE SUCH A SPECIAL AND PRECIOUS BEING?

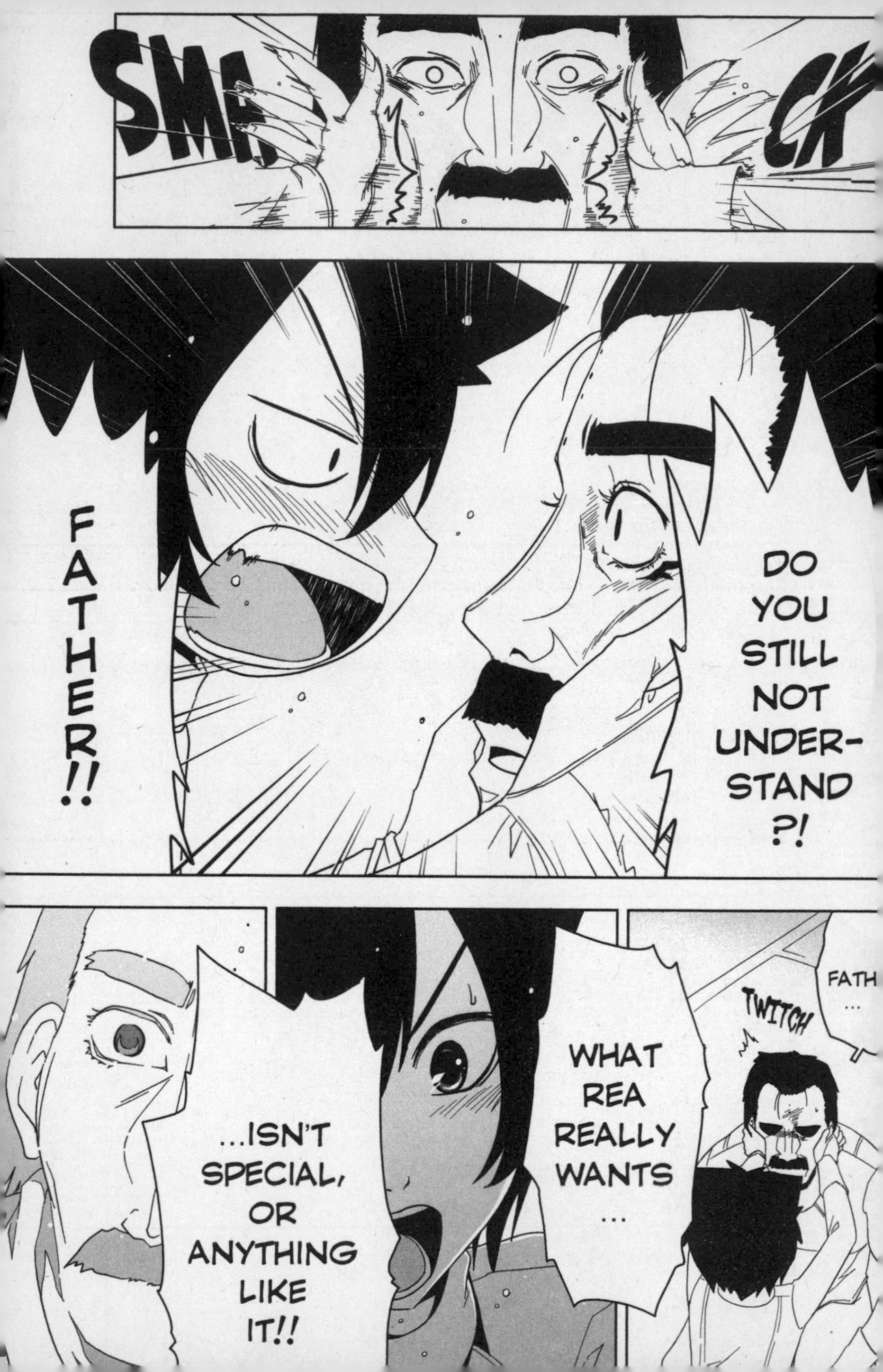
SMA CK
DO YOU STILL NOT UNDER-STAND?!
FATHER!!
FATH...
TWITCH
WHAT REA REALLY WANTS...
...ISN'T SPECIAL, OR ANYTHING LIKE IT!!

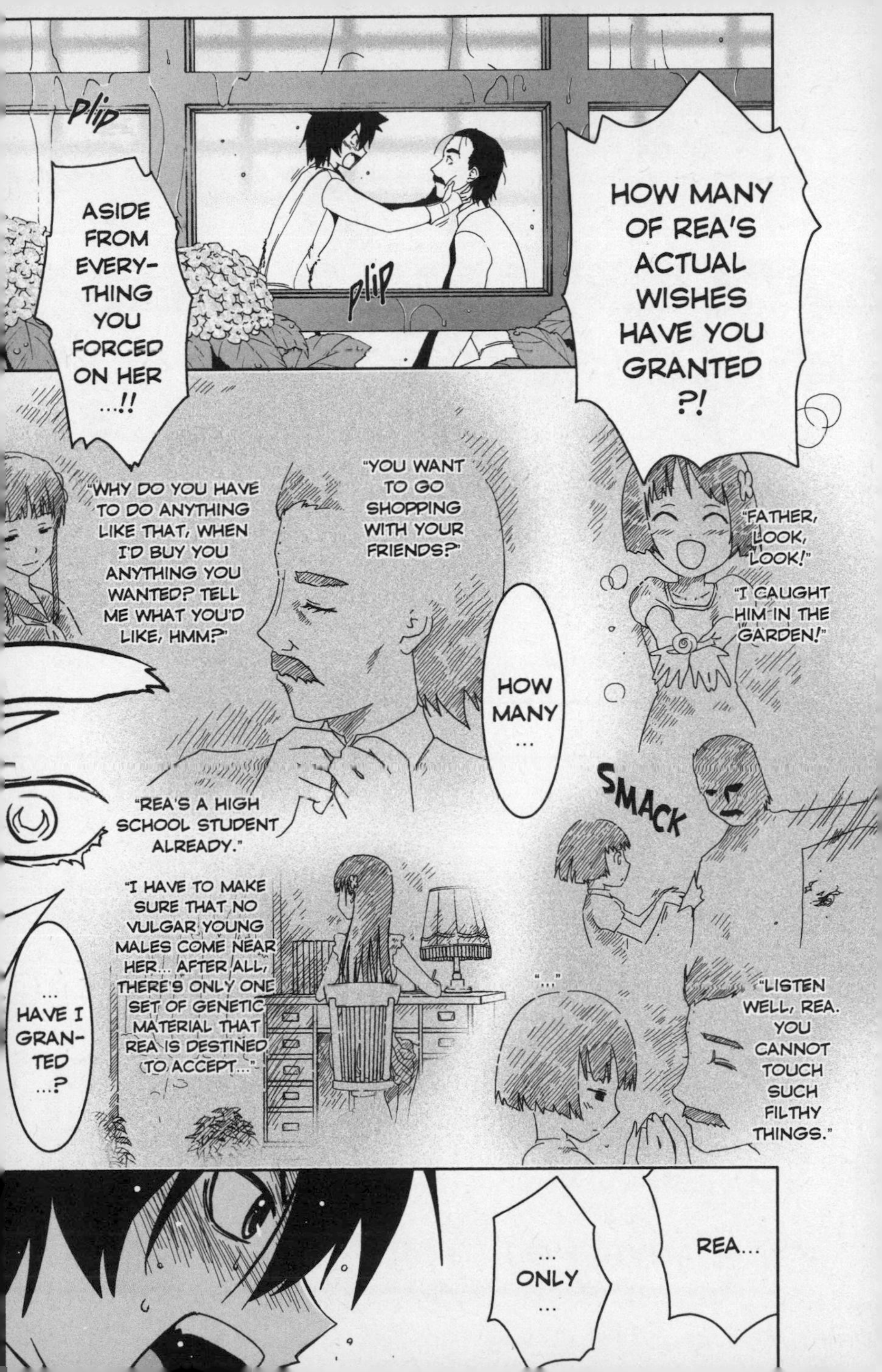
HOW MANY OF REA'S ACTUAL WISHES HAVE YOU GRANTED ?!
PLIP
PLIP
ASIDE FROM EVERY-THING YOU FORCED ON HER ...!!
"FATHER, LOOK, LOOK!"
"I CAUGHT HIM IN THE GARDEN!"
SMACK
"LISTEN WELL, REA. YOU CANNOT TOUCH SUCH FILTHY THINGS."
"..."
HOW MANY ...
"YOU WANT TO GO SHOPPING WITH YOUR FRIENDS?"
"WHY DO YOU HAVE TO DO ANYTHING LIKE THAT, WHEN I'D BUY YOU ANYTHING YOU WANTED? TELL ME WHAT YOU'D LIKE, HMM?"
"REA'S A HIGH SCHOOL STUDENT ALREADY."
"I HAVE TO MAKE SURE THAT NO VULGAR YOUNG MALES COME NEAR HER... AFTER ALL, THERE'S ONLY ONE SET OF GENETIC MATERIAL THAT REA IS DESTINED TO ACCEPT..."
... HAVE I GRAN-TED ...?
REA...
... ONLY ...

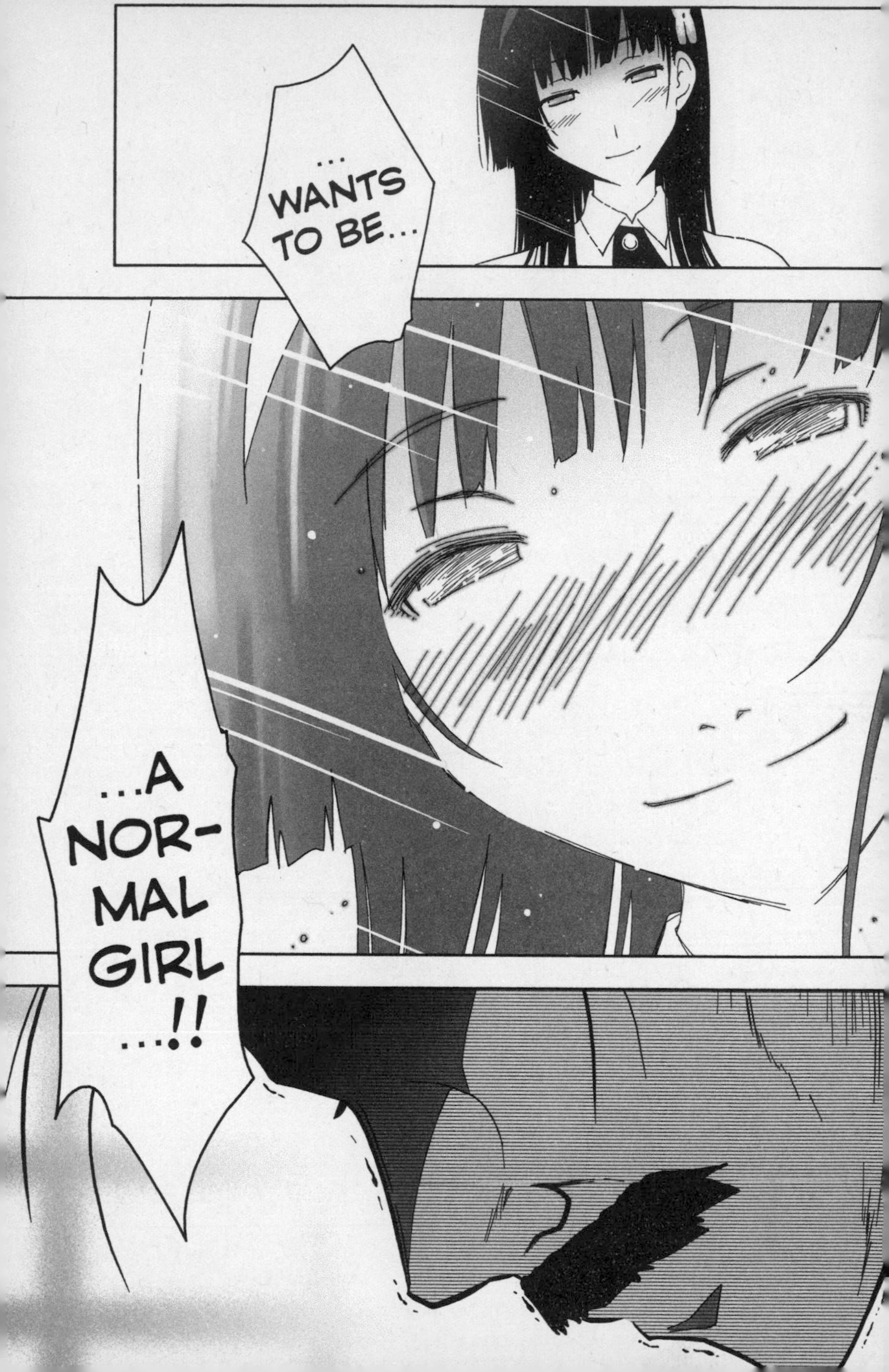
... WANTS TO BE...
...A NOR-MAL GIRL ...!!

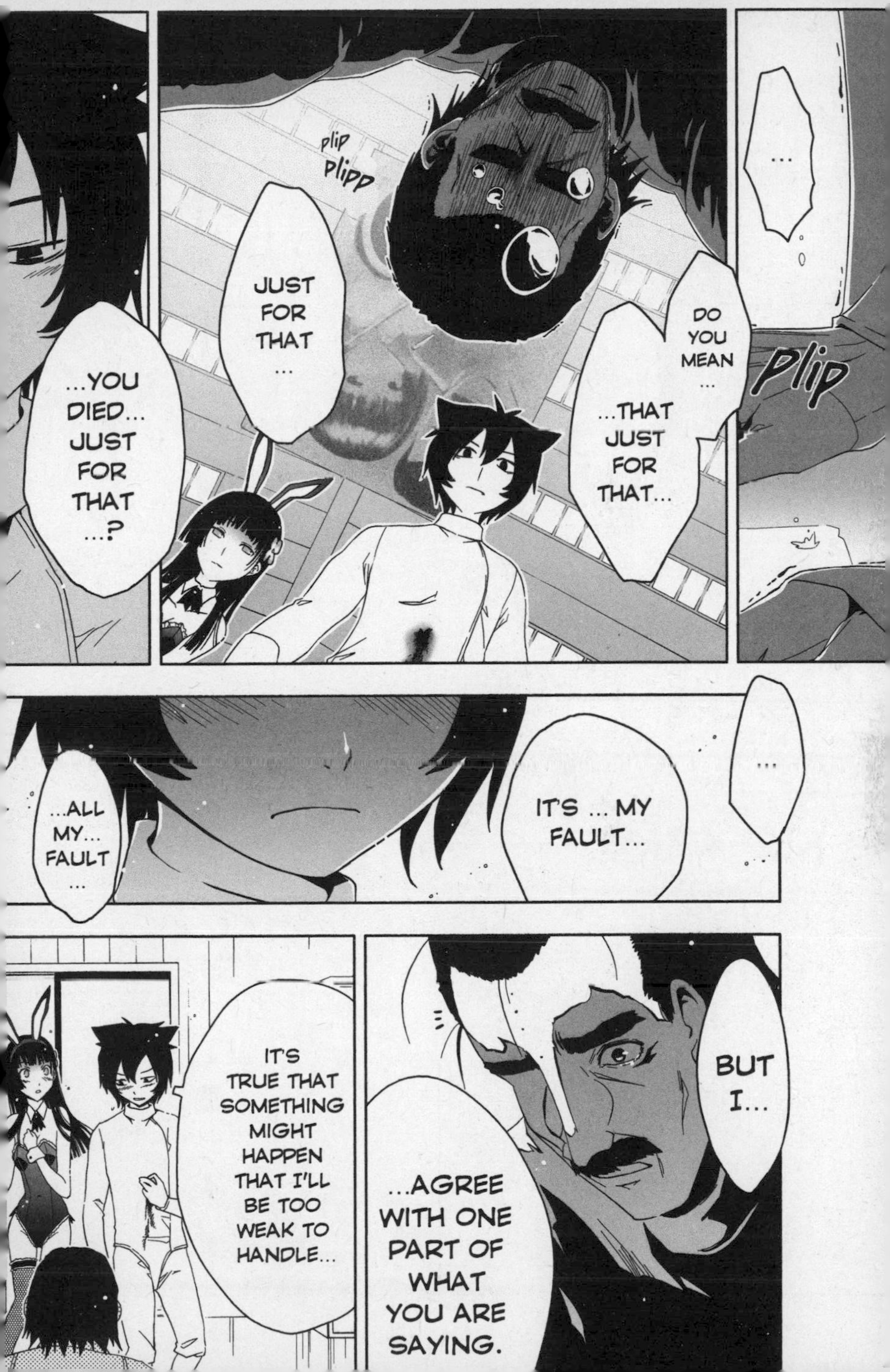
...
Plip
DO YOU MEAN ...
...THAT JUST FOR THAT...
plip plipp
JUST FOR THAT ...
...YOU DIED... JUST FOR THAT ...?
...
IT'S ... MY FAULT...
...ALL MY... FAULT ...
BUT I...
...AGREE WITH ONE PART OF WHAT YOU ARE SAYING.
IT'S TRUE THAT SOMETHING MIGHT HAPPEN THAT I'LL BE TOO WEAK TO HANDLE...

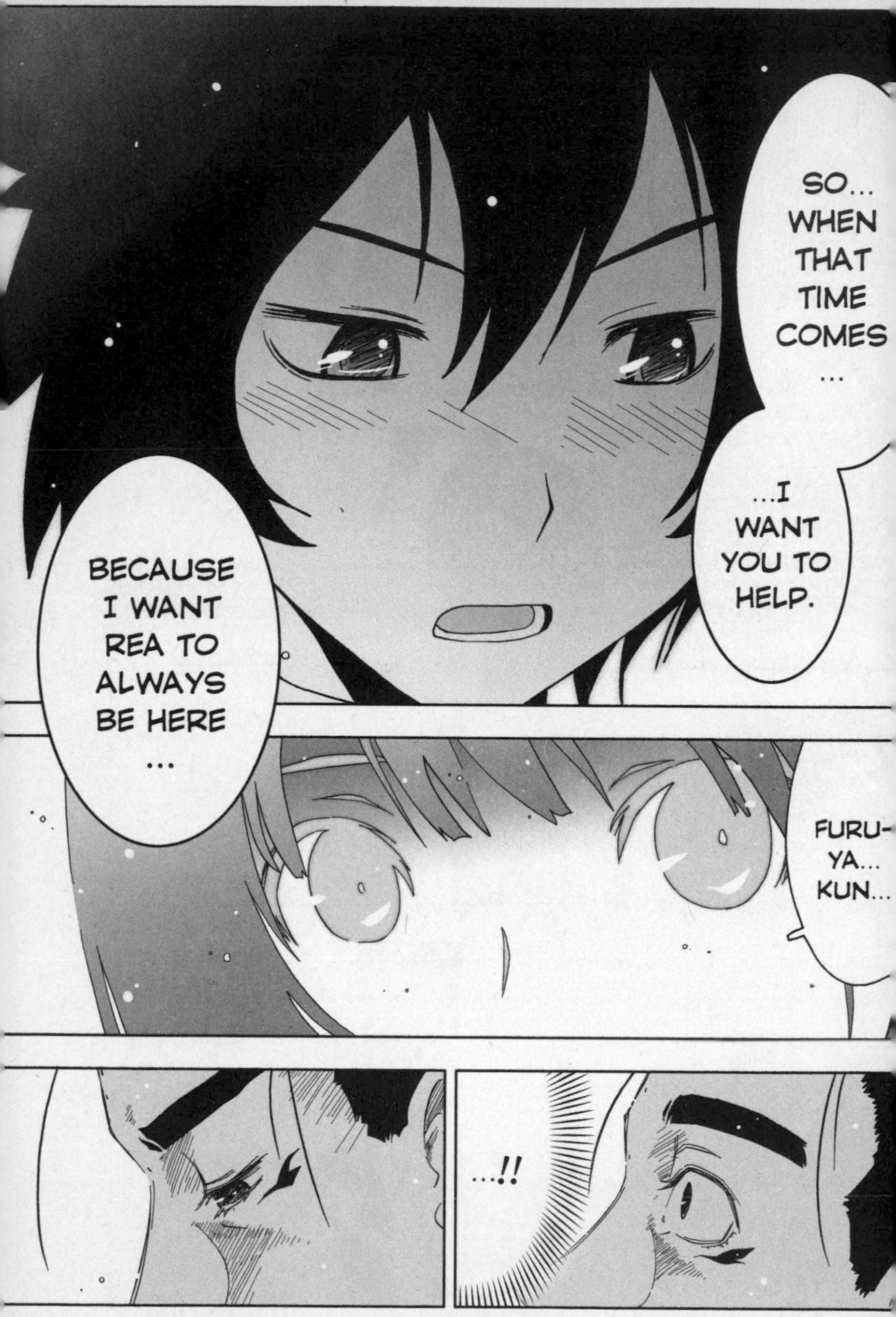
SO... WHEN THAT TIME COMES ...
...I WANT YOU TO HELP.
BECAUSE I WANT REA TO ALWAYS BE HERE ...
FURU-YA... KUN...
...!!

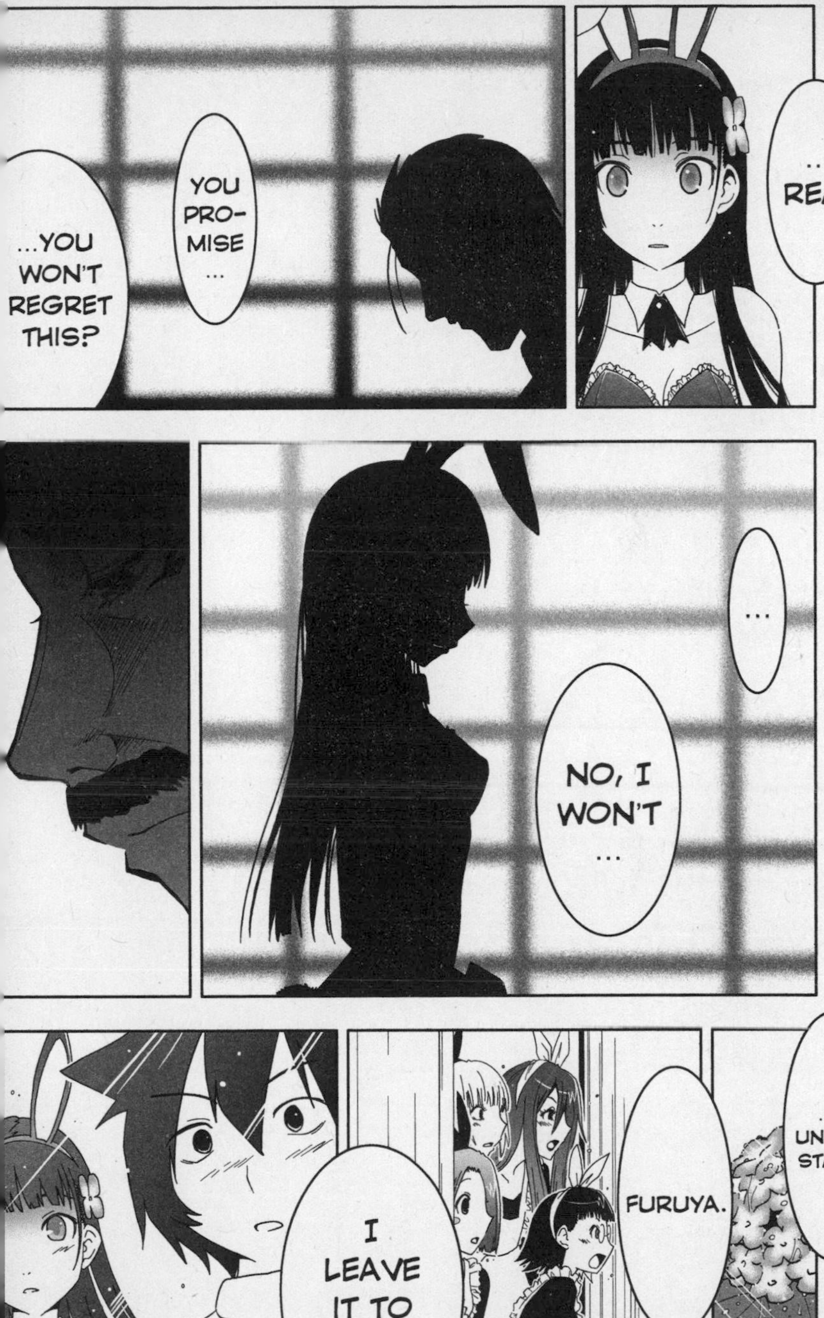
... REA.
YOU PRO-MISE ...
...YOU WON'T REGRET THIS?
...
NO, I WON'T ...
...I UNDER-STAND.
FURUYA.
I LEAVE IT TO YOU.

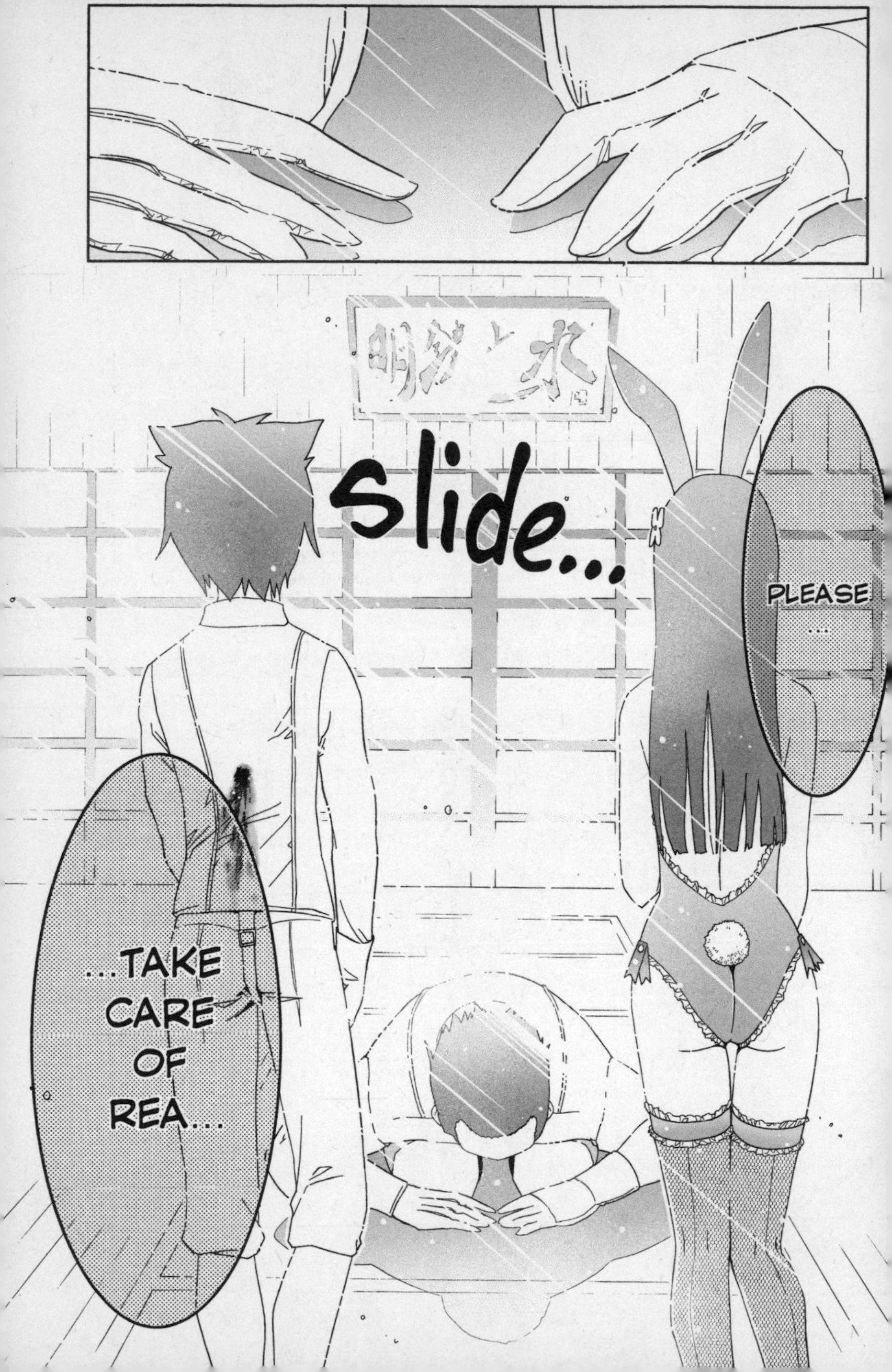
PLEASE ...
Slide...
...TAKE CARE OF REA...

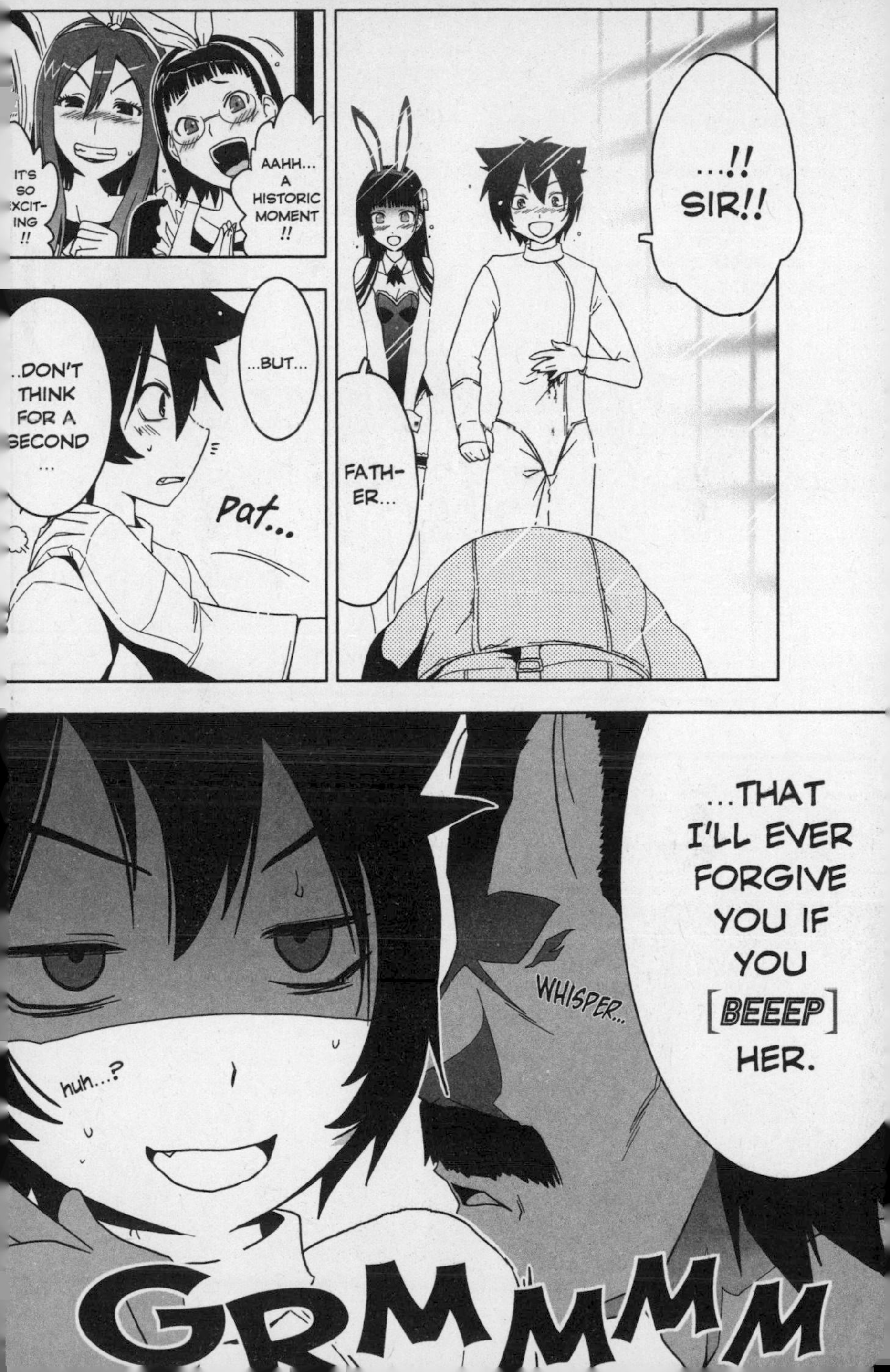
...!! SIR!!
FATH-ER...
AAHH... A HISTORIC MOMENT !!
IT'S SO EXCIT-ING !!
...BUT...
..DON'T THINK FOR A SECOND ...
Pat...
...THAT I'LL EVER FORGIVE YOU IF YOU [BEEEP] HER.
WHISPER...
huh...?
GRMMMM

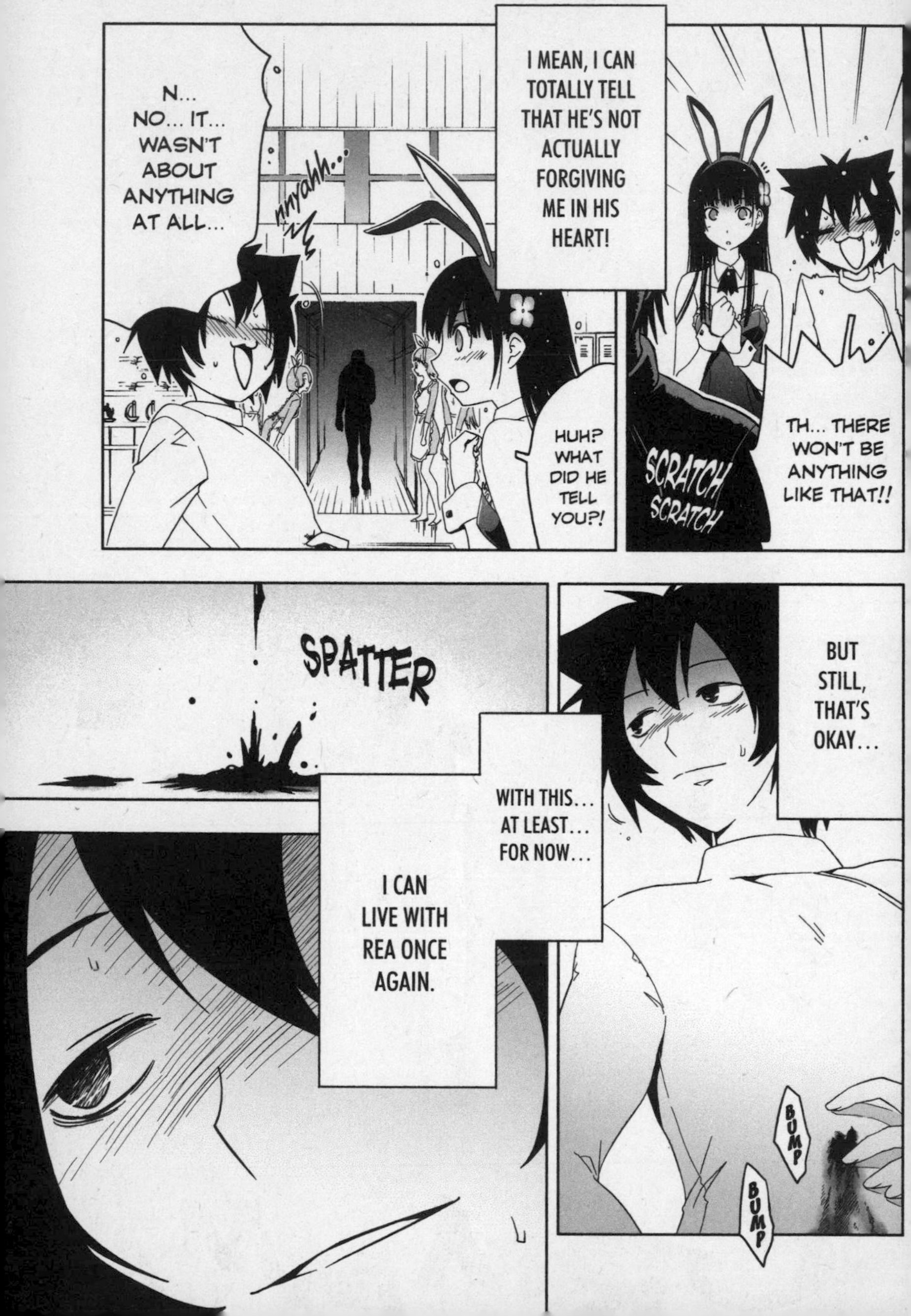
TH... THERE WON'T BE ANYTHING LIKE THAT!!
SCRATCH
SCRATCH
I MEAN, I CAN TOTALLY TELL THAT HE'S NOT ACTUALLY FORGIVING ME IN HIS HEART!
N... NO... IT... WASN'T ABOUT ANYTHING AT ALL...
nnyahh...
HUH? WHAT DID HE TELL YOU?!
BUT STILL, THAT'S OKAY...
WITH THIS... AT LEAST... FOR NOW...
BUMP
BUMP
SPATTER
I CAN LIVE WITH REA ONCE AGAIN.

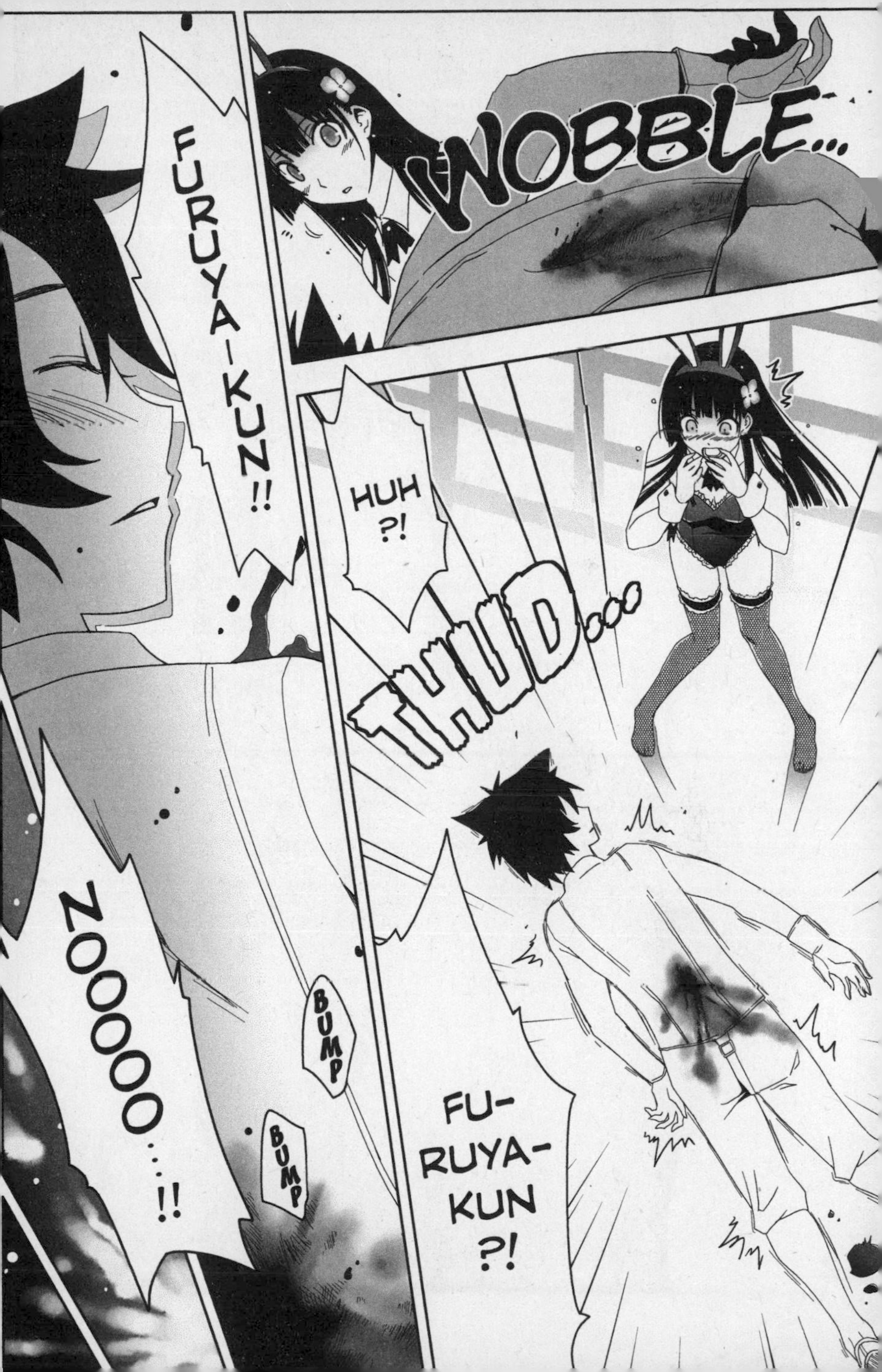
WOBBLE...
HUH ?!
THUD...
FU-RUYA-KUN ?!
FURUYA-KUN!!
BUMP
BUMP
NOOOOOO...!!

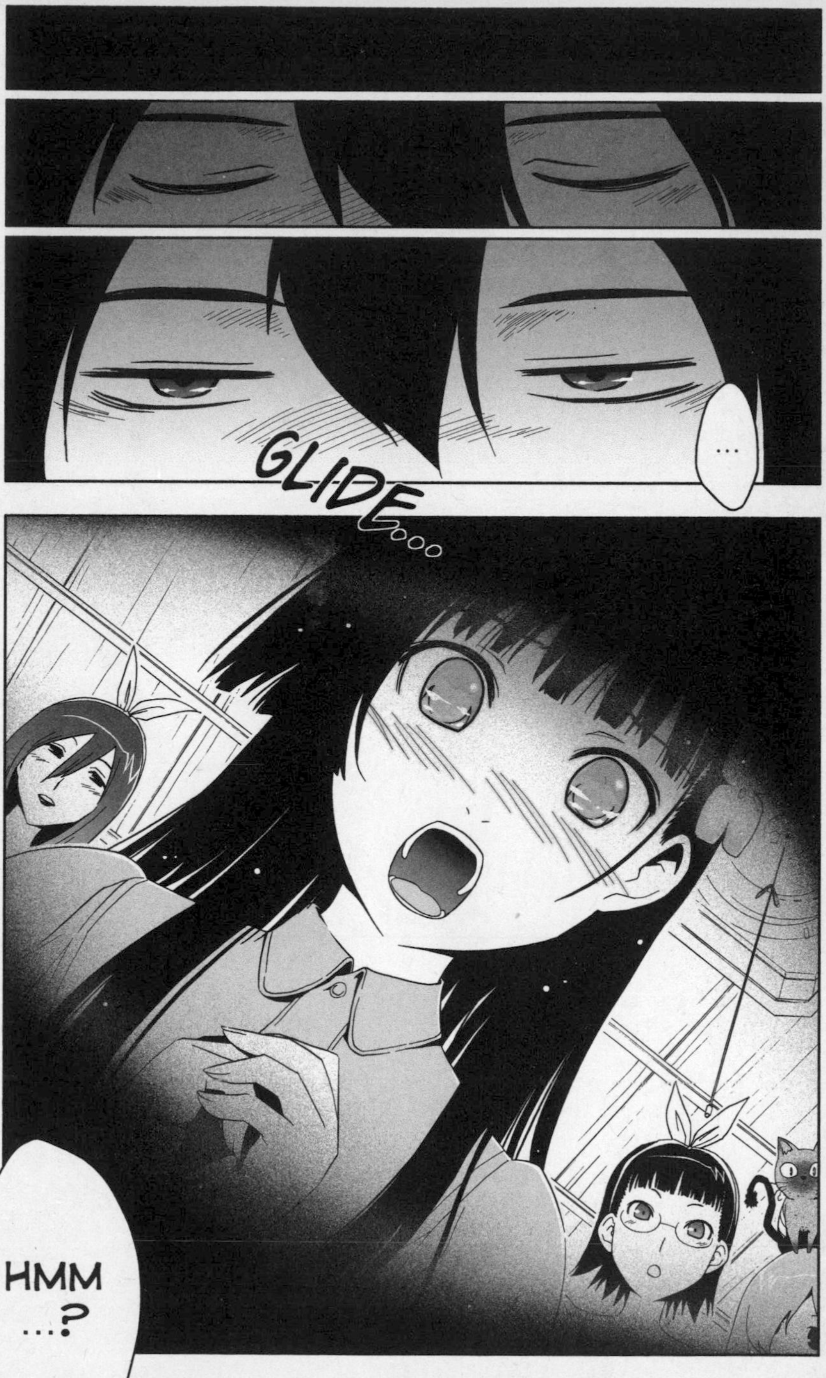
...
GLIDE...
HMM ...?

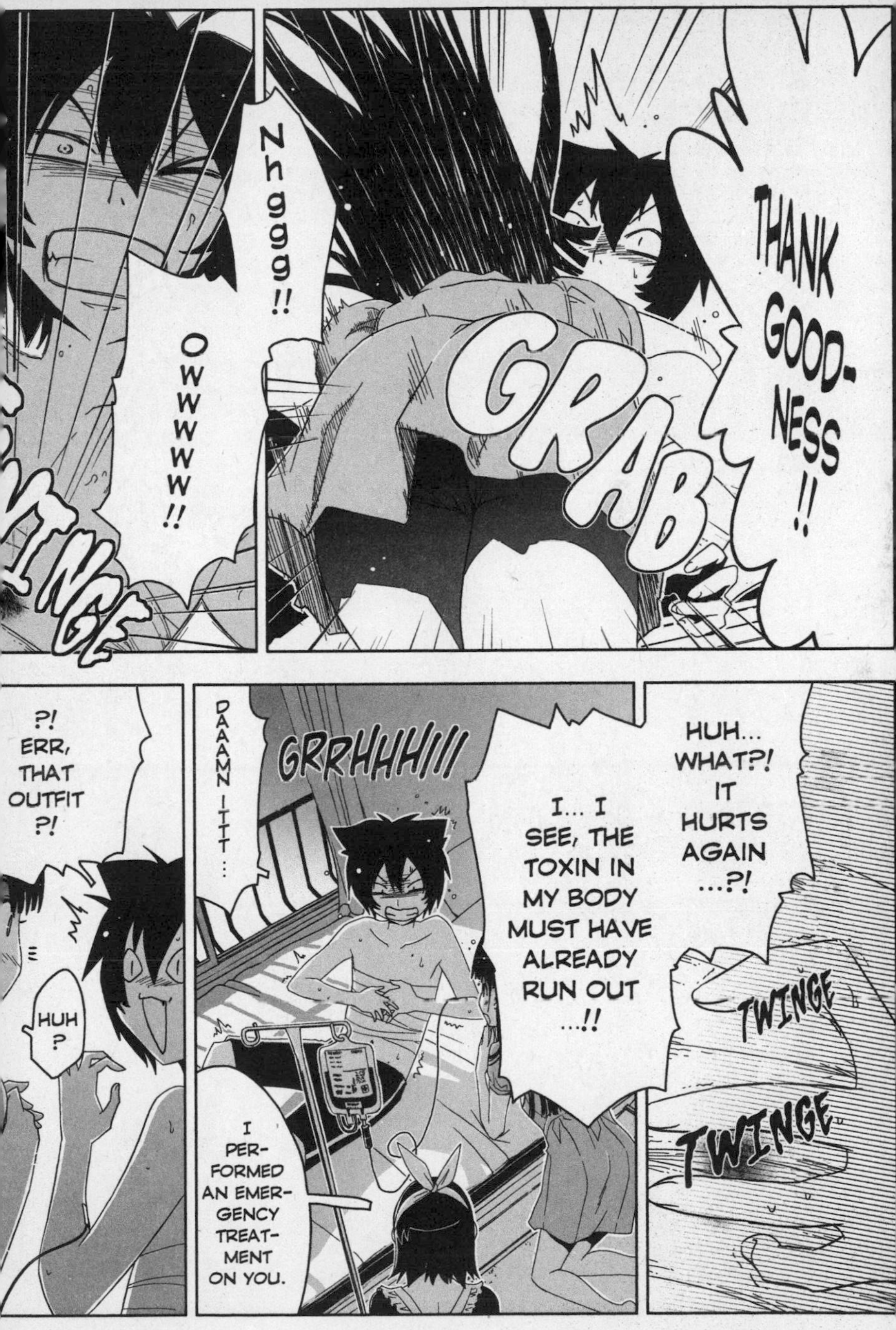
THANK GOODNESS!!
GRAB
Nnggg!!
OWWWWW!!
HUH... WHAT?! IT HURTS AGAIN ...?!
TWINGE
TWINGE
I... I SEE, THE TOXIN IN MY BODY MUST HAVE ALREADY RUN OUT ...!!
GRRHHH!!
DAAAMN ITTT...
I PERFORMED AN EMERGENCY TREATMENT ON YOU.
?! ERR, THAT OUTFIT ?!
HUH ?

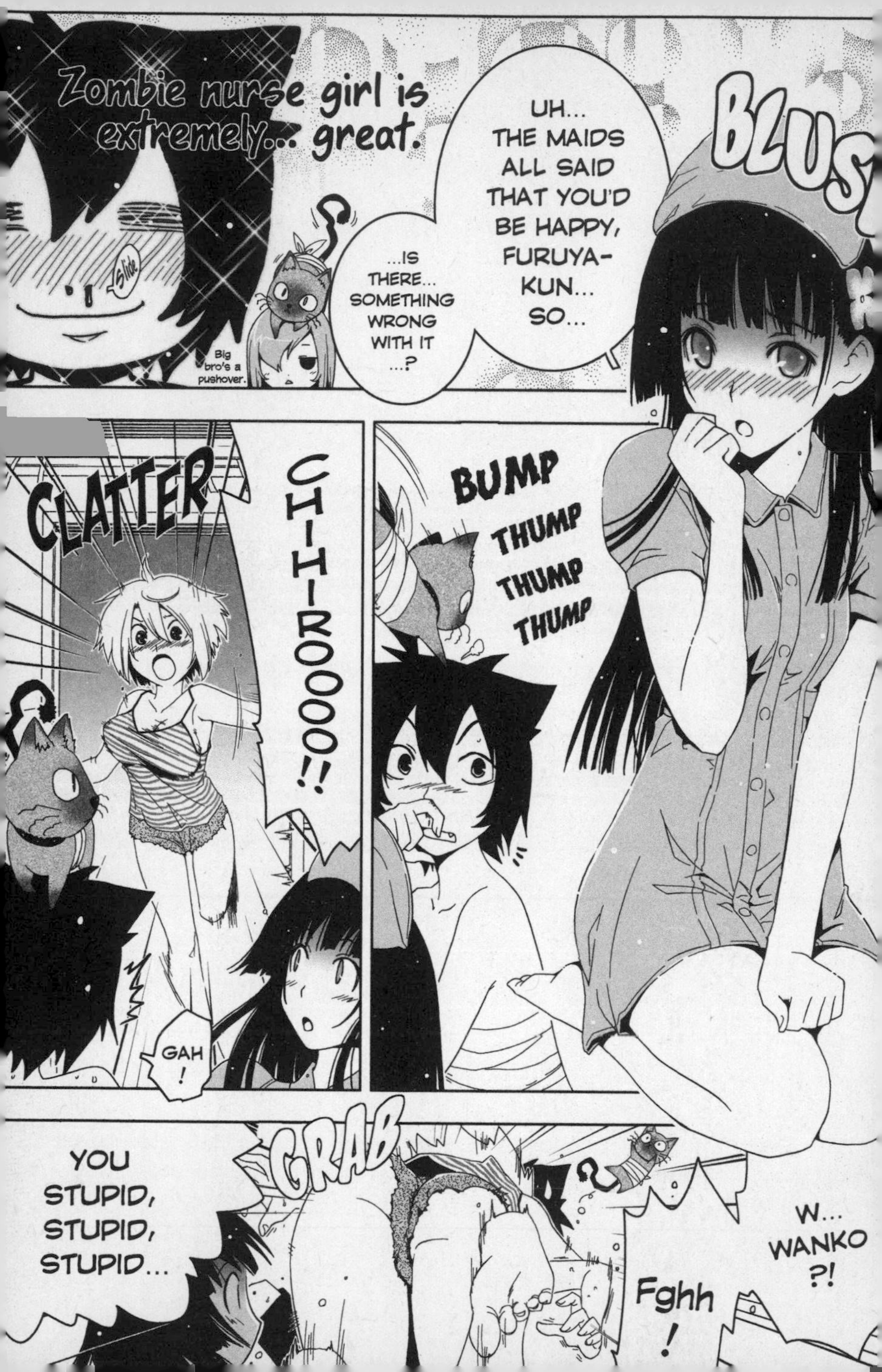
BLUS
UH... THE MAIDS ALL SAID THAT YOU'D BE HAPPY, FURUYA-KUN... SO...
...IS THERE... SOMETHING WRONG WITH IT ...?
Zombie nurse girl is extremely... great.
Slide
Big bro's a pushover.
BUMP
THUMP
THUMP
THUMP
CHIHIROOOOO!!
CLATTER
GAH!
W... WANKO?!
Fghh!
GRAB
YOU STUPID, STUPID, STUPID...

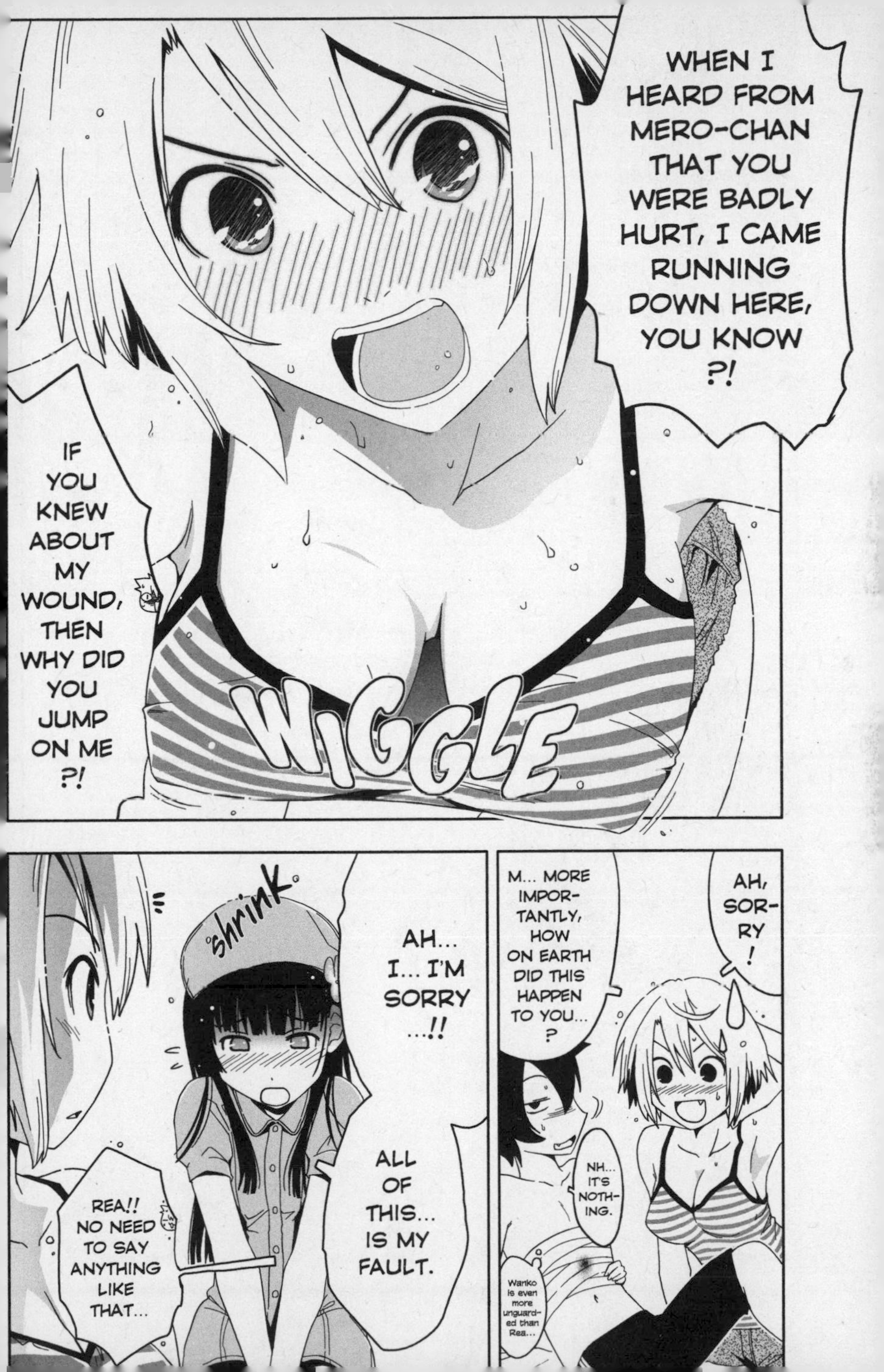
WHEN I HEARD FROM MERO-CHAN THAT YOU WERE BADLY HURT, I CAME RUNNING DOWN HERE, YOU KNOW ?!
IF YOU KNEW ABOUT MY WOUND, THEN WHY DID YOU JUMP ON ME ?!
WIGGLE
AH, SORRY!
M... MORE IMPORTANTLY, HOW ON EARTH DID THIS HAPPEN TO YOU... ?
NH... IT'S NOTHING.
Wanko is even more unguarded than Rea...
AH... I... I'M SORRY ...!!
shrink
ALL OF THIS... IS MY FAULT.
REA!! NO NEED TO SAY ANYTHING LIKE THAT...

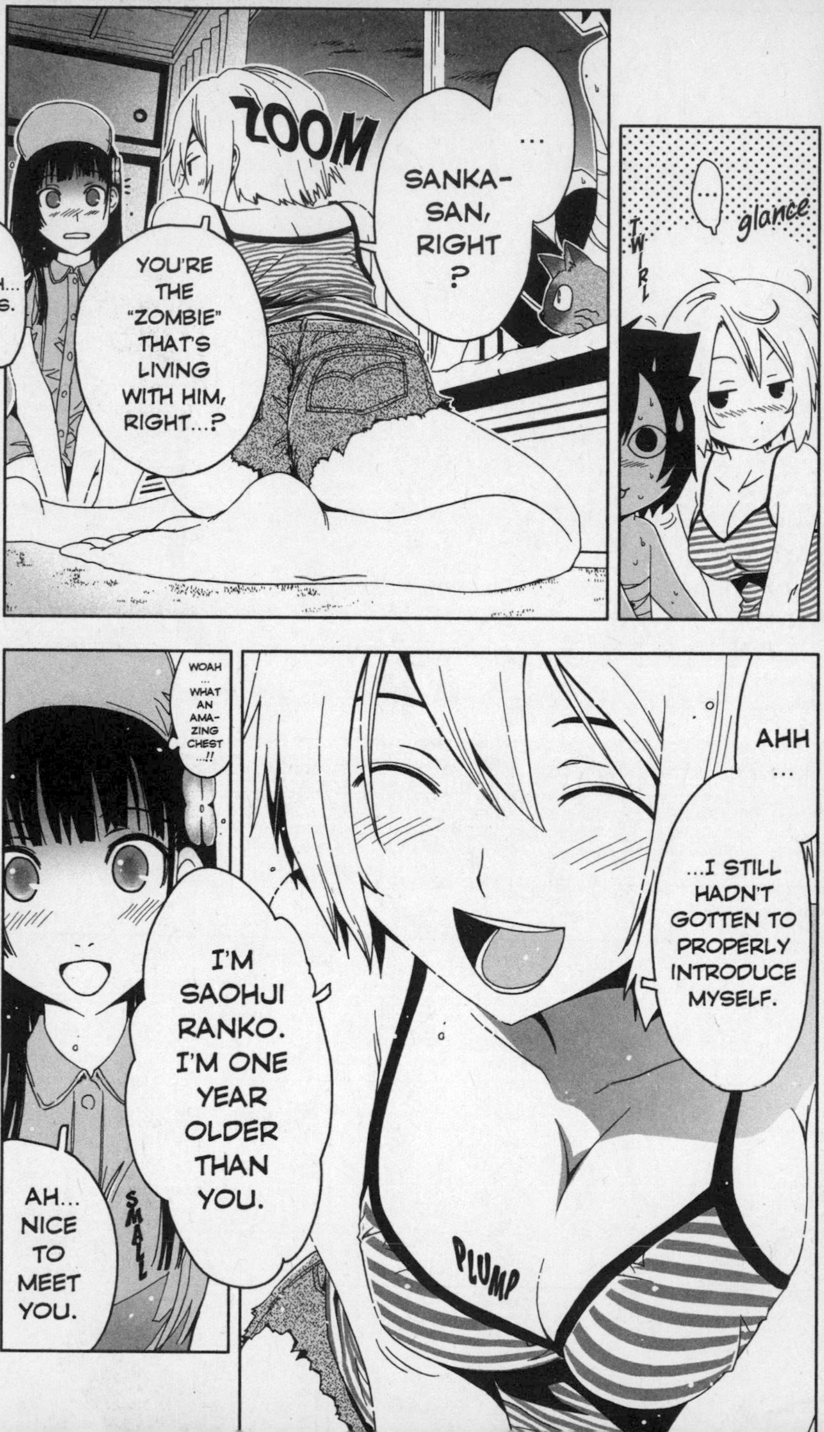
...
TWIRL
glance
ZOOM
... SANKA-SAN, RIGHT?
YOU'RE THE "ZOMBIE" THAT'S LIVING WITH HIM, RIGHT...?
OH... YES.
AHH ...
...I STILL HADN'T GOTTEN TO PROPERLY INTRODUCE MYSELF.
I'M SAOHJI RANKO. I'M ONE YEAR OLDER THAN YOU.
PLUMP
WOAH ... WHAT AN AMA-ZING CHEST ...!!
SMALL
AH... NICE TO MEET YOU.

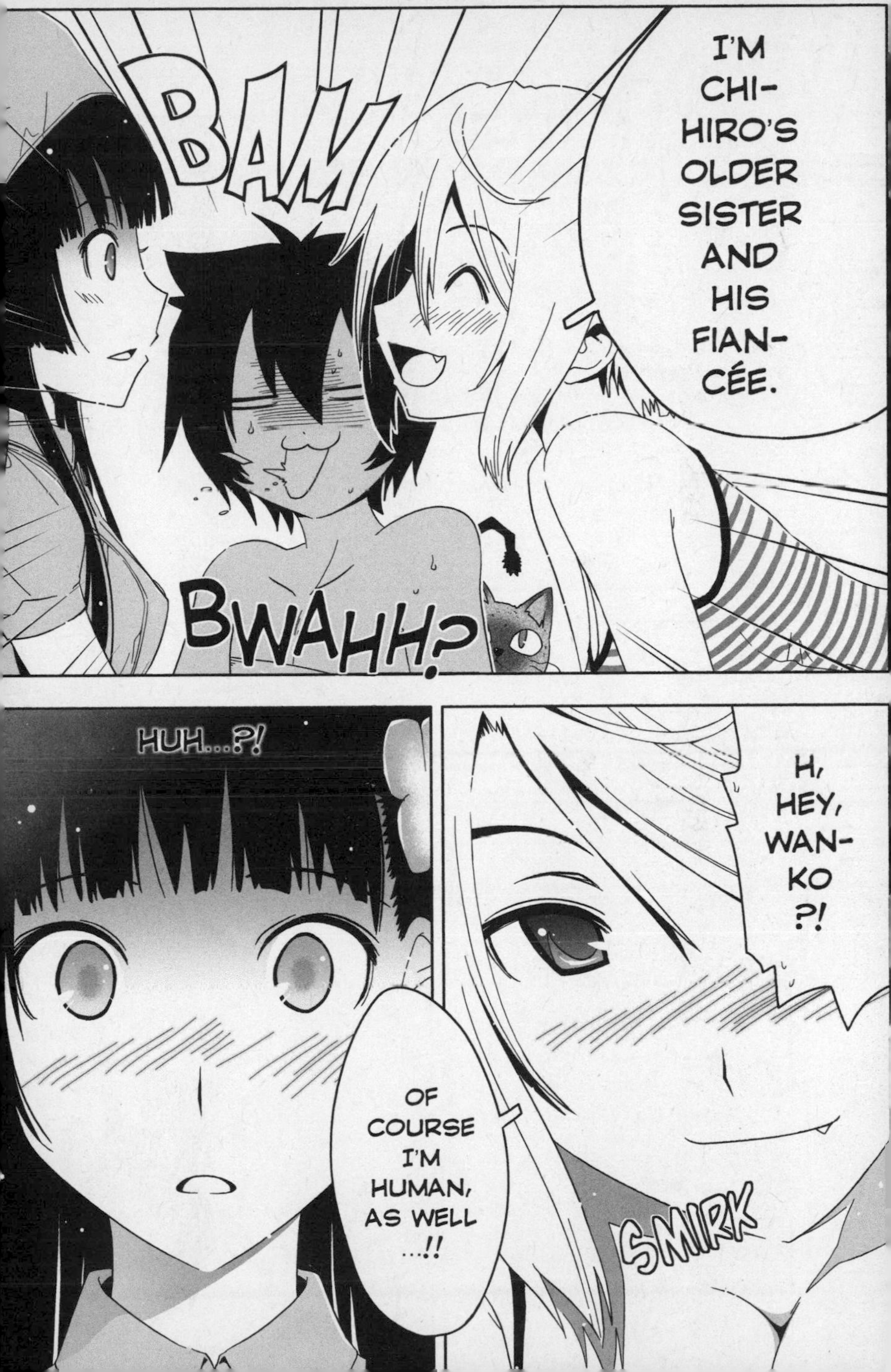
I'M CHIHIRO'S OLDER SISTER AND HIS FIANCÉE.
BAM
BWAHH?
H, HEY, WANKO?!
OF COURSE I'M HUMAN, AS WELL...!!
SMIRK
HUH...?!

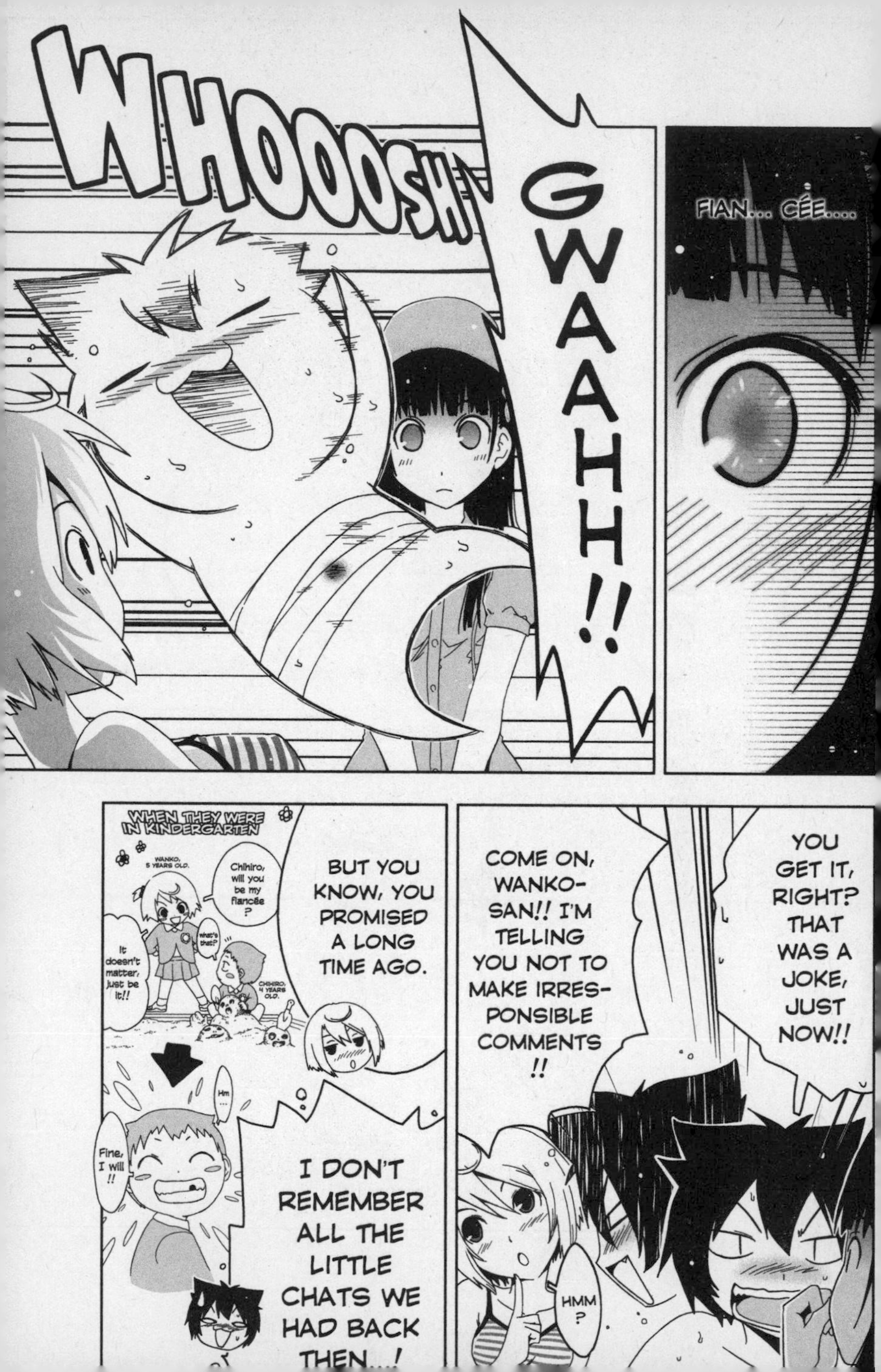
FIAN... CÉE....
WHOOOSH
GWAHH!!
YOU GET IT, RIGHT? THAT WAS A JOKE, JUST NOW!!
COME ON, WANKO-SAN!! I'M TELLING YOU NOT TO MAKE IRRES-PONSIBLE COMMENTS!!
HMM?
BUT YOU KNOW, YOU PROMISED A LONG TIME AGO.
WHEN THEY WERE IN KINDERGARTEN
WANKO, 5 YEARS OLD.
Chihiro, will you be my fiancée?
what's that?
It doesn't matter, just be it!!
CHIHIRO, 4 YEARS OLD.
Hm ...
Fine, I will!!
I DON'T REMEMBER ALL THE LITTLE CHATS WE HAD BACK THEN...!

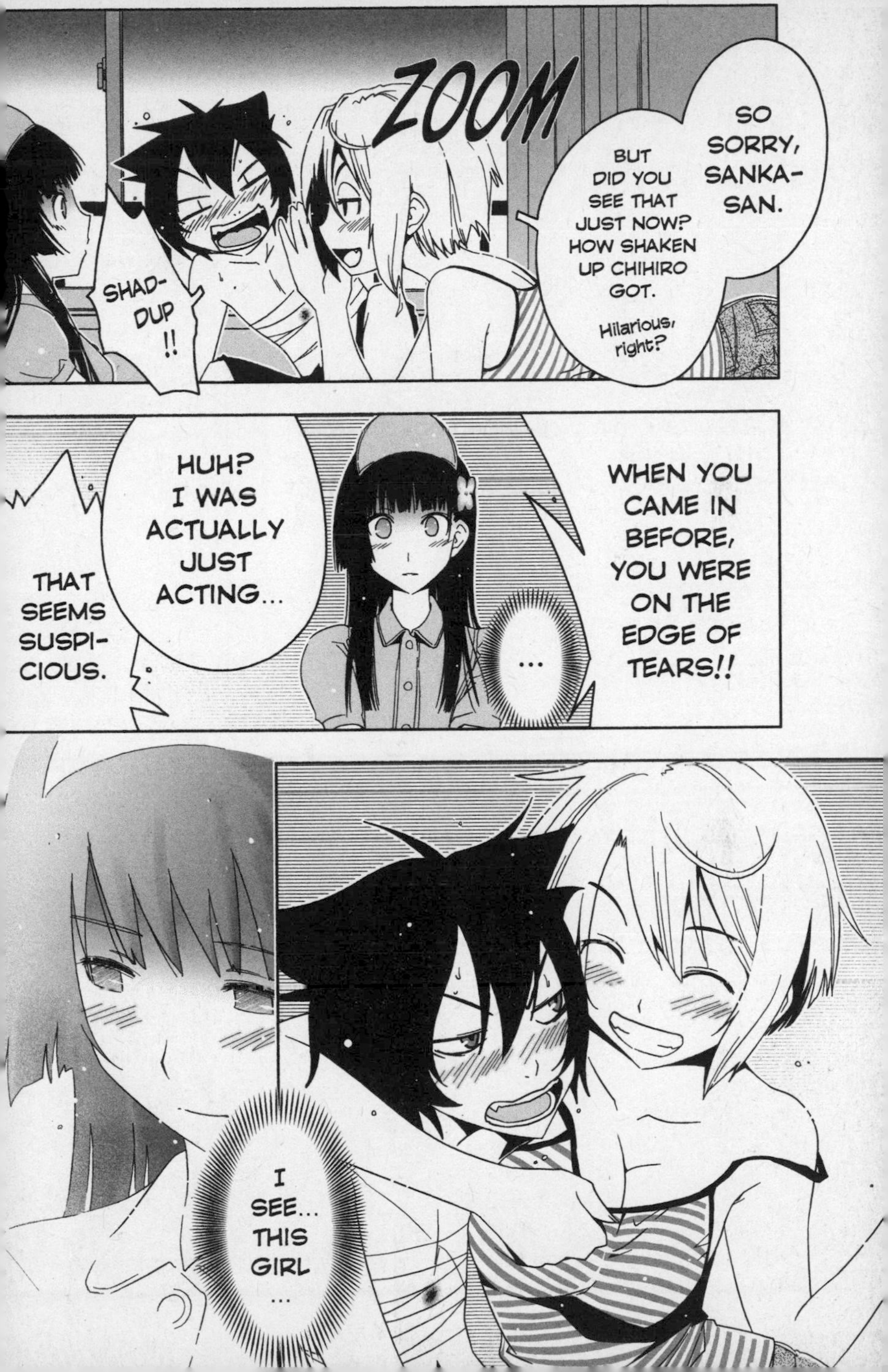
SO SORRY, SANKA-SAN.
BUT DID YOU SEE THAT JUST NOW? HOW SHAKEN UP CHIHIRO GOT.
Hilarious, right?
ZOOM
SHAD-DUP!!
WHEN YOU CAME IN BEFORE, YOU WERE ON THE EDGE OF TEARS!!
...
HUH? I WAS ACTUALLY JUST ACTING...
THAT SEEMS SUSPICIOUS.
I SEE... THIS GIRL ...

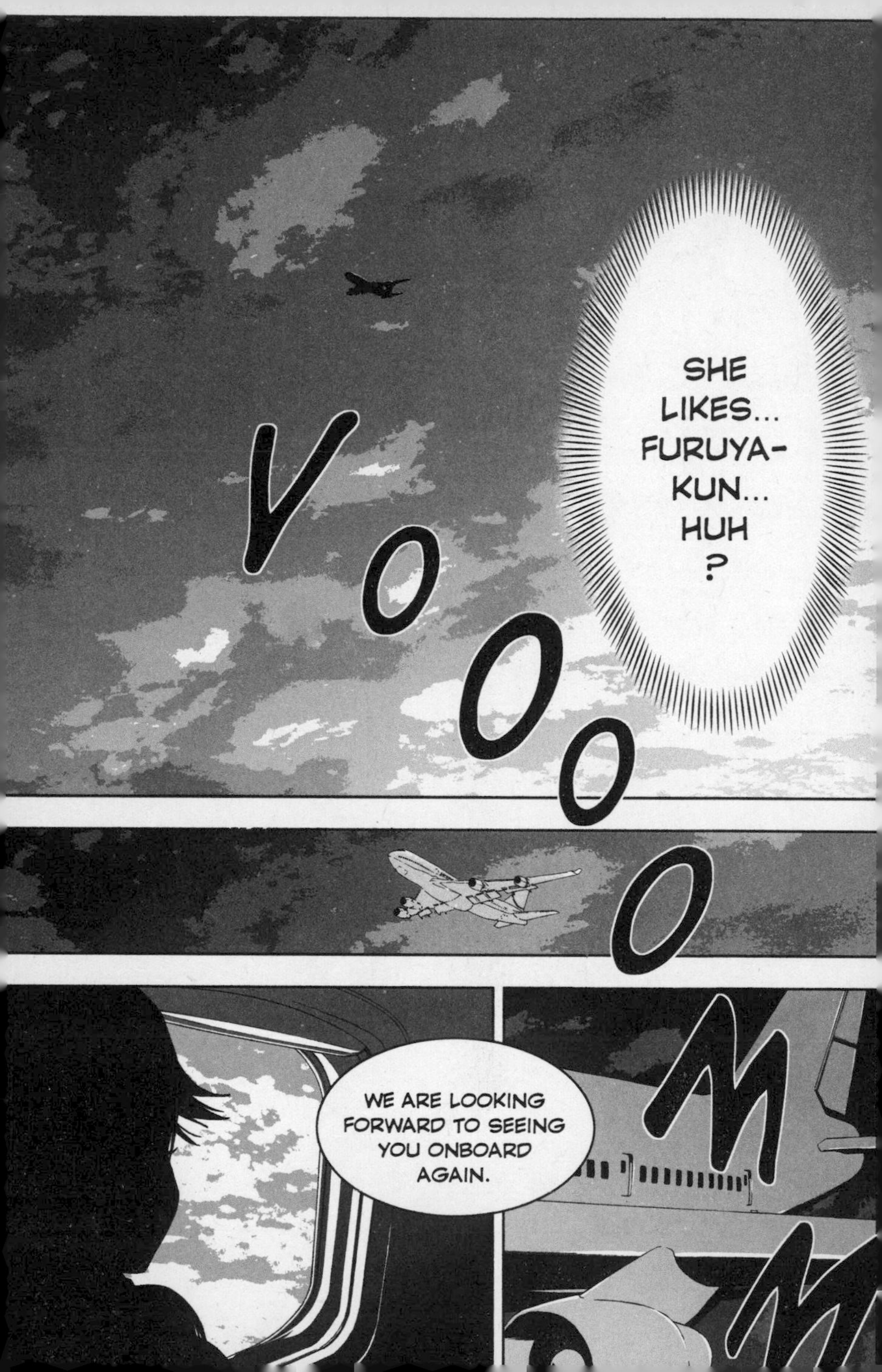
SHE LIKES... FURUYA-KUN... HUH?
VOOOOOMMM
WE ARE LOOKING FORWARD TO SEEING YOU ONBOARD AGAIN.

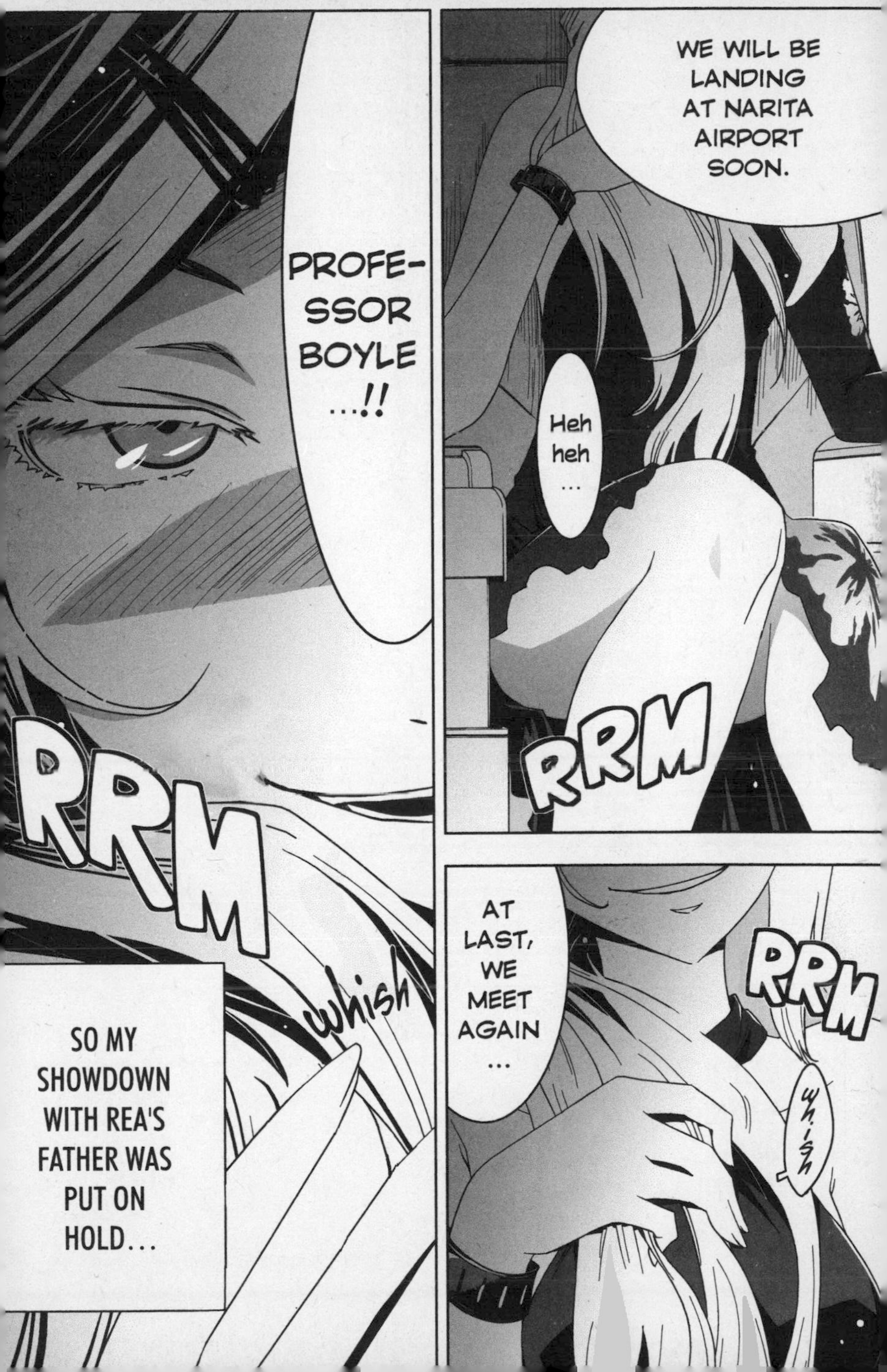
WE WILL BE LANDING AT NARITA AIRPORT SOON.
Heh heh ...
RRM
AT LAST, WE MEET AGAIN ...
RRM
whish
PROFE-SSOR BOYLE ...!!
RRM
whish
SO MY SHOWDOWN WITH REA'S FATHER WAS PUT ON HOLD...

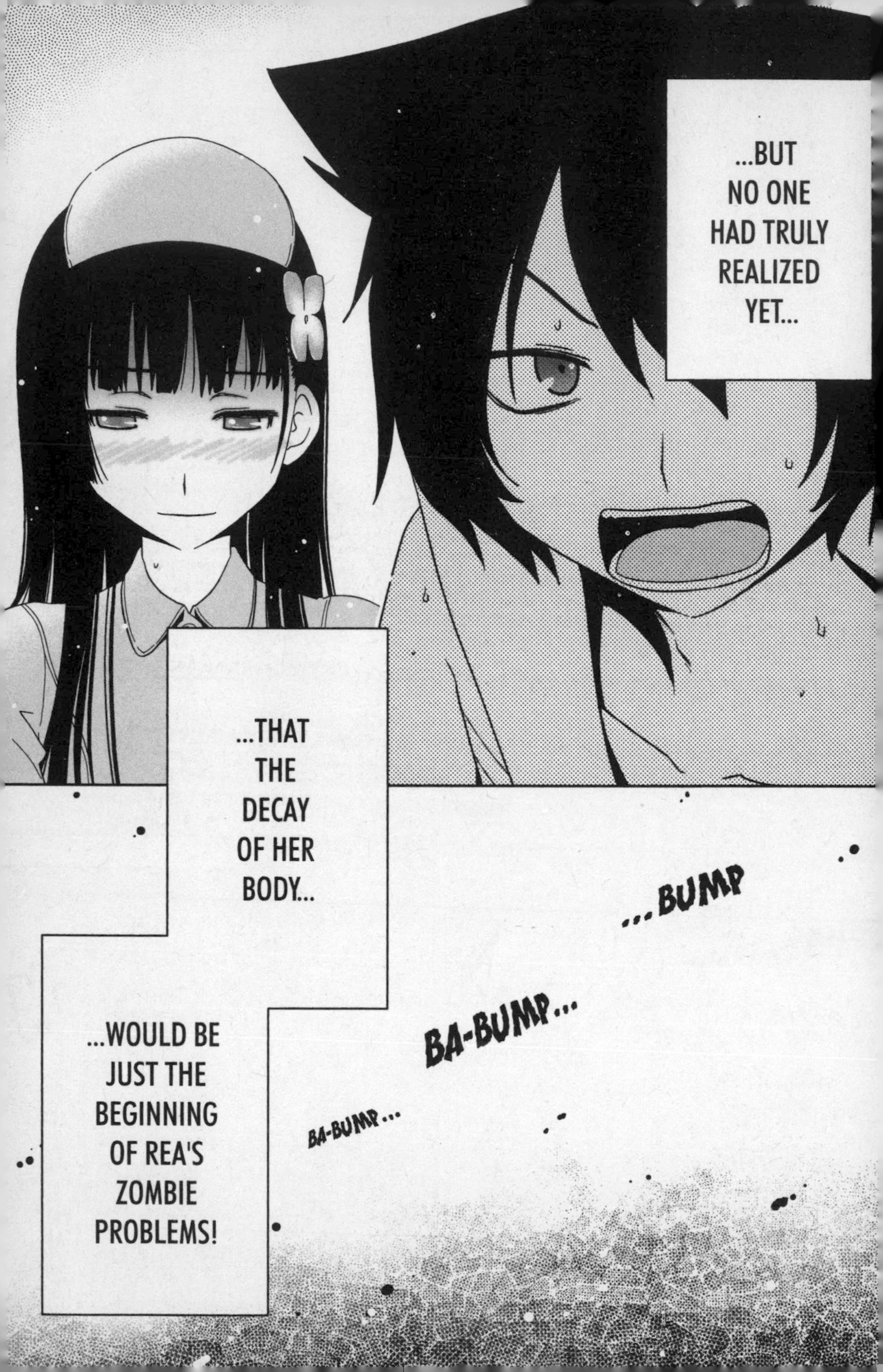
...BUT NO ONE HAD TRULY REALIZED YET...
...THAT THE DECAY OF HER BODY...
...BUMP
BA-BUMP...
BA-BUMP...
...WOULD BE JUST THE BEGINNING OF REA'S ZOMBIE PROBLEMS!

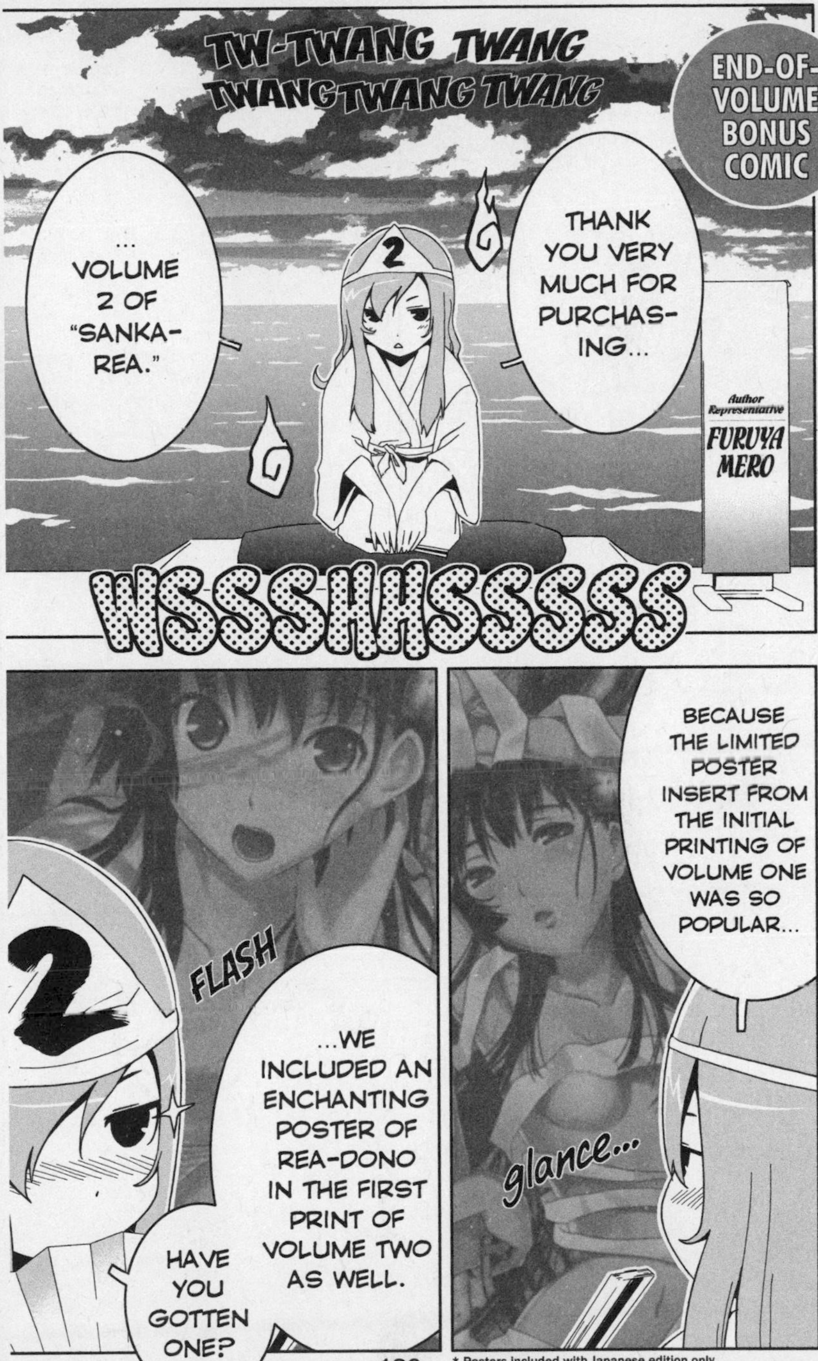
END-OF-VOLUME BONUS COMIC
TW-TWANG TWANG TWANG TWANG TWANG
THANK YOU VERY MUCH FOR PURCHAS-ING...
Author Representative FURUYA MERO
... VOLUME 2 OF "SANKA-REA."
WSSSHSSSSS
BECAUSE THE LIMITED POSTER INSERT FROM THE INITIAL PRINTING OF VOLUME ONE WAS SO POPULAR...
glance...
FLASH
...WE INCLUDED AN ENCHANTING POSTER OF REA-DONO IN THE FIRST PRINT OF VOLUME TWO AS WELL.
HAVE YOU GOTTEN ONE?

* Posters included with Japanese edition only.

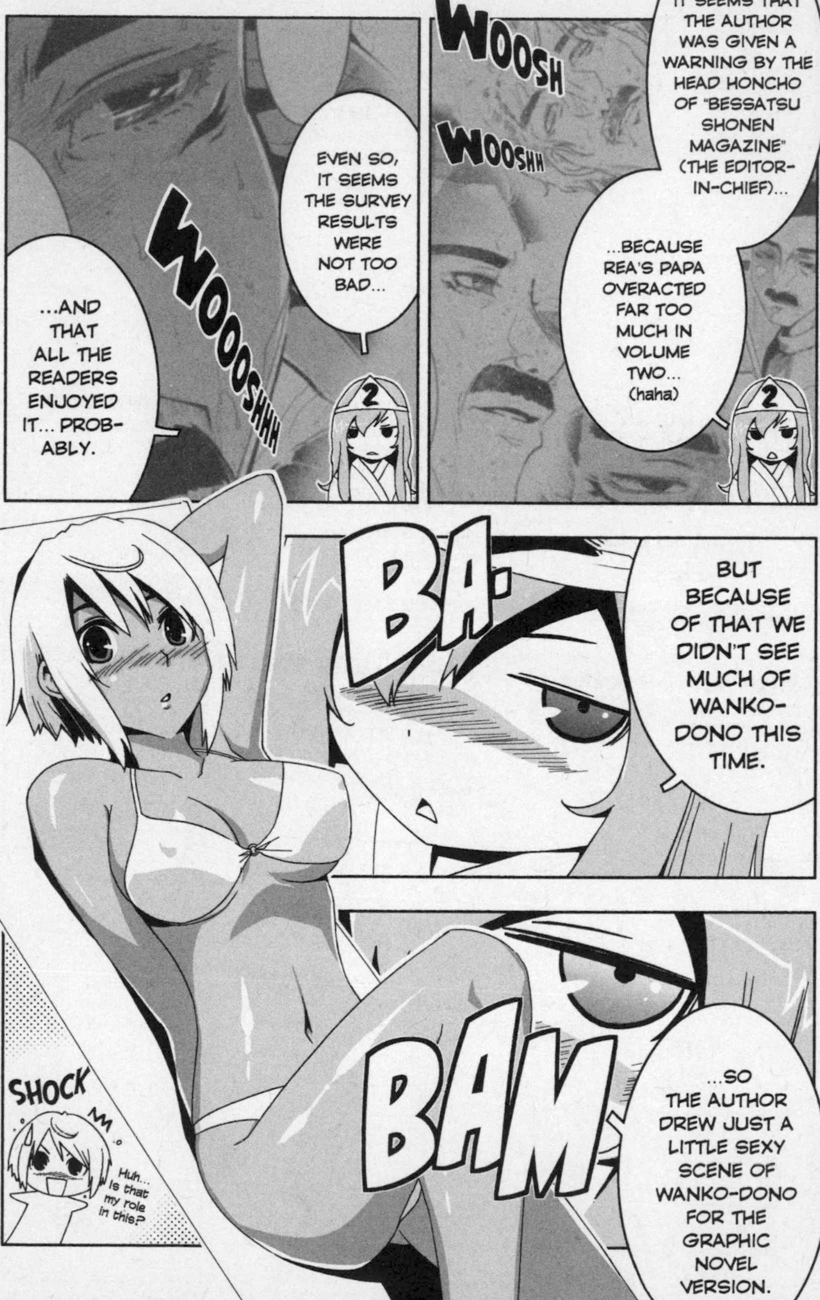
BY THE WAY, IT SEEMS THAT THE AUTHOR WAS GIVEN A WARNING BY THE HEAD HONCHO OF "BESSATSU SHONEN MAGAZINE" (THE EDITOR-IN-CHIEF)...
WOOSH
WOOSHH
...BECAUSE REA'S PAPA OVERACTED FAR TOO MUCH IN VOLUME TWO... (haha)
EVEN SO, IT SEEMS THE SURVEY RESULTS WERE NOT TOO BAD...
WOOOOSHHH
...AND THAT ALL THE READERS ENJOYED IT... PROB-ABLY.
BA-
BUT BECAUSE OF THAT WE DIDN'T SEE MUCH OF WANKO-DONO THIS TIME.
BAM
...SO THE AUTHOR DREW JUST A LITTLE SEXY SCENE OF WANKO-DONO FOR THE GRAPHIC NOVEL VERSION.
SHOCK
Huh... is that my role in this?

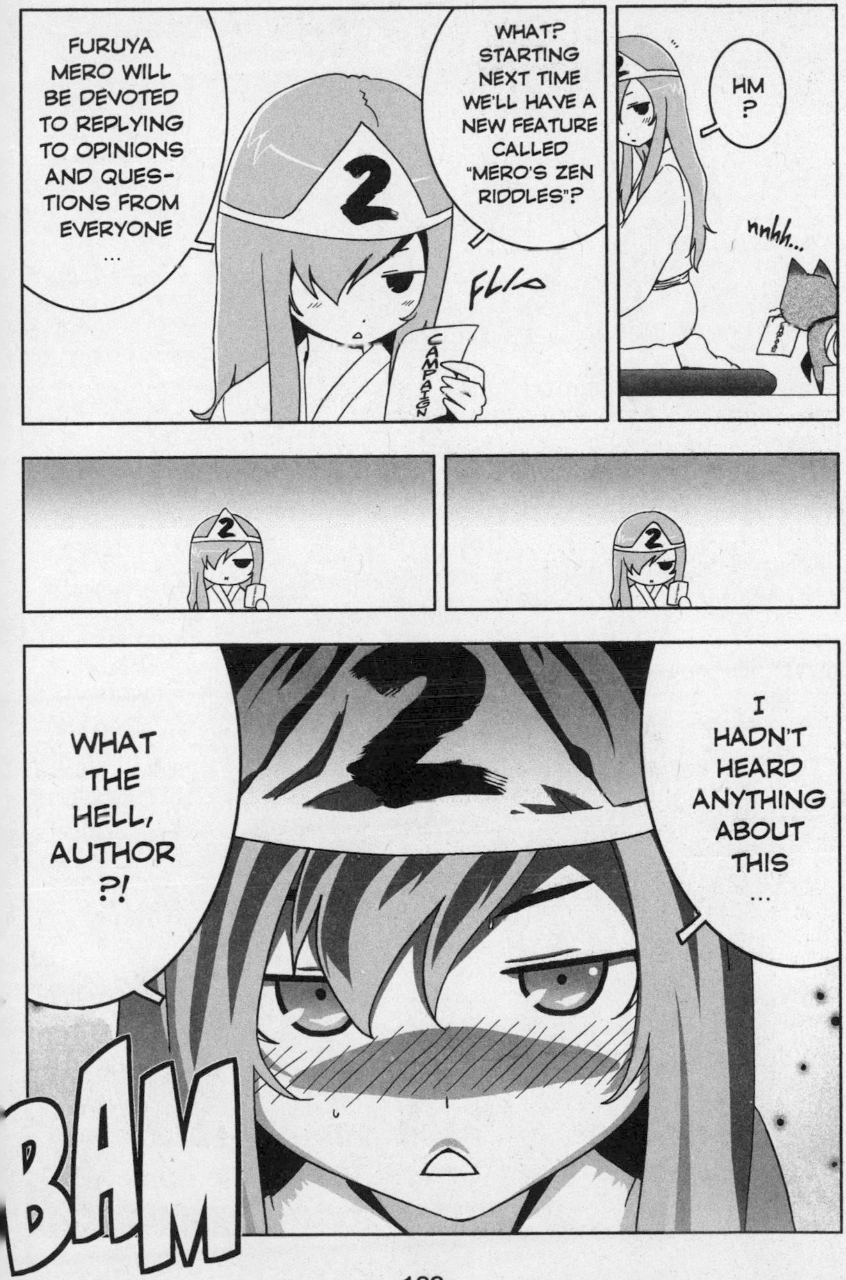
HM ?
nnhh...
WHAT? STARTING NEXT TIME WE'LL HAVE A NEW FEATURE CALLED "MERO'S ZEN RIDDLES"?
FURUYA MERO WILL BE DEVOTED TO REPLYING TO OPINIONS AND QUES-TIONS FROM EVERYONE ...
FLIP
CAMPAIGN
I HADN'T HEARD ANYTHING ABOUT THIS ...
WHAT THE HELL, AUTHOR ?!
BAM

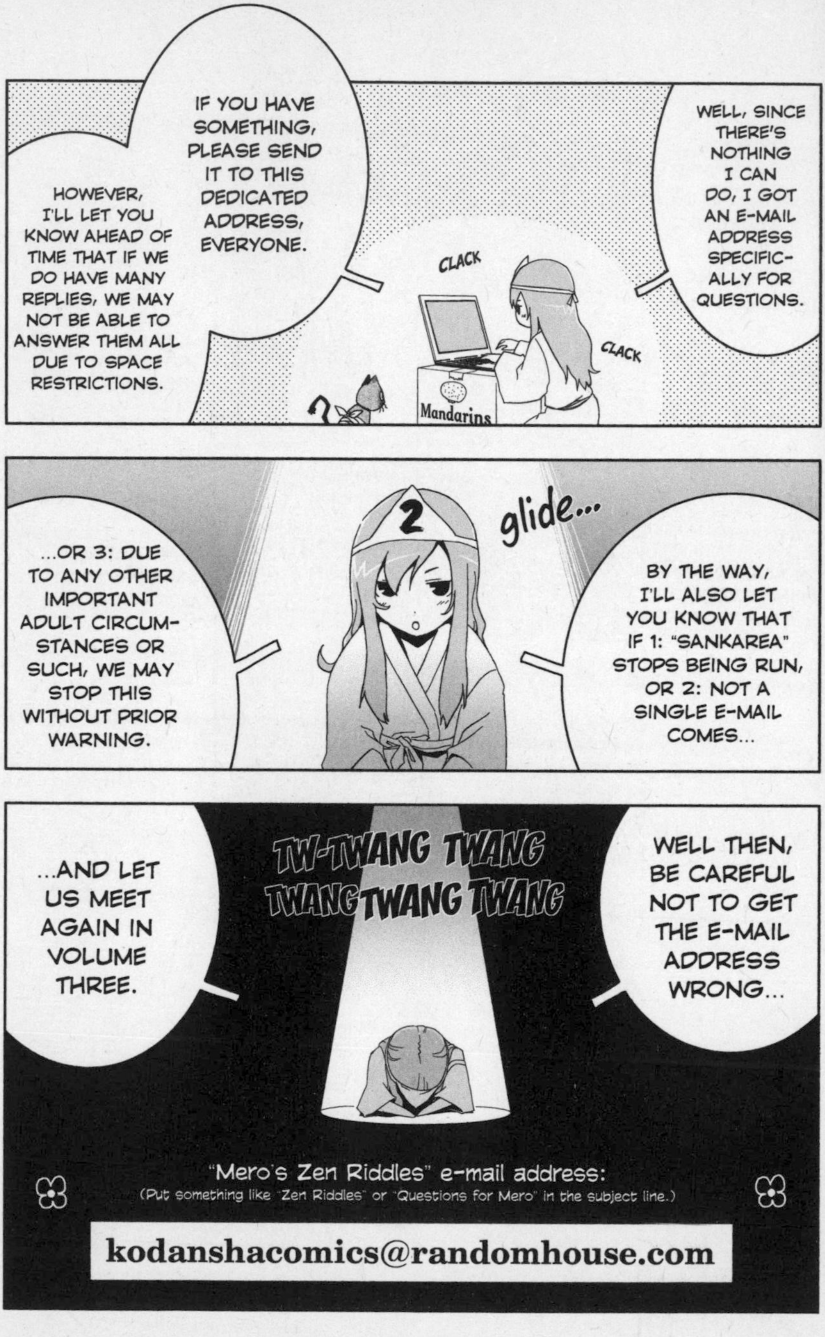
WELL, SINCE THERE'S NOTHING I CAN DO, I GOT AN E-MAIL ADDRESS SPECIFIC-ALLY FOR QUESTIONS.
CLACK
CLACK
IF YOU HAVE SOMETHING, PLEASE SEND IT TO THIS DEDICATED ADDRESS, EVERYONE.
HOWEVER, I'LL LET YOU KNOW AHEAD OF TIME THAT IF WE DO HAVE MANY REPLIES, WE MAY NOT BE ABLE TO ANSWER THEM ALL DUE TO SPACE RESTRICTIONS.
Mandarins
BY THE WAY, I'LL ALSO LET YOU KNOW THAT IF 1: "SANKAREA" STOPS BEING RUN, OR 2: NOT A SINGLE E-MAIL COMES...
glide...
2
...OR 3: DUE TO ANY OTHER IMPORTANT ADULT CIRCUM-STANCES OR SUCH, WE MAY STOP THIS WITHOUT PRIOR WARNING.
WELL THEN, BE CAREFUL NOT TO GET THE E-MAIL ADDRESS WRONG...
TW-TWANG TWANG TWANG TWANG TWANG
...AND LET US MEET AGAIN IN VOLUME THREE.
"Mero's Zen Riddles" e-mail address:
(Put something like "Zen Riddles" or "Questions for Mero" in the subject line.)
kodanshacomics@randomhouse.com

My type

I'm Sanka Rea.
I'd like to become friends with all kinds of creat-ures.
Oh, Mr. Hyena.
Hello.
CHF CHF
Oh, Mr. Vulture.
CHF CHF CHF
FLAP
Hello.
...I'm beginning to feel like the kinds of creatures that like me...
...tend towards a certain type...
Carrion Beetle

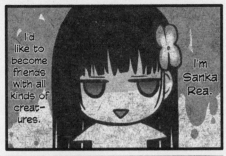

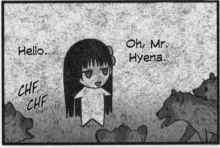

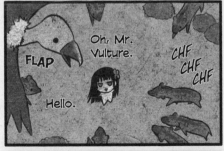

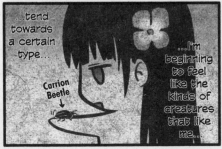

TRANSLATION NOTES

Honorifics: This series retains the Japanese honorifics. Here's a guide:
-san: Polite, equivalent to "Mr." or "Ms."
-sama: A term of great respect.
-kun: Used for boys or people in a lower position.
-chan: A sometimes cutesy term of endearment for girls.
-dono: A very respectful and now old-fashioned term.
-sempai: Refers to a student who entered school before you, or a colleague who entered the company before you. (The equivalent for your juniors is "kohai.")

p. 3, Heart Sutra
Sutras are Buddhist sermons or prayers. The Heart Sutra is probably the best known and most popular of all the Buddhist Sutras. Though they were originally written in Sanskrit, the version known in Japan has been transcribed into Chinese characters.

p.16, Namu Amida Butsu
A prayer involving saying the name of the Buddha, commonly used in Pure Land Buddhism. In this case, this scroll is a sample of Mero's calligraphic prowess as an elementary student.

p.20 Furuya Dohn
In some branches of Buddhism, priests and monks might have to take a vow of celibacy, but this hasn't been the case in Japan for quite some time. It's very normal for Buddhist monks to have families that live with them and work with them in their temples. Usually, this type of work is passed on from generation to generation.

p. 23 Kyoto Kaiseki
Kaiseki is the most representative type of traditional Japanese haute cuisine. It's extremely seasonal and local in choice of ingredients and the order in which guests are presented with the small plates of food is exceptionally structured. Kyoto is the region most typically associated with this type of cooking, and it seems Ranko's family runs a store that specializes in it.

p. 90, Meikyou Shisui
The Japanese version of a Chinese saying that means "A mind as serene as a polished mirror." It's often seen as calligraphy in these types of martial arts practice halls in movies and comics.

p. 93 Juon
Like the movie of the same name, the word "Juon" basically means "grudge," but only in the sense that a spirit or ghost who died a wrongful death might begrudge the living.

p. 100 Ran ran pi!
This is probably a reference to a Japanese McDonald's ad campaign in which Ronald McDonald says the nonsense phrase, "ran ran ruu!" Like most viral videos, this one's a bit tough to explain, so just punch "ran ran ruu" into YouTube.

p. 136 Kigurumi
A kigurumi (literally "clothing stuffed animal") is a full-body costume like a mascot costume. Pajama-style kigurumi became popular among some fans of Japanese street fashion around a decade ago.

p. 151 Fururin
Japanese movies often have a stamp on them that says "Eirin," short for "Eizou Rinri Kikou," or "Film Ethics Organization." This is the ratings board that determines who a film is appropriate for based on content. Having "Furu" replace "Ei" makes it sound like the "Furuya Ethics Organization," Furuya's very own (fictional) film content ratings board!

p. 186 Twang!
Here, Mero's dressed up like a ghost (because she likes to dress like a ghost...) and imitating a traditional Japanese storyteller, who was usually accompanied by the sound of a shamisen, a three-stringed Japanese banjo-like instrument. That's what is playing Mero on here.

ankarea: Undying Love volume 2 is a work of fiction. Names, characters, laces, and incidents are the products of the author's imagination or are used ctitiously. Any resemblance to actual events, locales, or persons, living or dead, entirely coincidental.

Kodansha Comics Trade Paperback Original.

ublished in the United States by Kodansha Comics, an imprint of Kodansha JSA Publishing, LLC, New York.

ublication rights for this English edition arranged through Kodansha Ltd., okyo.

irst published in Japan in 2010 by Kodansha Ltd., Tokyo, as *Sunkarea*, volume 2.

SBN 978-1-61262-352-8

rinted in the United States of America.

www.kodanshacomics.com

8 7 6 5 4 3 2 1

ranslator: Lindsey Akashi
ettering: Evan Hayden